Managing Multimedia

Project Management for
Web and Convergent Media
Book 1 – People and Processes

We work with leading authors to develop the
strongest educational materials in computer science,
bringing cutting-edge thinking and best learning
practice to a global market.

Under a range of well-known imprints, including
Addison-Wesley, we craft high quality print and
electronic publications which help readers to
understand and apply their content,
whether studying or at work.

To find out more about the complete range of our
publishing please visit us on the World Wide Web at:
www.pearsoneduc.com

THIRD EDITION

Managing Multimedia

Project Management for Web and Convergent Media

Book 1 – People and Processes

Elaine England
and
Andy Finney

 Addison-Wesley

An imprint of PEARSON EDUCATION

Harlow, England ■ London ■ New York ■ Reading, Massachusetts ■ San Francisco
Toronto ■ Don Mills, Ontario ■ Sydney ■ Tokyo ■ Singapore ■ Hong Kong ■ Seoul
Taipei ■ Cape Town ■ Madrid ■ Mexico City ■ Amsterdam ■ Munich ■ Paris ■ Milan

Pearson Education Limited
Edinburgh Gate
Harlow
Essex CM20 2JE
England

and Associated Companies around the world

Visit us on the World Wide Web at:
www.pearsoneduc.com

First published 1996
Second edition 1999
Third edition 2002

ISBN 0 201 72898 2

British Library Cataloguing-in-Publication Data
A catalogue record for this book can be obtained from the British Library

Library of Congress Cataloging-in-Publication Data
A catalog record for this book can be obtained from the Library of Congress

10 9 8 7 6 5 4 3 2 1
06 05 04 03 02

Typeset by 63
Printed in Great Britain by Henry Ling Ltd., at the Dorset Press, Dorchester, Dorset

Contents

How to use Books 1 and 2   xi

Introduction   1

Part I   **The Project Life Cycle**   3

1   **The background: multimedia and projects**   5

What is multimedia?   5
What is a multimedia project?   7
Summary   14

2   **The background: multimedia project management**   15

Multimedia: industry fusion or confusion?   15
Is multimedia project management the same as project
    management?   17
Organizational structure and its effects   30
The project manager as team leader   34
The role of the multimedia project manager   39
Summary   40
Recommended reading   40

3   **Scoping a project**   41

The initial phase of the project: are the clients ready?   42
Online interactive media scoping questionnaire   49
Offline scoping   68
Post-meeting responsibilities   74
Summary   75
Recommended reading   82

4 The proposal   83

The aim of the proposal   84
What it should contain   85
Description of the components   86
Online client-centred project scoping questionnaire   99
Offline client-centred project scoping questionnaire   105
Summary   109
Recommended reading   110

5 Contract issues 1   111

What needs to be covered?   112
Background to multimedia contracts   112
Refining the proposal into a contract document   113
Agreeing how to work together   117
Change management   120
Stages of a product   123
Responsibilities   124
Does education work?   125
Summary   128
Recommended reading   129

6 Agreeing the content   131

The importance of content   132
Whose role is it to define content?   134
Communicating the structure and content to clients and team   136
What affects content selection?   142
How to get content agreed   146
General principles for establishing content   148
Summary   149
Recommended reading   149

7 Selecting the media and techniques: the treatment   151

Constraints   152
Budget   153
Matching the media to the message   155
Video: background factors   157
Video   159
Audio   165
Computer and video graphics   167

Text 170
Where does this leave us? 174
Summary 175
Recommended reading 176

8 Interface design 179

What is an interface? 180
Interface design 181
Summary 197
Recommended reading 199

9 Contract issues 2 201

Introduction 202
Costing rights and clearances 202
The legal issues 205
Conclusion 212
Summary 212
Recommended reading 213

10 Selecting the team 215

Introduction 216
Identifying the skills needed 216
Skill-set profiles: core team 220
The extended team: skill sets 225
General support 232
Specialist support 233
Summary 240
Recommended reading 244

11 Testing 245

Multimedia and testing 246
What is testing? 250
What is a testing strategy? 255
Insights into software testing 259
Final sign-off 260
Summary 261
Recommended reading 261

12 Archiving 263

Archiving: the rationale 264
What needs to be archived? 264
Closing the project 268
Summary 268
Recommended websites 269

13 Managing small, quick projects 271

Putting this chapter in context 272
The smaller new media project life cycle 272
What are the risks? 276
Summary 295
Recommended reading 295

Part II Self Development 297

14 Team management principles 299

The project manager and team culture 300
Management styles 302
Teams: lessons learnt so far 306
Successful managers of creative teams 307
Characteristics of successful teams 309
How the organization can affect team management 314
Summary 317
Recommended reading 317

15 Rights, copyright and other intellectual property 319

Rights and wrongs 320
In the beginning 320
Some rights models 333
How to negotiate 337
… and finally, jurisdiction, distance selling patents and
   data protection 339
Summary 344
Recommended reading 345

16 Multimedia narrative 347

Rationale 348
What is multimedia narrative? 348

Broadening the definition of 'narrative'   352
Managing the development of narratives   354
In the meantime   355
Summary   356
Recommended reading   356

17 **Adapting projects for other languages and cultures** 359

Background   360
Assessing the scope of a localization project   361
... and does it matter?   367
Summary   368
Recommended reading   369

18 **Marketing implications for interactive systems**   371

What is marketing?   372
Why are these concepts important?   373
Marketing principles and new media   373
Know your customers   374
Know the competition   376
Know your strengths   379
Know the market   380
Know how to reach your customers with information and
      products   383
Know how to keep your customers   386
An introduction to market analysis   387
Summary   390
Recommended reading   390

Glossary   392

Index   418

Trademark notice
The following are trademarks or registered trademarks of their respective companies:

Acrobat, Adobe and Photoshop are trademarks of Adobe Systems Inc; ActiveX and Windows are trademarks of Microsoft Corporation; AltaVista is a trademark of AltaVista Company; Apple and Macintosh are trademarks of Apple Computer, Inc; DHL is a trademark of DHL; Doom and Quake are trademarks of Id software; FedEx is a trademark of FedEx; Google is a trademark of Google; Java and JavaScript are trademarks of Sun Microsystems, Inc; Linux is a trademark of Linus Torvalds; Netscape Navigator is a trademark of Netscape Communications Corporation; RealAudio and RealVideo are trademarks of RealNetworks, Inc; Sony is a trademark of Sony Electronics, Inc; Unix is a trademark of The Open Group; Vertabase is a trademark of Standpipe Studios LLC.

■ Who are they for?

These books provide a background to the management tasks you will need to use when developing multimedia projects. Book 1 takes the perspective of managing people and the production processes, and Book 2 covers the relevant technical issues. They are aimed particularly at people wishing to adopt the role of managing a new media development team. In this context multimedia development includes online projects for the World Wide Web or interactive television (iTV), or offline using CD-ROMs or any other appropriate interactive medium. Previous editions have proved useful whether the readers were already working in the industry or were studying ready to join it.

There are a variety of titles that are used to denote the team leader role – producer, managing editor, analyst, or senior software engineer, for example. The term 'project manager' is used here because it is a neutral term, which does not betray any media origins, since new media is produced from a fusion of talents across several media.

The role of 'account manager' is another term that is met in new media companies. The differentiation of a project manager and an account manager in terms of what they do in new media projects tends to be ill-defined. The account managers appear to have more direct contact with clients at the initial stages of the project and can begin the project definition phase and then pass it over to the production head of project. They may keep a general eye on the project progress and might be brought in during the project if there are any discrepancies. We will concentrate on the project manager role rather than account manager but we cover the definition phase of a project as if the project manager carries it out or when necessary uses specialists to help with the definition.

Our emphasis in the two companion books is the adaptation of project management theory and practice to multimedia projects. This approach offers insights to help you keep control of projects. Interactive media projects are notoriously difficult to keep within time and budget because there are so many variables. These books analyse all the variables within projects from clients to techniques; from team members to applying project management principles.

The material in Book 1 concentrates on the people and processes involved in the definition and production of a project. It follows the life cycle of a project. It broadens the understanding of the multimedia context for those with a single specialization such as programming or graphics, while giving a practical business and management slant for others. It also covers emerging trends in areas that although peripheral to the main processes at the moment, may become mainstream in the near future. This extra material is designed to help the self-development of multimedia project managers. Book 2 focuses on the media platforms and production processes. These have expanded quickly over the last couple of years and for this reason warrant a separate book for this edition.

These companion books will also prove useful for those commissioning new media, since the client's roles and responsibilities are defined in parallel with the project manager's. Book 1, *People and Processes*, clearly identifies the phases of a project and acts as an introduction to the process. Book 2, *Technical Issues*, can help those people commissioning projects increase their understanding of the range of existing interactive media and emerging interactive media. It can help them make the appropriate media choice for a particular purpose. It also covers the production processes so that commissioners know what will be involved and the choices they will need to make on quality levels.

■ The structure of the books

In *People and Processes*, Book 1, the core chapters are organized around the development of a project from initiation to completion. Administration, management and production processes are interweaved, reflecting the way they happen during a project. Because some phases occur simultaneously, the linear nature of the chapters misrepresents the overall process to an extent. However, we have tried to cover all the phases for developing a team-based, client-driven, commercial project. Initial chapters offer background insights into the theory of project management and how it relates to interactive media project management. The self-development chapters predict and cover salient issues for project managers to get up to speed with emerging issues and top up their knowledge. In *Technical Issues*, Book 2, the core chapters address the technical media issues and the associated production issues. They have a common structure with the chapters in Book 1 providing a consistency and integrity across the writing. These core chapters cover a project production process that uses the equivalent of some original video footage, a range of audio assets, commercially sourced and in-house-produced graphics, and text content.

We use a client-centred commercial project as the default in both books because it needs the greatest number of tasks and resources and involves all the management processes relevant to client, team, application development and budget management. There are, however, many varieties of projects, so the readers will need to select and apply the relevant sections according to their particular requirements. All projects need certain management processes but these processes can be streamlined if any of the following apply: you are working alone, no money is changing hands, you do not have a specific client, you do not have to clear rights in materials, and you are not using audio or video in the application.

Some readers of previous editions have asked for a definition of commercial versus non-commercial projects. Commercial as applied here implies that money changes hands for the exchange of services and goods: time and effort is accountable and budgeted against monetary return. This would include projects done for charities if not done voluntarily, for example. There are other types of multimedia projects. Some types of research, student assignments and self-development projects are examples of non-commercial projects.

Projects that don't require a team can of course be commercial. One or two multi-skilled individuals can produce excellent projects alone and would need many but not all of the aspects covered here. If you are working on these types of project you may not have as many administrative and legal aspects to cover as in team-based projects, but many will be the same, albeit on a smaller scale.

Website projects can use just a selection or all of the media, depending on the specific project but as the bandwidth available increases the media choices become more fluid so we cover all media in case the project demands them. Multimedia games and entertainment titles tend to have a different development cycle because they are driven by different tools such as games engines, need different skill sets and are market driven. International projects have more phases, and are referred to when appropriate.

For those who work in small companies with smaller, more contained new media projects, we have included a new chapter (Book 1, Chapter 13) focusing on the appropriate business imperatives and risks. The business case should help to guide your approach to managing projects. This covers the same core principles as the project life cycle chapters but aligns them directly to the business perspective. We hope that this perspective will prove convincing enough for project managers of short, quick projects to recognize the need for using the principles.

The Glossary will serve as a ready reference for any terms that need further explanation. We have tried to make it as comprehensive as possible, and it is also included in both books.

■ The structure of the core chapters

In each book the core chapters begin with a résumé of the project manager's responsibilities. This will prepare you for the concepts that will be covered and will help focus your interpretation of them on the role outlined. During the books, the complete range of responsibilities builds up into the equivalent of a job description. If you are not an interactive project manager and

Icon of project manager's responsibilities

Icon of theory
into practice

Icon of refer
to companion
website

Icon of
summary

Icon of
recommended
reading

you are reading the books for a general purpose, then you can skip the résumés and read the chapters for salient information.

During the chapters you will find suggested tasks. These are to help you transfer the principles into practical activities of relevance to your own situation. Because there are so many types of multimedia projects we have tried to stick to principles that can be applied across the greatest variety of projects. But the principles will serve you for your own situation only if you take the time and effort to apply them. The 'theory into practice' tasks can help you build up project-specific sets of reference materials that suit the range and type of projects you develop.

Where appropriate during the chapters you will be referred to the companion website for information that is represented better in an electronic form, and for practical exercises on visual and audio examples. See www.booksites.net/england.

Each chapter has a summary. This reinforces the main points covered in the chapter, but can also be used as a quick reference when you are developing a project and reach the phase being discussed. Some people prefer to read the summary before reading a chapter to decide if it has direct relevance for them. Others read the summary first to preview the chapter, to prepare them for it.

Where possible we have included recommended reading or website references at the ends of chapters, but a few of the aspects covered here have relied on practical experience and represent the authors' interpretation of that experience rather than insights from defined theory.

■ Acknowledgements

Many thanks to all those who gave their time and expertise to comment on the drafts and helped shape the book through to this 3rd edition:

Judith Aston, Senior Lecturer in Time-based Media, Faculty of Art, Media and Design, University of the West of England, Bristol, UK.
Stewart Atkins, Development Director, Traffic, UK.
Jardine Barrington Cook, Logica, UK.
Birte Christensen-Dalsgaard, The Danish State Library, Aarhus, Denmark.
Mark Dillon, Director, On-Line Services, GTE Entertainment, USA.
Steve Hope, Technology Trials Manager, Orange Personal Communications Services.
Bob Hughes, Multimedia Author and Consultant, Bristol, UK.
Peter Looms, Danmarks Radio/Television/Online, Multimedia Strategist, Denmark.
Peter Marshall, Technical Director, The Digital Television Group, UK.
Mike Philips, MediaLab Arts Course, School of Computing, University of Plymouth, UK.

Malcolm Roberts, Senior Manager, Bank of Montreal Institute for Learning, Scarborough, Ontario, Canada.

Gisella Rosano, Designer/Developer, Bank of Montreal Institute for Learning, Scarborough, Ontario, Canada.

Claus Rosenstand, Head of Board, InterAct, Aalborg, Denmark.

Henry Steele, Associate Professor, International Business and Marketing, School of Management, The Open Polytechnic of New Zealand.

William S. Strong, Partner, Kotin Crabtree & Strong Attorneys at Law, Boston, USA.

Charles Walker, Partner, Walker Tomaszewski Solicitors, London, UK.

Jonathan Wilson, Account Director, BBC MediaArc, London, UK.

We both recognize that many of our past and present colleagues have contributed to the span of experience covered here, and we thank you all – too numerous to name individually.

Finally we also recognize the debt to all the pioneers who persevered against the odds and kept the faith that interactive media would be mainstream. You were right.

Elaine England
Andy Finney
April 2001

■ Multimedia: the present climate

The numbers of people working in new media related jobs has increased dramatically over the last few years. The range and type of projects that people are involved in has diversified but at the same time multimedia has been integrated into mainstream business processes. This has resulted in a reshuffle and repositioning of new media companies on the one hand and the absorption of new media roles within traditional businesses on the other. All this has been driven by the force of the Internet and the speed at which it has become an essential business communication tool

Certain market sectors in new media have begun to consolidate. Specialist new media companies are lining up with them – e-learning and e-commerce are examples of these sectors. Some new media companies differentiate themselves from other companies by calling themselves web agencies. This indicates an affinity with the culture and approach of the advertising and marketing sectors and their clients are more likely to originate from those sectors. Although there has been consolidation within and across such market sectors, there have also been many mergers and take-overs leading to fewer but larger new media companies.

Meanwhile, traditional business sectors have moved to embrace the potential of interactive media because of the need to establish a business presence on the Internet. They have also begun to recognize the internal interactive communication potential of an intranet and its place in their business. They have either had to increase their own staffing to cope with developments or look to out-source the projects.

The maturing of market sectors and the increase in the number of projects have had an effect on the way in which projects are addressed by new media companies. Both the type of client and the business sector that they work for affect the management processes adopted inside the companies. This is especially true of the beginning of projects and the way in which they are initiated and scoped – we will look at some of the implications of this in more detail later. However, once the project moves to the production stage, the project cycle follows a more predictable path within all companies.

As the spread of Internet use gathers pace across the world, the importance of content in the native language is growing. This has an impact on the way in which some projects are developed if a company is responsible for delivering an application for different languages and cultures. Issues arising from these specialist projects need extra consideration and so there is a new chapter in this edition to make people aware of the implications.

People from television production often used to ignore interactivity as being irrelevant to them. However, the need to have a website associated with a traditional television programme and the arrival of interactive television has meant that people from that sector have undergone fast changes in attitude. They have had to face decisions of how to mix the linear TV programme and website to best advantage and now recognize that they need to consider how to make best use of the interactive power that set-top boxes bring to televisions. This is a powerful, rich sector and they bring their own skill sets and preconceptions to the new media mix. For this reason another new chapter on multimedia narratives has been added to this edition. Interactive scriptwriters will look for new formats so that they can develop content for the new generation of interactive TV viewers.

Finally there is another influential sector that has ignored the specialized interactivity related to the use of media despite being a cornerstone of interactivity itself. This is the IT or software sector. It has watched new media with apprehension, preferring not to have to worry about content within their applications because the code development process is difficult enough in itself. But the need for the development of large database programs to drive e-commerce sites on the Internet is as much the preserve of IT companies as new media companies. There has been – and continues to be – an uneasy battle over who should win business of this type. The IT companies need the 'softer' new media skills for the front-end look and feel of this type of project while the new media companies need the hard-core disciplined database development skills of programmers for the e-commerce engine. This struggle is still being resolved, but the size and power of the IT sector may well mean that it will engulf the smaller new media companies to get the balance of skill sets needed for the sizable Internet business projects.

From this snapshot we can appreciate that there's a lot happening quickly. There are many more people involved in producing interactive media. The need for processes to help manage the definition and development of such projects has increased dramatically. We hope that this updated edition will act as a guide for those involved.

The Project Life Cycle

■ Introduction

Part 1 is concerned with the production life cycle of an interactive project. We take the perspective of a project manager throughout the cycle. General project management principles are applied when they suit the interactive context, but as we'll discover, interactive projects demand different management strategies and procedures from non-interactive projects.

There are many strands within a project that can be part of the project manager's responsibilities: client liaison, team management, financial control, contract negotiation, all facets of application development from technical considerations to interface design, legal requirements, and testing, among others. It is an exciting and demanding role as well as a complex one.

As the digital revolution spreads into all traditional media sectors and the power of interactivity is realized, more and more people will find themselves heading up interactive project development teams. Training for interactive middle management has not been part of the culture of this embryonic industry sector. Often interactive project leaders are left to firefight and crisis manage; to sink or swim. As the sector matures we hope that this situation will change and that this project life cycle part of the book will provide constructive guidance.

The background: multimedia and projects

■ What is multimedia?

Multimedia is the seamless integration of text, sound, images of all kinds and control software within a single digital information environment.

TONY FELDMAN, MULTIMEDIA CONSULTANT

This definition applies to interactive media productions for distribution both online, such as Web pages, and offline, such as kiosks, DVDs and CD-ROMs. Throughout this book the term 'multimedia' is used to encompass both online and offline projects, and has relevance for other interactive media such as interactive TV (iTV) and on-demand services. The use of the word 'seamless' in this context is important from an artistic as well as a technical perspective. The viewer (or user if you like) of a computer should be cushioned from the technology as much as possible, and the designer should be able to choose the best medium to get the particular message across.

An 'offline' project is self-contained, does not interact with anything outside its immediate environment, and usually communicates with nothing outside the computer it runs on except for the user. An 'online' project needs to communicate with distant resources and sometimes distant users. Sometimes the application will actually be running on a distant computer, but more often your local application will be gathering information and assets from distant resources over a network. Some projects have elements

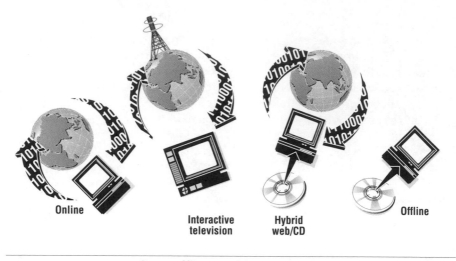

Online   Interactive   Hybrid   Offline
                television   web/CD

Online, offline and hybrid projects.

of both on- and offline projects, and we will refer to these as hybrid projects. Online projects, having originally been predominantly text and graphics biased, are now taking advantage of increasing bandwidth to integrate animation, sound and video, as and where appropriate. Offline projects are rarely constricted in their choice of media components nowadays. Just to confuse the issue, iTV projects can be any of the above since an interactive television application may be downloaded into the set-top box (and therefore start off online) but then run entirely in the set-top box without any other connection to the network (which means it needs to be treated as if it is offline when it is programmed). This is known as a carousel and is explained more fully in the iTV chapter (Book 2 Chapter 3). It depends on the configuration of the application and the equipment.

Multimedia has a chameleon-like ability to pretend to be many things. In designing an application you have the freedom to use so many disparate media types and techniques that it can be a challenge to understand which ones are relevant for a particular type of project. Animation, sound and pictures can help to attract your viewer to the screen on the one hand and make the most tedious of Help screens interesting on the other.

The disciplines of multimedia are as diverse as the media types. Familiarity and expertise are required in all the facets of media production as well as a facility with computer software and even journalistic skills. The skills you may need when working in multimedia production can include project management and cost control, understanding the way computer systems operate, understanding computer language logic, video and audio editing, text and image design and manipulation, interactive script writing, relevant market and user profile information, complex people management skills … plus the need to be able to integrate the disparate elements in a meaningful and appropriate way.

Of course there is a downside to this complex integration. Computer-related projects are notoriously difficult to scope and to budget, and this is often a problem for people coming into multimedia from other media backgrounds. Multimedia is more intricate, because you first have to decide on your delivery format from components that are constantly changing and shifting, and then once you have made a choice, this has an impact on how you can treat the content. This is analogous to building a videotape recorder at the same time as editing the tape. Coupled with this there is often a lack of knowledge of what can be achieved with the technology (and this applies to developers as well as the clients), as ever more is offered by developments in computers and other equipment. Software techniques change too, as do fashions in the tools that are used to build the final application. The pace of change in the use of tools is reflected in the changes in interface design and can be easily seen if we compare the look and feel of Internet sites over several years.

For people with a computing background there is the difficulty of scoping and specifying the way in which the application is to work, in the knowledge that the content and look and feel are usually more important than the computer program that controls and displays them. The software team leader will often be reporting to someone who may not share his or her specialist knowledge of computing. This person may find it hard to believe that superficially simple things can need difficult programming, and yet seemingly complicated changes in structure can be achieved by quick changes in the code.

For end-users, whether they are in a classroom, in the home or at work, multimedia improves the flow of ideas and information. It is a rich canvas on which to communicate, but this richness brings with it complexities and challenges, and quite often the only way to see what can be done is to try it.

■ What is a multimedia project?

☐ Varieties of project

A project in multimedia comprises a series of tasks that deliver a combination of media and have a computer component to integrate them. There are hardware-oriented multimedia projects where the aim might be to specify, introduce, and integrate a delivery platform, such as videoconferencing with a tailored user front-end, into an organization. There are software development projects that combine media components into an application to run on a delivery platform. The delivery platform will be one that can support an interactive combination of video, graphics, animation, sound and text. This could include anything from the Internet to iTV.

This book will concentrate on client-centred software development projects that need a team to work together to achieve the project. This type of project covers the majority of circumstances that will be met in both on- and offline project management and production. There are some multi-media professionals who carry out all aspects of a project alone, so they will not need the staff management aspects covered here. However, the principal stages of a multimedia project are the same. Managing the project cycle and handling clients need the same skills whether you are working alone or as part of a team, and whether you are producing on- or offline products. If you work alone or work for a micro company that usually has smaller projects, Chapter 13, *Managing small, quick projects*, takes a small business per-spective and shows how the same project management principles make sense for those circumstances too.

Projects can be initiated in many different ways. Often the client makes the first approach although many of the larger projects have a tendering process where companies compete by presenting or pitching their ideas to a tender board. Sometimes the sales force or the account managers drive the initial stages; sometimes analysis of market needs prompts projects. If people are involved in winning business when they do not have experience in the production processes involved, they need to be guided carefully in the questions to ask, how to estimate budgets, the contractual implications of their discussions and the expectations to set. They need to explain the production process that the company will employ via the project leader or equivalent. They also need to liaise with the production leader or project manager to ensure they do not inadvertently make false promises that the team will not be able to deliver within the time and cost. For many projects that go off the rails, flaws can be traced back to the initial stages of project definition so getting this part right is essential.

☐ Varieties of client

It will help if you consider that a client is anyone who has the authority to control time and budget, and has the right to sanction design decisions. This definition covers both internal and external clients. Internal clients are those who commission a project from within your own company, for example. External clients are people outside your company who commis-sion projects.

The process of developing a project is in principle the same for all clients except that the contractual agreements will probably, but not always, be more straightforward for internal clients – if such agreements exist at all. The company's internal procedures will determine whether formal agree-ments are needed between departments where budget transfer is con-cerned. You will still need to establish ways of working together, and the project will need to run to time and resource constraints. Beware the inter-nal client who does not agree the way of working, and expects you to do everything they ask in impossible times, regardless of your resources. Putting a nominal costing on your resource time is a good discipline even if you do not have to exchange money. It gives you a common ground for understanding if you tell the internal client that your section has spent the equivalent of a small fortune for them. It makes them think things through more carefully, and begins to educate them about the potential cost of changes.

Emerging models of development

A company's culture can influence the way in which they set a project up. Also, their predominant perspective will drive the way they choose to work with their clients. Because the number of companies involved in multimedia development has grown in line with the uptake of the Internet, it has become apparent that there are different working practices emerging. These form the basis of different working models. Since the online growth continues apace with ever-changing capabilities and the companies dealing with it are running to keep up with it, it leaves little time for reflection about working practices and whether they are optimized for the circumstances.

The insights offered here are embryonic but they try to explain why and how a project manager's experience in one company can be very different from another's in a different company. Clients can also find vast differences in working practice if they are working with several development companies.

The Internet is a communication tool that offers extra ways for resources to be used so there is a move for traditional companies to gear themselves up to develop for it. At the same time newer companies exist purely to develop for an interactive environment. The first type tries to work from their traditional working practices and the second is trying to find a good working model. Neither appears to have the right answer at the moment.

However, we can get closer to answers if we have a continuum linked to the attributes that clients might look for. As a good starting point for discussion we can consider new media companies that develop functional or creative websites. This perspective allows a better way of describing some of the tensions in working practices that occur in projects.

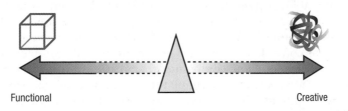

Functional   Creative

New media companies could use this diagram to plot where they think they lie between these extremes. This might help point to the type of gaps in their working practices that need filling. Interactive development companies that originate from the more creative end of the spectrum – perhaps those with roots in the advertising, graphics or marketing sectors, for example, have been used to having loose, open discussions and several stages of trying out concepts with the clients before moving towards a finished product. They continue to try to apply this practice with inter-active projects but find that it is a lot harder than previously.

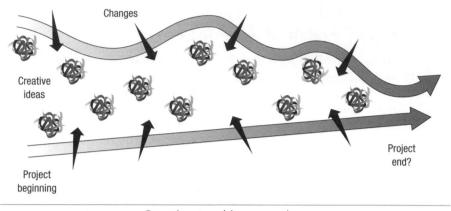

Changes

Creative
ideas

Project
end?

Project
beginning

Creative working practices

The problem is that this approach encourages constant change and refinement. The fluid exchange process is actively encouraged at the beginning and the clients get used to it. The companies then find it difficult to accommodate changes later in the project because rework becomes involved. The rework takes longer and has more knock-on effects than changes required for traditional media. It is equally difficult to establish that payment is needed to cover the changes and rework when the company has been flexible and accommodating at the beginning phases of the project. The refinement process takes longer for interactive projects, ties up more resources and is more difficult to predict than with the development of non-interactive creative projects.

The general criticism made of this type of company is that their applica-tions may look good but may not perform as well as they could. The loose informal process is not seen as efficient and it is easy for them to lose money by not being able to pass the real costs for development – including any changes – on to the clients. What is needed perhaps, is a process that allows a fluid phase of refinement then a focus for development where changes are discouraged or controlled so the project moves towards completion.

Interactive development companies that originate from the more func-tional end of the spectrum – perhaps those coming from software database systems development for example – are used to having a paid detailed definition stage prior to beginning production. They allow changes up until the specification is complete but once production is under way changes are discouraged or controlled. They have strongly documented and agreed project phases that carry a heavy admin overhead. These companies tend to be more concerned with the functionality than with the image portrayed. They are criticized for neglecting the visual impact and the market consid-erations of the applications. The functional companies need to incorporate

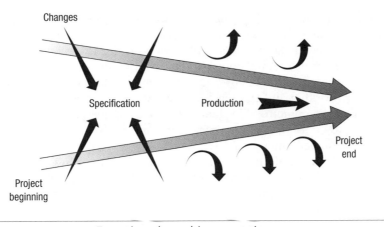

Functional working practices.

some of the creative processes to counter the criticisms but without causing the project to spin out of control.

The concept of phases of a project will be raised again later because interactive companies are beginning to develop varieties of models based on phases of production. This continuum introduced here can establish the start point of the process where companies can begin the definition of phases and move to establish practices that avoid the problems of the extremes.

☐ The client-centred multimedia project cycle: overview

During the definition stage of a project you are trying to get an understanding of what the client wants so that you can match their needs to a multimedia solution. This may need to be carried out quickly for a smaller project, so you work from assumptions and experience rather than facts. On the other hand the initial stage may be protracted with several discussions and levels of management involved from both sides before a general high-level understanding is reached about what the project means. We refer to this initial stage as 'scoping the project'.

Once you have scoped the needs of the project and have a timescale, you can begin to work out the costs so that you can formulate a more detailed proposal for the client. The proposal indicates the range and scope of the work you will produce according to the time and cost you define. In effect, it becomes your working contract. There are different names for this type of document according to the way a company chooses to work. We refer to a 'requirements agreement' in Chapter 13, *Managing small, quick projects*, for example, but it is effectively the same type of document as a proposal. The name 'requirements agreement' has stronger connotations than 'proposal' to encourage the client to move faster to a contract because of the collapsed time constraints in quick projects.

When the client accepts the proposal the project explodes into activity, with several layers of operations happening simultaneously. In the book we shall cover one strand or one major part of a strand at a time, but the project cycle diagram demonstrates the true nature of the process.

You need to establish how you will work with the client because you will depend on them at certain points to give you assets or decisions to allow you to continue the work according to schedule. While you are establishing the ways of working and the legal aspects of the contracts, work starts on the project development. The details of the content, platform, media and techniques to be used, style, interface and interactive design are firmed up and production gets under way.

The production could not happen without personnel, so the team is also being assembled by recruitment or by use of internal staff at this time. While the production team members are working together, the management aspects of teamwork come into play.

Of course, the actual asset production work – text, graphics, audio, video – that leads to integration of the assets gets under way. Coupled with production of the assets themselves is the administration of the rights in the materials used. This may not be a trivial task and depends on the number of assets that will be used and who owns the rights to them. There is a better consensus now on how to treat multimedia by those who hold or administer copyright than a few years ago. However, the process is still not completely standardized with the different rights owners across the media platforms.

Meanwhile, as asset production evolves, so does the testing to ensure that all the pieces will meet the specifications so that integration can take place as smoothly as possible. As the media components are integrated, the code underlying integration needs to be tested thoroughly in a variety of circumstances on the equivalent of the final delivery platform. The development platform may well have been different, and there are often adjustments that have to be made for the delivery platform to ensure that the software operates according to specification, or behaves properly on different browsers or different computers.

The client will be uneasy about giving final sign-off because they recognize that they lose any bargaining position they have at this point. As the manager of the project however, you have to have an end point that is clear, or the budget quickly turns into overspend. The precise terms for final sign-off need to be negotiated before the end of the project to help the process run smoothly.

Finally, it is tempting to consider final sign-off and delivery as the end of the project. For most projects it is, but many developers forget the importance of archiving the project in a systematic, well-documented way. If there is return business for upgrading the application or website, or if reuse of assets is needed for the same client in another project, you'll save time, confusion and money if it is easy to locate any asset, piece of code, or documentation that might be needed.

This then is the multimedia project definition and production process that will be expanded in the following chapters. There are many more stages that occur within each of the major stages identified here. These represent

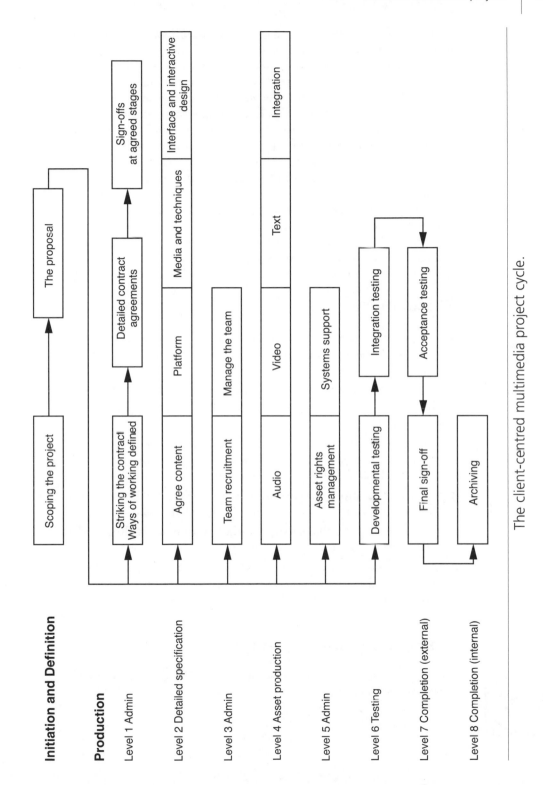

The client-centred multimedia project cycle.

the tip of the iceberg, so to speak. The simultaneous nature of levels 1 to 6 in the project cycle diagram should indicate the complexity of the interaction between the team members and the processes of production. This should also serve to demonstrate why project management principles need to be applied to help control this complex interaction.

Because there are differences in dealing with small projects, Chapter 13, *Managing small, quick projects*, is designed specifically for those who want to extract the most important project management points to apply in their set of circumstances. It is put at the end of this section because it also acts like a condensed overview of the whole project management life cycle and will be useful for all.

This book concentrates on the people and process management aspects of the development cycle so if you want to understand the background to more technical details of the platforms and asset production, they are covered in Book 2, *Technical Issues*.

■ Summary

- Multimedia is the seamless integration of text, sound, images of all kinds, and control software within a single digital information environment.

- The skills needed to produce multimedia are diverse. Working practices are still emerging and at present are often linked to traditional practices with limited success.

- The person responsible for winning the project needs to be guided strongly by company policies in what agreements to reach to avoid problems later for the rest of the team and company.

- Apart from competence in software and media design and production, cost control and staff management skills are needed.

- A client is anyone that has the authority to control the time and budget, or to sanction the design.

- A client-centred project follows stages of initiation, scoping and proposal definition, followed by production. The production phase has several levels, which are interrelated. It is not a linear process.

■ Recommended reading

There is no specific support material recommended for this chapter. The definitions are based on experience.

The background: multimedia project management

◼ Multimedia: industry fusion or confusion?

Because multimedia uses many skills, and because its people come from a variety of backgrounds, the multimedia environment does not have a single, defined way of working. New media companies tend to have a bias according to their origin and the background of their management. The bias can reflect advertising, video production, computing, publishing, TV production, journalism or interactive training/education among others. Functional specifications have to blend with storyboards, source code co-exists with time code, branding and imaging concepts merge with database engine definitions.

Each of these disciplines has different role names, phases of production, methods for documenting production, ways of working, organizational structures, and cultures. The individuals who work in the companies have their own specialisms. Some will recognize the environment they find themselves in, but many will not. They will have to adapt to the new terminology and structure.

Communication across the disciplines is problematic. Imagine a person with a web design background being asked to produce a website extension product on DVD, or someone with a video producer's background being

TABLE 2.1 Comparison of multimedia origins

	Advertising/ Marketing	Website production	Video/TV production	Computing	Publishing	Interactive training/Education
Roles	Creative director	Web manager	Executive producer	Project manager	Commissioning editor	
	Senior designer/ designer	Information/ Content architect	Producer	Analyst	Senior editor	Training analyst
		Technical architect	Director		Editor	Instructional designer
			Production assistant			
	Graphic artist	Web editor	Scriptwriter	Programmer	Author	Interactive designer
		Web programmer				
		Web designer	Video graphics artist	Computer graphics artist	Print graphics artist/Illustrator/ Cartoonist	
Production phases	Pitch/Tender/ Commission	Tender/ Commission	Pitch/Commission	Tender/ Commission	Pitch/ Commission	Tender/Commission
	Formulate strategy	Analyse	Research script	Analyse	Research/write	Analyse
	Conceptualize	Design		Prototype	Review	Design
	Focus groups/ user tests				Rewrite	Prototype
	Build	Produce	Shoot	Program	Proof	Redesign
	Trial	Redesign	Offline edit	Test		
	Refine		Online edit		Produce	Produce
		Publish	Distribute	Release		Test
	Release	Update			Distribute	Release
						Evaluate
Documentation (client/ commissioner receives)	Concept brief	Proposal	Storyboard	Functional specification	Proposal	Proposal
	Site chart	Script	Script	Technical specification	Drafts	Outline design
	Prototype	Rewrites	Rewrites	Change management procedures	Redrafts	Detailed design
	Trial results				Proofs	Sign-off agreements

asked to produce a functional and technical specification, or a programmer being asked to produce an interactive storyboard and assimilate time code data from an edit shot list. This happens.

Table 2.1 is representative of how each industry has developed its own way of producing a media product by dividing roles and responsibilities and denoting phases of development. (Note: approaches to production and names of roles vary within each industry so this table has been streamlined to allow cross-comparison of concepts.) As soon as an interactive application uses a mix of media components, aspects across these can prove invaluable for successful production. So if pieces of video need to be included in a website, aspects from the video/TV production cycle may be met if the website company subcontracts a traditional company to do the pieces for them. Alternatively, if the new media company decide to shoot the video pieces themselves, do they have the right skill sets and do their production phases allow for this?

Where does project management fit into this?

Although there are obvious differences, the industries share the production of media products. Their ways of working have evolved to suit the production methods for a particular medium, market and distribution cycle, in some cases over many decades. We often imagine television broadcasting to be a new medium, but it has been around since the mid-1930s, and drew on practices from radio and the movie industry.

They are all team-based, complex activities with a role acting as the team's main leader/coordinator. They are all producing a particular end-product as the result of the team effort. Each product has unique properties. These aspects are characteristics of project management, and they apply to interactive media management too.

A project manager is expected to produce a product by organizing and controlling resources according to planned expenditure, in a certain time frame, and to a defined quality level. This fits the description of a person in charge of a new media project. For the purposes of this book the term 'project manager' will be used to denote a person with this role irrespective of the specialist origins, where the role might be called many other terms as we can see from Table 2.1.

Is multimedia project management the same as project management?

Although project management methods offer a good basis for multimedia project management, there are limitations and confusions that need to be recognized and considered. Some of these are inherent in project management methods, and some occur because of the particular nature of interactive media.

Traditional project management principles were derived from engineering projects, where the link between time for production, the cost of the product, and the quality of the end-product was established. The principles state that if any one of these factors is changed, the others are affected. Once a project has started, the project manager needs to monitor changes and assess the impact on the planned time, cost and quality of the product.

Some of these principles were used as the basis for the computer-based project management software packages that exist today. They provide a method to help define the breakdown of the project into tasks and the sequence of tasks that need to be performed according to a time line. This is called a Gantt chart. Some tools link the use of resources to the costs incurred, and some attempt to link the dependence between tasks, time and resources.

Project management tools have proliferated in the last few years. Some are better for certain tasks and organizations than others. It is important for you to monitor developments in this field, as the tool that finally meets the real needs of multimedia projects will be invaluable.

Gannt chart example.
(Screen shot reproduced with permission from Microsoft Corporation and IST)

The tools have derived from the analysis of different sets of needs within the profession. Some have emerged from the administration of the management of the volume of electronic multimedia assets. They formulate tasks and times around the changes needed to convert the raw assets into the delivery of integrated assets. Others have emerged to try and make best use of the distributed online working environment allowed by the World Wide Web. Take note of the reference to Bulldog's and Vertabase's websites at the end of the chapter to see an example of each of these approaches to project management tools. Microsoft Project is derived from the more conventional project management wisdom of deciding milestones, tasks and resources. Different tools will suit different companies and ways of working and it is important to evaluate a spectrum of tools to decide which suits your particular company and preferred way of working.

The tasks, sequence of production, resources needed, and cost breakdown need to be defined in some way as part of the multimedia project manager's role, and this is not straightforward.

☐ Limitations of project management methods

Traditional project management methods tried to address the interrelation of the dependencies between tasks to the sequence of production and time. This was done using a technique called network analysis, which was also known as critical path analysis.

Network analysis encouraged project managers to use a diagram to show the logical links between tasks, illustrating which ones would be in simultaneous development and which ones were dependent on others' reaching a certain stage before work could begin. The critical path is derived from this

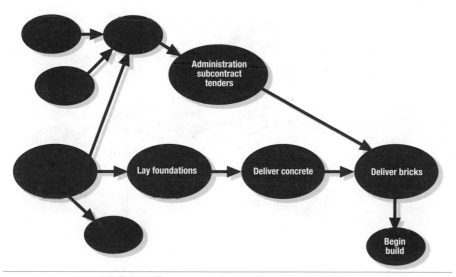

Multimedia network analysis: Example 1.

analysis. It is the sequence of development of tasks that allows the optimum progress through the project.

For example, in a building project (Example 1) the delivery of ready-mixed, quick-setting concrete is dependent upon the foundations being ready to receive it. If there is a delay with the foundations, the delivery of the concrete has to be delayed. The one is critically dependent on the other. But in this case the opposite is not true because the digging doesn't have to stop if the concrete is going to be late. The subcontract tender process for the bricks doesn't have to stop if the foundations are delayed.

Sometimes, however, the dependence *does* work both ways. Sometimes dependence states change. Sometimes something that was not dependent can become dependent. Sometimes something that wasn't critical becomes critical. It begins to sound mysterious – it is, and there are no set rules for when or why things change their nature!

To give a multimedia example, your project may be going well, and you have worked out the sequence of production with a good understanding of which parts can be under production simultaneously without affecting each other and which major parts need to wait for several processes all to be complete.

Example 2 is for the purposes of demonstration, and represents only a small part of the project. It addresses major parts of an offline project – like producing a marketing CD for example. We do not cover the detailed processes.

It shows that while computing and graphics tasks begin as soon as one part of the content/script is agreed, audio and video production wait until all the relevant content is agreed. This is usual, because audio and video production is often better done in one phase than in pieces. You want to hire a video crew or a sound studio for a voice-over only once for a defined

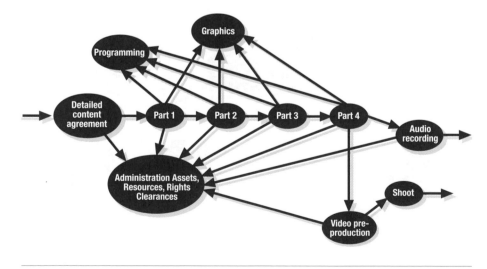

Multimedia network analysis: Example 2.

time, for example, whereas your graphics and programming resources have a longer commitment to the project.

But consider this problem while looking at the diagram. You are likely to know how many voice-over artistes are needed from the initial agreement of the structure of the application, but not exactly how much or what they will say until the whole content has been agreed. The client has specified that they want to use a particular artiste in this project because his voice has become identified with their products through advertising. He is an actor as well as a voice-over artiste but is known best for minor character roles.

The project is almost half-way through the content stage. You have had to adjust the timescale of developments because of hold-ups on sign-off of Part 1, but you are getting more confident that the next stages will run pretty smoothly. You decide to check out the availability of the artiste with an indication of which month you'll need him and most likely which week. You find he'll be filming on location for two and a half months around then for a TV series. He can manage to give you only one or two days, and these are a full month before your content should be finished if nothing else affects its planned progress. You can't afford to wait until he finishes his location shooting because the project release date is linked to a fixed conference day in your clients' organization, and you've already lost a lot of contingency time. Although you try to influence the client to change, they insist on using this artiste.

Completing the audio script now becomes more critical than completing the rest of the content. This is an example of something becoming critical when it wasn't previously a problem. The network analysis would have to be reworked in a radical way to separate out the way of working to achieve this. The voice-over date would be fixed, and would influence all the phases of production linked to it whatever else occurred in the project. Fixed dates and times have more effect on project development than anything else, so the sooner they are identified, the better.

In a similar way, the critical path of a website project could be affected by outside influences. Imagine you have begun a project to create a website for a medium-sized but successful business. They have agreed the general structure, budget and timescale. The website is due to be rolled out stage by stage, beginning with the corporate profile, then products and services, distributors, and finally a 'what's new' section. The content underlying all the sections is large, and needs separate sign-offs. You haven't yet completed the profile or obtained agreement on the general interface design. Suddenly, news of a new product is leaked, and the company decides to meet the demand for information on the Web, since their switchboard is being swamped with queries.

The information has to be accessible by the following Monday morning, three days away with only one day to source materials from others – they will disappear for the weekend even though you won't – write up the material and have it signed-off before constructing some temporary pages.

This leak of information and the reaction would obviously have a radical impact on any critical path that had been defined. During the day it emerges that this new product is dependent on two previous complementary products and services. This triggers debate in the company on whether these should be featured as well, or the new product information would not be clear enough. This means that you have to liaise with more people than originally expected during the day, and of course they are 'out on business'; you'll also have to produce some pages on existing products and link between them and the new one. You weren't due to begin that section for another two weeks!

Some of the problems in using network analysis are evident in this example. Although it was popular during the 1980s, its popularity has waned. The first difficulty is met when the level of detail needs to be decided. It is possible to clutter the diagram with connections between tasks very easily. A large amount of space is needed to outline a complex project, and relatively small changes can mean a complete reworking of the level of detail, as in the case shown above. Sometimes network analysis makes the process appear so complicated that there seems to be no clear development path. It is also difficult for others to grasp its meaning and relevance. It is very time-consuming to maintain if the project environment is prone to as many changes as online and offline multimedia.

However, the impact of the consequent changes in use of resources, different priorities for completing tasks, and the dangers of not meeting the date, need to be recorded in some way that all understand. At the moment this is usually done by word of mouth, backed up by an e-mail to the team – if the project manager is experienced. Project management software tools can show fixed deadlines in the Gantt chart, but the reasons behind the line-up of tasks is not clear, and with so much going on all the time it is sometimes easy to forget why you made a seemingly odd decision. This is why other documentation such as an e-mail project diary becomes important.

If we return to looking at project management methods and tools, the computer tools can prove useful in the planning stage of the project, particularly if the clients help to construct the schedule and agree to their time involvement on tasks. It also helps if they get an understanding of the process so that they can appreciate why you suggest certain solutions to problems that arise.

What is quality in interactive media?

The first limitation of conventional project management tools lies in the definition of quality. In engineering projects it is easier to specify quality in measurable terms: for example, the dimensions of the product, its durability, the physical mechanisms and how they operate, the components, and so on. But in any media project how is quality defined in measurable terms?

How do you measure multimedia quality?

It is easy to define technical levels of quality, such as whether the audio is mono or stereo, and whether it is encoded at a specific digital level, but the quality of design is more problematic. Without such a definition, it is very difficult to measure the impact of changes in time and cost on quality.

Project management tools do not help in defining the quality level that is agreed between client and producer. The link between time, cost and quality of product is not shown in any breakdown of tasks, or in the resource/cost schedule, and this is a problem. The three are interrelated, so that a change to any one will affect the others, but there is no direct correlation. There is a tendency for project managers to overlook the impact of time and cost on quality because of this. Because the quality level is not specified as exactly in multimedia projects as it is in manufacturing projects, for example, it is harder for project managers to define the impact because it is so intangible.

When people are asked to judge new media awards they come face to face with the dilemma posed by people having different perspectives on the meaning of quality in multimedia. The judges come from different backgrounds in interactive development, and so look for different features. These features are perfectly valid for each perspective, but reconciling them all can mean that it is difficult to get a consensus. It helps if the judges or the company holding the awards reach agreement on a set of criteria before making their decisions.

This difference of perspective on the nature of quality is similar to what happens within multimedia teams because the members come from different media backgrounds. It occurs between developers and clients for the same reason. There can also be a gap between the team's understanding of quality and that of their management. So the definition of quality in inter-active media is a major problem.

If we look back at Table 2.1, quality has been defined in different ways in the different disciplines. Video production produces a storyboard and script for the client to agree content and visual treatment. Computing uses a functional specification to define how the application will operate and a proto-type to show how it will look and feel. Publishing uses editors and peer review processes to control the quality of work submitted. Interactive training and education uses the outline and detailed design documents to agree the quality level of content and a prototype for the look and feel. Advertising and marketing like to gather reaction from the end-users to refine the impact of the product or concept. Website design documentation and agreement procedures have not yet been standardized. They are open to interpretation and multiple practices.

This highlights some of the problems in defining quality in multimedia. There are objective parameters for some of the technical aspects, but many subjective aspects for design quality. Each project will define its own 'quality' priorities according to the subject and the target audience.

How then can the time–cost–quality equation work for multimedia? It can only work with a guiding principle defined as quality – one so general that it will operate for all multimedia projects. The principle needs to be viewed with the understanding that it is only acting as a control mechanism for time and cost.

For budgetary purposes then, the following definition of quality will be useful. Underlying all the processes are the definition and agreement of content and its treatment. The content means the information that is going to be presented, and the treatment means which media and which techniques will be used, and what it will look like.

Design quality for media projects = Content and treatment agreement

This definition is intentionally broad, and can therefore be linked to whatever project is being considered. Some people will not accept this as a definition; they find that it omits aspects they would like to see covered. However, most problems during development relate to changes in the content and treatment. The overall aspects of robustness of the product and fitness for purpose for the audience are important, of course. But we have moved those to be part of the testing cycle, which moves in parallel with the development of content and treatment. These aspects are covered in Chapter 11, *Testing*, where we discuss how to devise a testing strategy to suit the client and yourselves. The definition of content and treatment above is used as a starting point and is expanded in Chapter 6, *Agreeing the content* and Chapters 7, *Selecting the media and techniques*, and 8, *Interface design*.

The definition of quality in interactive media can be split into each media component, and can be debated by each professional group. The concept of quality that is achievable in professional terms, and which is considered 'leading edge', may not be compatible with the quality that relates to that achieved by a particular team for the budget and time they have. The approach that needs to be adopted here is to set levels of quality that are appropriate and achievable for a given purpose to achieve defined results. It is a business-driven rather than a specialism-driven approach.

It is hard for professionals to accept the idea of producing less than what they consider 'top quality', as they tend to be judged by their projects in the eyes of their peers. Within each level of quality that is dictated by the constraints of the project, however, there is still room to be creative and professional, as well as aspiring for the best that can be achieved for that level. This dilemma of specialism versus business needs is one that underlies many a project conflict. It should be brought into the open, and the peer pressure relieved. It would help if this debate was addressed in all spheres and all courses as a priority for it remains one of the fundamental differences between the mock projects that students of multimedia carry out in an academic setting and the reality of projects in a business setting.

Time, cost, quality triangle.

How are time, cost and quality linked in multimedia?

The relationship between time, cost and quality is far from linear. If we consider a classic request from a client in a less complicated process than multimedia and study the effects, it will give a clear indication of the relationship between time, cost and quality, and demonstrate the principles that should be applied in multimedia.

'Oh! and there's just a small change ...'

You are a specialist furniture craftsman. A client has ordered an armchair in a particular style using particular materials, with a particular fabric and a particular fitting. You have worked out the cost and delivery time accordingly, to a formula that takes into account the type and availability of the materials and the complexity of production.

However, after a week, the client changes his mind about the fabric. What are the implications for cost and time? The knock-on cost will depend on how far along production the original request has got.

■ *Project management note 1. Change may have cost implications for administration and production.*
The original fabric could be at any of the following stages at different times of the process: it could have been cut out, or sewn, or fitted. So the customer may well have to accept some charges and a changed delivery date. In this case the fabric has been cut and sewn, so there is redundant work and materials, and rework. You will have to start the production again.

■ *Project management note 2. Change may have time implications because of rework.*
When you explain the time and cost knock-ons, the client insists that he really needs the chair in the original time. There may be no way that this can happen. You may not be able to achieve it, as the time limit may now be too short. The new fabric choice is from a special supplier, and is much more expensive than the original choice. When you contact them, they are out of stock. It will take time to order.

■ *Project management note 3. Change may make the project impossible to achieve if it results in factors beyond your control. Also, there are some processes that cannot be speeded up.*
If you make it into a special order where the workers will need to work overtime, more costs need to be passed to the customer.

■ *Project management note 4. If timescales are immovable but you have to absorb changes, the workload increases and causes extra cost.*
You might offer a standard fitted cover rather than a loose one, as this takes less time but is of a different quality. Alternatively, you might suggest a different style and shape for the chair that is easier and faster to produce.

■ *Project management note 5. The quality of the product can be changed to meet the time constraint.*
It has taken a few hours for you to assess the situation, time and cost implications and relay three alternatives to the client. You need a quick decision

because your new timescales and costs are based on starting immediately. Your client doesn't reply to your fax immediately. You phone his company the next day to be told he's out of the country on business for two days and isn't contactable! Your work's supervisor is reworking the production schedule and is on hold waiting for the decisions! The fabric supplier keeps phoning to ask if you're placing the order or not!

■ *Project management note 6. Never be fooled by 'it's just a small change'.*
Even though there were only three quality variables here – style, shape and fabric – it is easy to understand how a relatively small change can have significant repercussions according to when the change was requested, how far into production the product was, and how quickly new decisions are agreed.

THEORY INTO PRACTICE 1

Look back at the example and substitute the following. It should give you an insight into the repercussions of change in an online or offline multimedia project.

The style of the chair (type of wood, springs and stuffing)	=	Content agreed
The shape of the chair	=	Structure agreed
The fabric	=	Treatment of content agreed (usually known as 'look and feel')

Multimedia has many levels of quality and variables within each of the production processes – video, audio, graphics, text, animation, content treatment. Each of these has several stages to production, so any changes at any point can have upward, downward, backward, forward and diagonal effects.

The schedule and plan become difficult to change and update. You have to predict the time and cost implications of slippage, and this means consulting members of the team who will be affected by the proposed change. You also have to balance what can be absorbed with the effect this has on any contingency you had allowed in time and cost.

You have to agree the change and the knock-ons with the clients. Then you have to communicate the changes and the impact to the whole team because they are making decisions based on the time they're allowed. A change a day is not uncommon, so imagine the impact on your time from the administration of these changes.

So to summarize the limitations of trying to use traditional approaches to project management with new media production, the main difficulties inherent in the use of the project management methods and tools are as follows.

- The quality level isn't specified within the existing methods in such a way that the impact of changes on it is measurable. If there are changes, the project manager has to predict all the consequences and update the plan of time and costs accordingly. The tools are not dynamic enough in prediction of the impact on time, resource and cost in relation to quality level. The value of the network analysis technique from traditional methods is difficult to define. Its value even for traditional projects is questioned. The importance of defining the dependences and their changing states is right in principle but difficult in practice.

- In the armchair example, the quality was agreed in detail before the project started. In multimedia applications, the quality levels are often not well defined because the client and producer have little common ground in communication. When the multimedia specialists try to explain, their language is incomprehensible to clients. The clients can't specify what they would like because they are not sure what they can have to begin matching it to what they want. The producer cannot specify cost and time accurately until there is a clear specification, so a lot of time needs to be spent to understand the scope of the project. It is because of this initial effort that many development companies ask for staged payments to make sure that their costs are covered even if the project never goes ahead.

- If you start from a poor definition, the clients will make so many changes that the project will get out of control quickly. We will deal with how to get a good definition later. Even if you are market driven and not client driven, if you don't have a good definition at the beginning the product will evolve and take more time and effort to complete than might be necessary. Sometimes the time of release of a product to market is vital – in time for Christmas presents, for example – or the market's characteristics have changed and it is no longer receptive to the style of product.

☐ How the nature of multimedia affects the project management process

The time, cost and quality principles are important but do not translate directly to multimedia. They can be applied when a process is well defined and the clients understand their role in the development process. In the building project example the client and architect would have taken a long time to define the shape, structure and cost of the building before work commenced. The client recognizes that once the foundations have begun they cannot change the shape of the end-product. They may try to change the construction materials or some features of the building, but the points at which they can no longer affect the process are clear. The structure of a multimedia project is not as readily recognizable but the consequences of changes to it past a certain point in production can be as bad as changing the shape of a building under construction.

In part, this problem is due to the seemingly fluid nature of computer software. There is no definite relationship between the elements of a program that comes near to the definite way a building sits on its foundations. This does not mean that such dependencies do not exist. In the development of projects, good programming practices can minimize problems due to change – object-oriented programming and rapid application development (RAD) are elements of this practice – but they cannot remove the difficulties completely. For example, adding a section into a program where this requires another item to be added to a menu can be very problematic if the menu has been built up in a sophisticated visual style with many layers of video and stills. In website design there is often more flexibility, and changes can be made efficiently without major disruption if component parts of the site structure need changes. But many small changes quite quickly add up to days of extra work.

Multimedia management is much more like managing innovation. The process and end-product are constructed according to unique circumstances. Each multimedia application is handcrafted because the content is unique, even if standard tools are used. The personal qualities of the project manager – leadership style, team management, client management, credibility – come to the fore. Aspects related to general management, such as level of authority, level of control over resources, and level of control over budget, are connected to the structure of the organization where the project manager works. These can have a significant effect on projects, and can either help or hinder the project manager in developing a project.

Planning, monitoring, and control of time, cost and quality are still prime factors in a project management role, but because the whole environment is unstable and intangible, the complexity increases and the risks of failure are higher. The total organizational structure contributes to success or failure, but often the project manager has to accept the blame unfairly for setbacks.

Successful managers of innovation try to control the project earlier in the process than traditional project managers because the earlier control is taken, the sooner the risks from disrupted project progress decrease. The link between planning and control is stronger. Rather than just plan time, cost and quality, you need to anticipate risk areas and take measures to decrease the risks. This includes controlling the expectations of the client, the development team and the company management. In market-driven projects, you try to minimize risks through market analysis, by having strong distribution channels and through marketing and advertising the product to give it the maximum chance for success. So to manage innovation, knowledge of likely risks and how to cover them is crucial.

These personal and managerial qualities, like the concept of quality level, are not as definable as time and cost. They have to be put in context, in the environment where the project manager needs to operate. It is easy to recognize that multimedia does not have one environment but is a hybrid because of the range of skills of the people involved and the different approaches taken, depending on the bias of the company (see Table 2.1).

Because of this, only a few of the basic principles will be put into context here to demonstrate the extent to which a project's success can be affected by organizational structure, team leadership, and risk analysis. Each individual environment and mix of people needs assessment to reach a more detailed understanding.

■ Organizational structure and its effects

Because of the pace of change in business practices, many companies have flattened their levels of management to facilitate the faster decision-making that suits the business climate. Companies talk now of having an 'open' structure where they listen to ideas from all employees who then feel that they can have an influence on management decisions. This has been a noticeable trend. Multimedia companies have been innovative and small in general terms. They have naturally had a flat, highly communicative structure where ideas flow and each person influences the other. However, as multimedia has become more mainstream in business the small companies have often been taken over or merged into larger units where there is more definition of roles and more process-driven workflows. These can seem to work against the autonomous workplace.

If you are a multimedia project manager working in an organization with a traditional hierarchical structure, certain characteristics may have a tendency to interfere with your ability to get on with the job. You will have been assigned a project team, but some key members may continue to receive instructions and take their lead from their functional superiors. This is sometimes referred to as dotted line responsibility because of the way it is shown on an organizational chart, and is quite common in the technical side of media companies.

In multimedia the programmer may have a senior programmer and the graphics artist may have a senior graphics artist or creative director who set their standards of work and, in addition, will generally control their workload as well. They may be working for other project managers on other projects during the timescale of your project. In this case, their seniors will control their time and effort on your project. You may find that your programmer cannot complete the task you need on time because another project has been given priority.

You end up fighting for resources without the authority to influence the situation. This shows a definite role conflict. You cannot be held responsible for your project slippage if you don't have control of people's time. Control of time should be one of your biggest responsibilities. You might be able to allow your team member to work on some other tasks for their functional manager, but the manner and exact amount of time should be within your control and governed by *your* project demands. This type of conflict, which interferes with project progress, also applies to non-human resources. If your team members don't have access to the right equipment at the right time because others have been given priority, there are further hold-ups.

There is a need for shared resources in a business, and the management will only be seen to be doing their job if they try to get the most from the least, to increase margins. But there's a fine balance between downtime costs when sharing resources and savings from labour and equipment charges.

It doesn't take long for a hierarchical allocation of resources to get abused by those best placed to do so in the organization. This is mainly because everyone's projects fall prey to shifts in expected workloads and all is fair in a hierarchical war depending on your rank!

If you are working in an organization where functional and project managers coexist, both roles need to be tightly defined. The functional manager's role needs to change to a more generalist role because the project manager's role is specifically tied to the project and is therefore specialist. The authority over people and equipment for the term of the project has to be established, and it needs to rest with the project manager. If not, there is no real role for a manager of this type.

Any request for resource time or equipment that has been allocated to the project should go through the project manager. Otherwise, the programmer and graphics artist tend to agree to the extra work for the functional manager without being fully aware of the present status of the project. For example, they wouldn't know that you are trying to block a major change resulting from a phone call from the client at the moment they agree to extra work. You finish the phone call but have failed to block the change and need them to absorb the extra work on your project.

As the project manager's role is also to monitor the time and cost of the project, a functional structure may cause problems. Many multimedia organizations operate control over time and costs via timesheets. There needs to be some mechanism for monitoring time and translating it into real costs rather than projected costs, and timesheets are a well-accepted practice. However, there are many debates about how much time can be allocated to projects against time used for organizational administration, general meetings and the like.

If the internal and external resources for your project fill in timesheets, which go to the finance/accounts function, then it is their responsibility to have up-to-date records of costs per project for you to keep track of how much you have left to spend. The project manager has to make many decisions on reallocation of budget and spending. If the accounts section is behind with collating the hours from your project, you may not be able to get an accurate picture of how much you have left.

The project management tools have become more refined over the last few years and it has become easier for project managers to pull out the salient information on a project-by-project basis. Electronic timesheets from the whole team can be integrated into project specific reports automatically and a project status generated instantly via some tools. Some tools even generate invoices for the client broken down into the tasks and resources used for a defined period. The tools have and continue to adjust to suit working needs and it has finally been recognized that more and more companies are project-based. The fundamental problem of how accurate the timesheet information is, who, how and what factors influence the hours that are logged, remains problematic.

In a project environment the budget versus time information on the individual projects is necessary for the lower management levels. The same information still needs to be collated by department performance into top management financial information, of course. Accounts departments have to reconcile the overall project payments to overall spending, and reconcile it with the information from other expenses. They have different interests to serve in reporting the overall position to management.

The whole question of how the financial data for each project is kept, and who needs what information when, is a real problem. But as project manager you need to have detailed breakdowns of projected cost and actual costs to use in negotiations with the client. You need to make decisions on how much might be absorbed for small changes for the client as gestures of goodwill and when to charge for other changes because there is a real danger of the projects going over budget.

The structure of the organization will dictate who has what type of financial information, who can have access to which financial data, and under what circumstances. If there is the equivalent of a project manager role in the organization, the financial structure should facilitate this role and its needs as well as the executive management information. Without accurate records of cost, a project management role cannot be fulfilled.

A hierarchical organization will tend to have strict control over who can spend money. If the project manager or equivalent does not have a good level of authority over spending, projects may get held up waiting for the correct authorization. It is right that there is control over spending, but authority levels need to be allocated according to criteria worked out by the management according to the company's needs.

There are two points to note here. First, project managers will only spend wisely within a defined level if they have good information on current spending, otherwise they will be spending blind. So authority to spend should be linked to the responsibility for monitoring the overall budget of the project to avoid this. Second, if project managers buy a piece of software they have a responsibility to ensure that it is really necessary, that the company doesn't already have a copy, that the licence agreement is recorded and filed according to company policy, and that the correct people are fully informed of what they have done. This will avoid others replicating the same spending later through lack of knowledge of the existence of the software.

THEORY INTO PRACTICE 2

Your designer has met a problem that one piece of software will solve. The company doesn't own it. The technical director who must sanction software purchases is on leave, and the systems manager who acts as his unofficial deputy is on a stand at a conference for three days. You have a deadline in two days and don't have the authority to spend company money.

What should you do?

There are no wrong answers. Some might be better than others. Here are some replies from project managers. They might match yours and give you some new insights.

- Buy it myself and claim it back later on expenses.
- Never start a project unless you've agreed some authority to spend money unsanctioned.
- I used to buy things myself but it took so long and so much hassle to get repaid, I ended up out of pocket because I went overdrawn. They didn't care. Then they just expect you to do it all the time. It's in their interest, really. Now I just explain to the clients why I can't make the deadline – they have a go at the management, who have a go at me, but I'd get the software. One day they'll listen, I suppose.
- I'd find someone with some authority and get them to buy it. But it takes so much time to justify why you need it. They're always busy, and blame you for not sorting something out sooner.

In an alternative organizational structure, a team is constructed for a particular project under the project manager's control. The core of the organization is organized to support and facilitate projects, general administration and general management. The project team may exist for only one project and then be disbanded or moved into other teams.

This is more like the working practices of video production. The producer recruits people and facilities according to budget and needs. He or she has authority to spend within budget but has to report back within the company on progress and spending.

Within this type of structure there is more flexibility, which seems to be needed in creative projects, but the organization has to work hard to facilitate, coordinate, record and communicate. There are central needs that have to be controlled – allocation of team space, meeting space, access to phones, network and so on. The larger the organization the harder this becomes, and the informal ways need to become more formalized without becoming restrictive. This is the challenge for management.

Another set of working practices emerging for project-run companies is based on a retail model, in which people are tasked to develop new business for the company. Their salaries tend to be linked to commission based on the amount of business they bring in. Their skills of persuasion and influence are important, but there are dangers for the project manager and also the company under this structure. Because the new business developers need to win the business, they tend to offer too much on too little information and raise clients' expectations of what they will receive. One of the features of managing innovation that we mentioned earlier was the need to control expectations as early as possible. There is an inherent conflict between these roles.

Many new media companies that have an account manager role and a project manager or producer role have not defined the roles and responsibilities carefully. Apart from the dangers mentioned above, poor role definition causes gaps on the one hand and duplicated work on the other. Again, the management needs to recognize this, and then make decisions on how best to resolve it.

As website development has matured and the diversity of projects and their needs for this platform is settling out, it is easier to recognize when particular skill sets may be needed across companies to produce a complete site. This has led to new media companies working in partnerships with other companies for example. When a complex site is being constructed the front-end may well be developed by one company but the server side or back-end processes may well be developed and hosted by another. Some new media companies will encompass all aspects of development while others won't. A project manager's role shifts to encompass coordination between partnerships as well as production in this case.

These are only some of the differences in organizations and a project manager may move between several types of organizational structure in the course of a career. The strengths and limitations of the working environment affect the risks to projects so it is as well to become aware of them. You need to build in more contingency time for achieving tasks if the communication process involves other companies or if the organization is chaotic!

■ The project manager as team leader

A multimedia team can vary in size and skills. Different projects need different teams to achieve them. The team may grow and shrink during the course of the project. Parts may be subcontracted out if necessary. Sometimes a team member may take on two roles – graphics and authoring, for example. The team definition will begin from the definition of the major components of the project. Then those with skills that match the requirements will be allocated or recruited.

In terms of roles, a typical development team may have:

■ a leader, who might also use his or her specialism from a media background to contribute to part of the project development;

The project manager as team leader.

- someone who will agree the content and treatment/interface design with the client and the relevant members of the team;
- someone to produce the computer graphics;
- someone to program or, for web pages, write HTML;
- someone to program CGI for the back-end servers if needed on a web project;
- someone to arrange and manage the audio and video production, if these are necessary.

Over the last couple of years a project manager has also become involved with an extra stage that precedes production. When the definition of the project is complex the project manager may decide to bring in analysts or consultants. This will depend on how a company works, the type of client, their expectations and their position in their own company.

Defining the strategy of a business in terms of new media can be a major phase in itself and several parallel projects might spin out of the one strategy. Once the major strategy is defined, then the project manager can take over.

Within a project team there are also support roles that you'd expect to find as part of the organization structure, such as technical support and secretarial/admin. There are often important support roles that the organization may need to employ if they don't have the skills in-house and the project needs them: project/personal assistants, picture researchers, cartoonists, animators, rights clearer, video graphics artists, translators, specialist programmers, computing consultants and technical consultants, for example.

All the usual problems of personality conflict and professional conflict can occur in a team. But a leader of a multidisciplined, professional project team made up of individual specialists also faces people used to making and taking decisions for themselves within their own specialisms.

The control of a creative, skilled group is not easy. In multimedia, the members of the group all have a relevant perspective on the way the content should be structured and treated. All the key people will have some training in their professional background to analyse and treat information within their discipline. This is a potential strength but also a potential weakness of the group. The project manager will have a bias from a background specialism which will be evident in the perspective of the treatment.

The first management decision – of whether you will impose a general design solution on your team or involve them fully in the creative decisions – is often made for you, and is outside your control. An initial specification might have defined the media mix in general terms because of the budget agreed up front. For example, colleagues might have worked up the proposal for the clients because they had the time available. The budget for a CD-ROM might have been based on the cost of ten minutes of video for Windows, computer graphics (approximately 100 screens), a few five-second simple animations, 30 minutes of audio, and so on. It is possible that neither you nor your team members had any involvement in the initial specification. This is more common where the core functionality of a site is an online database that has been defined and possibly developed by another company and then your work might relate to defining the interactive front-end to add onto this. Or a company website might have been specified as a maximum of 18 pages of text and graphics, no audio, no video, and no animation.

This type of specification acts as a constraint under which you have to try to work irrespective of whether the detailed examination of the content indicates a different media selection mix. Most projects can't get off the ground without such a high-level specification. If the detailed understanding of the content suggests a better media mix, and you feel it is in everyone's interest to point out the improved benefits to the client, the same conditions apply to your suggestions for changes to the program structure as to suggestions coming from the client. You need to convince them to pay more or sacrifice some other aspects of the program.

This directive management approach to your team sounds harsh. However, if the time allowed for decisions at the beginning of a project is severely limited then this will be a set of circumstances where an initial directive stance may be appropriate. It does not mean that you continue to dictate solutions to the team. Wherever possible their input is needed to give a rounded product, so your management style has to adapt to the changing circumstances of the project as explained in Chapter 14, *Team management principles*.

The main difficulty is in deciding what treatments to use for the various parts of the content. The decisions are often made quite early in relation to the agreed budget. Your team will have plenty of ideas on what will work more effectively. They have freedom of thought in relation to the top quality that they could attain in their specialist areas, and are often frustrated by the decisions that have been made.

They are not subject to the constraints of time and cost in their thinking, and if they haven't experienced the difficult dynamics that occur between the company and the clients to reach enough of an agreement to proceed, they find it hard to compromise their enthusiasm and professional opinions. You need to make clear the reasons behind the decisions, and focus your team on tailoring their suggestions to improvements, consistent with the time and costs, that will serve the user best.

Some of the most difficult problems arise if your team members suggest ideas in front of clients. Once clients have been motivated by an idea that sounds good, you are in a vulnerable position. It is essential that you brief the team to make suggestions openly at any time *except* when they are in meetings with clients. In market-driven applications the working atmosphere is different. Creative brainstorming between the team members is common both before and during the production. Because all the decisions can be taken quickly and internally, more time is created for fine tuning and experimentation. This can still get out of control, so someone has to focus the team on the deadlines and call the tune of how much the changes are costing in terms of effort.

It also causes problems if your team members respond to clients' suggestions in meetings by agreeing that they can do what is wanted. They will be concerned to demonstrate their technical and professional competence. But it is not what is possible that is the issue, it is what is possible within the constraints. The team members feel free of the constraints and will not make the wisest decisions. This is a common cause of tension between creative decision makers and business decision makers. The project manager has a foot in both camps!

You need to make the reasons clear, and set ground rules for how team members communicate with clients. They should not make any agreements for changes unless they directly affect only the material they are working on and they can contain the changes within the next working deadline. You have to be kept informed of the changes if these are agreed independently with the client – on the phone, for example. If they receive requests from the client that fall outside these parameters then these have to be referred to you. Some clients may play you and a team member off against each other in order to achieve a change in the design. In this case it is important that your team tell you of anything of this nature that they discuss with the client.

When ideas are suggested by team members, your problem is to determine how much they can affect the quality without incurring time and cost penalties. If you do not allow them to shape the program in some ways you run the risk of missing out on genuine improvements, and of losing the team's motivation, trust and respect. If you allow them to influence the structure but don't control them, then there is a big risk of overrun on time and costs. You face a dilemma. Should you tap into the team's appropriate strengths only up to a level that can be contained within cost or budget, or should you fight on their behalf to convince your management and the client that the cost of the increase in quality is justified?

If the project manager shares a discipline perspective with a team member the balance of power in decisions can easily be unbalanced. It is difficult to listen to suggestions objectively when your own discipline is driving your thinking in a different direction. So the split role of project manager and specialist complicates the job.

Sometimes the timescale of the project is so tight that decisions have to be taken quickly and imposed on the team: so you may allow changes only for technical efficiency. The team will try to affect the structure and look and feel, but in this case you should focus them on the shortness of time and make sure that what is specified is technically possible in the time.

On other occasions you need to offer a defined time to the team to talk through the agreed outline structure and ask for any suggestions for improvements. This team effort is valuable at the early stages of the project. It is important that you influence their decisions on which suggestions to implement according to time, cost, and benefit to the user. The time for suggestions has to have a limit because the later into a project changes occur, the more impact they have on the remaining time.

You need to consider whether there may be hidden agendas. This is problematic if the suggestions are outside your own specialism. There may be personal motives driving the suggestions, as the members of the team may want to create an opportunity to try out some of the latest techniques purely to obtain the experience that will keep them abreast of the latest advances in their area. These might not be in the project's scope or interest. This is a balancing act, but you need to understand your team's motives and accommodate them within your constraints.

It is true that you cannot time creative ideas. Many good ones will occur during the project that will have to be rejected. As the detail of the content emerges, the conception of the best treatment will be affected. You do not want to discourage ideas. They are part of professional development, and there's value in the team's recognizing their worth. They will serve other projects because the factors that led up to the ideas will be recognized earlier in subsequent projects where it is easier to implement them.

Throughout the project, as team leader you have to represent the views of the users. They are the most important group but they may have no input into the project. The project's success depends on the users' reaction. Your decisions on which changes have priority over others should try to serve the users above all others. There are many interests that drive the project in one direction or another. Often the client's direction will prevail even when they make decisions that are counter to professional advice because they are in a position to call the tune.

If user interface and cognition are not your strengths, then identify the people in the team who have these skills. If necessary, bounce the suggestions off other colleagues who have strengths in these areas to test them out. You need to ask all those who make suggestions for change, including yourself, to define the benefit to the user. It is surprising how often this will help the decision making. If time, money and circumstances allow, small user trials can often help.

This has been a rapid overview of some circumstances and how they can affect the management role of the project manager. The full chapter on team management (Chapter 14) examines some of the principles behind management styles. Consequently, the pressure, time and cost constraints on decision making are less evident there. However, a project manager is expected to employ the appropriate style for a given set of circumstances.

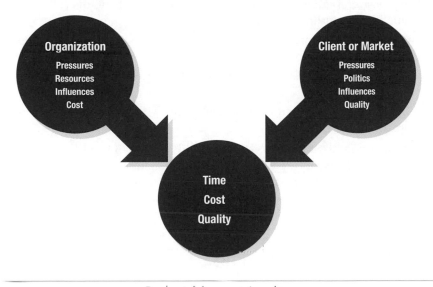

Project Manager's role.

The role of the multimedia project manager

It should now be clear that the project manager's role is to control the progress of the project against any detrimental influences to the time, cost and quality that can occur from the client, the place of work, the market forces, and the team. The needs of the user should drive priorities and decisions during the course of design and production, and that is true for both client-centred and market-driven projects, and for both on- and offline projects.

This is not a recognized definition within multimedia. Project managers, or their equivalent, have usually evolved from specialist roles of computing, graphics, video production, or interactive education and training. Many have received little or no exposure to general business and management principles. Any training is usually confined to professional development within their specialism. This is driven by the constant changes within the professional areas and the need to keep abreast of them. As the tools and standards become more stable, there may be more time to broaden the scope of their training.

■ Summary

- Project management principles unite the disparate ways of working in interactive media development.
- Not all project management methods transfer well to multimedia development.
- Time, cost and quality principles are important but the overall concept of quality in multimedia remains vague.
- The project's multimedia design quality = the content and treatment agreement reached for that project.
- The impact of changes on time, cost and quality can put the project at risk.
- Multimedia management shares similarities with the management of innovation.
- Anticipation of risk and measures of control are important.
- Organizational structure affects the project manager's role, responsibility, authority and control.
- The multimedia project manager has a difficult role as team leader because of the diverse, creative team.

■ Recommended reading

Block R. (1983). *The Politics of Projects*. New York: Yourdon Press Computing Series

Brooks F.P. Jr (1995). *The Mythical Man-Month. Essays on Software Engineering*, 2nd edn. Reading, MA: Addison-Wesley

Chicken J. (1994). *Managing Risks and Decisions in Major Projects*. London: Chapman & Hall

Reiss G. (1992). *Project Management Demystified*. London: E. & F.N. Spon

Webb A. (1994). *Managing Innovative Projects*. London: Chapman & Hall

Young T.L. (1993). *Planning Projects*. London: Industrial Society

☐ Project management tools – for multiple web-based projects

http://www.infoworld.com/testcenter/comparison/000131tcfeatures.html
  A comparison test of three web-based project management tools: Team Center, Team Play and WebProject

http://www.inovie.com/
  Example of a web-based project management tool and its features: Team Center

http://www.bulldog.ca
http://www.vertabase.com/about/index.html
  Tools developed by and for new media production companies Bulldog and Vertabase

3

Scoping a project

Project manager's responsibilities

- To ascertain the client's brief
- To attune yourself to the client and their culture
- To clarify unclear information
- To gather sufficient information to write an agreement document
- To explain any queries the client has
- To involve specialists as and when needed

■ The initial phase of the project: are the clients ready?

At the first few meetings with the client you are trying to establish whether they have a clear brief, if it is realistic in terms of the time for development, the expected use of media, and the results needed from the project. You need to understand these in order to define the cost and quality level that can be produced in the available time, and to define the number and type of resources you'll need for the project. If the client does not have a clear brief this often indicates that they have not yet defined their business strategy for the project.

There are several approaches that are used to help the definition. These approaches tend to reflect the particular bias of the company and the experience of the client. If your company is more on the creative side of multimedia development then perhaps the creative director and an account manager will work with the client to establish the initial brief. If your company is more attuned to the software development process, then the technical director and project manager might work to define the initial brief. If your company is more content driven than creative or technical, then an information strategist or business strategist might work with the client to arrive at a common understanding of the project brief.

The way in which initial meetings are conducted varies from company to company. Practice ranges from a single person trying to define the brief over several meetings to full-scale meetings attended by representatives of the main disciplines involved: production and management, graphics and software.

Many companies rely on the experience of the person or people conducting the interviews to ensure that relevant information is obtained. There is no standard approach, and this means that projects tend to evolve differently, displaying a variety of problems. This can often be traced back to early meetings where some vital facts or inferences were missed. So it is important for more than one person to take notes and for any unclear points to be revisited. The people involved at the initial stages of defining a project need to understand enough about all the processes in production to ask the right high-level questions. Then depending on the client's answers, they may need to draft in specialists from the team to determine the implications. It is useful to finish meetings by confirming the action points for both sides, especially if the clients have agreed to undertake some contributory work.

The fundamental requirement of these meetings is for you as a developer to interpret what your client wants, map this to the capabilities and constraints of a technology system and define how and what you can produce in a certain timescale for an amount of money. You are effectively trying to understand what reactions the client wants from the users via the technology – their objectives for using the system in other words. Unfortunately

this is not necessarily as simple as it might seem, because you and your client will probably have different backgrounds, and your client may be unfamiliar with the strengths and weaknesses of interactive media and what it can offer to their business. If you do not define what your clients are trying to achieve with new media, you will not be able to agree that you have provided what they wanted.

A clear, agreed definition of what the client says they want at the beginning of a project is essential. Then, if they want to change the scope of the project as new information arrives or if new people are brought into the project and influence its direction, you can demonstrate the change, evaluate the impact on the timescales and re-cost accordingly. Without the definition, the project can meander around, and it will be difficult to ask for extra time or costs for the changes.

It should be clear that deciding exactly when a project begins – so that your company can start charging for its time and expertise – is problematic. How many meetings can take place with how many people involved, for nothing? When can you and the client agree that the project has started? Multimedia companies have not generally been good at establishing this and this definition stage can last for a long time. In fact, in software development companies, the specification phase may be longer than the actual development of the application! However, the specification phase for software development is a known project stage and is charged for in their case.

If a new media project is won through a tender process then the winner knows that the project is deemed to begin after they have won. But all companies tendering for a project have to absorb the time and effort they put in to the initial presentations. This can be substantial if the process goes through the equivalent of several knock-out rounds.

If a project is not won through the tender process, how do both companies define the start point unless the developer indicates what will be offered freely and when charges will commence? It is obviously a delicate balance as the developer needs good relations with the prospective client and wants to show willing. It is becoming common for companies to establish a strategy of working that is defined in stages or phases and which is explained to the client. Then by agreeing that they have entered a phase, it is easier to agree where costs start within it.

For example, specify, build, test and deliver are recognizable as software development phases and these are sometimes used by new media companies that have a technical bias. Some other examples of phases used by new media companies include:

- discover, design, build, deploy
- relate, define, develop, test, release
- engage, develop concepts, implement, test, maintain
- analyse, design, engineer, launch, service
- initiate, scope, produce, test, deliver

It would be good practice for companies to spend time producing clear, flexible guidelines and checklists for stages of a project which could serve as the company's defined way of working. This should include reference to the actions the company will take for each phase and the documentation that will be provided or used at each stage. A defined process helps new staff gear up to the company's way of working quickly and also helps clients understand what will happen during the project.

It would be sensible to indicate when costs are likely to start within the first defined phase. Sometimes one or two meetings are enough to define a workable brief because the client is clear what is needed and you might have worked with them before. At other times, a great deal of time and effort is needed.

We refer here to this phase of a project as 'scoping'. In it we are trying to understand the breadth and depth of the project so that we can begin to estimate time and costs. To achieve this we can explain to clients that we try to reach a project definition through analysis in a 'scoping' phase within X number of meetings through the use of questionnaires. At the end of this exploratory meeting phase of X meetings we will both agree that if there are gaps in this analysis the clients may need more time to provide the answers, and that the time and cost markers will start for the project. We may well suggest that they work with one of the development company's appropriate people – strategist, consultant or analyst – on an extended scoping stage to facilitate them getting any necessary answers. As long as we have explained that this is how we work and that the preparation work is essential for the good of the project, these consultant costs can be timed and costed separately. The client would need to agree to this way of working up front, of course.

Some clients will have defined their e-business strategy for the whole of the company and be in the process of implementing their strategy by outsourcing specific new media projects. Then you would expect that they would be able to answer many of the questions that are necessary to help achieve a clear development path. The scoping phase could be relatively straightforward but you'd still be putting in quite an amount of time to achieve a clear definition. For a very straightforward smaller-scale project you may decide to offer the scoping phase free by using faster techniques and aids to help definition. These might include a template-driven approach to websites linked to different prices for different functions and ideas maps to focus the client on what they want. (See Chapter 13, *Managing small, quick projects.*)

☐ Extended scoping analysis techniques

If you haven't been involved in a project where defining the breadth and depth of the content and the range of functionality has been difficult, it will be hard to imagine. You may have been on the other end of one of these projects where the clients seemingly kept changing their minds because of new circumstances that occurred within their company. As a member of the development team you might have been kept running round in circles lining up the project first in one way and then another. Most of the answers to these problems lie in getting a consensus of opinion and direction from the clients. If their company hasn't provided them with a coherent direction for the use of technology, there are techniques that analysts use to help. Each specialist – the business strategist, training analyst, marketing analyst or the information analyst – has a particular way of eliciting information and then classifying it or ranking it into sections according to preferences. If your company is concerned more with the visual impact, the brand or image of the client and the emphasis is on the look and feel aspects of technology, then there is usually also an extended scoping phase in trying to arrive at a result that fits the subjective needs.

In the past, all forms of analysis have been time-intensive and time-consuming. The specialists needed to get a good cross-section of detailed opinions and sift them in various ways, then analyse and present the results. You can appreciate that just trying to tap into several managers across a multinational company to get one level of information might take weeks to set up, for example. Luckily technology has changed this. Now there are web tools that can elicit and sort relevant information quickly. Increasingly an ICT (Information and Communication Technologies) company's needs analysis can and will be done electronically. This includes new media projects so keep an eye out for the tools emerging.

One example of such a tool is Concept System. It is classified as a concept user interface tool (CUI). These analysis tools can help groups of people from across an organization to brainstorm, organize, rank, sort, cluster, prioritize, and action plan. It is this type of analysis that is needed at the beginning of projects to identify requirements. Then these can be mapped to the technology solutions in ways that allow the user to access what they need/want.

This CUI tool is based on pyschology techniques originating in the 1950s with George Kelly and his personal construct theories. His sorting and prioritizing methods lend themselves to computerization and have spawned several tools. But the added bonus of access to dispersed people via the Web and the ease of processing the material are making these tools more attractive.

Let's take an example of a large company wanting an intranet. They are having problems deciding what content it should cover. Obviously people from management and employees need to be consulted. Through applying the various techniques using a web tool, people from both groups move from brainstorming ideas to ranking concepts. Then they can compare one group consensus against another to identify points of common understanding against misunderstanding between the management and employees on this issue. This can help show ideas about the information to be included on the intranet that will meet most people's approval and so can be implemented more easily. The results of each analysis phase are reported visually via the Web and their significance is easy to grasp. (See the reference where there is an example of how the tool was applied to determine an e-commerce site's needs.)

This tool is quite complex and analysts need to be trained to use it effectively. Also, although these techniques can aid understanding, participants often find the tasks difficult and can get discouraged about completing them. In effect, the clients and their representatives have to reach a consensus through their own effort focused by the tool as well as the analyst. This is good for the analyst because it makes it harder for the company to turn round at the end of the project and say the developer's analyst gave bad advice about the content, the company image or whatever. But, on the other hand, the clients en masse may miss opportunities because they may not have clear understanding of the capabilities of technology systems. They will only encapsulate and consensualize ideas they currently understand. This mapping to the technology's strengths and constraints is an important item to introduce in some way. Tools may help but the analysts can still influence the final result based on understanding the wider picture.

Other forms of concept mapping are available to help analysts gather, sort and report both objective and subjective data. Subjective data has traditionally been more difficult to define. Concept maps can help determine content clusters – that is concepts that have commonality in some way that suggest they should be near one another, and flowcharting can help show relationships between the different pieces of a website for example. It is a good idea to draft a flowchart or an application map as early as you can in the scoping phase to help the client understand the shape and relationship between the parts of the whole. This can be refined as a visual record and it is certainly a good idea to include one with the agreement document at the conclusion of the scoping phase as a visual representation of the project. (See the references to flowcharting and ideas mapping tools in the references.) These tools can be used at the more detailed phases of project development and scripting too – wherever a framework example will make complex information easier to conceptualize.

Even recognizing these factors affecting the scoping of the project, it is not easy to gauge when a scoping phase will be straightforward and when it will not. There are further specialist projects within multimedia development that demand extra extended scoping analysis. A project that will be distributed in several languages in different countries needs careful attention because localizing or internationalizing projects can range from the relatively simple to extremely complex. Chapter 17 addresses the major principles that lie behind these projects. It will give a clear understanding of the issues and indicate the areas needing attention. E-commerce sites where a complex database of products has to be developed and the supply chain including distribution of products is affected because of the online focus also have specialist considerations. The amount and type of testing the client expects on a project is another difficult topic to check thoroughly but the issues need to be raised at the beginning because the range and type of testing greatly affects the time for development and the cost of the complete project.

Apart from specialist projects, there are extra considerations about web projects that a project manager needs to consider at the initial stages. These involve defining how much programming will be needed and which company resources will have to be involved.

To understand these special considerations we need to understand the production phases of a web project. These are divided into front-end, client-side development (by which we mean browser) and back-end or server development. Some projects are only concerned with front-end and browser development, others include the back-end as well. Different programmers

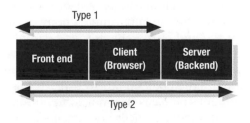

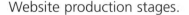

Website production stages.

tend to address the front-end and back-end programming stages even though the computer languages they use may be the same. They address different issues and apply different mind sets accordingly and in larger companies they tend to be found in separate sections if not separate buildings. (You will find more on the front/back divide in Book 2 Chapter 5, *Platform parameters*.)

If the project is going to concern all stages, then each part needs to be scoped. The programmers or web developers taking care of the browser development need to understand which browsers and platforms the application will run on and if they will have to maintain these as the browsers change. The number of browsers the application works with and whether it will be cross-platform or not affect the amount of development work. This will affect the time and cost of the project and so the project manager needs to get feedback from the right people to scope this stage correctly. Similarly, if the project will involve server-side development, the correct person has to be involved to scope the implications for resources, time and cost for this stage. If the application will depend on a large database to drive the information, then an information architect or database analyst may be necessary to help with the overall scoping.

A project manager cannot be a specialist across all areas but does need to recognize which stages of production will be involved and when to ask for specialist involvement on the scoping. One of the key indicators of whether all stages will be involved is the use of dynamic web pages. Increasingly larger projects involving websites involve the building of web pages 'on the fly' based on dynamic data transfer between the user and the information repository of the application and/or dynamic data updates from programmers into the information repository. Smaller web projects often use static data. If projects are going to contain dynamic data they will need questions asked about all the production stages. Otherwise the first two stages need to be covered.

So a general-purpose scoping questionnaire needs to ask the right high-level questions. If the initial answers indicate that there are specialist areas, this should trigger more backup questionnaires on these to refine the definition.

The following specimen questionnaire will provide you with a checklist and ensure a sound basis for obtaining the first level of information for an online interactive project. Each question category will be explained so that it is clear why the information is important. A copy of the online questionnaires is included at the end of the chapter, and can also be found on the website.

If you are working on an offline project there is an example questionnaire from an earlier edition of the book on our website. It has been moved there because the development emphasis has moved to online work.

Whatever type of interactive project you are involved with, the delivery platform of the project will have an influence on the overall look and feel and the type of interactivity. The budget and production time will affect your design decisions. The questions have to be tailored to the type of project. As there are many variables, we cannot include templates to cover them all. If you are responsible for interactive television programmes, you will need to use the following as examples to formulate a set of scoping questions. If you have a definite market bias – websites for large advertising companies, for example – then you will be able to refine the questions to suit your market. Hybrid projects such as a CD-ROM with volatile content kept on a website for pulling into the package as appropriate, for example, will need to combine elements of both of the questionnaires so refer to the offline one on the website as well as the online one outlined below.

It is the rationale and the principles of having a defined set of high-level questions for all projects that is important for you to grasp and apply for yourself suited to your own working conditions and set of projects.

■ Online interactive media scoping questionnaire

☐ Client's previous multimedia experience

Project name/no: _____

Contact details
Client/organization name: _____
Address: _____
_____
_____
_____

Tel: _____ Fax: _____ E-mail: _____
Website: _____

Project contacts:
Name(s): _____ Positions(s): _____
_____ _____
_____ _____
Direct line _____ E-mail: _____

Previous interactive media experience

Online
None ☐   A little ☐   Fair ☐   Good ☐   Experienced ☐

Offline
None ☐   A little ☐   Fair ☐   Good ☐   Experienced ☐

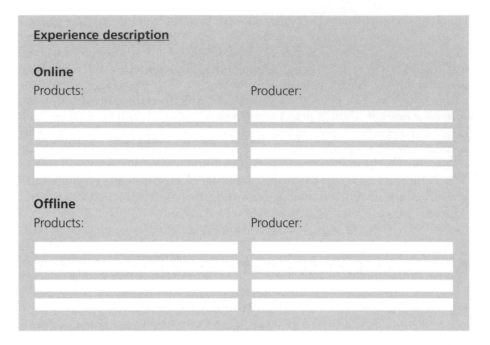

Prior experience affects everyone, and clients are no exception. It sets up expectations, which you need to understand. They may have had good and bad experiences. You can learn what they like and don't like in terms of ways of working as well as in interactivity. If they are return customers you need to find out as much as you can from the people who worked with them before. In fact you should have done this prior to the first meeting if it was recognized that they had been clients previously. Even if they are previous clients it is still good practice to find out what they particularly liked and disliked the last time.

You need to cover both on- and offline experience, whatever sort of project you are working on, as experience in one has both positive and negative impact when moving to the other, and colours expectations. For example, a client may have a large text-based website, which the user navigates by using a search facility, because the company deals primarily in information. Marketing consultancies would fall into this category, where they offer summaries of their respective reports to tempt people to buy the whole report. The text-driven nature of the website may well be the most appropriate way to convey the information. But if the company decides to develop a marketing CD, the interactivity of the website will not be the best model for the new purpose and delivery medium, even if they believe it will be. Some of the content may be useful, but it needs a new treatment to achieve the impact they want.

☐ Statement of what the client wants

Client's initial statement of what they want

It helps to formulate what the client says they want at the beginning of the interview. They may be very focused and know their needs precisely. In this case the rest of the questions confirm their needs and develop the detail. Or, they can be very vague. They may have a notion but not be able to define it precisely. The more precise they are the easier your job will be – unless they have misjudged what can be achieved or how to make best use of the medium. The more vague they are the harder you will have to work to get a good specification. An example of what you might enter here for a relatively small and straightforward project would be:

> *This is a specialist small firm producing garden furniture and ornaments. They want to set up a website to evaluate the potential for sales of their products over the Net.*

Notice that they have not said that they want to sell their products on the Net. At the moment, a database of products and payment structure for selling online would not be a confirmed need.

Alternatively, you might have put:

> *This is a specialist small firm producing garden furniture and ornaments. They think they want a webite but first they want advice as to what information to place there, some costings based on different types of site, and the type of benefits they could expect from their investment.*

This should trigger you to shelve the questionnaire, show them examples of your work, and demonstrate the features of some equivalent small specialist retail sites to help define the component parts of a site that would suit them. Once they have an understanding of what is possible they should be allowed to discuss the possibilities and probably return for a more productive meeting. It might help them to take the questionnaire away in this case so that they can prepare the answers to the queries.

In the case of a corporate client there might be several section managers involved. Then a more gentle lead-in where you try to understand their expectations of the processes involved, demonstrate some of your company's capabilities, listen to their reactions and explain your way of working might lay the ground better for the stronger analysis via questionnaire. The processes do not have to be rigid and can be tailored to suit the type of project and client.

☐ Type of project

The delivery medium affects the specific type of project that will be produced. Online projects serve a much wider range of needs than offline projects, and new uses are continually emerging as the Internet develops as an essential mass communication delivery platform. Classification of project types in this fast-moving marketplace has not yet become codified. So the following is offered as the starting point, and should be tailored accordingly.

Online project type

Internet ☐   Hybrid Web/CD ☐   Intranet ☐   Extranet ☐   Mobile ☐

Set up new facility _____

(If yes, domain name suggestions?)

_____

_____

_____

Add/change existing facility _____

Internet/intranet/extranet

It is important to clarify the differences between these three categories. The Internet offers general public access to electronic information. An intranet provides closed access to electronic information, and is usually company specific. An extranet allows nominated companies or individuals access to all or part of an intranet. If the site will be new then the company needs to put forward suggestions for its domain name. This is not always straightforward, as others may have already taken the most obvious choice. The sooner this is confirmed the better, and if they cannot come up with suggestions ask them to give you three approved alternatives as soon as possible.

The general scope of the project will be linked to the type of delivery and the access to the online facilities. Setting up a secure international corporate intranet and providing the design templates for each division to insert their own content while retaining the common 'corporate' approach is very different from designing a small company profile website to be published on the Internet.

In the intranet example the technical specification aspects can be complex, with several servers spread around the world and the security implications of linking them through the Internet. Such data links may already be in place but it is not uncommon for a large organization's IT structure to have grown spasmodically, and it may be difficult to find out exactly what is in place and who is in charge of the various parts. On the content side the number and type of templates will take a long time to establish, with the potential for cultural or linguistic differences and even office politics conspiring to confuse the issue. It may well emerge that a database might be the most efficient way of dealing with varying amounts of the data, and this might have to be built from scratch. Training people to input the data is likely to be necessary as well.

The small company website profile, on the other hand, may mean no more than several sets of pages linked by a straightforward structure with the option for the client to come back with material to update the pages as and when they wish. The technical and design aspects are much more straightforward in this case. The company will either have its own server or will be renting space from an Internet service provider (ISP), but in either case setting the website up on the server will be relatively straightforward. Hopefully the only awkward issue will be getting the right domain name. (There's information on how the domain name system works in Book 2 Chapter 2, *The Internet*, and some background on legal implications of the names in Chapter 15 in this book that covers intellectual property.)

Hybrid Web/CD

The term 'hybrid' can have many meanings. In Chapter 1 we have already mentioned a hybrid project as being a mixture of online and offline, for example a CD-ROM or DVD that links to a website. We can refer to this as an Internet/CD hybrid, or a Web/CD hybrid. This could be a disk that can take updates from the Internet, or it could be a website that picks its larger assets, such as movies, from a disc on the local machine. The term hybrid CD-ROM, for example, is also used to describe a CD that mixes different CD formats, usually CD audio and CD-ROM data.

It is more common than many realize that clients begin by wanting an Internet site but end up wanting a CD-ROM as well, and expect it for no extra cost! The CD often takes data from the site to feed into certain calculations, or refers out to extended resources found on the Net. Many clients imagine that once the data has been structured for the website it can be put on a CD and distributed as well. This is rarely straightforward, and the general expectations of the media to be found on a CD and how they operate are different from the Web. A hybrid Internet/CD project needs the information to be structured differently to optimize transfer between the different delivery mechanisms, and often needs a lot of extra data of different types. A shift in the target audience for the CD is common, and this means that the new market sector or specialized sector needs new information.

A hybrid project needs to combine elements of this questionnaire and the offline questionnaire. In your negotiations they should be treated like two separate projects and costed as such, taking into account any overlap of assets and data. Often the client does not understand the term 'hybrid', and it raises the idea for them to consider. In this case, you should take the opportunity to explain the issues and indicate that if they want a CD-ROM it needs separate specification and costing.

In this way there are no hidden expectations, and they will expect separate costs to be associated with a CD-ROM from the beginning of the relationship. If they originally reject the notion but suddenly change their minds in the middle of the project and want a CD, you will be able to remind them of the discussion and indicate that they originally wanted a website only. Accordingly, the assets and information have been oriented to that delivery platform only, and a CD will mean more work for you and therefore cost more now than if they had decided on a hybrid in the first place. As long as you have covered this earlier, it makes extra payments more palatable to the client even though they are usually annoyed – more with themselves, it should be said.

Mobile

Because of the success of mobile phones – in Europe particularly – many new media companies have been asked to develop projects for WAP or mobile. Their clients want to break into the interactive communication market. These projects count as online because the interaction takes place over the network. The phone is likely to have a tiny web browser built in and text is displayed on the mobile phone's view screen. Although the amount and type of information is limited by the tiny view screen, the telcos have been keen to understand what the public will access in this way and to establish a presence for the better interactive communication that will be offered through interactive video phones or more likely hand-held PDAs. Fortunately as even small PDAs are produced with high-resolution colour screens, the inadequacies of a WAP phone display will no longer be the main limitation. In the short term the issue is bandwidth, and even in the future mobile devices are likely to have less bandwidth than fixed ones. Because WAP in itself is arguably a passing phase, the term 'mobile' has been used here to describe the more generic project type. (See Book 2, Chapter 4, for the technical background about mobile communications.)

☐ Market sector of the client

Market sector			
Commercial ☐	Corporate ☐	Government ☐	Education ☐

The major categories of commercial, corporate, government and education are included as an indicator of your potential administrative overhead. As a rule, small commercial sites allow you more freedom and versatility when compared with the others. Decisions can be given to you faster, and your work can progress more smoothly. With the other three sectors, and with large commercial clients, it is often much harder to get clear statements and directions. You may be held up for long periods waiting for confirmation of how to proceed even if you follow the advice given in other chapters about establishing authority and sign-off. The internal cultural and political nuances associated with large commercial sites or the other three sectors cannot be ignored in your attempt to size up the scope of the project.

Project bias

Project bias	Importance ranking	Size of section (large, medium, small)
Company profile		
Information gathering		
Information dissemination		
Retail (products or services description)		
Database access/development		
Online transactions		
Marketing/advertising		
Redesign site front-end		
Branding/image rework		
Others (specify)		

The projects will often span several of the components under this heading, and it helps to understand this as soon as possible. The bias on the type of data will help to determine the type of interactivity needed, which will in turn have an effect on the programming and design. A recruitment agency website, for example, may need part company profile, part information gathering (prospective job candidates), and part information dissemination (database of current jobs on offer). These begin to give a good indication for the scope of the project, as you may then try to refine exactly what is needed under each component. You should be beginning to recognize the need for coordinating and agreeing the essential aspects of content for the company profile, form design for form filling, several layers of search facility, and so on.

If the site is to have a retail bias then an online database of products and services with online and offline payment options may be necessary. The company may already have a digital database and may link this to product availability and dispatch. On the other hand, none of these may be in place and all may need to be developed from scratch. Commercial online database development may be part of your skill base or you might have a partnership or alliance with a software company to develop this part of the project while you develop the front-end. The important thing is to realize that this needs precise definition by a competent person.

If a sizeable database is part of the brief whether the project is e-commerce or a volatile information site, a separate questionnaire would need to be completed with the client's software representative and your senior database member of staff to ensure the scope of that pure software development is thoroughly understood. Other aspects are related to this definition. The security of online transactions is an issue that necessitates clarification and firm agreement. The type of encryption and secure servers would also need to be defined. The specialist questionnaire needs to check on the company's policy for exchange of data across its systems and across the firewalls it might have as security. All these can have implications on the size and true scope of the project and need understanding by the right people.

If the brief shows any marketing and advertising bias, this indicates the need for a clear understanding of the image the company wants to convey and who they are trying to reach. These components have a particular bearing on the look and feel of the site, and have to have careful treatment. The same is true if you are asked to redesign a site. In this case your client will be expecting to improve their image and may have identified necessary new components. Because the medium is so volatile, the breakthroughs in programming suddenly allow new features of interactivity or design. Redesigning sites is often connected with introducing these new features. As they occur frequently, it is not uncommon for high-profile sites to be redesigned every six months or so. This creates a drive for others to keep up with fashion, and causes a ripple effect across other sites. However, while new web browsers bring new technologies and techniques to the web designer, not all web users keep up with the trends, and so any use of new web features has to be made knowing that not all potential viewers will see them. The amount and type of log analysis on user behaviour that would be collected and pre-release user trials would also need consideration for these types of projects.

☐ Importance ranking

If the clients have identified several components, use the ranking column. Because the amount and type of information can be infinite, you need to get the client to recognize their priorities. This is to encourage them to be realistic, and to help you to apportion your effort. If, later, the client does not like your quote, it will help you make edit decisions to prune the material that is least important to them. They may well say that each component has the same importance, so you might enter equal ranking numbers for them. The aim here is for you to understand if and where there might be leeway. An alternative way of approaching this quick form of ranking with clients is called MoSCoW. This gets the client to define what they must have (M), should have (S), could have (C) and want (W) but will wait for next time. The principle is the same – clarifying the most important needs for the client. You may find that you need to do the more extensive scoping analysis at this point because the clients are not able to define their needs. Refer to the earlier section, 'Extended scoping analysis techniques', for more information. The MoSCoW principle comes from rapid software application development processes and is part of a complete methodology for handling fast production of more traditional projects. We have just borrowed the high-level idea here not the whole process so recognize that people from software backgrounds may think that using this acronmyn indicates you will use the complete methodology. It is important that you are clear if you are using it all or not. (See the references for more information on Rapid Application Development.)

☐ Size of section

The amount of information you are given to structure for the site affects the time needed to complete the project and therefore the cost. Although it is all relative, you have to try and understand the amount of material within each section to get a feel of how to apportion time and resources as well as cost. One company's expectations of a company profile might be succinct and neatly contained in a few pages; another might see the profile as a major component, with several subsections and lots of media. They might both have ranked the profile as the most important to them, but their expectations of how you will deliver it can be very different. These queries might tease out several aspects that are important for you to note, so have some blank sheets ready. They often prompt healthy discussion between the client's representatives themselves, and they may want to consider their options before they answer. That's fine. Get them to note down the queries they want to discuss but continue with the questionnaire, as other questions might prompt similar responses and they will need to go away to consider their answers to all of them. If you are getting the impression that the clients have a lot to think through, or recognize they have time constraints to make their decisions and would be receptive to help, it is at this stage that you could remind them that an analyst or consultant from your company could facilitate their discussions. These people could help them align their decisions to their business strategy while firming up their directions ready for this project. This service would be offered with a price tag but once the client's awareness of the issues has been raised through the questioning process they should have more confidence in you and recognize the value of the offer.

☐ Browser/platform expectations

Browser/platform expectations

Either:

Developer policy accepted i.e.

Development only for X browser and X versions on X platform   Yes ☐   No ☐

Or:

Client wants:

Browser(s) _____

Versions supported: _____

Plug-ins _____

Platform(s) _____

Allow Java?   Yes ☐   No ☐

Allow JavaScript?   Yes ☐   No ☐

Allow ActiveX?   Yes ☐   No ☐

Or:

Client does not know.

Client contact name for answers _____

                        Tel: _____

                        E-mail: _____

This is the section where you are trying to understand how much extra programming will be involved to make the application work for particular browsers and their various versions and whether the application needs to work cross-platform or multi-platform. Do they want to make use of browser programming with Java, JavaScript or ActiveX (noting that this choice has implications for cross-platform compatibility)? Will they use plug-ins even though some users may have to download them to view the pages? It is likely that your client will not know the answers to this and you may need to talk to the client's technical representative. You may have the opportunity to influence the decisions here if you have access to data indicating the highest used browsers and platform. However, your client may have better data on the specific target users from their own research and understand the target audience better particularly if you are developing an in-house application for a large company. The significance of the browser and platform was much less of an issue a few years ago but as the capabilities and functionalities have increased, the workload for getting an application to work across versions and types has increased as well. Many new media companies have been caught out by this and as a result are now stipulating which browsers and versions they will support as a matter of company policy. This means that if the client has different needs or won't accept company policy, they will have to pay extra for the work involved for their specific requirements.

☐ Site maintenance

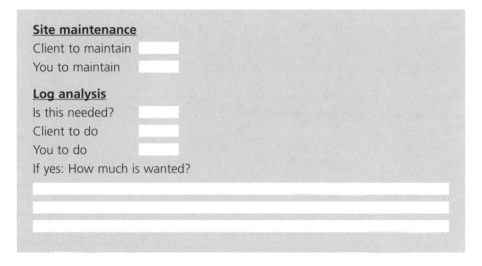

Site maintenance

Client to maintain
You to maintain

Log analysis

Is this needed?
Client to do
You to do
If yes: How much is wanted?

It is important to raise site maintenance early in the discussion. If the client is going to update the content, you have to know the competence level of those who will be involved so that you can design templates accordingly. You may have to provide training as part of the deal, and this has to be costed. If you are going to maintain the site, a whole set of agreements on how often, how much, and what to do about introducing new elements will be needed. Maintenance is often forgotten, but is crucial for all companies to consider. Many still underestimate the ongoing involvement in updating content on a site after its launch – and the ongoing costs. The responsibilities should be sorted out early on to avoid difficulties later. Remember that a website is more like a magazine than a book – it needs to be updated regularly to stay alive. In fact, some websites are more like newspapers, and update very regularly – even continuously. Even if your client is going to take responsibility for updating the content, you may be asked to host the server or co-locate a server or rent space on the client's behalf and a program to manage the website's content – a content management system – might be needed. You need to get an understanding about what this means in terms of ongoing effort and costs from your technical backup. Also, the client may want you to provide log analysis reports on the site daily, weekly or monthly. It depends what information they want and in what form, how much effort and cost this will generate so more precise detail is needed before you add this in.

The analysis of the logs of use of websites has become increasingly important as the market data and usability data they can provide indicate trends of use. The work involved means setting the logs up and perhaps writing programs to interpret them in meaningful ways for the client. If the client holds their own servers, their own people should handle this aspect for them. But if you are hosting their site, or if another company hosts the site for your client, you may need to take care of these aspects on your client's behalf. Defining whose responsibility and how much work is involved will affect your company's time and costs.

☐ Benefits/achievements wanted

Benefits/achievements wanted

Not applicable [   ] (Reason) [   ]
[   ]

Through this site the organization wants to achieve:
1. [   ]
2. [   ]
3. [   ]
4. [   ]
5. [   ]
6. [   ]
7. [   ]
8 [   ]

The users of the site will benefit from or fulfil needs by:
1. [   ]
2. [   ]
3. [   ]
4. [   ]
5. [   ]
6. [   ]
7. [   ]
8. [   ]

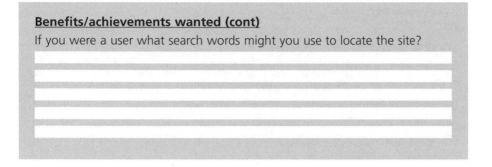

If the client has been able to define their initial statement earlier, this set of questions will probe their understanding to clarify their thinking. It is not easy to define objectives for the company or for the users, but if the client does not attempt this, the specification will lack direction, and will tend to meander. You will be given mountains of information to structure for no real reason unless you get the client to focus on these core issues. It is their responsibility to provide the answers to these questions rather than for you to surmise why they want the site and what they expect from it in terms of their company and their own clients. By asking the clients to imagine a user or customer deciding on search terms to use with a search engine, you help clarify key items of need that the users may have. Ask the clients to prioritize the terms they put forward and this will demonstrate what they consider the most important parts of the site to be.

Multimedia companies are realizing that if the clients have not thought through their complete online business strategy they will not achieve what they need to from the project. Then it is common for them to turn round and blame the developer for the lack of achievement. It is important to be diplomatic at this stage but it is at this point that it becomes clear that the client is entering into the unknown. You can jump into the abyss with them if they will pay on an ongoing basis. With this scenario you will probably have a stop/start progression where you develop lots of prototype concepts that are thrown away. Then a direction is finally forged and the real production process begins. In this case the risks are much higher and you'd need to establish strong controls over project phases and costs. Clients rarely agree to a time and materials budget since they cannot predict how much budget they will need to cover an unknown development time and cost. However, you will be in that precise situation if you leap into the unknown without setting up the correct parameters to cover your time and costs.

☐ Access and use

<table>
<tr><td colspan="2">**Access and use**</td></tr>
<tr><td>The audience/users</td><td>Access to what information</td></tr>
<tr><td>Internet</td><td></td></tr>
<tr><td>General public</td><td></td></tr>
<tr><td>Specific market sector(s)/
  age groups</td><td></td></tr>
<tr><td>(specify)</td><td></td></tr>
<tr><td></td><td></td></tr>
<tr><td>Intranet</td><td></td></tr>
<tr><td>Corporate/government/
  education/other:</td><td></td></tr>
<tr><td>In-house (all)</td><td></td></tr>
<tr><td>Exec</td><td></td></tr>
<tr><td>Managers</td><td></td></tr>
<tr><td>Sales force</td><td></td></tr>
<tr><td>Other</td><td></td></tr>
<tr><td>Extranet</td><td></td></tr>
<tr><td>No. of sites to connect</td><td></td></tr>
<tr><td>Who will need access</td><td></td></tr>
<tr><td>(specify)</td><td></td></tr>
</table>

This section will encourage the client to clarify their thinking even more. The benefits and achievements section will have given you high-level company and user needs, while this section will give you more detail about the content in relation to the user. The connection between the users and the reason they want access to certain types of information is the most important one to establish, whatever the medium. The type of user influences the structure and the level of interactivity. Consider how you might design information for 5 to 7 year olds to access as a resource from the Web, compared to designing it for teenagers accessing information on their favourite pop group, or investors checking their portfolio shares on an investment company's website.

The same information may need to be accessed by several different types of user, and this will determine the range, depth and structure of the information. The analysis for this section can be complex, and stimulates most discussion. But it is wise to raise the issues quickly so that the client realizes that, with so much on offer, it is no mean feat to prioritize the categories and match them to the reasons why the user will want to access them. This section will need to be refined and reworked at subsequent meetings in conjunction with the benefits and achievements section above.

If the client has not considered access and use in enough detail, ask them to make it an action point, and request written replies within a specified period. They need to prioritize the range of information types and the sorts of user they expect or want to attract. You will not be able to do a good cost analysis until you are confident about these features, and about the amount of information that needs to be gathered and structured. Don't worry if your client thinks you are asking them to do too much. Very often clients do not understand the process, and have not been able to raise the right issues for themselves. This is why they may appear vague. You have to raise the right issues and then they can respond to them. Alternatively, if the client has not thought the project through in enough detail, they will probably not have planned enough resources from their side as a result. By raising the issues, you help them to clarify their involvement. It is at this point that the client may be receptive to the idea of using your company's information architect, strategist or equivalent to help with this phase – assuming you have them.

If you don't have higher-level consultants and you will be clarifying the situation yourself, then you need to have established the amount of your involvement before you commence charging. This will be easier if you have indicated to the client that you'll use the initial questionnaire to establish how long it might take to get to definition stage. Then if the questioning process reveals that getting the project definition will take more than a couple of meetings, you can demonstrate this to them and offer to help them define their project as a paid pre-project stage. Remember, the common goal for both of you is to start the project from a clear definition of what is expected from both parties in order to progress through the stages smoothly and purposefully towards a known finishing point.

☐ Emotional reaction considerations

Emotional reaction considerations
Typical user reaction/first impression to main screen: Key adjectives(s)
Re the company/organization represented

Re the content of the page

Typical user reaction to time spent on the site

There is certainly a drive to make online experiences focused and productive as usability issues are taken into account. This has been needed.

But it is also true that the subjective elements have an impact that may be more difficult to measure. They exist and should not just be ignored. Usability principles can be applied to many answers given here as to use of colour and layout perhaps, but style is combination of subjective elements.

It may well be that no strong style is indicated by the adjectives the client uses – that you are asked to produce a clear but neutral experience. However, the opposite may be true and this helps to understand how visually driven and perhaps how much time and involvement might be needed from creatives in your team. If your client is expecting something that makes the company stand apart and the main experience from the site should be excitement or elation, then this affects the whole treatment not just the visual elements, for example.

People can react in many ways to this section and the adjectives can help bring some subjective elements to the fore. When branding and image are major concerns of your client, online communication is part of their company's integrated approach that is designed to act not just in isolation but to contribute to experience over time and across communication channels. They may well have selected you, the developer, because of the connections with the branding and image market sector. Most web agencies aligning themselves to this sector have more detailed approaches to eliciting the image needs of their clients but the majority of other developers might recognize that it is an area they have neglected completely in the past. The scoping checklist 2 in Chapter 13, *Managing small, quick projects*, tries to tie the client down to a style faster by providing a tick list of adjectives as an aid and could be worth considering if you feel it would help.

☐ Media mix

Media mix					
Client's media expectations	None, wants suggestions		Animation		%
	Text	%	Audio		%
	Graphics	%	Video		%

The client may have a vague conception of their site in terms of the media they expect to see as part of it. It is good to get these expectations out in the open, as you may well already have an indication of which media to use based on the emerging understanding of the audience and content. Allow them to state what they would like or expect, and use this to explain why you would not recommend video or audio, for example, in their case. Alternatively, according to what they say you might find yourself arguing for the inclusion of some video and audio for a particular section where you feel that higher-end users would respond well to the added cachet of those media, even though the client has seen the site in terms of text and graphics only.

☐ Content (existing assets)

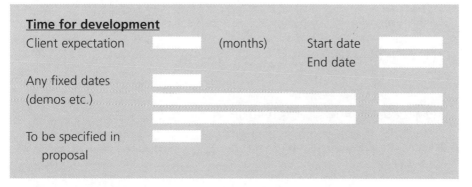

Content (existing assets)			
Written		Contact:	
Relevant databases	Spec:	Contact:	
Graphics/stills	Spec:	Contact:	
Audio	Spec:	Contact:	
Video footage	Spec:	Contact:	
Content experts		Contact:	

The cost of development in any interactive medium is affected by the number and type of suitable assets that the client already has, as long as their specification will retain enough quality for reuse in a new way. Perceptions of quality in integrated media are different for online and offline delivery. Lower quality is tolerated in online delivery because of the limitations of the delivery system. This is constrained by the bandwidth of the connections and the power of the computer receiving the data. Sites have to be optimized for a spectrum of uses, and for users who will have varying computer power and speed of Internet access. If a complete mix of media is needed, then compromises have to be made to optimize across this range. Many sites remain heavily text-driven with some graphics because of these considerations. The client may not be fully aware of the possibilities or of the compromises needed. The sooner you can contact the relevant people and understand what assets are available the better. You should be able to work out the gaps, check the rights position, and cost the reworking of existing assets and the generation of new ones. Don't forget to keep checking back to your relevant team members about the assets you find and the implications this has for them. This will help you define costs for this stage better.

☐ Time for development

Time for development				
Client expectation		(months)	Start date	
			End date	
Any fixed dates				
(demos etc.)				
To be specified in proposal				

There is often a mismatch between clients' and developers' expectations of the development time that is needed for a project. Clients do not usually appreciate the complexity of some of the processes involved. Their expectations may be impossible to achieve, and the scope of a project may have to be reduced to meet a definite timescale.

You need to understand any factors that are driving clients in their decisions on the timescale to see if they might be negotiable. This is why any fixed dates become important. This is the right place to establish as much as you can about the client's needs for completion, because this will help to determine how much content and what media might be achievable. You might suggest scheduling completion of one component before another in order to meet their needs, or you might be able to suggest publishing components as soon as they are ready, with placeholders in the other sections, or developing skeleton pages in each component just to give a feel for the overall structure. Online delivery is more flexible in this regard than offline, where prototyping tends to be more complex.

☐ Special considerations

Special considerations

Database development/online transactions

Company specialist and extra questionnaire needed   Yes ☐ No ☐

Client contact for this extra software analysis

                                    Tel:

                            E-mail:

Dynamic pages required.

Company server-side specialist and extra questionnaire needed   Yes ☐ No ☐

Client contact for this extra server-side
   software analysis

                                    Tel:

                            E-mail:

Testing strategy

Company standard (specify)

Focus groups

Usability testing

User trials

Stress/load testing

Other

Localization/internationalization

Not needed

Needed (further analysis to be done)

Accessibility factors mandatory   Yes ☐ No ☐

The Project Bias section should have alerted you to whether the construction of an online database and all that is involved with that will be necessary. This confirms if the software specialist has to perform a separate analysis and lines up the right contact to help get the information quickly. The answers to the project bias section should also have alerted you to the need for dynamic pages and the need for back-end programming. The implications for the amount of resources and work need to be assessed by a specialist.

As indicated before, testing and localization issues can be complex. Your company has to decide what they offer as standard testing for all projects – which will be included in the costs – and what extra categories they are prepared to support or manage as a subcontract. Refer to Chapter 11, *Testing*, for a full understanding of the categories mentioned here. You need to produce a subset of questions to use with your clients to explain the various options and firm up the type and amount that they want. Then you'll be able to cost this accordingly.

If there are any multicultural or multilingual facets to the project, another subset of questions needs to be devised to determine the exact requirements. These extra questionnaires are as much a resource for you to raise the awareness of the client as to exactly what is involved in these processes as to help you determine the true scope of the project. Refer to Chapter 17, *Adapting projects for other languages and cultures*, to develop a fuller understanding of the issues when developing projects for different languages. Accessibility factors concern users with special needs. (See Chapter 8, *Interface design*, for more.)

☐ Budget

Budget

		£/$ approx	
Budget holder:		Position	
Tel:			
E-mail:			
Project costs to be prepared and negotiated			
Separate costs to be put forward for maintaining and updating			

In an ideal world (for the developer), projects would be scoped and specified and clients would then pay for work done on a time and materials basis. Unfortunately, clients will usually want a fixed price agreed up front, and will not want to change that even if circumstances change. Doubly unfortunate is the difficulty of accurately costing any software project, let alone one with as many constituent parts as multimedia. For the sake of this discussion we shall assume a fixed-quote budget is wanted.

This can turn into a see-saw battle. It is common for the client to withhold their actual budget figure because they know you will scope to the top of that budget. Many clients prefer you to draft a few alternatives with a range of costs so that they have an indication of the quality and cost. Then they can negotiate from a better position.

Some clients will be inexperienced in the costs of multimedia projects, and will expect you to be able to give them an estimate during the first meeting. This is unfair, but it can help if you have ready some examples of the range of costs that can be incurred for projects of different length and different quality – to help them understand a top and bottom price.

You can't really work out an estimate unless the client has specified the size of the project and the expected media mix, and you know the usual production charges per minute of your company and can make a good guess at any extras such as the costs of rights clearances. Even then, considerations of content, existing assets and use will affect the costs, and we have gathered only first-level information about these. You need to explain why it is difficult to cost, and which factors affect the cost.

The people you are dealing with may not necessarily be the budget holder: they may have to refer the decisions on in the organization, and negotiate themselves in turn. It is important to know whether they have the authority to release the budget themselves, because if their decisions can be changed then you have to take this into account, for two reasons. First, you need to be talking directly to the top decision makers to keep the decision time and sign-off time as short as possible to avoid delays in the project, since end dates are rarely as flexible as start dates. Second, you need to find out whether the budget holder will have any authority over the content before he or she releases the budget. You do not want to work for agreement with your client only to have their boss make changes.

Organizations work in different ways, so you need to find out how the client's authorization to spend operates, and what controls are in place to stop it. This can affect the turnaround time for decision making throughout the project, and it will help if you sort out your approach to this as early as possible. If you are to propose costs for maintaining and updating the site, the person who has to accept the long-term budget costs may not be the same as the company project manager you are dealing with, so make sure the right information is passed to the right person, to save difficulties later.

■ Offline scoping

Because the proportion of offline projects has fallen so dramatically in the last couple of years, we have omitted the offline scoping questionnaire from this edition. It is available on the website in case you need to refer to it as a starter for a template document. There is a worked example shown at the end of Chapter 4, *The Proposal*, as part of 'Theory into practice' Task 4 if you want a quick printed reference. Here we will cover the points that are the most relevant differences to take account of if you are developing for offline rather than online.

☐ Offline considerations

Type of project

Often clients have no understanding of the different categories that exist to describe an offline multimedia project. It will help them and you to shape their ideas if you can begin to categorize the type of information that they want to communicate.

There are many differences between working on commercial, corporate, international and government projects. The scale is different. The components and resources needed are different. The budgets are handled and reported in different ways. The way information is structured will be affected by a company culture and image, or by the specification that's worked out by the international partners. There will be conventions and controls in corporate work from other parts of the organization – corporate communications departments, also known as 'style police', for example. The administration involved for an international project is far greater than usual. You might be one of several project managers of various levels and with differing responsibilities in an international project. The nature of the project itself might be more complex because of internationalization or localization issues. See Chapter 17 for more on these specialist projects.

There is one key difference between an online project such as a website, and an offline project, especially a CD-ROM that will be widely available. The offline project will be essentially 'fixed in stone' when it is complete and there will be little if any opportunity to change anything or fix errors. To anyone used to the flexibility that a website offers in this regard, this is a difference that has to be remembered during the whole production. This means that the client, as well as the developer, has to be absolutely sure about the project.

Multimedia presentation

While there is still a gap in the quantity and quality of assets that can be easily distributed on the Web, the strengths of developing a CD still count in certain circumstances. Presentations to high-profile audiences set up expectations of high-quality video, sound, animations and graphics. Most of these presentations tend to be produced for large corporations whose executives need to demonstrate an internationally competitive company image. The tools for computer-based presentations have made it possible for many to produce the lower-level forms of computer-based presentation, but when image, style and impact are expected, the higher-end assets are important and still work better offline.

Developing a presentation CD tends to be a quick, high-pressured project because there is a definite immovable deadline – the day of the internal or external presentation. Also, decisions to use the more complex high-production multimedia elements – such as video graphics, animations or original video footage – are often taken late. The projects are of a shorter duration than many of the other projects, and are usually meant to last for approximately 20–30 minutes. They can be an aid to a speaker who talks to and around the visuals, but it is becoming increasingly common for them to form the basis of a standalone demonstrator for conference stands or general publicity as well. This would then give the project a dual status of *presentation* and *point of information*.

It is also increasingly common for the speaker to publish the presentation or aspects of it on the company intranet, or on the Internet for public access. You need to fully understand the exact uses of the end-product to understand the true costs and to design as economically as possible, across the various forms of delivery if necessary. You should recognize the *hybrid* nature of the project if it will have a dual purpose that includes online aspects. You need to take note of the requirements necessary for the alternative delivery. A separate specification of the hybrid part will be necessary to make sure you know exactly what is wanted. If extra information for a different audience is needed for the hybrid part this will mean extra work for you, which needs to be costed.

These are not easy projects, but there is a tendency in the industry to give them less credence than the production of larger applications. The shorter timescale increases the difficulty and the risks. They are harder to control, and there is little room – if any – for contingency. Also, since they often involve the projection of corporate image, the company's style guidelines have to be taken into account and this can be a cause of frustration for the graphic designer as well as causing delays on vital approval stages.

Because they are high-profile, high-pressure projects, you need to establish a strong, clear method of working and agreement procedures. Any delays are critical.

Training

Training applications can be either commercial or corporate. Some that begin as an in-house corporate product can later become commercial if they are offered for sale outside their original target company. Several of the larger organizations produce their own applications. Others commission multimedia companies to produce them for in-house use. If the training application goes on general sale through training distributors then it is a commercial venture. It is important to remember that a change such as this may affect the type of rights that need to be negotiated for the original project.

Because training applications were always a strong sector when offline production dominated, there are many open learning centres that have been set up. These contain workstations that can play CD-based training as well as access online training. The rich media possible on the CD still makes more sense for training purposes especially for soft skills where behaviour and reactions can be portrayed better via video. So this sector continues to produce CDs although online and perhaps hybrid projects are more common.

Training has its own methods of working. There is a strong emphasis on defining the expected changes in the user's behaviour as a result of using an application. Data collection for evaluation might form part of the specification. There are differences between structuring information for learning and structuring it for information transfer, and these need to be addressed. The techniques for ensuring cognitive retention are different from those designed for immediate reaction to such things as strong visuals.

A recent major initiative in training has been the move towards accrediting work done in the workplace. This has meant defining skills and competences that underpin various roles in the workforce and then sorting them into hierarchical levels. Many vocational bodies have been involved in this definition, and their own qualifications have been restructured accordingly.

The trend towards doing more on-the-job and on-site training rather than sending staff away on courses opened opportunities for multimedia developers. The use of the Internet and company intranets for training has increased dramatically in the last couple of years making e-learning one of the strongest market sectors for development. Companies are attracted by the convenience, access and costs of training via online delivery.

Point of information (POI) kiosks

There is a range of applications that fit this category, from tourist information systems to applications in museums that give specific information about exhibits. These applications are often intended for use by the general public. Some are based in the reception areas of large corporate organizations, where a more specialist slant needs to be taken for the type of audience.

Kiosks were a significant development sector for multimedia and continue to be but in an adapted form. Increasingly now they are linked into the Internet so any volatile information is kept updated. Since the kiosks are usually specially designed systems, the hardware configuration can be chosen to be the best for the task, with few constraints other than cost.

Publishing

Publishers are not having an easy time adjusting to electronic content and all that it appears to offer. Traditional publishers (which in this context includes record and audiovisual as well as book publishers) experimented with offline projects, and some set up their own production facilities. However, the promise of the CD consumer market was not fulfilled. The distribution channels for offline proved difficult and were not fully taken into account because the consumer has to have easy access to the products to be able to buy them.

The Internet presented new challenges. This provided easy access to information about the products and the facility to buy relatively easily. The perceived success of Amazon as an online book distributor paved the way for it to move into delivery of other products as well. The word 'perceived' is used here since there appears to be disagreements as to whether they are profitable or not.

Some CDs still get produced when the power of offline media makes sense. So games based on successful book characters for the younger market might make sense. Increasingly support materials based around books or published materials are placed on publishers' websites.

Education

Ownership of content becomes an important issue and the ability to reuse such assets in other forms or as the basis for new development depends on ownership. If you do not own the content, you have to start from scratch every time. This overlaps with rights management, which will be covered later. This is a market that has increased in the past few years. The standardizing of curricula means that there is a potentially large market.

The popularity of the Internet as a multimedia information and reference source shared between millions of users was first spawned through its use in universities. Although it started as a text-driven method of communication, it has moved rapidly into a distributed multimedia channel. Access to the Net is being encouraged throughout education. Relatively quickly it has been recognized that there should be consolidation of materials and distribution around the common curriculum. The numerous small companies producing educational CDs are being superseded by larger companies doing deals at county level with educational authorities. They offer to install – or even lease – equipment, deliver large amounts of online materials and resources and maintain the system. A complete solution is attractive – and this is becoming the norm. Again, the CD resources are being superseded by the capacity and easy updatability of the online resources.

Edutainment

Many CD's that were published fell into a category called Edutainment and the market continues but has slowed because of the move to having resources on the Web. However, the richness of the media mix and the speed of the resources attract the home owners of computers to buy them for their children's general education. They can span both the consumer and education markets if they have been designed carefully, indicating which stages of the curriculum they cover or contribute towards as well as having wider appeal because of the subject matter. These increasingly have a hybrid component as well, via the publisher's website.

Entertainment

Entertainment is another category that is aimed at the home and business markets. Games, quizzes, titles built around celebrities such as pop stars or actors, and even television soaps would be examples from this section. Many of these now have hybrid components as well.

Reference titles such as atlases, road maps and encyclopaedias have made their mark, and are popular. They obviously benefit from the users being able to access the Web to update any volatile data or to have access to extra information on topics. These products can have quite extensive websites attached, so you need to understand how large these will be and exactly what data is expected on them. They need separate specification, and can be considered a separate project in terms of time, resource allocation and costing.

The popularity of DVD videos and the extra information that they include in a limited interactive form also fall under this category. A DVD disk might be DVD-ROM, which can be treated like a CD-ROM but with much greater capacity, or it might be a DVD video disk designed to be played in a DVD player. Because DVD video has been adopted by a large enough market, offline interactive entertainment development for DVDs has grown despite the small amount of interactivity usual on such applications. Adapt the online questionnaire to help scope the hybrid web aspects of the CD or DVD projects.

Reference

Reference titles were popular and one of the most successful sectors for CDs. The interactive search facilities offered by the technology made sense when people were trying to locate specific information quickly. However, the rise of the Internet offers the same functionality with the bonus of more up-to-date material since updating volatile data is easier and cheaper online than offline. For these reasons there is a decline in producing reference materials offline and the trend is to offer them on subscription or as part of a company package deal for online facilities.

International projects

These types of project, particularly if they are related to government research, demand a good deal more administration than others. Many extra levels of communication and documentation are built into the project plans to ensure that the progress of the project is monitored and recorded. These projects follow international project management principles, and as such are well structured and defined. The projects start with a specification stage, and then contracts and resources are allocated according to this.

In funded research projects, for example, there may be a process of external review where experts are called in at regular intervals to analyse and comment on progress. The funding and budgeting structures are very different from those for other multimedia projects as the funding organization may have its own conditions to be met. Your company may have to meet the equivalent of the fund, in money or in time equivalent, or in the value of the assets you bring to the project.

Major international projects often break new ground, so developers can find themselves working with untried technology and software. This undoubtedly makes the projects higher risk, and contingency time has to increase because of the risks. This applies to any research project.

Technology doesn't stand still, so there is constant prototyping and trialling of new technology platforms and tools. In tool development it is common for the software to be tested by people outside the company that is writing it. The final stage of this is beta testing, when the writers think the software is finished and it is up to you to test this claim. There are very good reasons for wanting to build multimedia projects with beta versions of tools, not least because of the lead it might give you over your competitors. On the downside are the difficulties caused when the tools do not come up to expectations, or when bugs are found. As a developer you may be the first person to really try to build an application with this new tool, and it can be surprisingly easy to 'break' it.

■ Post-meeting responsibilities

You should be in a better position to decide if the definition of the project is going to be straightforward or not. You may need just a couple more meetings to be able to put forward a clear proposal with costs or have agreed with the client that someone will be helping them to establish the requirements based perhaps on a day rate based on time and cost. Clients may need to get back to you with some of the information you've requested – the benefits to the user, for example. Make sure you agree a timeframe within which to receive the information. A lot of time can be wasted during these early stages, which can affect the start and end date of the project and therefore what you can produce.

If the client doesn't get back to you in the agreed time with the right information, take this as an indication of what they will be like to work with, and make a mental note that if the project goes ahead you will build in contingency time at points where the client needs to find information or give decisions. This may seem a harsh judgement, but you'll need to make many decisions on very limited information. As one of your main responsibilities you need to identify potential risk areas and start trying to minimize them. This type of decision making is characteristic of managing innovation.

You will have information to check out from the meeting as well. If the client has given any contact numbers for further information you need to pursue these to firm up on facts. The client may think there is little visual data available but the contact may be able to indicate that there is good source material of the right specification to help with the project.

Once the scoping questionnaire is complete, make a copy and send it to the client as a record of the meetings and of the information given. Get into the habit of dating the documents for the day of their dispatch as well as having the date of the original meeting. This can often prove important later in the project, particularly in corporate projects.

Organizations are changing their focus all the time, and staff changes occur during projects, so you can find yourself working with a new person who has a completely different perspective on what the organization wants in a particular area. From his or her perspective, the new person will be quite right to point out some fundamental changes that he or she was aware of at a particular date, but you will be able to show that this was not the information you had. If he or she wants major changes then the project has to be re-scoped at the client's expense.

THEORY INTO PRACTICE 3

Look back over the scoping questionnaire. Would you be confident in using it with clients? Without looking at the text, can you give reasons why you need each category of information?

If you are working with specialist client-centred projects, what extra questions need to be answered to scope your project?

If you are not working with client centred projects, what equivalent questions need to be answered to scope your project?

◼ Summary

- If possible establish the client's expectations and needs for the project in detail, the assets they can bring to the project, the audience profile, and the budget.
- If the definition is not going to be straightforward, offer a paid pre-project stage to help them define their requirements.
- Record the meeting clearly to form the basis of the proposal.
- Assess whether the brief is realistic in terms of development time, the use of media, and the client's expected outcomes.
- Give clear requests for further information from the client within a timeframe.
- Follow up any information you need as soon as possible.
- Send a record of the meetings to the clients.

■ Online client-centred project scoping questionnaire

<u>**Project name/no:**</u>

<u>**Contact details**</u>
Client/organization name:
Address:

Tel: Fax: E-mail:
Website:

<u>**Project contacts:**</u>
Name(s):   Positions(s):

Direct line   E-mail:

<u>**Previous interactive media experience**</u>

Online
None ☐   A little ☐   Fair ☐   Good ☐   Experienced ☐

Offline
None ☐   A little ☐   Fair ☐   Good ☐   Experienced ☐

<u>**Experience description**</u>

Online
Products: Producer:

Offline
Products: Producer:

Client's initial statement of what they want

Online project type

Internet ☐   Hybrid Web/CD ☐   Intranet ☐   Extranet ☐   Mobile ☐

Set up new facility

(If yes, domain name suggestions?)

Add/change existing facility

Market sector

Commercial ☐   Corporate ☐   Government ☐   Education ☐

Project bias

	Importance ranking	Size of section (large, medium, small)
Company profile		
Information gathering		
Information dissemination		
Retail (products or services description)		
Database access/development		
Online transactions		
Marketing/advertising		
Redesign site front-end		
Branding/image rework		
Others (specify)		

Browser/platform expectations

Either:

Developer policy accepted i.e.

Development only for X browser and X versions on X platform   Yes ☐   No ☐

Or:

Client wants:

Browser(s)

Versions supported:

Plug-ins

Platform(s)

Allow Java?   Yes ☐   No ☐

Allow JavaScript?   Yes ☐   No ☐

Allow ActiveX?   Yes ☐   No ☐

Or:

Client does not know.

Client contact name for answers

                                         Tel:

                                         E-mail:

Site maintenance

Client to maintain

You to maintain

Log analysis

Is this needed?

Client to do

You to do

If yes: How much is wanted?

Benefits/achievements wanted

Not applicable [ ] (Reason) [ ]

Through this site the organization wants to achieve:

1.
2.
3.
4.
5.
6.
7.
8.

The users of the site will benefit from or fulfil needs by:

1.
2.
3.
4.
5.
6.
7.
8.

If you were a user what search words might you use to locate the site?

Access and use

The audience/users   Access to what information

Internet [ ]

General public [ ]

Specific market sector(s) [ ]

(specify) [ ]

Access and use (cont)

Intranet

Corporate/government/
   education/other:

In-house (all)

Exec

Managers

Sales force

Other

Extranet

No. of sites to connect

Who will need access

(specify)

Emotional reaction considerations

Typical user reaction/first impression to main screen: Key adjectives(s)

Re the company/organization represented

Re the content of the page

Typical user reaction to time spent on the site

Media mix

Client's media expectations	None, wants suggestions		Animation	%
	Text	%	Audio	%
	Graphics	%	Video	%

Content (existing assets)

Written			Contact:	
Relevant databases		Spec:	Contact:	
Graphics/stills		Spec:	Contact:	
Audio		Spec:	Contact:	
Video footage		Spec:	Contact:	
Content experts			Contact:	

Time for development

Client expectation ⬚ (months)   Start date ⬚
                                  End date ⬚

Any fixed dates ⬚
(demos etc.) ⬚ ⬚
⬚ ⬚

To be specified in ⬚
  proposal

Special considerations

Database development/online transactions

Company specialist and extra questionnaire needed   Yes ☐ No ☐
Client contact for this extra software analysis ⬚
                                            Tel: ⬚
                                        E-mail: ⬚

Dynamic pages required

Company server-side specialist and extra questionnaire needed   Yes ☐ No ☐
Client contact for this extra server-side ⬚
  software analysis

                                            Tel: ⬚
                                        E-mail: ⬚

Testing strategy

Company standard (specify) ⬚
Focus groups ⬚
Usability testing ⬚
User trials ⬚
Stress/load testing ⬚
Other ⬚
⬚

Localization/internationalization

Not needed ⬚
Needed (further analysis to be done) ⬚
Accessibility factors mandatory   Yes ☐ No ☐

<table>
<tr><td colspan="3">

Budget

</td></tr>
</table>

Budget		
		£/$ approx
Budget holder:		Position
Tel:		
E-mail:		
Project costs to be prepared and negotiated		
Separate costs to be put forward for maintaining and updating		

■ Recommended reading

As this chapter was based on experience, there is no reading material recommended.

☐ References

Kelly, George (1963) *A Theory of Personality*. New York: W.W. Norton

Concept user interface (CUI) tool

Concept Systems Inc have a web-based analysis tool, Concept System
http://www.conceptsystems.com/

Flowcharting and idea mapping tools

Ryerson's school of Radio and TV ongoing research into Charting Multimedia,
see Resources – Flowcharting
http://www.rcc.ryerson.ca/rta/flowchart/index.html

Axon Idea processor also possibly for eliciting concept maps with new clients.
A visualization tool for thinkers it says!
http://web.singnet.com.sg/~axon2000/

Rapid application development

DSDM (Dynamic System Design Methodology) model where MoSCoW rules are applied
in the design and iteration stage
http://www.dsdm.org

The proposal

Project manager's responsibilities

- Given the brief, to offer a realistic, fair deal in the timescale and budget for the client and the development team

- To make no false promises

- To make decisions based on the facts and your assessment of risks

■ The aim of the proposal

The proposal will summarize the development decisions, and these will be based on the information you have received from the client, on your experience, and on the discussions you have had with colleagues about the possible alternatives for the treatment. If special analysis was used during the scoping phase from business analysts, software analysts, information architects, branding consultant, training analysts or whoever was appropriate for the particular project, obviously their findings will help drive the requirements that you need to encapsulate into the agreement document with the client. Different people have different names for this type of document but the aim of all of them is the same.

The aim is to give the client a clear, high-level understanding of what the project will do, what it will contain and how much it will cost. For online projects this needs to be linked to the plug-ins and browsers that will be used, and whether the nature of the site needs static pages, dynamic pages or a combination of them. (See Book 2 Chapter 5, *Platform parameters*, and Book 2 Chapter 9, *Integration*, for more on these aspects.) For offline projects the approach needs to be linked to the platform that will be adopted and the reasons for the choice. The proposal should include a suggested schedule for development of the main stages, or milestones linked to payments, as well as the overall cost.

The clients need enough information from the document to make a decision on whether it fits their needs and the budget expectations. They want to be convinced by the relevance of your suggested treatment for their needs. It helps if there is an outline of a core set of components with indications of what might be cut without affecting the core functionality too much. This allows the client the option of pruning if the proposed cost is too expensive. The opposite is true. It is also good to include extra components that are attractive and perhaps innovative – ones that would make the difference to the site – that are suggested with extra price tags. This method sets up good practice for the rest of the project. It establishes that extra pieces cost more and if the client requests more, you will define them and cost them.

If the client did not pay separately for the scoping phase of the project because it was relatively straightforward to define their high-level needs, they may have approached a few companies for the project, so your proposal may be in competition with others. This leads to pressure to offer more than is appropriate, and sets up risks for the development stages. You have to balance your responsibilities to the clients, to your company, and to the development team.

To help you maintain a balance, it is good to base your decisions on what would be safe to offer for the time and cost, and what would be foolish to offer for the time and cost but would be exciting and innovative. You can then work out a range of best alternatives that would allow some shift from

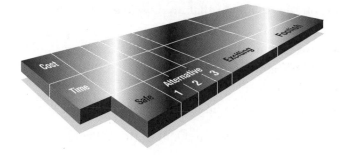

Offering alternatives.

the safe baseline, but not too much. This keeps the project challenging without making it impossible. This approach also helps you define the one or two additions you can put forward with the extra cost tags for the client to consider.

The main difficulty should be obvious. You have to commit the company and team to a plan of work for a cost that is almost certainly based on incomplete information. A complete understanding of the amount and nature of the content is not reached until later in the development. You need to compensate for the unknown by building in a contingency over the development stages. You can build this contingency into the overall cost, or you can include it item by item. Alternatively, if the client accepts this, you can be specific about some areas and say that others contain unknown factors, which may affect the cost. This could be due to the need for research that is impractical before the project starts, or it might be because of third-party costs such as rights.

■ What it should contain

The proposal should not be a long document. It needs to make its impact quickly and clearly. You will not be able to go into great detail because so much of the content information is unstable. You should also indicate that the document, as its name implies, is suggestive not prescriptive. You will need to adjust some features as the amount and nature of the content become explicit, so you need to make sure that the client understands this, and that it may result in shifts in cost.

The proposal should cover the following:

- general introduction and/or executive summary;
- statement of what the client wants from the website or application;
- statement of what the users need from the site or application;
- description of the general treatment and reasons for choice;

- variations on the treatment that are possible;
- outline diagram of the proposed structure;
- description of the human resources needed;
- work breakdown and schedule;
- cost/payment structure;
- company statement of the limitations of the proposal.

Each of these will be explained in detail in the following section.

Description of the components

General introduction and/or executive summary

This will collate some of the data from the scoping questionnaire: the definition of the type of project, its purpose, a description of the numbers, and the type of audience. The decisions on the online platform – or the equivalent system for offline – could be included here. Give the reasons why electronic media was chosen as the vehicle for delivery. It is worth considering whether there should be an executive summary at the beginning of the proposal. This becomes more useful as the length of the document increases, and basically provides a resumé of the proposal. It is different from an introduction in that it will summarize the decisions and may even give a cost. The person who will find an executive summary useful is anyone you would expect to read the final part of the proposal – the budget – first. Executive summaries are more common when the document will be read by several managers in the client company and discussed severally before a decision to go ahead is given. The new media company you work for will usually dictate the exact nature and even name of the 'proposal' document.

Statement of what the client wants from the project

The statements that the client has given at the first meeting(s) need to be shaped into a sharp, business-focused account. It is helpful if you can use phrases and terminology that reflect the business area of the client. If you have attuned yourself to their business approach during the first meeting(s) you will find it easier to write to suit them.

You may not have attended the initial meeting with the client, because companies work in different ways. You may, for example, be verbally briefed, or passed notes from initial meetings conducted by others to work into a proposal. Some companies split the responsibilities between people who land the business and people who manage the development teams. Exactly who writes the proposal or equivalent may not be straightforward. However, if you have to write them, you have to work hard to understand the client's business and to show that you understand it. This can be as simple as realizing that people from an audiovisual background often find the term 'user' rather unfriendly and might prefer to think about 'viewers'. Those from a journalistic background might be more comfortable with 'the reader' for online projects.

It is useful if you can explain some of the positive factors that the inter-active media environment will add to help the client achieve their needs in relation to the users.

This section might be a summary of one or more documents or reports from the specialist analysts if they were called in to help with the definition or scoping phase to work with the stakeholders to reach a clearer under-standing of what was wanted.

Statement of what the user needs from the application

The client will have interpreted the needs of the users in the scoping phase or the scoping phase might have included surveying a representative sample of the intended users. This might have been in conjunction with an analyst or as a result of the questionnaire used to scope the project. You should summarize the user needs and you can also add your experience of the users of an application from a professional point of view. It is important to state that the users' experience of the application must be the focus of con-cern for all. You can predict the interactive level needed from the program to suit the users. If there are examples of attributes from similar programs that have appealed to this type of user, you should introduce these here. If the client has requested extra stages of specialist testing such as focus groups or user trials these could be indicated here.

Description of the general treatment and reasons for choice

There is no right or wrong answer to deciding on the treatment for the topic for your clients. It might help you to consider that, for the same project, dif-ferent companies would suggest very different treatments for a variety of reasons. There are certain guiding principles, but the general treatment might be the combination of ideas from several strands of experience within a company or it might be up to an individual to define an overall approach. The ideas should reflect the aims of the client and the needs of the users, and it is important to explain why the suggested structure will achieve these.

There are differences in the treatment of the next few sections for on- and offline projects, and so they have been split out for clarity. The pro-cesses you should use are common to both, so they are then brought back together for consideration.

Online projects: treatment

Your experience will be influential when defining the treatment. It is a good idea to have walked your client through several sites at the initial meeting, noting their general reaction to structure and interface design. It helps to explain the reasoning behind some of the structure decisions and levels of interactivity and, most particularly, to begin to focus them on the needs of the users rather than on personal preference. See Chapter 8, *Interface design*, for more on this aspect. If you have managed to influence them with this exercise, then your proposed treatment will extract features they liked and ones you know will suit the needs of the users.

The home page is all-important. It sets the expectations, structure and image for the rest of the site. It serves the purpose of giving a mission statement or an overview of what is on offer. The users want to have a quick, clear understanding of what is available. If they enter the site seeking specific information, then they want the categories to point to where they can find it. If they come to the site for entertainment or amusement, then the page set-up should reflect this. The home page also has a secondary function when the site is indexed by a Web search engine. Some engines index a site from hidden information in the page headers (called meta tags); some work with the title and text in the page; some use both. The home page is also the starting point for a search engine working through the whole site, just as it is for a human visitor, and both need to be taken into account for the design.

Clients tend to underestimate how difficult it is to categorize and classify information and provide apposite summaries for people. Many want to put in too much inappropriate text, not understanding that users adopt different reading techniques for the Web. See Chapter 8, *Interface design*, for more on this.

For the proposal you may not have had time to prototype a home page completely, but it would be good to show the general structure and the number of elements that will be included for branching off to other pages. This is sometimes referred to as a site map. (Note that this can be confused with another use of a 'site map' which is a text hierarchy sometimes included on the live site, so the term application map, information structure, application architecture or site reference map might be better.) A diagrammatic representation of the content and functionality branches is a good idea, with a statement of the reasons for them, and showing how their structure relates to the needs of the user and the wishes of the client.

Each section of the site should be mentioned in terms of its expected size, the media components and reasons for the media choices, and the estimated time needed to complete the content and design for each section. You will have to work hard to get a feel for the size and complexity of the sections because your cost quote will be linked to these.

At this stage it is impossible to know how long it will take to get the right information together for the respective sections, or how much there will be, but you'll have a better feel than the clients. It may well be easier for you to talk in terms of small, medium and large sections, representing each by a banding of pages and a complexity indicator: the following are offered as an example but you'd need to adjust these according to your way of working:

- Small = 5–10 pages
- Medium = 10–20 pages
- Large = 20–30 pages
- Very large = 30+ pages

Pages here are taken to mean submenus and the content associated with each. There could be several levels in one section according to the split in information.

In the section audit table (Table 4.1), complexity can relate to the media production components, the content, the programming, or all three. You may rank each of them as low, medium or high. For example, a section that relied on pulling information from an existing database and adding a new front-end could be small in size of pages displayed, medium in terms of complexity for media, and low in content production and programming because the database exists. However, later you may find that the database is relatively old and needs a complete overhaul to port it to the Web. Now the content would have to shift to high; the programming would increase and the cost would move accordingly.

T A B L E   4 . 1 Section audit.

Section name	Size (pages)	Complexity			Development time + Testing + Rework	Cost
		Media	Content	Programming		

When you have a good grasp of the complexity and size of the whole site, you are in a position to determine the resources you'll require and the time that they may need. This assessment can help you in costing the project. Different companies have different ways of costing. A lot depends on whether all the resources are in-house or whether extras need to be sourced. Allow some contingency for flexibility to make the inevitable adjustments.

This analysis is based on static pages of HTML. If the information is volatile, and the clients want to be able to update it themselves, or if the site is exceptionally large, pages probably need to be generated dynamically. Many such websites are actually generated by purpose-built databases. If the site is both large and structured, with a large number of pages that contain similar layouts of differing information (such as a catalogue), then a purpose-built database should be considered, and a database programmer needs to be involved to make a different form of analysis from the one discussed here.

Rights clearances are generally fewer in number and involve fewer types of media for online than for offline, but they still need to be considered and costed accordingly. If you are reusing assets from the client's company, they need to have the right to reuse those assets in electronic form. It is prudent to ask the client to double-check this. See Chapters 9 and 15 for more on the legal considerations. New assets or ones that do not wholly belong to the client will need to be cleared and paid for. The number of assets that require this will depend on the media mix you are using and on the size of the site.

In your time for development, consider the resources and time that will be used for production. Don't forget the time for testing and rework, and for trials with user groups if necessary. Testing and trials are often forgotten, but they can eat up time and resources. You should establish exactly how much of this the client requires and build it into the equation. It is common for clients to forget that you asked this. They often reject the idea at first but change their minds later. So keep good records of their response to this, and put it in writing to them confirming that they do not want user trials or extra testing apart from your own in-house verification. If they suddenly decide that they want to do an internal trial with colleagues, you'll then be in a position to negotiate for the time and rework that this always produces.

When drafting the proposal, refer back to the scoping questionnaire and list the client's wishes/objectives for the site and their user needs. Show how your company intends to achieve the objectives in the treatment of the content for each section (Table 4.2). This then links your decisions back to specifics that the client understands. They should recognize your concern for their needs and their own client's needs. This should help instill in them trust and confidence in you. It also provides guidelines for your decisions.

If there are any objectives for either client or user that are not met in the sections as agreed by you, you can either point this out to the client, asking for clarification of the content that might meet the need, or put forward a range of suggestions of what you could do to meet the needs. In this way you

TABLE 4.2 Section related to needs.

Content section	Client need satisfied	User need satisfied

can spot gaps between the client needs and content areas. A similar process is explained for offline projects in more detail below, and it may help you to refer to that explanation.

For each section, as you describe the approach that will be used check the media list that the client may have given you in the scoping questionnaire. You may not meet the expectations they had, if you have valid reasons. You should indicate your reasons for media choice for each section linking it to the objectives and user needs.

Offline projects: treatment

This presumes that you have completed the equivalent of a scoping questionnaire with the clients (one is available on the website as a resource) and you have a clear enough way to move to a proposal. You need to cover the main areas of content, and indicate how they will be linked. A diagram, along the lines of a flowchart, would be useful here. The media selection for each area of content needs to be discussed and the reason for the choice of media explained. It helps at this stage to indicate the total number of minutes of material that each section will contain, as this will later provide the editorial control over the amount of information contained.

For example, if you suggest 10 minutes of audio and graphics and 3 minutes of video in one section, but later as the detail comes to light it becomes clear that it will need 15 minutes of audio and graphics to do the

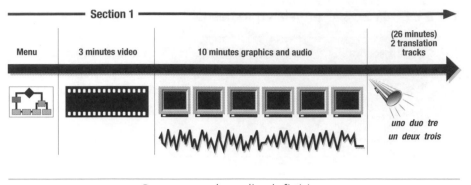

Content and media definition.

topic justice, then you have the power to bargain for extra money for the extra time. Equally, if later there is not enough content to put in this section you might suggest cutting out the 3 minutes of video here but adding 3 minutes in a more suitable place.

You arrive at the content and media definition process by matching the content suggested by the client against their needs, to find out if there are gaps. Then it is easier to concentrate on filling the content gaps in relation to the needs that have not been covered. This type of exercise can focus creative brainstorming from your team to fulfil definite purposes rather than have complete free play with ideas. The aim is to suggest content and treatments that will cover all the wants and needs at some stage.

Once you have recognized how the content might suit the purpose, you should begin to get a feel for the best media to use. As you decide on the treatment you should check the needs of the users, as this can influence your decision. This is the most creative aspect of the decision making, and is where most of the risks are taken, because assumptions have to be made on availability of material, suitability of treatment, and reactions of the client. At this point you can suggest some timings and an overall duration for the section, but these will change as you work out costs later.

So the decisions about treatment can be influenced by, and need a balance between, the needs of the user, the type of materials available, the time to produce, and an appreciation of the cost. It is this simultaneous weighing of several factors that makes multimedia decisions a complex skill.

Remember to include built-in Help and preference selection if these are appropriate. Help can either be general – ideally your functionality should be simple enough to require minimal extra Help – or context specific.

Choose the media that you think would best suit the content you decide on. At this stage you should not worry too much about platform or media constraints. Add these onto the page or spreadsheet so that it is easy to change them later. It helps to differentiate the ones that originated with the client from those suggested by your company members.

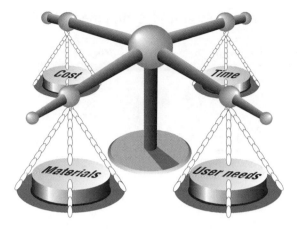

A question of balance.

Choosing media won't be as easy as it sounds, and it can help if you brainstorm with colleagues. One category of content should serve more than one requirement, so that you keep control of the amount of material even at this stage.

When you've got a feel for the content range, you need to look at the expected media mix if the client has stated one, and check it off against the treatment you've suggested. The platform decisions can affect media decisions, so take this into account now, changing the treatment accordingly. But keep a record of what you had intended, as you might find this can influence the client later. If a platform isn't stipulated, make your decision based on any strategy that the client has indicated and the needs of the users. Indicate the reasons behind your choice of platform.

Put a total time on each category, with the time for each media component broken down into constituent times. For example, you might have decided to set a scene with 2 minutes of video and then allow the user to choose between five points of view about this video. If each interview was 1½ minutes with audio over graphics, the total for that category would be 9½ minutes.

Then cost the media components. You need to refer to past experience – both your own and that of your colleagues – to do this. Companies work in different ways for costings, so you'll need to adjust this part accordingly. Some will give estimates based on the combined staff and production costs related to media components. For example, a company might have tables of costs per half hour of different video formats – full drama production on location, full drama production in studio, studio interviews, location interviews – and you can cost each type of video production according to your estimates. Another set of tables might list the digital conversion costs and so on, so you gradually apply the tables to the components you have

TABLE 4.3 Identifying costs from staff, time and rights breakdown.

Internal	External	Time/weeks	Cost
Area 1			
Jake (graphics)		1	
Sue (″)		1	
	Area 1		
	Phil (script)	$^3/_4$	
	Phil (audio)	$^1/_2$	
Area 2			
		Total	

Rights clearances		
Category		**Cost**
Stills		
Music		
Voice-overs		
Video footage		
	Total	

suggested to arrive at the total estimate. It is important for the tables to be current in this case.

Another way of costing starts with the staff and the time needed as shown (Table 4.3). Apply internal and external costing rates according to the roles and general salary levels for the role. The time for which the staff will be needed depends on several factors – new material development, complexity of the graphics, use of animation and special techniques, and so on.

It helps if you look at the costs of a recent project to estimate an average time for production of graphics per day. This is an inaccurate rule of thumb since the difficulty of graphics production varies according to content, so take this inaccuracy into account in your estimate. Gradually build up the picture of how much time the content would take to research, process and produce.

Rights clearances can be very costly, so they need to be considered here and refined later. Work to an estimate of how many voice-over artistes you might need, and for what length of material. They are costed per hour even if there is only 10 minutes' work. You also have to consider how much and what type of music – library, commissioned, recorded – as these have variable costs too. If you have to clear permissions from picture libraries or companies there will be costs attached. The same is true if you will be using existing footage from a film library. All these factors will affect the costs that you need to build in to arrive at a realistic offer to the clients. See Chapter 9, *Contract issues 2*, and Chapter 15, on *Rights, copyright and other intellectual property*, for more detailed information on rights.

On- and offline projects: common ground

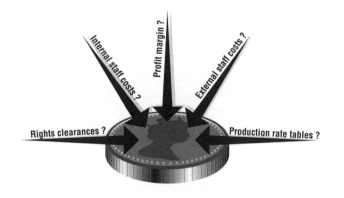

Cost considerations vary.

Some companies work to a defined profit margin, which needs to be added to the staff and production costs. Other companies have built this into the daily rates that you apply, so you should understand how your company is working to make sure that you have accounted for all the factors.

When you have your total time and cost, go back and look at the time and budget that have been stipulated by the client. Then you can make editorial decisions on what to cut or add, depending on the match between the two. You should also assess how much of the cost is real external spending and how much is in overheads such as salaries and hardware amortization. The amount of money you actually have to spend to carry out the work should influence whether you ask for some of the money in advance. Smaller companies often need to request an up-front payment to cover the initial work because of the importance of cash flow to the company. (See Chapter 13, *Managing small, quick projects*, for a more refined project management outline for small businesses.)

Variations on the treatment

These will come to light as you apply the process described for defining the treatment for online and offline respectively. If you need to cut any major features to suit the budget, you could add them to the proposal as extras for consideration, suggesting to the client that these would offer value to the user, and the reasons for this. You would already have the extra time and budget implications worked out for the features so you could build these into the variations on offer – with their respective price tags.

Outline diagram of proposed structure

A site map of the proposed site structure really helps communication with the client, particularly at this initial stage. The map will need to be refined, if and when the project progresses. See Chapter 6, *Agreeing the content*, for an example and more on site maps.

Description of the human resources

List and describe in general terms the roles that will be part of the project. You will probably have a core team, with extras to supplement it at key stages. Most clients are surprised at the numbers involved, and it shows the complexity of the project in terms they understand. You do not need to put in the time that the people will spend on the project at this point, even though you have had to do a rough estimate for the overall cost implications. The possibility of using multiskilled personnel for more than one task is something you should be aware of, but for the time being it should not be reflected in the proposal. The point of the proposal is to sell the ideas and suggested treatment to the client. You will be able to manoeuvre time and cost better later if you have not made strong commitments here. You will need this leeway because of the instability of the development process.

Work breakdown and schedule

Even if you have used a computer package to help with your scheduling and costing (see the example budget template on the website), it is wise to leave the description of costs for the client to a minimum, for the reasons already stated. You, however, have to have as detailed a breakdown as possible for yourself and your management, to create whatever figures are given in the proposal. Remember, different companies have different policies on how to approach budgets. If you are a contract project manager, check that you understand how to work out your budget according to the company's template. Some will include stationery and couriers in their overheads, for example. Others will expect you to project figures for these specifically for the project. The way contingency costs and profit margins operate will be company specific as well.

For scheduling, it will be enough at this stage to state the start and end dates for each of the options, with general timing for research (outline and detailed document dates) and key development stages, often called milestones. For more complex projects you might break the work down into work packages, each of which has a budget and timing and one or more deliverables.

Time and costs for testing

It is easy to forget to include phases for testing the application, but these can take a significant amount of time. You should take the lead here in specifying how much can be absorbed into the development time and what sorts of testing are recommended. It is important to have established your testing strategy at this point and negotiate with the client so that a realistic level of performance is achieved for the time allowed. Chapter 11, *Testing*, describes how to devise a testing strategy, and how to explain the options and implications of decisions to the client.

Cost/payment

The total cost should be given, with indications of the company's payment policy. Most companies ask for staged payments to improve cash flow, and to cover themselves for unforeseen circumstances where the project might be stopped or delayed. The stages are often linked to key deliverables or milestones of production. Companies will define these in different ways but many link staged payments to:

- the agreed prototype front-page look and feel;
- the phase or phases leading to the detailed agreement of content;
- the content's look and feel;
- the first working example of the code and navigation;
- the near-final stage, sometimes called the beta;
- delivery of the final version of the project – a fully functioning site for online or a golden master for a CD-ROM, for example.

Limitations of the proposal

Because the proposal is based on a limited understanding of the overall content, there need to be indications of this to allow for changes from the developers as their understanding deepens.

If you have based any of your decisions on material that will be supplied by the client you will need a proviso that this is subject to the material being of the right type and quality. Otherwise you will need to revise your estimates of how much material will need to be produced.

If the client does not turn the decisions around or provide materials within a timeframe that has been agreed, you need to have the right to charge a fixed overall day rate for downtime. Behaviour from the client like this can hold the project up significantly but having this proviso focuses them and can help keep the project running smoothly. For example, if someone who usually gives sign-off to a stage is away on holiday for 2 weeks, do you have to wait before you proceed? If the clients know they will incur costs they are more likely to delegate decisions in their absence or take measures to ensure they do not hold progress up.

Technology production is changing rapidly all the time so costs vary quickly. It is wise to put a time limit on the offer subject to costs being reworked. You need to point out that the start dates are dependent on the client's agreement to proceed being given in time and that any delay for the start would add time to the finish date. It is surprising how often clients return to you after the start date with agreement to proceed but still expect you to complete in the same time without cutting any of the production.

☐ Conclusion

Proposals often need to be turned around quickly. They are difficult documents to draft, and there need to be clear guidelines to help with the drafting according to company practice. It is management's responsibility to ensure that these guidelines exist so that whoever writes a proposal for the company covers the scope in the way that serves the company best. Bias within the company towards any specific origin, such as video production, will affect the components in the proposal.

The principles that underlie a proposal are the same, however. The client will be looking for clear statements of what the company can offer in the time and for the price. Their attitude will be affected by their own bias towards media and the needs of the project. They can be influenced by good ideas that show value. To define the added value of one form of media or treatment over another requires professional expertise and experience.

It is rare for the proposal to be accepted outright, and the client will negotiate on the range, type and composition of the content as well as debate costs. You face a problem if you give a more detailed breakdown of costs at this stage because you have been working from a hypothetical mix for the team. For example, you may have presumed that you could have an internal graphics resource at one cost, but until the project becomes a reality the allocation of resources is notional. It might transpire that all internal resources are booked on other projects for the period, and that a completely new freelance team needs to be formed.

THEORY INTO PRACTICE 4

You have been asked to draft a proposal because there is a deadline and your colleague is sick. She attended the briefing meeting with the client, and all you have to work from is the completed scoping questionnaire. You have one working day to complete and fax it to the client while coping with your ongoing projects. This sort of timescale is not unusual. Remember this next time you look at a program and criticize the treatment.

You have a choice of two completed scoping questionnaires – one online and one offline. Using the information given, derive a proposal for one of them.

■ Online client-centred project scoping questionnaire

Project name/no: Wrap-it Com/106

Contact details Jeff Standing, President

Client/organization name: Wrap-it

Address: 29 Westbery Avenue

Mission Quay

ONTARIO K3X 4T5

Tel: (613) 555 7171   Fax: (613) 555 7289   E-mail: standing@wrap.intmail.com

Website:

Project contacts:

Name(s): Jeff Standing   Positions(s): President

Stella Carpanini   Production Manager

Direct line: as above   E-mail: as above

Previous interactive media experience

Online

None ☐   A little ☑   Fair ☐   Good ☐   Experienced ☐

Offline

None ☑   A little ☐   Fair ☐   Good ☐   Experienced ☐

Experience description

Online

Products:

Website as part of trade	Small Business Alliance
association package. Standard	
Templates, little feedback	

Offline

Products: Producer:

Client's initial statement of what they want

This is a small firm specializing in all forms of wrapping paper/goods for crafts people/
hobbyists. Customers are now asking why they cannot order online so they want this
implemented. They feel their present site looks and feels dated. They want better
information on hits/enquiries/sales. As the company is Canadian they need the site to be
in both English and French. They will supply text and translations about products.

Online project type

Internet ✓   Hybrid Web/CD ☐   Intranet ☐   Extranet ☐
Mobile ☐
Set up new facility ▭
(If yes, domain name suggestions?)
Already in place but need to move from last company who hosted the site to us.
Add/change existing facility ✓

Market sector

Commercial ✓   Corporate ☐   Government ☐   Education ☐

Project bias

		Importance ranking	Size of section (large, medium, small)
Company profile	✓	3	small
Information gathering	✓	1	n/a
Information dissemination	✓	2	small
Retail (products or services)	✓	1	medium
Database access/development	✓	1	medium to be developed
Online transactions	✓	1	medium
Marketing/advertising	☐	☐	
Redesign site	☐	☐	
Others (specify)	☐	☐	
Image improvement through general look and feel	✓	1	

Browser/platform expectations

Either:

Developer policy accepted i.e.

Development only for IE browser and current versions on   Yes ☑ No ☐
  PC platform

Or:

Client wants:

Browser(s) _____

Versions supported: _____

Plug-ins _____

Platform(s) _____

Allow Java?   Yes ☐   No ☐

Allow JavaScript?   Yes ☐   No ☐

Allow ActiveX?   Yes ☐   No ☐

Or:

Client does not know. ✓ (We need to propose answers as has no one in-house)

Client contact name for answers   _____

                            Tel: _____

                       E-mail: _____

Site maintenance

Client to maintain   ✓ (content)

You to maintain   ✓ (server)

Log analysis

Is this needed?   Yes ☑ No ☐

Client to do   _____

You to do   ✓

If yes: How much is wanted?

Referring pages, number of visits, duration of site visit, profile of use by hour/day,

_____

Benefits/achievements wanted

Not applicable [＿＿＿＿＿＿＿] (Reason) [＿＿＿＿＿＿＿]
[＿＿＿＿＿＿＿]

Through this site the organization wants to achieve:

1. Offering new service to customers
2. Increased inquiries about products
3. Increased sales online
4. Enhance image appropriate for niche market
5. Seen to keep up with competitors' Web presence
6. Platform for offering special deals cheaply and quickly
7. Profile of customers using new service
8.

The users of the site will benefit from or fulfil needs by:

1. Up-to-date information on the company and products
2. Clear, fast access to information wanted
3. Access to new product details before other customers
4. Access to special deals advertised on Web only
5. Quick, easy enquiries via e-mail
6. Fast response to enquiries
7.
8.

If you were a user what search words might you use to locate the site?

Craft, Craft supply/supplier, packaging hobby/ies, Wrap it, bags, boxes, gift wrap and
equivalent terms in French

Access and use

The audience/users		Access to what information
Internet		
General public	✓	All
Specific market sector(s) (specify)	✓	All

Company traditionally deals with specialist craft packing needs. Wins business on small
runs others won't do. Could be useful to general public who have craft hobby/interest.
Note: the client liked the features and feel of our paint manufacturer site (Cozy Colour)
best but could not afford the treatment once told the cost.

Access and use (cont)

Intranet

Corporate/government/
   education/other:

In-house (all)

Exec

Managers

Sales force

Other

Extranet

No. of sites to connect

Who will need access
(specify)

Emotional reaction considerations

Typical user reaction/first impression to main screen: Key adjectives(s)

Re the company/organization represented   Efficient

Artistic

Re the content of the page   Inviting

Clear

Typical user reaction to time spent on the site:

Pleased with range of products

Good value

Media mix

Client's media expectations	None, wants suggestions	✓	Animation		%
	Text	%	Audio		%
	Graphics	%	Video		%

Content (existing assets)

				Contact:	
Written	✓			Contact:	Nigel Benson
Relevant databases	✓	Spec:		Contact:	Lindy Cortez
Graphics/stills	✓	Spec:		Contact:	Nigel Benson
Audio		Spec:		Contact:	
Video footage		Spec:		Contact:	
Content experts	✓			Contact:	Nigel Benson

Time for development

Client expectation [2] (months)   Start date [January]

End date [February]

Any fixed dates [   ]

(demos etc.) [   ] [   ]

[   ] [   ]

To be specified in proposal [   ]

Special considerations

Database development/online transactions

Company specialist and extra questionnaire needed   Yes ☑ No ☐

Client contact for this extra software analysis [n/a]

Tel: [   ]

E-mail: [   ]

Dynamic pages required

Company server-side specialist and extra questionnaire needed   Yes ☑ No ☐

Client contact for this extra server-side [n/a]
    software analysis

Tel: [   ]

E-mail: [   ]

Testing strategy

Company standard   ☑

Focus groups   ☐

Usability testing   ☐

User trials   ☐

Stress/load testing   ☐

Other   ☐

Localization/internationalization

Not needed [   ]

Needed (further analysis to be done) [Yes as French version needed too]

Accessibility factors mandatory   Yes ☐   No ☑

Budget

[   ]   £/$ approx

Budget holder: [Jeff Standing]   Position [President]

Tel: [see above]

E-mail: [see above]

Project costs to be prepared and negotiated

Separate costs to be put forward for maintaining and updating

■ Offline client-centred project scoping questionnaire

Project name/no: SMCE/67

Contact details

Client/organization name: Brentfields Museum

Address: The Parade

Brentfields

Tel: 234 444   Fax: 234 445   E-mail: jane@brentfields.org.uk

Website:

Project contacts:

Name(s):   Jane Morris   Positions(s):   Exhibition Organizer

Libby Turner   History Curator

Direct line   E-mail:

Previous interactive media experience

Online

None ✓   A little ☐   Fair ☐   Good ☐   Experienced ☐

Offline

None ☐   A little ☐   Fair ☐   Good ☐   Experienced ☐

Experience description

Online

Products:

Offline

Products: Producer:

Project type

Commercial	☑	Corporate	☐	Government	☐
Presentation	☐	Point of information	☑		
Training	☐	Publishing	☐	Hybrid CD/Web	☐
Other	☐	(Specify)			
Education	☐				
Edutainment	☐				
Entertainment	☐				
Reference	☐				

Content (general statement)

What's the project about? Why multimedia?

As part of its centenary celebrations, the museum is putting on a special exhibition. There will be five sections covering 20 years each. Each section will feature the five most important acquisitions during the period and have mini exhibitions of work of two/three key local people who won international fame during those times. The history of the museum will run as the main theme throughout the sections.

The multimedia application is needed as a centre point for the exhibition area, which will be shaped like a star. The client wants it to complement and extend the other exhibits.

Content suggestions

There's a family portrait of the museum founder and records about the family, which they feel could offer good background material. They have a full record of special exhibitions held over the whole period with a copy of the accompanying catalogues, which Jane thought might be useful

Audience/users

Commercial		Corporate	
General public	☑	In-house (all)	☐
Specific market	☐	Exec	☐
Sectors (specify)		Managers	☐
		Sales force	☐
NOTE: More schools and retired people form the audiences. Also, tourists, surprising number of foreigners.		Other ☐ (specify)	

Estimated number of users (approx.)

1–100	☐	5000–10 000	☑
100–500	☐	Other	☐ (specify)
500–1000	☐		
1000–5000	☐		

Estimated number
of systems   ☐1   **Location:**   At the museum in the centre
of the exhibition

Benefits/achievements wanted

Not applicable [   ]   (Reason) [   ]

The organization wants the POI:

1. To inform people about the history of the museum
2. To be the centre point of their centenary exhibition
3. To add to the visitors' experience in some way
4. To demonstrate the museum's contribution to the locality
5. To instil local pride in the local visitors
6. To encourage people to come to the centenary exhibition.

The users need the POI to be:

1. Easy to use very quickly
2. Attractive
3. Motivating
4. Brief and to the point but stimulating
5. Memorable
6. Suitable content for all ages.

Content (existing assets)

Written	☑		Contact:	John Barnes, Records
Video footage	☐	Spec:	Contact:	
Graphics/stills	☑	Spec: photos/slides (top quality)	Contact:	John Barnes
Audio	☐	Spec:	Contact:	
Content experts	☑		Contact:	Jane Morris, Libby Turner

Time for development

Client expectation   `3.5` (months)   Start date   `1/5/01`

                                                End date   `15/8/01`

Any fixed dates   `✓`

(demos etc.)   `Exhibition opens`   `15/8/01`

To be specified in proposal

Platform

Existing platform(s) ☐   Specification: `none`   Nos:

Location:

Client's suggestion   Specification: `none`   Nos:

Location:

Reasons:

To be specified   ☑

in proposal   Factors to consider:

`Robustness, child-proof, vandal-proof, to fit in with exhibition`

`style and decor`

Emotional reaction considerations

Typical user reaction/first impression to main screen: Key adjectives(s)

Re the company/organization represented   `Up-to-date`

     `Modern`

Re the content of the page   `Attractive`

     `Clear`

Typical user reaction to time spent on the site   `Interesting`

     `Easy to use`

Media mix

Expected length of programme/how long a user would take to complete (hrs/mins)   50 mins

Client's media expectations					
None, wants suggestions			Text	5	%
Video	60	%	Graphics	10	%
Audio	15	%	Animation	10	%

Special considerations

Company standard ☑
Focus groups ☐
Usability testing ☐
User trials ☐
Stress/load testing ☐
Other

Localization/internationalization

Not needed

Needed (further analysis to be done) ☑

limited to ease of use + clear English + 1–2 pages Outline summaries in French, Japanese, Spanish (main tourist sectors)

Accessibility factors mandatory   Yes ☑   No ☐

Budget

£48,000   £/$ approx

Budget holder:	Mike Vincent	Position:	Finance Director
Tel:			
E-mail:			

Costs to be proposed and negotiated

■ Summary

- From the information given, present an understanding of the approach, schedule and cost. If working on an offline project explain the platform choice.
- Work from the client's objectives for themselves and the users.

- Take into account any content suggestions from the client and match these to the objectives.
- Find the gaps left in the objectives, and devise content and treatment to fill them in the time allowed.
- For online projects, check that the media mix is suitable for the content, the users and the download time.
- For offline projects, check that the media mix is suitable for the content and the users.
- Check that the media mix can be achieved by the platform.
- Cost the proposed treatment, and refer back to the client's budget.
- Tailor the treatment to the budget. Don't forget to include a testing strategy, with options for clients to make decisions on.
- Define the resources that are needed.
- Explain any limitations of the proposal.

■ Recommended reading

As this chapter was based on experience, there is no recommended reading.

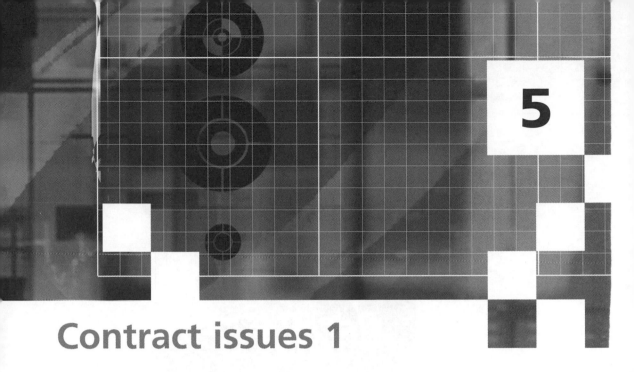

Contract issues 1

Project manager's responsibilities

■ To rework the proposal document's specifications, schedule and costs according to discussions until contractual agreement is reached

■ To be able to understand concerns of members of the team about narrative structure

■ To educate clients in ways of working together

■ What needs to be covered?

Benefit and burden.

A contract is an agreement between parties that defines the benefits and responsibilities for those concerned. Multimedia contracts will involve several documents and several parties. You will need agreements not only with the clients but with your staff and with any companies you work with during the project. In this book we shall cover contractual aspects in several chapters because we are following the stages of the project development, and the various issues have more relevance at certain times during development.

The chapters that will deal with specific contractual issues are: this one; Chapter 9, *Contract issues 2*; and Chapter 15, *Rights, copyright and other intellectual property*. In this chapter we shall refine the proposal into a contractual document, and suggest forms of agreement on how you and the clients should work together.

■ Background to multimedia contracts

The various industries involved with new media have their own ways of reaching contractual agreements. Publishing and computing are generally the most formalized. The arrangements in training vary according to company practice, and video production often still works on informal arrangements.

Multimedia development is a combination of stages from the different media production processes, and so it is difficult to apply one form of agreement that will satisfy all the stages. Your clients may well have background experience in commissioning some of the media components, and will have expectations from the previous work practices they have encountered.

It is difficult for a client to trust something that is expensive and unknown. Consequently, inexperienced clients feel they need to exert more control over multimedia projects than over other projects. They want to understand the processes that lie behind a project's development; they want to feel that they are getting their money's worth. As a result they query more, they hesitate to make decisions, and they want justification for actions. If they come from an audiovisual background they are also likely to take a detailed interest in the audiovisual content – if any is involved.

Because of this climate of uncertainty and apprehension, it is important to agree how to work together to help smooth the production path. Once you have set up a working relationship with a client, or if they understand multimedia production because they employ it themselves, this assumes less importance. Throughout the book we take inexperienced clients as the base because they have the most needs to consider and are the most likely to benefit from a set process. However, it is of course a mistake to underestimate the knowledge and experience of clients. Your way of working needs to be balanced against their experience.

◼ Refining the proposal into a contract document

As soon as it becomes clear that the new client has not rejected your proposal out of hand, and wants further discussions, you need to listen carefully to their redefined needs, and then recost and refine your budget. The sooner you recognize any major differences between the initial proposal and the final work specification and costs, the better. If you are still at a negotiation stage, you can influence the budget. Once the amount and type of work has been agreed, you lose this facility, or at least make it much harder for yourself to justify more time and money.

In the rush to produce a proposal you are guided by the media components that are required and the amount of production that these will take. You may have applied a house formula for production costs, or have relied on your experience to quote a production figure. You may have defined the number of staff that would be needed and estimated the staff costs based on a split of some internal and external resources. You will have guessed at a figure that might be needed to clear rights from film or picture libraries, if necessary, and estimated voice-over costs, again if necessary. Many of the cost components would of necessity be vague at this stage. You wouldn't know exactly how many pictures of what type were needed or from where, for example, and this can affect the cost significantly.

However, as soon as the specifications and timescale become tighter, you need to break down the costs so that you are sure that you can achieve the project according to time and budget. This means establishing how long and at what rate the staff will be paid, and the maximum that can be paid for each component to stay within budget. It also means refining the estimate of what rights might need to be cleared, how many stills to be cleared at what maximum rate, and so on.

You were asked to outline the major cost components in Chapter 4 to serve as a quick assessment of costs. Here, these will be expanded.

We left the proposal document at the point where it was handed to the client for the first time. In the first draft of the proposal, you may have offered the client a range of options and costs. If the client wishes to proceed, negotiations will then take place between you to refine the specifications of deliverables. You have to record all the changes from the meetings, and rework the costs and schedule accordingly until agreement is reached. The final proposal document will form a major part of the contractual agreements between you and the client because it will specify the work tasks, schedule and cost. The sign-offs are also contracts. They are agreements that demonstrate that certain parts of the work have been completed satisfactorily.

During the proposal refinement, you need to carry out a detailed budget breakdown based on resources, acquisitions and clearances. The client should need only the high-level summary that was contained in the original proposal, with milestones and sign-offs indicated in the schedule. But your estimation techniques should become firmer to allow you to feed better figures into the summary. (See the budget template example on the website.)

The charts that we used in the first proposal document cover the right areas to prompt you to arrive at estimated figures, but Table 5.1 indicates the amount of detail that you should be aiming at in discussions with the clients, and provides a checklist to make sure you do not overlook anything. Your project may not need all of these resources, so you can cross them out. Alternatively, you may have special resource needs to add in.

There will be a wide range of rates that fluctuate according to the internal charge-out rates for company staff who work on the project and freelancers who are brought in to supplement them. You can't affect the internal rates, but the external ones can vary a good deal. As you gear up to start the project you should try to get a feel for which resources will operate as in-house ones and which you'll need to recruit. Take a near-top rate for any freelancers to give yourself some leeway when you are recruiting, because your recruitment decisions will be affected by the budget you've allocated to specific tasks, the skills of the people interviewed, and their rates. However, if cost was an issue with your client from the first round of the proposal, you may need to use a lower middle rate and cut the quality of the freelancers employed.

An explanation of how you arrive at your team mix, and the roles of the various people mentioned in the listings, is given in Chapter 10, *Selecting the team*.

TABLE 5.1 Multimedia project resource costs.

Resources	Initials	Internal/ External	Rate per day	Days/weeks needed	Cost
Management/administration					
1. Project manager/Web manager					
2. Information/business analyst					
3. Project assistant					
4. General production assistant					
5. Secretarial support					
				Subtotal	
Video production					
1. Director					
2. Producer					
3. Production assistant					
4. Camera					
5. Lights					
6. Sound					
7. Grips					
8. Make-up					
9. Continuity/props/set issues					
10. Logging					
11. Scriptwriter(s)					
12. Video graphics					
13. Offline editor					
14. Online editor					
15. Film/picture reserach					
				Subtotal	
Audio production					
1. Production manager					
2. Scriptwriter(s)					
3. Editor					
4. Voice-over artiste(s)					
5. Musicians					
				Subtotal	
Stills/graphics production					
1. Production manager					
2. Graphics production					
3. Picture researcher					
4. Animator					
5. Photographer					

TABLE 5.1 (Cont)

Resources	Initials	Internal/ External	Rate per day	Days/weeks needed	Cost
6. Lighting					
7. 3-D modeller					
8. Graphic designer/web designer					
9. Scanner/digitizer					
10. Art director					
11. Illustrator/artist					
12. Typographer					
				Subtotal	
Database development					
1. Database architecture analysis/definition					
2. Data collection/management					
3. Integration/development					
4. Indexer					
				Subtotal	
Design/documentation					
1. Interactive designer/information architect					
2. Instructional designer					
3. Interface designer					
4. Web editor/scriptwriter					
5. Subject matter experts					
				Subtotal	
Computing and integration					
1. Programmer/web programmer Software engineer/author					
2. Technical manager					
3. Network manager					
				Subtotal	
				Total	

It is important that all the new details in the specification are recorded in the refined proposal document so that the new agreements are clear. It is easy to confuse points that have been raised, discussed but rejected, and points that have been accepted at this stage. Good records need to be kept of the meetings during this time particularly.

The refined specification will help to determine better costs and scheduling than in the original document. Your objective is to get the client to sign the document understanding exactly what they will receive for the time and money. Both you and your team will benefit from a sound specification with clear deliverables.

■ Agreeing how to work together

If we examine the logic behind agreements – and contracts are agreements with responsibilities on both sides – then agreements are made on understanding, and understanding comes from knowledge. We should be asking ourselves how we can give the client knowledge about the working processes of multimedia development and their responsibilities in this. It is easier to reach an equitable agreement if both sides understand what is involved and what each one is expected to contribute.

Larger companies – both developers and clients – will more than likely have a set of standard terms and conditions. These set out the general way the company deals with contractual agreements. Often these will have two parts to them; the first outlines a set of principles that will be applied to each contract and the second part is drafted according to the principles specifically for each project. The first part tends not to vary unless any of the principles is renegotiated. The second part links these standards to the particular project aiming to define the time, cost and deliverables in a way that will demonstrate that the contract has been completed satisfactorily. (You will usually find in an agreement that the standard terms, sometimes referred to as 'boiler plate' are placed after the terms specific to the project.)

However, the terms and conditions rarely explain in enough detail what the development means in actual practice. If there are formal contract terms you will need to check them to see if there is enough to help you in agreeing the precise way of working. If you or the client vary each other's terms and conditions because often there are one or two clauses that go against each other's 'ideal' way of working, it is best if you have the changes checked out by a legal representative. More formal agreements are necessary to establish ownership and rights, for example, and these will be discussed further in Chapter 15.

The proposal document is often used as the basis for the agreement of the second part of the set terms and conditions so it is a useful exercise even when there are more formal contractual arrangements. When there are no set terms and conditions to work from, the proposal will in effect become your contract. (Because 'terms and conditions' are legal documents and need to be kept up to date by qualified people, we do not include examples ourselves. Fortunately standard contracts for many purposes are available in book form, from trade bodies and even from some law firms.)

The education of the client will continue throughout the project, but it is helpful to indicate what is going to happen at the beginning of the project. Once the project proposal has been accepted, the successful completion relies on both parties. At certain points the development company has to

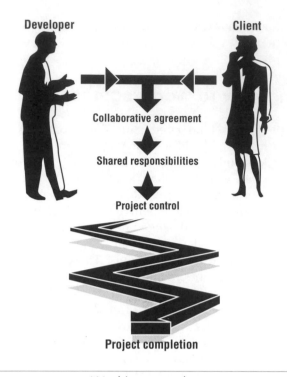

Developer

Client

Collaborative agreement

Shared responsibilities

Project control

Project completion

Working together.

pass control to the client and cannot proceed without agreement and the subsequent handing back of control.

The real problems lie in the definition of a client's role. Clients hold the balance of power because they are paying for the service. The customer is always right from a retail perspective. But in a collaborative process, where you depend on the client to provide some of the materials and decisions according to a schedule, you should not be held responsible for deficiencies that originate with the client, nor for the impact these have on the development process. It is perfectly acceptable for the responsibilities of both sides to be agreed.

The client's responsibilities need to be defined, and you should get their agreement that they will accept the consequences of time, cost and quality changes if they do not fulfil their side of the bargain. This might include a fixed day rate cost for downtime if the client does not get materials or sign-offs back to your team and they cannot continue with the project as a result. The converse is true, of course: the company and project manager also have to accept responsibility and liability for not fulfilling their own responsibilities.

There is one other aspect to take account of in a client relationship. Even if the client has agreed to the defined dates and processes, the project may be revised in terms of the priority level it receives from them because of other factors. Your contacts within the client company will be subject to their own pressures from their own organization, and internal matters will often be given higher priority than external projects. You need to understand the pressures they are under, because these will affect the project.

Every multimedia project is unique because the products are tailored to circumstances. Some may be similar to others, but they all have some aspects that are characteristic of the tailored approach. In principle, though, they all follow certain stages and rely on certain points of agreement or acceptance.

The way of working may not be defined in a company but it will help your role if you explain the way that you want to work with your client. A definition that is company based carries more weight, and it means that there are prior examples that you can use to show the client. It is in your interest to encourage the management to define the stages of documentation and the ways of working. As long as these remain defined at the level of guidelines, they will be flexible enough to allow the project manager to decide exactly which combination may be right for a particular project.

You will find the following useful to give the client once there is agreement to proceed with the project:

- Online – a short non-technical description of the platform that the client will be using – Internet, intranet, extranet – the range of possible media related to plug-ins and bandwidth, and the stages in producing these media components. A glossary of the more technical terms used within the description is also useful. Some short case studies often prove useful too.

- Offline – a short non-technical description of multimedia, its media components, the stages involved in producing and refining each component, and relevant platforms. A glossary of the more technical terms used within the description is also useful. Some short case studies often prove useful too.

- A short description of the phases of a project that your company has decided to work to, how changes are dealt with and the payment structure according to the phases.

- If your company hasn't decided on the phases then give a general indication of stages that the projects go through, indicating where sign-off is needed. For online, this could be related to the stages of producing a small, medium or large site. The company's approach to changes needs to be stated clearly. The stages may include proposal, outline design, detailed design, testing, and so on. It is wise to break down the sign-off into component parts or you may find that disagreements arise about what a sign-off actually meant.

- A general description of your responsibilities and the client's responsibilities to ensure a smooth project.

- Sample copies of sign-off forms.

■ Change management

In the previous chapters we have seen examples of the impact that changes in the project can have. There are different causes of change, but one of the most common is an alteration to the work specification. The work specification is stated in the proposal, and once this is signed it is a contract. If a client asks for changes, they are asking for alterations to the contract. They need to recognize this. Agreement on ways of working together needs to address how any changes to the agreement should be handled.

The computer industry has had to develop some form of control to contain the impact of changes once production has begun. This is called change control or change management. It is becoming more commonly used in new media companies, as they recognize the recurring problems of changes and the consequences of the company's having to absorb overruns on budget.

Some argue that the agreement between client and company should be based on trust. These companies see change control as a mechanism that interferes with the client relationship. These companies tend to come from the more creative end of the spectrum where previous client relationships for delivering traditional media were looser.

Trust comes from understanding and respect. The difficulty with new media development is that clear understanding of the production processes and where latitude is acceptable have not become part of a common shared experience. The understanding of ball-park costs are not common either so the shared basis that underpins successful loose agreements are not in place. This actually leaves the production company more vulnerable than they realize.

Mainstream computing still suffers from mistrust, but this has shifted towards better acceptance as the mystique has disappeared and its potential has become more widely accepted. Software engineering has shown that any changes in a project need to be carefully controlled and monitored, because the consequences of changes can be disastrous.

Several things can happen. If the change is not communicated to all of the team, people working on different parts will end up working in different directions. Then the pieces will not fit together, parts of the program that worked stop working correctly, and a lot of time is spent unravelling the problem. Version control is also used in software engineering so that everyone can check which version of the program they are using by looking at a version number and date. Version control helps to avoid wasted effort, but it is changes that drive the need for new versions, so change control precedes version control.

It is not always immediately obvious that a change will have spin-off consequences, even if the whole team is informed. With offline projects a change to some graphics may cause programming problems, extra audio or video may make the program too big for the disk or platform to run efficiently, and adding an extra section may cause stripping down of the code and rebuilding because a programmer plans coding based on an understanding of the total way the program needs to work. With online projects, many changes can usually be accommodated more easily than with offline, but they can still have ripple effects across work already completed, causing more rework than expected.

Communicating the change may seem trivial, but the team is usually an extended one in which some processes are performed off-site. Contacting several people to communicate a change and then ensuring that they remember to carry it out is not trivial. Even identifying the change can be problematic unless each tiny component has a unique identifier of some sort.

Apart from informing everyone, any documentation will need to be revised and extra copies given out. This takes time in itself. Documentation for a multimedia project can run into several hundred pages, often with illustrative graphics. If individual sheets are sent out, it is easy for them to disappear in a paper chase, particularly if several changes are made per week. It is also common for changes to be made to previous changes as an original idea is refined. It should be obvious how easily chaos can occur.

Clients need to understand the possible consequences of changes and accept a procedure for implementing change. Software engineers recommend using a change request form, which would have the following features:

- Project name
- Date
- Change initiated by
- Change description
- Requirements affected (with identifying numbers)
- Other program effects

- Other system effects
- Planned start and completion
- Resources affected (personnel and schedules)
- Approvals (this could include the systems manager, development manager, configuration manager, quality manager, program manager)

This makes it clear that any change needs to be considered by all involved for the possible impact and the time for implementing the change to be agreed. A similar process is needed in multimedia development.

At the moment, given the way multimedia is working, this level of what will be seen as bureaucracy would be totally unacceptable. The equivalent approvals needed might include: client, development company director/account manager/finance director, technical director, project manager, web designer, programmer, graphics artist, video director, video graphics artist and so on.

Development time is always at a premium in projects, and administration suffers. Because the project manager's role is often split between developing part of the project according to a specialism and the overall management, any lengthy administration procedures would add to an already over-burdening workload. But without some form of change control, the project can quickly degenerate.

The form as described above does not work for a client-driven project, because if the client initiates a change they are not in a position to describe the change or its possible impact in ways that can be understood by the team. The project manager has to work with the client to derive a description, and then check out the consequences. In this way the communication time increases in a client-driven project.

The form also does not work for every multimedia project component. It has been drafted for changes to the code and structure of a program. Multimedia changes might affect these but there are also changes requested in graphics, audio scripts, video scripts, video graphics and text scripts.

In offline projects, if a careful object-oriented approach to the software design has been undertaken then quite a lot of the changes to the content will not impinge greatly on the software. The difficulties that changes cause are also related to the time in the project when they are made, and whether the components have been integrated with others.

With online projects, the impact of changes can be as great as in offline if the more complex coding – such as Java – is being used. Otherwise, changes to HTML code are comparatively straightforward. But asking for a few pages within a section that demand a new structure that has not featured before is a significant change even though the pages are part of a section.

If the client is made aware of the last opportunities to make changes for each of the components, the project can run more smoothly and truly trivial changes can be accepted willingly. It is right for clients to adjust components until they are satisfied with them or until the agreed timeframe for adjustment has lapsed. If clients agree that after sign-off of each stage any changes will incur time and cost penalties, the developers have some form of control.

A compromise solution is needed. This is why it has been suggested that client education needs to address changes. If clients can understand the complications that can arise, they will be more disposed to stipulate their requirements carefully at the beginning and within the adjustment leeway. If they understand that, after sign-off, changes will be costly and time-consuming, they will be more careful in suggesting changes.

■ Stages of a project

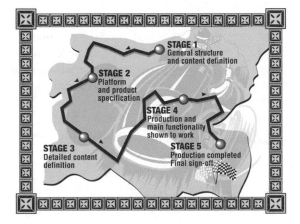

A project generally follows these stages of development:

1. Agreement to the overall structure and major content/development areas (the proposal or sometimes the outline design should stipulate these). Sign-off stage 1 and 2.
2. Agreement of the system's technical capabilities for online projects or platform for offline projects, and product specification for both types of project. These can be in Sign-off 1 or 2.
3. Agreement to the detail of each component: text, navigation methods/menus, audio, graphics, video. These can have individual sign-off stages if the scripts are produced separately.
4. Agreement that the package operates as stipulated for Phase 1.
5. Agreement that the product has fulfilled all specifications and is concluded. Final sign-off.

If sign-off dates are set within the schedule then last change dates can be set ahead of these to allow the last set of changes to be carried out and checked. The overall timing of the project will affect how much time is allowed in total for each stage.

The client needs to know how the project will develop and what they will be expected to do at each stage, so that they can plan their time and effort. If your company has decided to use defined phases then your agreement list as outlined above should have the phase headings as the titles. Then the client can see the work tasks that will be performed under each phase and the sign-off points linked to them.

■ Responsibilities

If a list of responsibilities is agreed, this will give commitment to the project as well as educate the client in how it will progress. The list needs to be tailored to the type of project and company practice. Agreement to the responsibilities is best achieved formally, with signing and dating, rather than verbally.

The lists below show the responsibilities for a project manager and a corporate client respectively. Although the project manager's list will remain relatively constant for client-driven projects, the client's responsibilities will need to be tailored to the specific project.

Project manager's responsibilities

- To work with the client to produce a mutually acceptable proposal that outlines the project content, timing and budget

- To produce a detailed work schedule consistent with agreed start and finish dates, which will map out phases of production

- To monitor and record time spent on the project

- To keep clients informed:

  - on general progress, e.g. a written summary every week/month

  - on any slippage as it occurs and actions to be taken to remedy it

  - on any suggested changes to the specification arising from technical or design factors as soon as these occur

  - on any other factors that affect the project as soon as they occur

- To ensure that each component part of the project is produced to the right technical specification

- To ensure that the structure and approach to the program are agreed and signed off by the named contact in the client organization

- To ensure that the content/script is agreed and signed off by the named contact in the client organization

- To agree the number of turnaround days for the client organization for any decisions/revisions on any of the parts of the project

- To provide deadlines for the client for:

  - the last round of changes on parts of the script (the number of times a client can make changes will depend on the overall time limit of the project and can vary accordingly)

  - the latest time that changes can be made to any graphics/animations

  - the latest time that changes can be made to any audio/video/music

  - the latest time that changes can be made to any text

- To get final sign-off for the completion of the project

The client's responsibilities

- To prepare a clear brief for the developers

- To work together on the detail of the specification

- To inform the project manager of any factors that will impinge on the project as soon as they occur

- To appoint one sign-off person in the organization who will be able to devote adequate time across the whole project and whose agreement will be binding

- To agree any subject matter with experts from the company who will need to be involved and ensure that they offer adequate time in accordance with the schedule

- To keep within the turnaround time agreed, or accept revised time, cost and quality penalties

- To agree that any changes made after deadline dates or sign-off will incur time, cost and quality penalties

- To agree that any slippage caused by delay of any type by the organization will incur time, cost and quality penalties

- To help the developer gain access to any people or materials in the organization who will aid the project

■ Does education work?

It works slowly, and a project operates better if the client has some understanding than if they have none. However, there are several issues that will arise irrespective of setting up these measures of control.

The client may be anxious about sign-off points because they recognize that they are points of no return. (A sample sign-off form is provided for reference.) They may delay signing because they say they are unsatisfied, but the longer the delay the more the end date will need to slip. The partnership aspect of working on a project needs to be made clear. The final product can only be finished on schedule if the components are produced according to schedule. Both of you may need to compromise on some aspects to achieve this, so that the components may not be the absolute best that could be achieved but they are the best in the time available. If you continue to strive for the best with refinement after refinement, the project is in danger of never being finished. To put this dilemma in perspective, the film director François Truffaut once said that he started every project wanting to make the best film ever made but that as the work progressed he ended up thinking himself lucky just to be able to finish it at all.

Project name:	Wrap-it
Project No:	Com/106
Client name:	Wrap-it

Components for sign-off Phase 1 Title _____ :

Outline design including: Structure map with main content sections defined
Overall treatment of each section
Length for each section
Schedule
Sign-off authority

Signed on behalf of the company:	**Signed on behalf of the client:**
Name: _____ (printed)	Name: _____
Signature: _____	Signature: _____
Date: _____	Date: _____

The client will be subjected to pressures for change from other factors. If their organization changes their approach or a key member of staff, the content and structure of the original specification may become outdated. This is not a problem if extra time and costs can be established. But with corporate projects particularly, the release date is often linked to high-profile events, which cannot be changed. Your client has to produce something that is in tune with the tenor of the organization at that time. They get trapped politically, and you are ensnared in the consequences.

Another problem that still occurs with clients is the thorny problem of their agreeing to one thing on paper but imagining the end result will be visually different. The discrepancy between actual visuals and a text description of visuals, and the difference between static and moving items, always cause problems. This is the reason why prototyping parts of the project will be valuable.

With online projects, prototyping is quicker and easier, and really helps to smooth the process. With offline projects prototyping tools have improved, and it is easier than it was, but the process still takes enough time to need scheduling into the plan.

Clients will become suspicious if you make changes but prevent them from making changes without adjusting the time and cost. This is difficult to justify, but the only way to explain it is to refer to your proviso in the proposal and outline designs, where you reserve the right to adjust according to the detail that emerges. You need to remind the client that you have made provision for your changes in the estimate of time and cost based on the experience of the range and type of adjustments that occur as the content firms up from a development point of view. You have taken the risk in agreeing to produce a partially defined product to a fixed rate. You may be very wrong in the estimate and have to absorb far more than experience dictated. However, if the client asks for changes to the specification, then you have the right to revise the estimate.

If a project has a short lifespan then some of the phases may well need to collapse or not occur. The tendency is to work according to verbal agreements during a short project. Unfortunately, the tighter the project turnaround, the stronger the need for tight specification with no changes, and the client needs to be aware of this. It should be up to the management of the company to explain the risks to a client of undertaking a complex task with a short timescale and how it will affect quality and working practice. This is difficult because the thirst for business can outweigh sense. However, multimedia development is being influenced more from the software engineering experience and companies are now more confident of discussing the risks and penalties attached to development that takes place in stringent timescales.

There is one further issue to consider regarding the final sign-off: the completion of the project. With an offline project such as a CD-ROM there is a definite psychological point where a golden master is handed over to the client for replication. With a website this does not usually happen. The site may even have been visible on the Web, albeit hidden away, during the production process. In this case the client may not feel that the process of production is ever complete, and will continue to ask for small changes. (This is a totally different issue from maintenance of a site since, in essence, a website should continually evolve: we are considering the job you initially set out to do.) To help overcome this you may like to give your client a master copy of the website on a CD so that the psychological handover is actually carried out. Do this even if you have installed the site on the client's server.

THEORY INTO PRACTICE 5

Choose one of the tasks outlined below. Select the one that suits your type of project best.

Online
1. Write a brief, non-technical account of online production for prospective clients. You will need to indicate the possibilities of the use of different media, their advantages and disadvantages according to bandwidth available.
2. Then write a concise introduction to the project life cycle phases of your company. Indicate the actions you will take and the documentation you will give the client during each phase. Include a description of what signifies the end of one phase and the beginning of another. Explain what is involved for the prospective client.

Try out your account on a few people representative of your client base and evaluate whether you have succeeded in improving their understanding of the ways you need to work together.

Offline
Try writing a brief, non-technical account of multimedia for prospective clients. You will be trying to convey the complexity and interdependences of each of the media strands without confusing the reader. You will need to mention the stages of development of each component. Video production could include the following, for example: decisions on video quality and final digital type, research, script, storyboard, shoot, offline edit, online edit, digital conversion, integration.

Your purpose is to give the reader an appreciation of the number and type of stages that a multimedia application can have so that they can understand why it appears to take so long to produce.

Try out your account on a few people representative of your client base and evaluate whether you have succeeded in improving their understanding in the ways you need to work together.

■ Summary

- Clients often suggest changes to the proposal document, which means that the specifications, schedule and costs need to be reworked.
- The final agreed document forms part of the contractual agreement between you and the clients, as it states the work to be performed, the schedule and the costs.
- It is important to firm up the details so that you can refine the costs – particularly on the resources and rights clearances – if there are any.

- At this time it becomes more important to know which team members will be in-house and which will be subcontractors, to cost more effectively.

- The lack of understanding about multimedia development leads to difficulties between the company and the client.

- Educating the client eases the difficulties. Successful development depends on a partnership in which each side contributes.

- Building in control mechanisms based on change management and sign-off points helps to achieve steady progress.

- Defining the responsibilities of work practice helps to achieve a smoother way of working together.

■ Recommended reading

Brooks F.P. Jr (1995). *The Mythical Man-Month. Essays on Software Engineering*, 2nd edn. Reading, MA: Addison-Wesley

Burdman J. (1999) *Collaborative Web Development: Strategies and Best Practices for Web Teams*. Reading, MA: Addison-Wesley

Humphrey W.S. (1990). *Managing the Software Process*. Reading, MA: Addison-Wesley

Agreeing the content

Project manager's responsibilities

- To ensure content integrity and information structure is suitable for purpose and audience
- To establish time for business, market, architecture and/or content research if necessary
- To influence the client's selection of content
- To guide the client on commenting on content
- To agree turnaround time and number of revision cycles
- To get sign-off on content scripts

■ The importance of content

The common thread joining all the types of interactive development lies in the desire to communicate. This might mean communicating information or designing an experience. The interactive platform provides the communication channel to another person where we want our material to generate some form of reaction. In Chapter 2 we saw that design quality for our purposes is defined in terms of content and treatment. If a positive reaction is caused then the connection is made and communication takes place. If however, there is a negative reaction, the faults will often lie in the content, the treatment, or a combination of both.

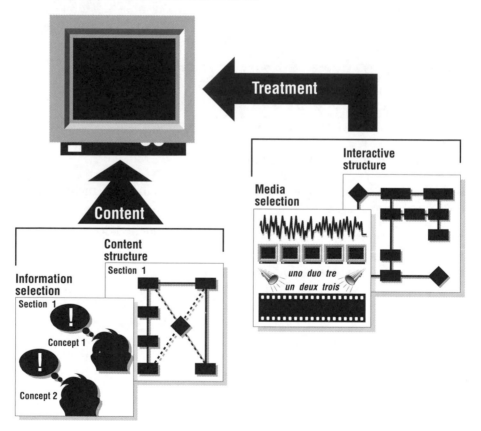

It is difficult to isolate content from its treatment, so we need to take the definitions further to help this process. Content means the messages or information contained in the product, and the way these are arranged. This includes the structure or architecture of the application. Treatment means the media, the techniques associated with the media, and the user interface that is chosen for the product. This is usually known as the look and feel. In some offline applications the treatment dominates because there is little or no content – games programs and some entertainment applications, for example, if they are activity or action based. This chapter does not apply to these kinds of application.

Over the past couple of years, the importance of e-commerce and e-publishing sites has made the structure blocks that contain the content a more prominent component for developers to take into account. Because the content may be volatile and need updating – daily news for example or prices of goods – the container blocks for the content need to remain static for efficiency while the specific volatile items of information contained in them might change. Essentially this is a non-technical description of a database. When databases are involved, the structure of the content blocks and the way they relate to one another is as important as the content that is put in them. The site's architecture has a bearing on the way the user navigates the site. In other words, it affects the feel. The number of components has implications for the layout and therefore can impinge on the look. But the specific visual impact on choice of shapes and colours within a layout remains relatively open.

The economic efficiency of maintaining larger sites means that more and more are moving towards 'template' structures for dynamic data in their websites. The drives to change information and update online sections regularly and efficiently are becoming the prime considerations in business. So even the more conventional websites for medium to large companies are becoming more mechanical, more consistent across departments, more integrated with the total communication branding of the company and more user aware. With these types of applications, determining the site structure blocks is important and is affected by the type of content that will be put inside the blocks.

For large database-driven applications – e-commerce sites are prime examples – the definition of the database engine is a major component. The number and type of fields, whether the database is relational or not, size and complexity and other factors, will influence the product information or general information contained in the fields. The structure and content of the whole database is masked to the users who are only concerned with the pieces of information that have relevance for them. They will use a search or select mechanism to see certain combinations of the data. It is at this point where the information meets the user that the transfer of meaning starts. This drives the need for the developer and clients to agree the precise details the user sees and its layout on the screen.

Of course, this assumes that the database has been constructed with the right details and the ways to access them. If you are just remodelling the front-end of a website and have not constructed the database, this may cause problems. The database may originally have been constructed for offline and professional access rather than for online and general public access. The functionality may have to be reworked. You need to recognize the extent of the work involved here early enough to get the project scoped correctly. It will take a specialist to check and keep checking the needs and expectations of the client against the database structure.

Reworking a database is not a trivial task. So even if your responsibility appears to be front-end work, you may need to appreciate how this can impact on other spheres and if you should take this into account. The general information on content selection and agreement will apply for these front-end projects during this chapter, but the definition of data fields and database functionality will not be addressed as it belongs more to software development specialists. However, as we move towards full development of multimedia databases, this distinction will blur.

The links that web work has to such fundamental business processes as the core company database has brought web developers to work closer not only with general management but also with other specialists. The use of business analysts, information analysts and technical analysts at the outset pre-development stage of a project is growing. These stages have a lot in common with more traditional IT development projects where the specific content is less important than the information structure. Consequently, more traditional companies have become involved in this type of development and have different working practices as outlined in Chapter 1.

Because the information that reaches the user is dependent on the way in which the database is structured, it is important for the people involved with the structure definition and the interactive definition to collaborate. On top of this they both need to understand from the right technical people, that the proposed solution will fit the client's technical capacity and configuration.

The definition we use for content and treatment remains true and can still be applied allowing for the expansion because of the database considerations mentioned above. Content in its widest sense is now receiving better recognition as to its real value. Previously more importance was often given to the visual treatment than to the messages. Since multimedia is about communication this acceptance of the importance of the content correctly balanced by its treatment is a good step forward.

The quality of the content depends on a number of factors: the selection, breadth, depth, appropriateness for the audience, pace of delivery, how all this is structured, and the sequence in which it is presented. The media techniques – use of graphics, animations, hot spots, audio, video, and so on – can only serve to help the content achieve its purpose better; they cannot make up for poor selection or lack of content integrity.

■ Whose role is it to define content?

In new media production there has been no specialist role devoted to defining the content of a project. In part this is because a lot of the ideas for the content often came along with the brief. Now however, there can be several people involved depending on the type of application. The specialist role has been present in the traditional training industry because there has always been a training needs analyst defined as part of the team. This content-focused role has carried through into interactive training development.

Now equivalent analysts who help define content for different types of interactive projects are emerging. The project managers might have a background in analysis of some type and perform the scoping themselves or they may work alongside several analysts to help shape the project in a way that will provide a good solution for the clients but remain workable by the team for the time and cost.

As indicated in Chapter 3, *Scoping a project*, if the brief has not been well defined and the client cannot answer salient questions, you may suggest that they use your company's business analyst, information architect, technical analyst and whoever else you think may help them reach a clear definition of what they want. When the applications involve database definition, the structure of the content blocks (e.g. the records and fields) may need to be done in conjunction with a business analyst, information analyst and/or technical analyst. When the applications are part of the branding strategy of a company, input from a marketing or branding specialist might be needed.

If your company does not have these analysts you might suggest that your project manager work with the equivalent in the client's organization to reach a definition. There is a problem if neither you nor the client has analysts at this level when they are needed. You do not want to begin a project without a clear brief because this holds the highest risks. Equally, you do not want the client to go to another company for this first part of the project in case that company then lands the development of the project as well. You may consider partnerships with consultancies that offer analysis but do not do development so that you can call on them to help as a subcontractor. Much of this negotiation depends on the size of the client's company, their expectations from the application and the way your company chooses to work. For smaller projects the project manager collapses several roles into one and takes more responsibility. However, the clients themselves also take more responsibility and make decisions that imply the direction they want, based on their knowledge of their sector.

For other media sectors and applications, different specialists have traditionally filled the role of defining the detailed content. The author, editor, and scriptwriter have fulfilled the function for print, and video. Instructional or interactive designers have fulfilled the role for training applications. The interactive designer works with the commissioner or nominated subject matter experts to define the content of the training content. He or she recommends an overall interactive structure for the main sections, and then works through each section defining the detailed content with its accompanying detailed interactivity.

Graphics, whether video or print based, has always had a supportive role except in very specialist areas such as full film animation. As a result, graphics artists usually creatively interpret other people's scripts. They extend, shape and reshape the ideas, adding their dimension of visuals. However, those that have experience in interactive user interface design and human factors are now finding more roles open to them in helping define the content architecture for applications.

Technical writers who are experienced in developing multimedia Help screens for use in offline programs have skills that could be applicable to defining content in new media applications. They have learnt to become surrogate content experts on each application they worked on. Subject matter experts (SMEs – Note: this acronym is also used outside interactive design to mean Small and Medium Enterprises) have always been involved in defining content for media where applicable but they need to be teamed with interactive designers when working on digital applications for a balanced skill set unless they have interactive experience.

The role of the web editor has become established, particularly where a website is committed to daily updates, new stories and so on. The role is similar to that of a traditional editor or managing editor because in many ways a website has much in common with traditional print-based media, especially magazines. This does not imply that the editor makes decisions on the structure of the website – although this may be a part of the role – but that the editor provides the content to drop into predefined sections.

■ Communicating the structure and content to clients and team

☐ The structure

Websites have tended to grow larger and larger as companies understand how to utilize them more effectively for more people. Many sites have needed redesigning to cope with the extra content. The original site structure was based on certain premises about the amount and type of content but as this changes, the way to give clear access to the right information for the right people also changes.

Companies just beginning to develop an e-presence have greater expectations about what the site will do for them and this is based on looking and learning from other companies and other websites. They are more focused and demanding. However, often they want to put too much content forward – not understanding the way in which their users wish to relate to the material. Too much content from your clients can be as difficult to manage as too little.

It can really help to give your clients an overview of the structure, the routes or navigation and the balance of the material that will go into their site and the earlier they grasp this and agree to it the better for your project.

Using a visual overview in the form of flow charts is common with offline application development. This also helps the project manager to define where the media elements will be in the program, roughly how much of each will be needed and whether it will fit on the chosen delivery mechanism such as a CD or DVD.

As websites become more complex, the need for a visual reference point between client and developer has become stronger. Various types of site maps can provide these reference aids that can also be used diagnostically when redesigning a site to compare the existing structure with the proposed new structure or to demonstrate what has changed and where the changes have been made on a site for maintenance purposes. Structure maps can be identified for diagnostic purposes in existing sites taking various forms – from text tables with various levels to visual metaphors. (See Paul Khan's online articles – in the Recommended reading, classifying site structures using a visual perspective.)

It is important to differentiate between image maps and site maps. Image maps are graphics on a web page that have interactive 'hot-spots' defined in them and have links attached to those hot-spots. Image maps were sometimes used as actual front pages for websites – as the navigation method. A site map shows the structure of a site in a diagrammatic way. It is often used as a text overview of the site contents and accessed from the front page. Image map front pages were popular until their poor loading times and lack of usability were recognized as being detrimental to users. These maps were produced by designers for users whereas we are focusing on site maps generated during the development process for communication purposes between clients and the development team.

The next figure shows an example of a site map used for communication purposes across front-end and back-end teams during the development of the online training project and is compared with the actual front page contents listing of the project that appears on the site.

Some tools are available and automatically map sites that exist. (See the Power Mapper reference at the end of the chapter, as an example.) They offer to produce several types of maps that suit different purposes and clients. These can be live maps that activate the appropriate page for the client to check the detailed new information on a new section for example. Live maps only work for existing structures so you need to fast prototype some pages for your projected site structure for new sites if you use this type of tool, or use a standard chart package or similar to produce a visual representation for your team and clients. (See the references to flowcharting and ideas mapping tools in the references.)

In effect, agreeing the structure moves your client towards understanding the navigation paths and functionality of the site.

The detail

Once an overall structure is agreed for both online and offline, the detailed information or experience need to fit within it. There has to be agreement on the amount and nature of this detail and this can involve several people from the client's organization. They have to see and agree the detail. This

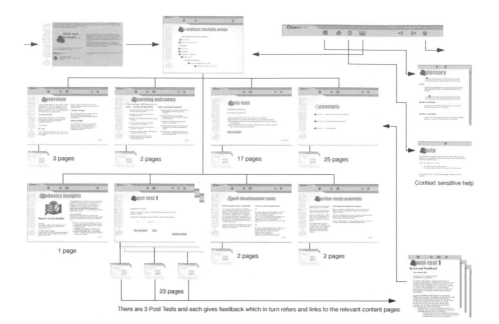

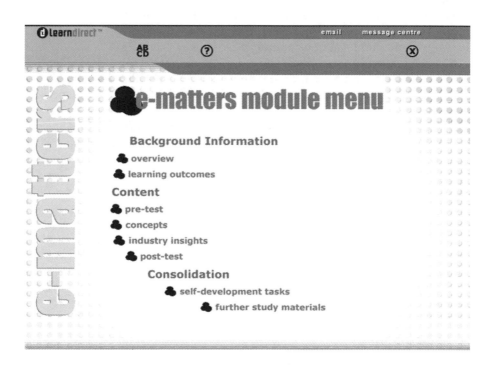

Site map and front page contents
(one on top of the other for comparison)
Used with permission of Ufi Ltd UK

includes agreement on graphics and layout. Many forms of scripting for different types of interactive materials have evolved. Sometimes online projects skip a formal printed version of the detail because the client relates directly to the evolving application on a web address that has restricted access for the development teams. For speed of turnaround and when you have a good working relationship with your client, this is very effective. However, if several people from the client's organization are going to comment and if their views are different, you may end up constantly reworking and getting nowhere if there is no consensus and no one sign-off point. A lot depends on the circumstances and the agreed working practices in these cases.

If the proposed application needs specific detailed content and treatment, the person who defines this will have to record this in some way. Interactive scriptwriting needs additional skills over and above those writing for linear media projects. Perhaps the best way to understand this is to compare scripting for linear media with that for multiple media.

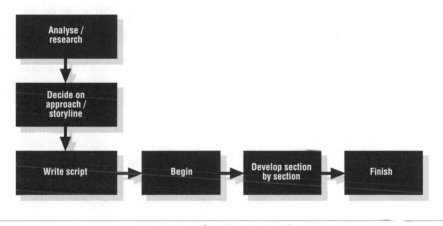

Scripting for linear media.

The skill base needs to change from the equivalent of working in one dimension to working in 3-D. This is not meant to belittle the skills of working in one medium, which has its own complexities of selection, treatment and techniques, but rather to show the scope of the additional knowledge and skills needed. New media scripting is more like designing a relational database of knowledge on a subject suitable for different levels of ability and a range of audience profiles. (Compare the last diagram with the next.)

It is the appreciation of interactivity and how it affects content that is important, and is lacking in the traditional content definer's role. Competence in scripting in non-interactive media is a good base to start from, but it takes extra knowledge and skills to become a good interactive, all-media scriptwriter. In the past, multimedia scripting has relied on ad hoc solutions either from a person who has gradually acquired the skills through experience or from a team contribution from specialists of single media.

There are courses now that are beginning to address interactive writing, and with the rapid progress of online materials plus the interest in interactive TV this role is beginning to get the recognition that has been denied until now.

The journalistic skills of a web editor capitalize on skills used in print-based roles, but as more media become commonplace on sites the role will expand to cover the audio and video aspects of communication as well as print. The role will then need the wider skill set.

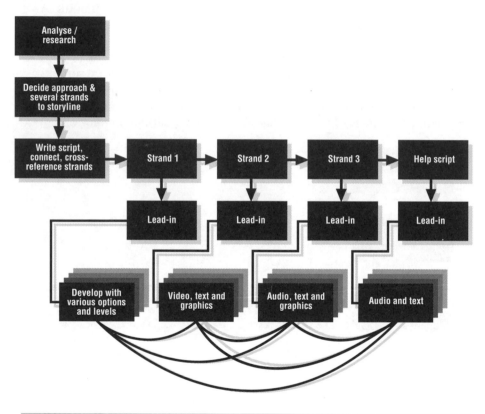

Scripting for multimedia.

Scripting for multimedia

The diagram demonstrates that scripting for multimedia needs a complete understanding of the component parts of the content, and the places where there may be occasion for the user to move sideways or diagonally through the content as well as up and down. It is also important to remember that an interactive viewer has control over the order in which the information is presented – there is no definitive beginning, middle or end although there might be an implied one in the structure. Alternatively, the program might need to track what the user has done and tailor access to the rest of the information accordingly. The content is intertwined with media types and techniques because they affect each other, but the possible impact of media and techniques will be covered separately in Chapter 7.

The main sections of content in an application might involve the use of different media, and may well have had different people script them. This might mean that they have component integrity but not cross-component integrity. Another problem might be that each section has different weighting – one could be 2 minutes long, another 20 minutes long. Unless there is good reason, different treatment of the depth of the content risks leaving the user puzzled and dissatisfied.

The purpose of the communication affects the breadth and depth of the content. People absorb different types of information in different ways and for different reasons. It is no good people using a point-of-information tourist kiosk to find out the opening hours of a castle, for example, if they have to watch and listen to all the information on the castle before that information is given. This is acceptable for a television travel programme but not an interactive system. Interactivity is meant to enhance access to information, not hamper it. You may need to second-guess the user during the early design stages and, if you have the luxury, test your assumptions in user trials.

Multimedia scripting is complicated and demands a complex set of skills. These include:

- making decisions on what material is relevant;
- deciding which media would be right for the purpose;
- scripting various levels of materials in different media;
- providing the cohesion between the levels by providing navigation diagrams/flowcharts;
- understanding the user and the implications of user choice on the structure of the material;
- being able to communicate with and instruct the programmer;
- keeping the vision of the whole while dissecting it into fragments;
- organizing the material into a detailed design document that the team can understand.

There are many ways of scripting projects, and it is beyond the scope of this book to cover the detail of how to script. The references at the end of the chapter will point you to several resources that do provide this. We are concerned here with identifying the driving background factors that affect content.

With the coming of interactive television, the potential of interactive drama scripting is being recognized and researched. This could expand the repertoire of interactive scripts and encourage the reskilling of TV and film scriptwriters. The premises driving the structures of the dramas – or in more common TV terms, the formats – are covered in Chapter 16, *Multimedia narrative*, and the technical attributes of interactive television are covered in Book 2 Chapter 3.

■ What affects content selection?

☐ Influences on content: business and retail

From previous chapters we have seen that there are many factors that can affect the length of a program and its media components. Most of these have been driven by business principles of scoping a solution according to time and cost. These undoubtedly constrain the amount of content and the way it might be presented. But the content still needs to have integrity and cohesion, whatever the length or treatment.

In Chapter 4, *The proposal*, the wishes of the client and their perception of the needs of the user were used to help make content decisions. Multimedia development itself is thought of as a service industry and is subject to the retail pressures of giving the client (or your customer) satisfaction and the retail premise that the customer is always right. If you are actually developing a project for a retail client like a shopping chain, however, they are middlemen acting on behalf of the user, who is ultimately the customer for the product you are developing. The client should know more about the customer's profile than the developer, so their perception can be useful and their organization should have access to market research on their customers. However, general understanding of a market sector and understanding of the equivalent online market sector can be very different so this has to be taken into account. Decisions on the content mix should reflect market trends and intelligence. Anyone making decisions on content for a retail product should try to tap into the specific online market research. Online customers/clients/users are a specialist section of a market by nature of their way of seeking information. Market sector research on online use has become increasingly important and should have a strong influence on what content is provided, its style, and its structure. (See Chapter 18, *Marketing implications for interactive systems,* for more on this.)

An obvious problem is the restricted time available between meeting with the client and completing a proposal, making a pitch for a tender or whatever way is being used for landing the project. As discussed before, you should try to convince the client of the need to gather market intelligence to help with the decisions on the quality of the content and treatment. This should be done by one or several of your company analysts if you have them or by the client's own analysts if they have them. If they don't grant this then you can only do what you can do in an amount of time you specify according to the resources available and whether the client will pay for this service or not. Unfortunately, clients will often think that the lack of knowledge at this point is due to your inadequacies rather than theirs. It should be their responsibility to state clearly what they want, and they should know what they are trying to achieve with the particular market and why but in the emerging e-business market this is not straightforward.

The client also has a responsibility for the level of quality in the program, and if they choose to curtail quality of content selection because of time that is their prerogative and risk, but they need to recognize that this is what is happening. There are other occasions where the client dictates the content completely. They may insist on a body of content that is inappropriate for an interactive medium. They may insist that a large amount of information is covered when the user may be likely to spend relatively little time on the application. Content inadequacies are not always due to developers.

When you cannot create the time and backing to get relevant information, a few telephone interviews with relevant people from within and outside the organization may help to indicate trends in the customers' behaviour. This can trigger thoughts about relevant content areas. Finding out what is irrelevant is equally useful because you can cut it out of the range.

Influences on content: training applications

The concern with cohesion and detail in training stems from the need to test the strength of the overall message and of each of its component concepts. It is likely that the users will be tested or have their performance evaluated after doing the programme and you can only test what has been taught. Care is taken in presentation of ideas to maximize comprehension and make tests fairer.

It becomes important to know the user's entry level of knowledge in the subject so that the interactive designer can make decisions on what to leave out as assumed prior knowledge. A thorough understanding of the audience is essential to keep the content relevant.

The structure of the content in this case is driven by theories of learning. The content needs to be assessed in terms of complexity, and the concepts need to be introduced in a sequence that aids retention. Reinforcement is important, as is the chance for the user to apply the knowledge in some way to make sure that it is retained in the longer term, not just stored temporarily in short-term memory.

The distinction of knowledge and skills is useful. Knowledge can be taught by sequential building of facts and concepts from easy to difficult, general to specific. Skills are acquired by the application of combined strands of knowledge to particular circumstances – knowledge in action, so to speak. Some techniques are better than others for demonstrating and explaining the different types, and these will be covered in Chapter 7, *Selecting the media and techniques*.

Lately, the emphasis on knowledge and skills has transferred to competences. This movement has taken place to help people achieve qualifications in the workplace. People naturally employ knowledge and skills to do their jobs. The definitions of the competence levels that are needed to do various jobs have been analysed so that an employee can use examples of work and interpersonal skills to offer to an assessor to achieve a qualification.

This is a reversal of the ideas of traditional qualifications, where people are isolated to learn theoretical principles that are tested and then applied later. It recognizes that application is the true test of worth and that many are already applying themselves in ways that demonstrate mastery of certain skills without traditional qualifications. The structure of the content of these qualifications depends much more on giving enough information for the learner to perform self-assessment of their skill level and present themselves for independent assessment when they are ready.

The construction of educationally sound tests and assessments is complicated. The determination of the content and structure of tests has a wealth of professional experience in its own right. Because the content and assessment of a topic should be worked out simultaneously in a training or educational programme, it is important to have a training or educational professional involved when developing such a programme. A distance learning professional, instructional designer or interactive designer may well have a better appreciation of the interactive treatment of content and tests than a classroom professional in this case.

☐ Limitations

Traditional learning theories do not link content to media use except to recognize that people learn in different ways so that using various alternatives will help transfer the concepts to the majority of people. The areas that have tried to investigate which media is better than another for presenting information are distance education and instructional design. Instructional design has enjoyed more popularity in the USA than in Europe. Europeans often use the term educational technology rather than instructional design. These areas attempt to understand the way media stimulate reaction, and have value for interactive developers. The ideas behind instructional design and media will be covered in Chapter 7.

Although training and educational applications have principles that can be applied to guide content selection and structure, these principles do not transfer directly to other types of application. When the burden of proof for transfer of information is taken away there is more freedom. The principles of

- repetition,
- the use of remedial modules,
- ongoing checks for comprehension,
- setting up situations for the user to apply the knowledge,

do not have to be applied in non-training situations.

It should be evident that the content of training and education packages has recognized principles that should be applied to ensure content integrity for the purpose. Establishing content for other applications is not so clear cut, and there is the added difficulty that the strengths of interactivity are not yet currently understood in a consumer sense.

Yet unless content is taken more seriously, one part of the quality equation will continue to be neglected. Online training has its own considerations. There are many ways of structuring web courses. Often the type of interaction online may be traditional distance media components: texts, videos or CDs mailed out to you, with the added bonus of e-mailing your tutor and contributing to discussion groups with other students on the course, for example. However, there are also complete web-based courses constructed to be fully online where all content is transferred and tested via the Web or company intranet. In between, you can find all manner of combinations. The principles outlined above as considerations still apply, because they underpin all attempts to ensure transfer of knowledge and skills.

THEORY INTO PRACTICE 6

Apply the content integrity test shown below to three new media products, both online and offline.

Content integrity

Application/Site name

Online _____ Offline _____

Platform _____

Purpose of package

To inform _____
To entertain _____
To train _____
To educate _____
To sell _____

	Inappropriate				Appropriate
	1	2	3	4	5
1. General coverage of subject matter	☐	☐	☐	☐	☐
2. Breadth	☐	☐	☐	☐	☐
3. Depth	☐	☐	☐	☐	☐
4. Suitability of content choice of major sections	☐	☐	☐	☐	☐
5. Suitability for audience	☐	☐	☐	☐	☐
6. Suitability for purpose	☐	☐	☐	☐	☐
7. Weighting for each section	☐	☐	☐	☐	☐
8. Access to information within sections	☐	☐	☐	☐	☐
9. Access to information across sections	☐	☐	☐	☐	☐

Content integrity

By the end of the session:

	Yes	No	N/A
(a) Were you taught the necessary knowledge/skills?	☐	☐	☐
(b) Did you reach the required skill level?	☐	☐	☐
(c) Was there feedback to remedy poor performance?	☐	☐	☐
(d) Was the content offered in a variety of ways?	☐	☐	☐
(e) Was there extra information for remedial purposes?	☐	☐	☐
(f) Was there extra information for advanced learners?	☐	☐	☐
(g) Were there opportunities to apply the knowledge/skills?	☐	☐	☐
(h) Was the material motivating?	☐	☐	☐

All applications

	Yes	No
Would you recommend this application in terms of content integrity?	☐	☐
Why? _____		
Would you recommend this application overall – media treatment, and so on?	☐	☐
Why? _____		

■ How to get content agreed

There are stages of refinement in the production of content, and sign-off should follow these. The first stage is to agree the major sections or topics that will be addressed, and to indicate the volume of content for each section. This high-level agreement should set the scope and balance of the application. This usually happens at the proposal or outline agreement stages of the project, as explained in Chapter 5, *Contract issues 1*. The content structure maps discussed here are relevant in helping to focus the client and to continue to focus them during the stages of development. You may use an embryonic one in a proposal where the highest level sections are identified. This may change and be refined as the detail becomes clearer. The original will serve to show where changes have been agreed and if extras have been added that necessitate renewed schedules and costs.

Stage 2 for content agreement occurs as each major section is drafted. Here there is another dilemma: the more clients see, the more they want to change or at least influence the development. There is also a strange but common reaction to make changes for the sake of change – perhaps to show that they have actually looked at the online material or script!

New media scripting is not standardized. Some companies begin from a storyboard approach, emphasizing the visual and layout elements. Other companies use predominantly print to describe the content and interactive linking via a number system or other such denotation system.

Both forms are professional forms of scripting, and often provoke the wrong responses from clients. The client may well end up focusing on details of the visual when they need to define the content. Or, with an interactive print script, they often get lost in the instructions, and may well end up rewording instructions to the programmer rather than editing the text relevant to the content. There are many ways to script, but it is wise to introduce your clients to your method and educate them in how to read and comment on scripts. The references at the end of the chapter cover techniques and specific ways of scripting. The subject is too large to cover here, as it needs a book in itself.

Another problem to watch out for is when clients rewrite scripts in an inappropriate way. With online text scripts they tend to want to put too much information in each section, and do not appreciate the 'scan and dip' mentality of the Web user. This behaviour affects the amount of information that is presented at any one time. Many people do not recognize how varied styles can be, or how the impact of the communication is affected by this. The client may alter the tone or style so that it becomes inappropriate for the purpose. This is clearer when applied to other media scripts, as explained below, but the same is true for altering styles within text scripts.

With offline scripts, for example, the client might change short, informal audio scripts into formal speeches or text appropriate for business reports because they're used to that variety of English. Also, they are reading the script in a written form without projecting the script into its proper setting, and so they react to it as written English. If such changes were made, they would act as a good example of the style of English becoming inappropriate for its purpose. Its weighting would be affected as well, if the type of information was intended to motivate, not to inform. If your client is able to alter the proposed online material directly online at your trial site during development, then it needs to be changed by the right person in the company – someone who will be writing for that section and for the appropriate audience once the application is live. (The comments made here about varieties of English are equally applicable if you are developing your material in any other language. See Chapter 17, *Adapting projects for other languages and cultures*, for a more detailed account of the processes.)

You face the most difficult problems if the client does not approve the script for audio and video sections. If they react after the recording or video shoot has taken place it is expensive and time-consuming to rework these, so control has to be established at script stage. You can minimize the risks by allowing only your one sign-off authority to make any comments or changes to the script. Do not allow your designated sign-off contact to hand it out to others as this starts a paper-chase reaction with people disagreeing with colleagues' suggestions as well as the original! This takes weeks to sort out for each piece of script, and involves rewrite after rewrite, because once people have been involved they want to stay involved. This is more characteristic of large corporate projects than others. This is why it is important to get as high a sign-off as possible from the client organization because others will tend not to disagree with the authority figure.

In a business application the sign-off authority may well insist on delegating someone with more expertise in the area to agree the script. This is fine as long as you get it in writing that this delegate has absolute authority in this case and that the main sign-off authority will not countermand any of the delegate's decisions. This might sound harsh, but once you have been involved in a script paper-chase, whether for on- or offline projects, you'll try anything to avoid it again. It is one of the major causes of slippage in projects, and one that is unstoppable once it is in motion.

A useful tip for audio and video is to keep the client away from scripts and instead to do mock voice-over tapes without professional artistes. This helps to set the style and setting better for the client. It adds an interim stage but allows changes without too much time and expense.

Lastly, you can educate again. If there is a standard way of scripting for projects in-house, you could arrange for a previous application demonstration with accompanying pieces of script. Then you could talk the client through the process of matching the paper to screens. This can prepare them for meeting their own paper script and attune them to what the different pieces mean, who they are aimed at in the team, and what their role is. Online projects are easier than offline in this respect because it is so much easier to make changes to text within websites.

You need to ensure that the client understands how many revisions they are allowed per script. Otherwise you can find that instead of the changes becoming fewer as revisions go on, they become more. This happens when the client gives more time to their script reading as the point of no return approaches. They need to understand that their time investment should actually diminish as the scripts progress, and that they should merely check that their requests have been complied with, not begin to read the whole script again. The project manager can influence clients by explaining how many revisions are allowed – dependent on the time available – and that the first reading should be the most thorough to set the conditions for changes that diminish through the revision cycle.

■ General principles for establishing content

- Irrespective of the project being on- or offline, the purpose drives the selection of content, whether in terms of information, promotion, entertainment or education.
- The age range of the intended audience can influence content selection.
- Market trends can influence content selection.

- If you are doing a project for a corporate client, the company's culture can affect content selection. Sometimes the developer, despite trying, cannot influence this in order to achieve the best result.

- The purpose of the project will indicate the length of time the user is likely to spend on the system, and this determines the depth and breadth that the content needs to have.

- The length of the sections of the application and therefore the depth and breadth of the content should take access and attention span into consideration. This is particularly important in online, point-of-information and kiosk applications.

- Content that dates quickly should be avoided, or put in a format that is easily updatable, unless the client accepts the consequences.

■ Summary

- Content = the structure blocks, the messages or information in the package. Treatment = the media selected, media techniques employed, and the interface.

- The quality of content = the selection, breadth, depth, appropriateness, pace and sequence of presentation.

- There is confusion over whose role it is to define content, content quality and integrity.

- Scripting for new media needs complex skills: the more media elements are used the more complex it becomes.

- The purpose of the project and the business sector it is being developed for influence content selection. The client may provide or influence the content.

- Get sign-off agreement to the content stage by stage.

- Control the sign-off process carefully – it is a high-risk area for project management.

■ Recommended reading

Bonime A. and Pohlman K.C. (1997). *Writing for New Media: The Essential Guide for Writing for Interactive Media, CD-ROMS and the Web*. New York: John Wiley & Sons.

Boyle T. (1997). *Design for Multimedia Learning*. Englewood Cliffs, NJ: Prentice-Hall

Collis B. (1996). *Tele-learning in a Digital World: The Future of Distance Learning*. London: International Thomson Computer

Duffy T.M. and Jonassen D.H. (1992). *Constructivism and the Technology of Instruction: A Conversation*. Hillsdale, NJ: Lawrence Erlbaum Associates

Ellis J. (1992). *Visible Fictions. Cinema: Television: Video*. London: Routledge & Kegan Paul

Gagné R.M., Briggs L.J. and Wagner W.W. (1992). *Principles of Instructional Design*, 4th edn. Orlando, FL: Harcourt Brace Jovanovich

Garrond T. (1996). *Writing for Multimedia: Entertainment, Education, Training, Advertising and the World Wide Web*. Boston: Focal Press (This has script examples.)

Korolenko M. (1997). *Writing for Multimedia: A Guide and Sourcebook for the Digital Writer*. Belmont, CA: Integrated Media Group

Naidu S. (1994). Applying learning and instructional strategies in open and distance learning. *Distance Education*, **15** (1), 23–41

☐ Web map tool

This creates several forms of 'live' structure maps as it analyses a site. Good to use with clients' representatives to demonstrate the content range and structure once the site is built.

Power Mapper.
http://www.electrum.co.uk/mapper/

Dynamic Diagrams Inc
http://www.dynamicdiagrams.com/

Look at seminars at this site by Paul Khan. Comprehensive articles giving an Information Architect's perspective on principles of structuring sites and examples of site mapping; good explanation of various types; see links for maps tools too.

1. Designing Information Architectures for Web Publishing
2. Mapping Web Sites, May 1999

☐ Flowcharting and idea mapping tools

Ryerson's school of radio and TV ongoing research into charting multimedia, see Resources – Flowcharting
http://www.rcc.ryerson.ca/rta/flowchart/index.html

Axon Idea processor also possibly for eliciting concept maps with new clients. A visualization tool for thinkers it says!
http://web.singnet.com.sg/~axon2000/

7

Selecting the media and techniques: the treatment

Project manager's responsibilities

- To define the project constraints that affect the use of media and techniques

- To understand the strengths and weaknesses of each medium

- To involve experts from each medium for the detailed treatments, if possible

- To keep the focus on interactive use of media and the needs of the user

- To keep abreast of research because this area has few guidelines to date

■ Constraints

☐ Online or offline platform

It may seem to be counter-intuitive and negative to start from the constraints that affect the development team, but in reality this is usually what happens. For online projects you need to understand what specification of machine the users are likely to have and perhaps more importantly which browsers they have or want to work with, and start from there. With intranets and extranets you will be able to get a fair idea of the machine's capabilities from the client. Someone in the organization – usually the IT department – will have a profile of capabilities within the company: there may be only one combination of browser and computer on their network. If they do not, you'll have to balance the time to find out against a good guess based on the information the company can give you. You are trying to understand what media components will be accessible to all users and design the site accordingly. It is no good producing a high-end Java-based website with RealVideo, for example, if the majority of your projected users will not be able to view it successfully.

Make it part of your task to get sign-off for the base range of machine and browser capabilities you will design for, as this will pay dividends later if complaints start coming in. For example, you might be told about people not being able to read the new corporate mission statement from the CEO as the text disappears on the right-hand side on the intranet. Your client might have insisted on a layout of graphic banner and text that only suited a large screen despite your best endeavours to persuade them to design for smaller ones. So their wishes overrode your experience, people with smaller screens appear to lose text and the result appears to be bad design.

If you are designing a general website, you need to make your decisions based on the type of information you are trying to convey, the purpose of the information, the image your client wants to project, and the profile of the users. Added to this, you need to keep in mind the market information about the best fit of target machines, browser use, and your audience.

For offline projects, if a client specifies a platform you need to find out as much as you can about it quickly, because many organizations will customize standard computer set-ups. This will affect your decisions about what is possible, what is likely, and what is impractical, because of the platform's capabilities and limitations. This is especially true for the range and technical quality of the media components that it is able to support.

If the platform is already in place – perhaps in hundreds of installations – then you may find that you have no leeway and will have to work with the hardware provided. This could be equipment that is several years old. As technology advances quickly, this can mean that the team has to work to a much lower specification than they would like. With this situation, if there is a possibility that the client would upgrade their systems to allow better use, the arguments need to be made early for them to find the extra budget.

They need to understand the factors that have driven the decisions for your solutions so that they recognize the constraints their systems might be imposing and the benefits that a better system would bring.

For both types of project (online and offline), if you demonstrate examples of previous work to a client you should exercise care. If there are features and quality levels that are not possible for them to have with their online connections or their offline equipment, this needs to be made very clear indeed. It is difficult for anyone, let alone the client, to see some stimulating demonstrations that imprint themselves on the memory while listening to passing remarks about why some of these features will not be possible. They will often hark back to these features later and comment on the difference in quality that they are getting. They will have forgotten that it is the constraints you have identified that cause the restrictions.

Another problem occurs if clients see or read about the latest developments in technology and expect to be able to have them when you are already halfway into the project. Clear, straight talking backed up with written records is the only way to cope with the change in expectations as clients become more versed in multimedia and its possibilities. This change is healthy for the next project because specifications will be clearer, cleaner and faster.

It is more useful if you can show a client examples of the range and type of features that their particular circumstances can handle.

■ Budget

☐ Online projects

The more media you use, the more production costs increase. Your client may want a full range of audio, video and graphics, but expect not to pay a lot more for the higher production values. One of the problems of online productions is that clients expect production to be fast and cheap. They are fooled into equating ease of access with ease of production. If this is the case then an explanation of the production processes and relative costs of a few minutes of audio, video and a range of graphics from animation to stills will be invaluable to shape the client's expectations. See Table 7.1.

☐ Offline projects

The biggest constraint on the selection of media and techniques is the budget. Many clients do not have systems already in place so the outlay for both the platform and the application is expensive. Many projects of this nature are pilot projects, and so clients want them done cheaply even though their purpose is important. Pilots are used to impress the organization to move towards using new media. The purpose and budget do not match well, so you may have to work hard to compensate. Many companies are not

TABLE 7.1 Media components.

Component	Type (Q = quality)	Cost	Production time	Notes
Video	Drama	High	Long	Rights and clearances can be costly and time-consuming
	Interviews	Low to medium	Short to medium	
	Location 'documentary'	Low to medium	Medium	
Audio	Drama	Medium	Long	Good voice-over narrators and actors for drama can be expensive
	Interviews	Low	Short	
	Narration	Low	Short	
	Music	Low to medium	Can be off the shelf	
Computer graphics	3-D animation (Hi-Q)	High	Long	Production time longer than video graphics but usually better value for large number of graphics
	3-D animation (Med-Q)	Medium	Long	
	3-D animation (Low-Q)	Medium	Long	
	Static graphics (Hi-Q)	Low to medium	Medium	
	Static graphics (Med-Q)	Low to medium	Short	
	Static graphics (Low-Q)	Low	Short	
Photographs	Film based	Low to medium	Short to medium	Wide choice of libraries at varying costs. Do-it-yourself an option
	Digital	Low to medium	Short	
	Library	Low to medium	Can be off the shelf	
Text		Low	Fast	Can sometimes be costly if licensed or needing special fonts (in offline)
Translations	Video soundtrack (timed)	Medium	Medium	Check results with subject expert if possible. Remember different languages take different space/time
	Narration (timed)	Medium	Medium	
	Narration (not timed)	Medium	Short to medium	
	Text (constrained to space)	Medium	Short to medium	
	Text	Medium	Short to medium	

considering offline applications as they feel that online offer the best solution for them. However, for particular purposes and clients, the full media experience offered offline can still be a better solution until such time as the bandwidth for the Net allows otherwise as a matter of course and/or iTV becomes a viable option.

Resources

Within each kind of medium there are a range of possibilities that affect the cost. You therefore need to decide the best for the purpose, platform, price and user. The costs are not straightforward, since they depend on other factors: for example, access to the right equipment at the development site, the need to hire facilities, whether the right expertise is in-house or if there is a need to hire it. Your resources can constrain you to work in certain ways.

Table 7.1 gives guidance on some of the media components, their major categories, and the relative development times and costs for any project. This presents them in general terms, and the time and costs need to be considered in a work context to refine the generalizations.

Once you understand the constraints you are working with, the challenge is to produce the best within them. Constraints do not stifle creativity: they shape the way it can contribute. Each combination of media, message, techniques and interface can have unique features that are suitable for the content and the users.

Matching the media to the message

If the developer has complete freedom, there are definite occasions when one medium will convey some concepts better than others, and there would be a natural selection – video for coverage of action-based events, for example.

The power of a medium does not just lie in the way it offers us messages – audio, visual, text, or combinations of these. It is also dependent on the techniques that have evolved in each medium – sequencing, ways of editing, morphing, time-lapse photography and so on. This power is difficult to analyse, because it is very subjective and difficult to identify which techniques or which combination of them have caused a reaction. The power of the media, messages and techniques is released only when the person receiving the messages interprets them, so we need to consider the skill level of the recipient as well as the impact of the techniques themselves. Basically, the ease with which viewers 'read' the grammar and syntax of media changes. It becomes more sophisticated as the media develop. However, this interpretation is not a conscious activity. The techniques have symbolic significance and influence the viewer's interpretation in this way. This is why the change in speed and quality between audio/video and higher-end graphics through the distribution capabilities of online need to

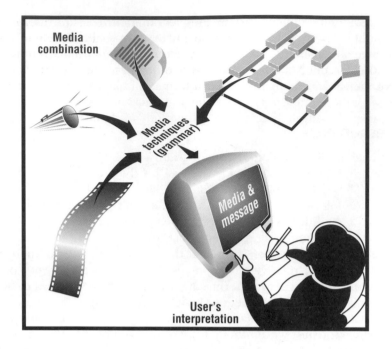

Media and message.

be considered carefully, since the consequences can affect how the users receive your messages.

The impact of each media component depends on a combination of the quality of the content, the medium itself, and the techniques employed by the media specialists. For example, a great deal of research has been done with printed text. Specialist techniques would include decisions on layout, use of space, length of sentence, readability, style and tone among others. These fine details all contribute to the quality of the product and to increased reception of the messages by the reader. Some of these can be useful for screen-based text, but the size of the screen and the electronic nature of the environment mean that parameters that work on the page have to be adjusted. Web pages have already changed their style several times as more has been learned about how readers are utilizing the variety of features presented to them on screen. It is accepted now that readers skim for headline interest and click through when motivated by interest. If the information is not clearly presented it will be ignored and the user moves on. The tolerance for the amount of text that a user will read from a screen is much lower than with printed matter. Web design researchers recommend up to 50% less text should be used electronically to convey concepts when compared with printed matter. (See the Usability section in Chapter 8 for more on this topic.)

There are two problems with making recommendations for use of media components. The first is that new forms or new quality levels of display are constantly emerging, and these evolve quickly, particularly for online projects. The second is that research into different forms of media and their relative merits for imparting similar information has been inconclusive. As there is conflicting information on the 'right' use of single media, decisions on the use of multiple media or combinations of them remain subjective, based on experience.

In view of this we shall present the individual media and discuss their strengths and techniques. We shall indicate wherever possible where the context and platform may influence use, and how multimedia may cause extra considerations.

■ Video: background factors

As video becomes easier to use and control in digital form, its use in general multimedia applications is increasing. Developers find it as liberating as digital audio, but its use needs to be considered wisely within the constraints that still operate. Online use depends heavily on the bandwidth available (either for downloading or for streaming) as well as on the characteristics of the intended audience. With offline projects, not all systems allow full-screen video, and the size permitted affects the type of content that should be communicated. Even the term 'full screen' can be misleading, since the video often fills the screen only because it has been expanded to do so. MPEG as used in DVD is a case in point, since the real resolution of MPEG-2 is usually that of television, which is about the same as a 14-inch computer monitor. When a DVD is displayed on a high-resolution computer screen, the pixels of the digital image are blown up to something like four times their original area.

It is easy to demonstrate the size versus content issue when you consider the inappropriate use of video for a well-known theatre drama that was transferred to CD-ROM and shown in an inch-square box! At the time of development that was the technological constraint for video on the system: the video couldn't be any bigger. With online projects you have to consider whether the size of the video materials, the speed of transfer, and the quality really achieve what is wanted.

Remember that users are familiar with good-quality visuals because of television. Their expectations are high, and they will be critical of poor quality, as will your clients. Any undue waiting during the use of the system also causes universal annoyance, so this needs to be avoided or made explicit to the client from the beginning. If you remember the example of 'Just a small change' in Chapter 2, it is easy to get carried away once the project is under way and agree to what appears to be a small change. It would be tempting to include extra minutes of video because the material that is shot is so good, but the repercussions need to be thought through from every angle – space, speed of interaction, sacrifice of other material.

Drama needs to be displayed in a size that is large enough for detail to be visible. This would seem to be a self-evident guideline, but sometimes the drive to try out what is possible with technology seems to blunt common sense. A talking head, shown in close-up, is likely to be satisfactory in a small window, but the same could not be said of a group of actors in a dramatic scene, or several people in a discussion. Anything that relies on wide shots of detailed scenes will suffer in such circumstances. The video needs to be big enough to suit the circumstances for the user. This is true for both on- and offline projects. This definition allows for a drop in video quality that people find acceptable if the items are breaking news stories for example. Here, the overriding circumstance is time rather than quality.

Video in a kiosk, as another example, should be at least half-screen since the user tends to stand further back from the screen than if sitting at a system: usually at arm's length. Kiosks also tend to be used for communal viewing because people often share the interaction.

Online and CD-ROM users tend to operate on a one-to-one basis with the application and sit very close to the screen, so there is a case for the video to be smaller. However, this should not affect the size to the extent that the video cannot be viewed adequately. An option for offline is to allow the user to choose whether to view the video in a window with other screen components around it, or to see it blown up to fill the screen. Blowing up video to fill the screen does not increase its resolution; it merely makes each pixel bigger, so the image will tend to look 'blocky', and it is possible that the computer will not be able to play the expanded video smoothly.

From these few examples it should be evident that the strengths of a medium are affected by the total context in which it is used. The guidelines for the use of media that will be cited here need to be adapted to the context of platform, the needs of the user, and interrelation with the other components. Many of the existing general guidelines do not indicate that these factors affect the decisions for use. A lot of the educational research guidelines do not recognize that their own context and purpose affect the validity of their findings for other types of media use. For example, a completely incongruous use of sound effects juxtaposed with weird graphics that make no sense would break all the rules for design, but it could also be very powerful in an entertainment application for that very reason. This type of use would fall foul of guidelines for both general and instructional use of media, however.

■ Video

Video is already a combined medium because it generally uses sound to accompany the pictures in some form. It is the current medium that gets closest to reality, since our lives are full of moving images and sounds. (Immersive virtual reality is another contender, but the image quality is not yet realistic although getting better.) Watching and listening are the natural way we process our understanding of the world, and we are comfortable with this realistic medium.

Film and television have developed some interesting techniques that relate to the treatment of information and its sequence of presentation according to time. Our own perception of time in the form of days, months and years is always linear and, to start with, the so-called grammar of film making followed this convention. But over time, as audiences grew accustomed to watching movies, film makers began to change the grammar to enhance the story-telling abilities of the medium. Time becomes non-linear and therefore closer to being interactive. The use of flashbacks or parallel action, for example, allows a non-linear progression through information so that the viewer gradually builds up a complete picture. Action replays allow a concentrated focus on particular events. These non-linear techniques provide a basis for helping people to relate to other non-linear techniques that come under their control as computer interactivity is added to sound and motion. It is interesting to note how these techniques have also infiltrated written literature.

Video can be used for a whole spectrum of purposes – explanation, humour, demonstration, exposition, fiction. In general it is used for appealing rapidly to the senses and transferring impressionistic information very quickly. Viewers cannot absorb and retain all the information that passes, so they filter it according to their preferences and prior understanding. This happens internally as the video passes across viewers' consciousness, but computer control will allow a greater manual selection of preference within a topic. Viewers will be able to preselect pieces to view. This is a proactive filter of information, although they will continue to filter the detail of the information even as it is delivered.

This control that the computer element allows when added to sound and motion means that information can be marked unobtrusively into smaller units of meaning than usual, so that each piece can be searched and selected. This might mean in practice that the equivalent of a 20-minute video programme could be classified into themes or sections, and viewers might select to see two or three minutes of the material most relevant to them rather than watch the whole programme.

Of course this level of control will be more useful for some forms of information than for others. Drama needs to develop and the story needs to resolve over a period of time, for example, so tiny pieces might be disconcerting, even frustrating. But put in a learning context where, for example, specific use of gesture or look is being studied by actors and actresses, such fragmentation can still be very useful.

The type of application will govern the amount of control and the size of the pieces of information. Kiosks, for example, will need to offer people fast, interesting information. Advertisers are used to getting their messages across quickly but powerfully, so developers could learn a lot from their techniques. Advertisers are the masters of short sequences of video, and they innovate continually to motivate people.

Because of the constraints of the delivery system, online projects for the Internet generally use video for short, high-impact sequences. This keeps transfer time down. The messages tend to follow precepts from advertising so that entertainment is the prevalent style. (Although streaming allows video of any length to be shown this is almost always used to view self-contained material in its own window – even in its own player environment – rather than being integrated into the web page.)

The combination of sound and vision can appeal to people's logic, imagination and feelings. But sound and static visuals can do the same, so what is the difference? The difference lies in how much viewers bring to the interpretation of the content and how much they have to do to construct meaning. The combination of sound and moving images is easier to process because viewers' senses are fed with stimuli that are realistic and are absorbed effortlessly and almost unconsciously. Static images and sound require viewers to contribute more to their interpretation.

In the extreme case, when only text is used, readers have to consciously apply decoding techniques to extract meaning from the letters. The skills of reading take several years to learn because the information is removed from reality into a complete system of symbols. There are various levels of symbolism used throughout the mix of media but there is a gradual move from the realistic to the symbolic as you move from video to text. When the mixture uses more symbolic elements than realistic ones the viewer needs to decipher more, and this takes more effort.

Viewing and listening are not passive processes, and this is often forgotten. The combination of vision and sound is more powerful for most people because they stimulate reaction more easily. They appeal to a larger range of possible reactions. Stimulation and motivation are closely linked, so it is easier to motivate the viewer to respond to an appropriate mix of sound and vision.

Appropriate use is the key factor, and the more media that are combined the harder it is to keep all the factors appropriate. For example, an historical video needs to ensure historical accuracy to be convincing. This includes location, location detail, dress, accents, type of language used, type of music used, and so on. Exactly the same criteria need to be applied to interactive video sequences. Details such as the tone and look of the presenter – even their accent – need to be appropriate for the purpose or the audience. Carefully and correctly chosen, they can be the making of the application. Any music used can motivate, can be ignored, or can actually demotivate the audience.

Most people are used to controlling videos in a limited interactive manner on their VCRs. The controls allow a combination of forward, back, scan, play, stop and perhaps slow motion. Viewers cannot jump around the video following links or backtrack to the point they started from. They are used to a semi-interactive environment within the one medium, and this limited control over a linear piece of video has become standard in interactive systems as well.

DVDs take interactivity a little further. The film is chunked into the equivalent of chapters so that the viewer can jump closer to a position they want rather than scan through the whole film till they reach the part they want. DVDs offer extra information around the film because they have far more capacity than tapes or CDs. These extras are also perceived to give added value because the cost is higher than the equivalent video tapes. Extra commentaries on the film and interviews with the director and key actors are frequently offered and extra material or scenes that were cut in the final edit might be included. This all adds to the experience to motivate the viewer as well as making use of the high quality digital capacity offered by the medium.

Interactive TV is limited at present and research is trying to establish what viewers want from interactivity in this form. The sheer capacity of digital cable and satellite systems allows interactive users to select a camera angle to view sport and enjoy action replays whenever they want. Receivers with built-in storage allow viewers to even pause live programming and then pick up later without missing anything. Other research is trying to identify formats in interactive drama that people might like. This is covered in Chapter 16, *Multimedia narratives,* and the technical introduction to iTV is covered in Book 2 Chapter 3.

☐ A few finer points of visual grammar

When film was invented it was believed that the camera had to remain static. The action was framed as if it were on a stage and the film frame was the proscenium arch. In time, directors and cameramen developed the techniques of framing, moving the camera and editing and, as they did so, the audiences learned with them. Today an audience is sophisticated enough to know that if the film shows a car drawing up at a building, the camera looks up to zoom in on a window, we cut to inside a room, and two people walk through the door, then those people were in the car and the room is the one we looked up at. The film is edited to remove time and so speed up the action.

At a simpler level the very way in which a shot is framed can convey information. If, during an interview, the camera gradually moves close in to the speaker, then the impression is of sharing in a secret or of some momentously important point that is being made. Often this visual metaphor will override anything that is actually being said.

The way a face is framed in a picture is important. This is true for stills as well as for movies. The face should have space to look into, otherwise the effect will be unnatural. The strongest points in an image are a third of the way across or up and down the image. You can increase the impact of an object by framing it to make use of this rule of thirds.

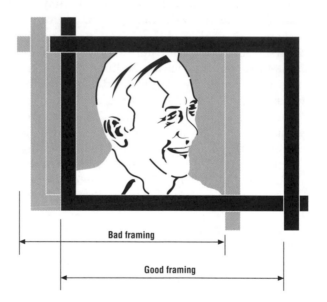

Bad framing

Good framing

Of course, there are more straightforward ways of drawing a viewer's attention to something, such as zooming in on it or panning to follow it, and viewers now know these conventions. You might, if you are feeling devious, actually distract the viewer by using the visual grammar to draw attention to something completely inconsequential so as to hide the real action, which can be revealed later. This technique was used to great effect by Alfred Hitchcock in his films, and if done well, as he did it, can completely unnerve the viewer. There is the way the viewer is made to identify with first the girl and then the private eye in *Psycho*, only to have them both killed. In *The Birds*, there appears to be something significant about the two lovebirds that the hero and heroine are carrying, but in fact they are another of Hitchcock's McGuffins, as he called them.

However, the quality and size of video sequences in online projects should affect the filming effects. Using close-up shots has already been mentioned, but with the extreme data compression used for video on the Web it usually pays to avoid fast smooth action or combined pans and zooms since they tax video compression algorithms. The alternative is to accept that movement may be jerky.

Video and applications for education and training

It may seem odd to single out training and the use of video but there are many factors that make the imparting of information for learning different from its use for other purposes.

As explained in Chapter 6, *Agreeing the content*, if the user is going to be tested on the knowledge and skills covered in the application then the information needs to employ certain structures and techniques to aid this. One of the strengths of video in other contexts – the ability to cover a great deal in a short time – is not necessarily a strength in a training context because the user needs to absorb more of the detail. This explains why there appear to be inconsistencies between educational research findings and general practice in the use of video. When the viewers have no control over the medium – as in television – they cannot look at the material again for revision. They have the one chance to listen and absorb – unless they have taped the material, of course.

Video players and computer-based interactive materials offer the means to control the video and so provide viewers with the opportunity to revise the information if necessary. Computer control can offer more than just replay opportunities. It can be used to pinpoint the concepts the user finds difficult and re-route to remedial material where the concepts are offered in a new way with different explanations.

Role-plays and simulations are recognized as good techniques for demonstrating skills in action. Video is very good for showing interpersonal skills, whether handling meetings or dealing with difficult customers. An interactive role-play could allow the user to take one side of the role-play while the video character asks or answers questions accordingly via prompts through the computer. This is an example of the combination of video with computer control and text with audio, serving the educational purpose possibly better than a linear video. The other obvious advantage is the use of the computer for testing the transfer of knowledge during and at the end of the application. A computer mixture of media-based information can also provide a superb reference set of materials where the learner is asked to research or discover information.

There are several defined approaches to the way people learn. People have preferential learning styles – the way they prefer to absorb, process and classify information so that it makes best sense to them. Educationalists can choose to present information based on a progression from easy parts to more difficult ones. Alternatively, it can be left to learners to impose a structure on

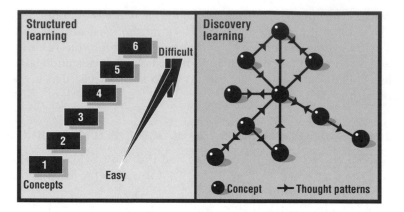

Structured learning/discovery learning.

the information through discovering links themselves. This is called discovery learning. The only problem is that discovery learning takes longer, and there is no guarantee that what is discovered covers the whole range that would be appropriate. Luckily, multimedia can be set up to cover both approaches with the same data, depending on the requirements.

There has recently been a large expansion of the use of online for education and training. This market will continue to grow. Traditionally the education market lags behind commercial markets in terms of its access to high-tech equipment because of the costs involved but this is not necessarily the case now since governments are investing heavily in ICTs for education in a bid to produce enough computer literate employees for the future information society. Developers of online materials need to consider their specialized market and understand if there are restrictions on higher-level access that affect their design and quality decisions.

It is difficult to make a case for using video online at the moment because of the special educational needs. The sequences may need to be longer to explain processes and other concepts in a variety of ways to suit various learners. Length of sequence is a problem online. Also, the attention to detail is important. Any decline in quality makes it harder for learners to discriminate specific meaning if it is tied to the visual. Furthermore, the size of the video window becomes crucial because there may well be more than one viewer in an educational group – more like the parameters that drive kiosk layout as mentioned earlier than the one-to-one use where smaller visuals may be acceptable.

The development of online training courses may well have different considerations, particularly if you are developing for corporate rather than for public use. The firm may have better faster online connections on their intranet, which might release more opportunities for using video effectively in the course.

Hybrid use has become a bridge when online access is limited. Any video might have been put on a CD or DVD so that the user can refer to it efficiently without the fear of delays in downloading or corruption in transfer. However, the production and distribution costs of the associated CD or DVD will push budgets up. In this way it is noticeable that decisions on when and how to include video in projects are driven by a complex set of interrelated factors.

■ Audio

Audio is a very versatile medium, which will usually be an integral part of any video but can be used alone or to accompany graphics, text, or both simultaneously. In offline projects, it uses relatively little space so can be used quite freely. The space it consumes depends on the quality level used but the levels are easy to choose because there are guidelines on matching the types of audio information to the quality level. These are explained fully in Book 2 Chapter 6. Audio seems to be less popular on websites than video and animations. Background audio, either as a digital audio file or as MIDI, is possible but the general reaction to background sounds has been negative (so if you use it please allow users to turn it off). Audio clips, especially RealAudio streamed sound (both live and recorded), is quite common and is even used by 'radio' stations that exist only on the Web. The quality is poor compared with FM broadcasting (although it continuously improves), but the attraction of listening to radio from the other side of the world has always attracted enthusiasts. Perhaps web radio is the new short-wave experience.

In offline projects, before audio was common in digital form, text and graphics had to be used for all information. This made explanations onerous. Screen after screen had to be used for the main content and all the Help explanations. Access to relevant pieces of the information became problematic because there was so much of it. Applications tended to be tedious and linear.

Audio liberated developers from lengthy text explanations. The main problem is overuse because audio is cheap and efficient. Its efficiency fails when too much information is given too quickly for the user to absorb and there is no opportunity to repeat it. The effectiveness of audio is increased when it is used to support text and graphics appropriately. This means that information, like video, which addresses both sight and sound senses achieves even better reception by the user. The use of audio feedback for Help in offline applications has increased, mainly because it can be played at the point in the programme where the user needs it. This means that users do not lose their place in the programme, and the audio supports the visuals that are on screen with extra explanation. It can be repeated easily. The alternative used to be endless scrolling text boxes, which took the user away from the main programme and could cause disorientation.

Audio includes speech, music and sounds. Both radio and television have developed techniques to use with sound that make it a sophisticated medium, but as it is so easy to listen to, the sophistication is not appreciated. The sympathetic blend of music and speech with variations in pitch, volume and style can add greatly to static pictures and text. These can be effective alone, of course. But it is precisely because listening is effortless that the subtleties of its qualities have been almost completely ignored in projects, to their detriment.

It is no accident that both radio and television choose to introduce many programmes with a signature tune. It identifies the programme (a form of branding), and it settles the listener and viewer to be receptive to what is coming next – or brings them in from the next room. It also emphasizes the end of the programme. During the programme it can form part of the continuity strategy to blend segments together when there may be little overt connection. In a non-broadcast context such as video or multimedia some music at the front end also helps the viewer to adjust the sound volume and even check that the sound is getting through.

Sound can be evocative. It can appeal to emotions and in this way influence the reactions of the listener. It can set an atmosphere. These are good points for applications that need to persuade, such as presentations, demonstrations and point of sale. Equally, it can jar and demotivate when used wrongly.

Most applications fall in a neutral middle ground in their use of sound. They have missed opportunities – but the opportunities are difficult to spot. Few recognize the full potential of a well-planned and well-executed sound track. The extra effort means extra money and time for something that is intangible. It is hard to prove its real worth until you compare an application that has professional touches and another that does not. Listen to the examples and explanations on the website to improve your appreciation of sound quality for on- and offline.

Sound has its own techniques to appeal to the listener. A fade-up implies that the listener is eavesdropping on something already under way, and a fade-out signifies that we are moving on and leaving them to it. Sound effects can be humorous, intriguing or realistic. Ironically, sound effects are not always what they seem. You can try this experiment. Take a piece of paper and crunch it up into a ball. Open it out and gently manipulate it. The sound is not unlike the crackle of a fire. Crunching quarter-inch audio tape (should you happen to have any around) can sound like walking through grass, and we all know about horses and coconut shells.

Interactive sound does have differences for developers to consider. Sound used on computer systems to attract passers-by irritates other people who might have to stay in the vicinity. Kiosks and demonstration programs can be prone to this misuse. A phrase becomes annoying if it is repeated often as the user navigates around the system. Developers need to consider how sound can have a good initial impact but then becomes irritating. They might need to consider giving control to the user so they can switch it off when they want. Alternatively developers can build in control themselves where repetitive audio turns itself off after a couple of times of use by the same person.

Another problem with kiosks, and any other installation in a busy area, comes from high levels of background noise. Any sound needs to be carefully manipulated to make sure that it is still audible over any extraneous noise without sounding distressingly loud.

The use of sound in a website can be unpredictable. Sounds that play when the user clicks on a link are straightforward: because the user selects them, the user wants to listen. As has been mentioned, background sounds can be an irritant, especially when what might be precious bandwidth is being used for sound that is arguably superfluous. For this reason, users sometimes configure their browsers to turn sounds off just as at one time many people surfed the Web with images turned off so that the pages loaded faster. This means that you cannot guarantee that the viewers of a web page will hear the sounds.

■ Computer and video graphics

Computer graphics systems, whether they are on desktop machines or on dedicated sophisticated television or video graphics machines, are capable of very impressive results. Desktop computer graphics are very versatile, and can range from simple line drawings to 3-D animations. More than any of the other components, they can be manipulated to suit the budget allowance. However, many of the specialist skills within graphics are still needed. Original material might need to be created, such as cartoons for example, before it is processed and integrated into an application. The manipulation of source materials and their successful integration are the two computer graphic processes that figure most in multimedia. Their quality can be affected by the platform and software.

The strength of graphics is to provide a visual stimulus that can trigger reaction in the user. It can be the prime source of the reaction, or can offer support for other media components so that their impact is improved. In offline projects, systems have become more sophisticated and have more memory, and Internet connections have become faster, so it is easier to use many high-quality graphics. This has changed the look and feel of websites and applications considerably away from a text, menu-driven approach to a visual selection in the form of icons and moving graphic menus.

The use of graphics has grown quickly for online applications, but the restrictions on access because of the need for plug-ins and extended download times still mean that care and thought should be given to the size and complexity of the graphics, balanced against their real value for the site. There has been a move away from using large image maps as first pages because many users wouldn't wait for them to download. Their use demonstrates a mismatch between their potential for visual impact and ease of navigation around the site and the time it took for them to download, demotivating the user to the point of not waiting to access the site. Some sites also had no text information at all on the first page – it was all in the image map – and this made it difficult for web search engines to index the site. On the positive side, better tools have become available for compressing online graphics to decrease their size without noticeably affecting their quality so it is important to keep abreast of new functions in software as these can affect the media selection and particular quality level of graphics in your applications.

Even though graphics can be realistic – as realistic as photographs – their advantage over video stills lies in their ability to be representational in a symbolic sense. This can add a dimension, a unique style and feel to an application or site. The style is often set by the home page for online and the first main selection screen or menu for offline. It usually is the key feature, the hallmark of a program, and one that is used the most and seen the most by the users. (There are some pointers to websites showing examples of different front page graphic styles and an example main menu for an offline application discussed on our website.)

Sophisticated graphics allow superimposition of one picture on a representation of itself and animation could add to the understanding of transformation. For example, this technique can be very effective when there are layers of visual material like the bones, muscle, tissues and skin of a person or animal that need to be shown or even the relationship between the outside of a machine and its internal parts. This type of technique is found useful in developing analytical and discrimination skills, and so can be extremely useful for educational purposes. However, these considerations may work well for offline but not for online for the reasons stated before. The delivery system needs to be capable of utilizing the features of graphics that are educational.

The use of graphics in education and training applications

As with the use of video, there is research that applies particularly to the use of graphics for instructional purposes. The choice of a particular type and style of graphic still lies in the joint decisions of designer/producer (or whoever takes this role) and the graphics artist, but they can both be served in making a selection by some of the insights from this research.

Instructional graphics have been categorized into representational, analogical and logical:

■ **Representational graphics** share a physical resemblance with the object or concept that is portrayed. An example of this might be a picture of a particular style of architecture that demonstrates the points that are

being addressed. A photograph of machinery, for example, would also be representational.

- **Analogical graphics** display something that has similarities with the issue under discussion but in an abstract way that uses analogy to help convey meaning. An example would be a time-lapsed video graphic that used a leaf decaying as an analogy to the decline of a dynasty, corporation or whatever, as shown here.

- **Logical graphics** are symbolic representations in the form of flow charts, graphs and charts. The flowcharts describing linear and multimedia scriptwriting in Chapter 6 are examples of logical graphics.

It was found that although learning theory recommends the use of graphics to support and extend text to aid comprehension, this was being ignored in computer-based courses. Representational graphics were used the most, and analogical the least. This may be related to the history of education and training, where text has played the dominant role. The visual side of communication needs to be recognized in those teams involved with developing interactive education and training so that the effort put into defining well-structured content achieves better success with a balanced use of media. This might be achieved by making sure that a graphics specialist works closely with the person whose role it is to define the content.

The instructional use of animations has also been researched, and these findings can be applied across different types of applications. It was found that users can be easily distracted by other factors, so that the relevance of the animation is only partially understood. This is particularly true when the users are inexperienced in the subject matter.

The guidelines recommend that animations are kept simple enough to be understood, but sufficiently complex to convey the important information. Users can fail to notice aspects if too much happens at once. Because of this, the use of cueing strategies such as narration and the use of colour becomes important. They help to direct attention to salient parts of the animation at the right time. It is recommended that users should be given control of parts of the animation such as the speed, triggering factors and so on, as this involves and focuses them. Animations were found to be good for representing motion, trajectory, spatial organization, and otherwise invisible events, but their overuse can be distracting.

For online projects, though, the use of all forms of graphics has to be balanced against the most likely configuration and speed of transfer as discussed earlier, together with their educational impact. The impact can range from motivational to instructional, and the range of type of instruction is diverse, as noted above. There are ways to juggle the size, quality and speed of download of graphics, and these techniques can be particularly valuable in instructional materials.

■ Text

The value of text tends to be overlooked by multimedia specialists, but it is an integral part of any application and needs to be thought through as carefully as the other media components. Strangely enough, the treatment of text in online and offline projects displays the most difference between the delivery systems. Whereas a few years ago, text used in offline applications was a dominant feature on screens, the amount and function of text has changed as the other media components have come to the fore. Many of the problems that made it difficult to integrate all the offline media components in a digital domain have now been solved. Previously, text had to bear most of the communication load, aided with some graphics. Even the graphics were limited, since they took up a seemingly enormous amount of disk space. Now, although space can still be an issue, things are easier because the storage capacities of disks have increased dramatically. The opposite is true of online projects. Text still dominates here, and although the barriers for using other media are being eradicated, the biggest one – that of the configuration of the most common user base system – is holding progress back.

In offline applications, the function of text information in multimedia has become supportive rather than dominant. It is used most for Help explanations, reinforcement or summary information, summaries of decisions made by the user, titles, names of hot-spots, and quick-scan information such as opening times and admission charges in a tourist application.

Poor typography is immediately evident beside the quality of the other media components. For an application to have integrity, its components need to blend into one another without any noticeable drops in quality. This may not be easy. If text has been added to the video at the video edit, other text added over computer graphics, and some screens are text screens alone, the difference between them can be very great.

This is because the final integration process can affect each component in slightly different ways, and can have a knock-on effect. Text is one element that suffers in video encoding, for example, because its sharp edges do not respond well to the compression and often become fuzzy. Of course, if text has been added into each component, control over font use, characteristics and size needs to be consistent across all and has to be established early. It may be better to generate all the text with the computer to maintain stricter control, but decisions such as this have to be made by the core team members.

When text is a dominant media component, as often happens with websites, it is important to pay a good deal of attention to screen layout, readability and legibility. This mirrors the problems that offline had a few years ago. Cascading style sheets allow greater control over typographical and other layout and with care can allow a page to look almost the same on a range of computers and browsers. To supply a document for printing out or offline reading, the best current way of presenting a totally controlled typographical style is by means of the portable document format (PDF) used in Adobe Acrobat. This format now also supports dynamic media types and hyperlinking and, ironically, can be used to capture a website for offline reading.

Making text easy to read is more complex than many people imagine. Readers are adept at deciphering text, but their job can be simplified or complicated by the techniques employed in the layout of the text. The users of the application will have certain objectives once they see text, because they will make the decision whether to read it thoroughly or not. They will employ their own reading strategies of skimming and scanning the information to appraise it. It surprises a lot of people to find that many readers of Western languages do not start to read at the top left of the screen. They may not scan the text from left to right until the bottom right piece of text. Instead, they may skim the headings to get the gist of the material; they may scan the material looking for a keyword that could indicate that the information they require is in the vicinity.

These types of strategy are used more often when the text is giving information, as opposed to text that narrates or explains. In sound there is a phenomenon called the cocktail party effect, whereby listeners will clearly hear a single word across a noisy room just because the word has a special meaning for them, such as their name. When a viewer picks out a word from text, a similar phenomenon is occurring. Of course, the word may be misread, or hyphenation, if used, may result in anomalous groups of letters being at the start of lines or even change the meaning of a word depending on the language being used.

The layout can help the reader by having clear headings or markers of some type. Line length is also important, as the comfort of eye span across words is linked to the length of a line: you will notice how many web page designs have gradually increased the amount of white space on the screen for layout purposes while setting the length of lines for readability. They may use multiple columns for better readability too. Because screens are generally small, it is tempting to cram as much text as possible into the space. However, this works against readability. Because of the limited space, it seems logical to have a small font size and as many words to the line as can fit, but this will only increase the difficulty of reading. The eye has a tendency to wander between lines if there is small type and long lines. The size of the font will also affect the legibility of the text. You need to consider the distance of the viewer from the screen when making decisions on how large and how much text will be viable.

The use of space helps reading because the reader needs natural prompts to understand how much concentration and attention to give to the information. If there are few or no paragraphs, the reader quickly reaches overload. Headings stand out if there is space around them, but if you need to sacrifice space, other cues can help. The use of bolding, colour and size can help to establish the importance of some parts of the text over others. (See the website for examples of readability and legibility.)

The use of colour alone to distinguish some text from others should be handled carefully, because a sizeable minority of the general public suffers from colour blindness – particularly red and green tones. It is also wise to remember that not all cultures share the same general reading pattern of left to right, top to bottom. If the text is going to be translated there is more to consider than whether the translations will fit into the same space: English is substantially shorter than any translations into most other languages. The lead block of text may be better placed in a completely different part of the screen according to the reading conventions of the country.

Text is still a powerful way to communicate. It allows readers a lot more control than the other media components because they control their pace of reading. They decide how and when to assimilate the information. They can re-read and pause, if necessary, to think things through. It is a versatile medium, which has changed with the times.

The use of computers has changed the way that text is organized, and this in turn affects the way people relate to it. They need new reading strategies to suit the new types of organization. Developers need to understand that just because reading printed matter can be taken for granted, reading on computer screens cannot. The use of layers of text instead of pages, as used in hypertext and Windows for example, represents a different form of structure for text. The stacking of related and unrelated information needs readers to develop new reading strategies. They are expected to keep track of detailed lines of investigation across time and space instead of reading sequential text that has been pre-ordered in logical patterns that they recognize.

The research on hyperdocuments and the confusion that they can cause in readers is fascinating. Readers can easily get carried away when they select link after link across cross-referenced text until they lose sight of their original line of investigation. Worse than this, they find they are lost in the depths of a seemingly never-ending document.

The Internet is a case in point. Unless a site is carefully designed and has good 'signposts' (either visual or text) to remind people where they have come from, and where it is logical to move next, they can get lost in the maze. The 'back' tracking facility that is now a feature of the World Wide Web stemmed from the unreliability of the human mind to keep track. There have been several attempts to build three-dimensional 'worlds' that mirror the structure of a website and assist navigation around it. This may not be a big issue for many designers, working on websites with simple structures and only a few dozen pages, but for the Microsofts and Sonys of this world the Web presence is substantial, and care is taken in helping visitors to find their way around. (See Chapter 6, *Agreeing the content,* for more discussion on structures of websites.)

Overlapping windows that have many selection possibilities can present a daunting image for newcomers. They forget what they have opened, forget where a particular function is hidden, and may never be able to find something because they do not know what it is called. With the spread of interactivity to television there will be many potential users with little or no experience of computer desktops, and for them overlapping windows on screen are unfamiliar.

These initial problems will multiply as text documents themselves become multimedia documents. In multimedia documents a piece of sound information will be cross-referenced to a bit of video, which will be cross-referenced to other sound, text and video components. Multimedia archiving and office automation are accelerating, so this scenario is no fantasy. (See more on archiving in Chapter 12.) There is much to learn from the analysis of reactions of users to the new forms of structuring information on computers and luckily usability information is increasing and becoming more accessible because of the Web itself. (More on this aspect will be covered under the 'Usability' section in the next chapter.)

Overview maps of multimedia applications are becoming common; when users complete a section, the map indicates that this has been done. The concept of a bookmark is also being used more frequently. This records how much of an application users have completed and what remains to be seen so that when they return to the application they can continue where they left off. The Bookmarks or Favourites facility of a Web browser can serve much the same function.

The difficulty for the developer is to decide how computer literate the audience will be, and how much guidance will be needed in the form of help explanations or aids such as route maps. These are aspects of the computer interface, and will be dealt with in Chapter 8.

THEORY INTO PRACTICE 7

Getting lost with associative logic is easily demonstrated if you play a game of verbal associations for a minute with a friend. One person starts with a word and the other has to reply immediately with the first word that comes to mind. At times this can operate like a trapdoor, where the association works in one direction but becomes virtually impossible to trace backwards. It is difficult to retain the thread of connections for long unless they are recorded.

Look at the following example and try to guess the flow of logic of the blank spaces. The answer is provided underneath the diagram.

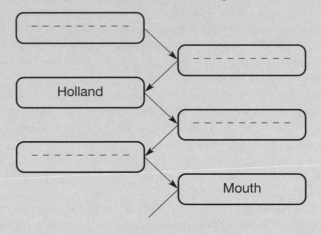

Lost in hyperspace.

Answer: Light, Bulb, Holland, Cheese, Food, Mouth

If you think that was difficult, remember that in hypermedia there would be multiple choices at each point.

■ Where does this leave us?

Media selection will remain complicated because of the constraints, whether these are mechanical or influenced by humans. It is a complex subject, that needs much more attention, but because interactive multimedia is still embryonic there are no set answers yet. We can only try to understand where and why one combination succeeds while other combinations fail. There needs to be broader research that crosses the traditional media demarcation zones so that interdisciplinary insights can emerge.

THEORY INTO PRACTICE 8

Try to write a text set of instructions to go with these graphics for a Web page for a motor parts company. Think your way carefully through the diagrams, imagining you are carrying them out, or ask a friend who has never changed a windscreen wiper to read them to see if the instructions are clear.

After completing this, go to the website, Chapter 7 Support Material, Windscreen wiper example 1. What difference does the sound commentary make to your understanding?

Finally, look at example 2. What difference does the movement make? Is animation more effective than video would be in this case?

All information can be represented in text, sound or visuals, or a combination of these. Media selection means making the best choices given the limitations of the distribution system, the audience attributes, the purpose of the work, and the time and cost.

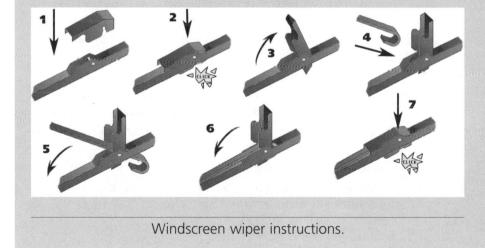

Windscreen wiper instructions.

Summary

- Understand your constraints and work within them.
- Research offers few conclusive principles to help match media and message in specific multimedia contexts.

- Video:
  - The display size of any video needs to be appropriate for the content, the needs of the viewer, and the method of distribution.
  - Video uses more space and/or bandwidth than other media, and may affect the interaction speed.
  - Video use for education and training has extra considerations from research.
- Audio:
  - Audio is a versatile medium, which is cost-effective.
  - It can save the overuse of text when this is an option.
  - It appeals to the emotions.
  - Its range and scope are unappreciated to date.
  - Care is needed to avoid sounds that become irritating when repeated in an interactive environment.
- Computer graphics:
  - These are versatile and have a wide range of quality.
  - They can offer realistic and symbolic representations.
  - Educational research findings have value for all applications.
  - They handle transformations between layers of visuals well: for example, skin and bones.
  - The use of video and computer graphics needs to be related to the delivery channel limitations.
- Text:
  - This is used extensively in online but less so in offline; care should be taken to keep its quality in line with other media components.
  - It can be difficult to integrate text and maintain its quality in offline projects.
  - Layout, size and legibility are always important.
  - The new ways of organizing text in interactive environments can pose problems for readers. Ensure that Help and aids are provided.

■ Recommended reading

Bordwell D. and Thompson K. (1993). *Film Art: An Introduction*. New York: McGraw-Hill

Boyle T. (1997). *Design for Multimedia Learning*. Englewood Cliffs, NJ: Prentice-Hall

Clarke A. (1992). How are graphics used in computer-based learning? *British Journal of Educational Technology*, **23** (3), 228–33

Clarke A. (1994). *Human Factors Guidelines for Multimedia*. European Commission RACE ISSUE Project 1065, HUSAT Research Institute, Loughborough University of Technology, UK

Collis B. (1996). *Tele-learning in a Digital World: The Future of Distance Learning*. London: International Thomson Publishing

Dix A., Finlay J., Abowd G. and Beale R. (1998). *Human–Computer Interaction*, 2nd edn. New Jersey: Prentice Hall

Ellis J. (1992). *Visible Fictions*. London: Routledge & Kegan Paul

Foley J.D., van Dam A., Feiner S.K. and Hughes J.F. (1990). *Computer Graphics, Principles and Practice*. Reading, MA: Addison-Wesley

Gagné R.M., Briggs L.J. and Wagner W.W. (1992). Selecting and using media. In *Principles of Instructional Design* (Gagné R.M., ed.), 4th edn, pp. 205–23. Orlando, FL: Harcourt Brace Jovanovich

Jonassen D.H., ed. (1982). *The Technology of Text*, 2nd edn. Englewood Cliffs, NJ: Educational Technology Publications

Koumi J. (1994). Media comparison and deployment: a practitioner's view. *British Journal of Educational Technology*, **25** (1), 41–57

Leher R. (1993). Patterns of hypermedia design. In *Computers as Cognitive Tools* (Lajoie S.P. and Derry S.S., eds), pp. 197–228. Mahwah, NJ: Lawrence Erlbaum Associates

Lowe R. (1993). *Successful Instructional Diagrams*. London: Kogan Page

Milheim W.D. (1993). How to use animation in computer assisted learning. *British Journal of Educational Technology*, **24** (3), 17–18

Monaco J. (1981). *How to Read a Film. The Art, Technology, Language, History, and Theory of Film and Media*. New York: Oxford University Press

Neilsen J. (1990). *Hypertext and Hypermedia*. New York: Academic Press

Preece J., ed. (1994). *Human–Computer Interaction*, 1st edn. Wokingham: Addison-Wesley

Watson R. (1990). *Film and Television in Education*. London: Falmer Press

Interface design

Project manager's responsibilities

- To recognize that different types of interfaces are needed for different types of application whether on- or offline

- To understand the components of an interface and their significance for users

- To analyse the target audience to meet their interface design needs

- To test the elements of the interface early with the target audience if at all possible

- To champion usability in the team and with clients

- To take accessability factors into account

■ What is an interface?

All online and offline websites and applications have an infrastructure that links the component parts together so that users understand what is contained in them, how the information is organized, and what they need to do to activate the separate pieces. An analogy that is often used refers to navigation within the application and the routes that the users can explore.

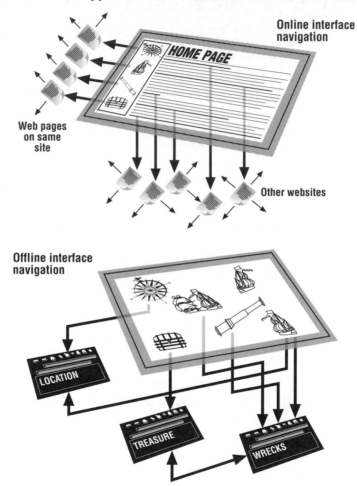

The interface design issues we will concentrate on relate to this structure. At a detailed level it means the selection screens where choices are given to the user, the style with which the selections are denoted, the transitions from one part of the application to another, how options are linked or cross-referenced, and the method of input for any data the user needs to give. Offline applications have evolved their interface style from text to icons or visual markers. Online has followed the same evolution as visuals became easier to transfer and download. Initially, the interface of a web page was defined by the browser, and often consisted of little more than underlined links between pages. Sites now include features such as drop-down menus and roll-over buttons that were once the preserve of offline applications.

Since online design is becoming more able to match many of the capabilities of offline we shall use the word 'application' in this chapter to include websites as well as disk-based projects; and the issues will be just as important for interactive television and other developments.

■ Interface design

If you glance back at Chapter 4, *The proposal*, you will see that the foundations for the interface needed to be laid then. The main content sections were suggested and agreed. This gives a shape to the intentions of what the site or application will contain. The decisions about the content will indicate the best way of organizing the information, and will take the audience and platform capabilities into account. Even at the proposal stage the decisions will be shaping the interface in a particular way, since the amount of material and the number of sections it will have tend to contribute to the style of the interface. In the more complex projects one or more analysts may need to be involved to help shape the definition of the content structure to the needs of the company and the users as discussed in Chapters 2 and 6.

When text is the dominant medium, interactive applications have tended to be structured through menus. The user makes a choice that leads to another text menu and so on. The user goes down through the levels and returns by selecting Back, Exit or the equivalent. This leads the user back through the levels to the top menu. This type of structure is known as a **tree structure**. Many websites follow this basic pattern using levels of headings and drop-down lists.

There can be variations on this structure, in which the user can select other routes to return to the top level instead of the reverse decision mode. It all depends on the links between the content areas and the options the users are given to move around the program. The tree structure has survived text menus, and can now be identified with icons instead of text on the menus.

As it became easier to incorporate graphics into interactive applications – CDs allowed far more space for them than floppy disks did in an offline context, for example – icon-driven menus started to become common. Icons have certain advantages over text. They can take up less space. They are not language-specific. They're more aesthetic and appealing. They can make access through an application easier. However, the research on the use of icons has inconsistencies. Sometimes they're good and sometimes they're bad. All the issues of perception and cognition for a particular group

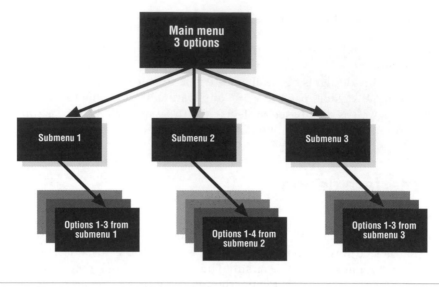

Diagram of tree structure.

of users come into play when addressing human computer interaction and readers are encouraged to do further reading in this area. The main issues can only be touched on in a chapter of this size.

What are icons?

The research on icons can be linked with that on signs and symbols called semiotics. In multimedia any pictorial representation that a user can select is called an icon. But in the theory of signs, icons are images that are readily recognizable. They are not symbolic; they are realistic to the extent that they are recognizable without explanation. Commonly, icons in multimedia encompass the complete range of images from abstract symbols to realistic representations. The user quite often has to learn what the symbols mean to be able to use the icons effectively. One distinction that is sometimes made in multimedia relates to the use of high-quality graphics that are so realistic they are like small photographs on the screen, and these are called picons. If there are the equivalent of icons with moving images that can be selected, these are sometimes referred to as micons. (Examples of icons, picons and micons can be viewed on the website.)

In the theory of signs, icons can be classified into iconograms, picto-grams, cartograms, and diagrams to help define their individual functions. Iconograms are like picons – realistic pictures. Pictograms are equivalent to icons, and so are related to more symbolic, abstract images. There is no equivalent of the miniature moving image in sign theory as by nature it is a study of static images.

■ Considerations for designing icons

Interactive media permit the combination and manipulation of information in new ways. Icons form part of the relatively new interactive vocabulary for the general public. They show that the user has choices, and try to indicate what sort of information can be activated if the icon is selected. However, current interface research could learn from past research. This has shown what happens when new techniques that are symbolic are used when the user does not have the ability to decode the meaning.

There are classic examples of cross-cultural misinterpretation that it would be wise to note as new forms of structuring information emerge on interactive platforms. Health educationalists in developing countries found that commonly understood visual techniques used in Western communication were completely misunderstood. In Peru, when demonstrating how to identify and eradicate lice, they used magnification to show the insects in detail. This only served to distract the viewers. They did not link the enlarged visual image to any insect they understood and so did not think the information relevant to them. The modern equivalent may relate to the use of new techniques for manipulating information, such as the use of icons. The use of a trash can icon to represent getting rid of unwanted files has been noted as culturally unsound for many countries that do not share this method of disposal. (Chapter 17, *Adapting projects for other languages and cultures,* looks at this and other issues in much more detail.)

As soon as you begin to design an interface it becomes obvious that some concepts will be difficult to encapsulate into an icon. Even something as simple as Exit is not that simple. There may be several forms of the concept 'to leave' in the program. Users may need to leave a section but stay in the application, they may want to leave the application completely or they may want to leave a screen, check something and return to the same screen.

The functions have similarities, and so any icons used to represent these functions might need to have similarities. But as there would be different results when using these icons, they would need some differences as well to indicate the different consequences of use. First, this example shows that an application can need many icons to indicate the functionality. Second, it shows that it can be difficult to choose symbolic pictures that demonstrate the functionality clearly. Designers also need to take into account that there will be a saturation point for the number of icons a screen can support. Even though icons nominally take up less physical space than text, graphics take longer to download and take up digital capacity.

If there are many icons, users will take longer to learn their meaning. In some multimedia examples, especially where users are not expected to spend much time on the system – kiosks, are an easy example but some websites operate for quick checks or updates on a situation too – it is best to limit the number of icons to the minimum. Users will want quick access directly to information.

Some concepts are by their nature more abstract than others and are difficult to represent visually. In packages where the concept 'save' has been needed to indicate the transfer of work to disk for storing, various icons have been used to indicate this meaning. Many have tried to follow the principle of relating icon use to everyday objects, but this can lead to strange anomalies. The 'save' icon has been represented by a piggy bank and a monetary symbol. There is a link between save and money, but the money-saving metaphor is out of context in an application for storing information. Quite often an icon showing a floppy disk is used, but not every computer has a floppy drive now.

Using everyday metaphors helps people to remember icons if and when the set of icons relate to an overall metaphor. The overall metaphor of a book or an office has been used successfully, with individual icons relating to specific details consistent with the metaphor, for example. But some of the concepts of dealing with information electronically, such as Undo, are new, and these pose problems for relating to everyday items in ways that will make sense. A compromise solution seems to be more common now, where an icon is used and its text name is either written in a text bubble that appears when the cursor is placed on the icon, or a roll-over text graphic replaces the icon when the cursor is placed over it. The balance between download time and understanding the icon quickly needs to be struck in online applications.

These techniques will provide answers for some of the problems, but not for all. Guidelines for international use advise against the use of text names in this way because they cause problems in translation. Often translations cannot be fitted into the same space as an icon so text bubbles offer more flexibility but may not be as aesthetically pleasing.

The arguments about interface design seem to lead you round in circles. The guidelines can seem inconsistent because of the complexity of the field. However, a lot of progress has been made because of the use of icons. Their use has widened the use of computers from specialists to the general public. Overall they do provide better access to the functionality despite their limitations. Instead of having to remember sets of symbols and codes, such as computer languages, icons provide prompts to help anyone activate the power hidden in applications.

Web design has gone through phases. As it started out as primarily a text-driven medium – but is evolving as rapidly as the access and bandwidth allows – icons tend to be collected together in a bar at the top or left of the screen. For a time, image maps that used visuals to give an impression of the range of the whole site were popular as navigational aids instead of icons. But the users were not happy with the amount of time it took for the maps to download, and the danger was that they did not wait and went on to another site. Micons are appearing in the form of flashing, rolling adverts or banners within the general layout of the online screen but again the users do not seem to be reacting well to these either.

☐ Get to know your target audience

The more you understand your target audience, the better your design will be. At present the hardest audience to design for is the public because although their use is gradually being analysed and lessons drawn from this, there is relatively little profile of use for different sectors and age groups. But this will improve steadily over the next few years.

However, at the moment if your project is tied to a specific target group it is best if you spend time building up a profile of them, their multimedia literacy level, what they would like from the application, and their expectations of what information/results they want from the interactive application.

Consistency in look and feel is a factor that needs attention across all media used to convey information, particularly if branding and image are important to your clients. Consistency of visual style across media helps users to identify a product. It can also provide a sense of harmony that contributes to a feeling of satisfaction for the user.

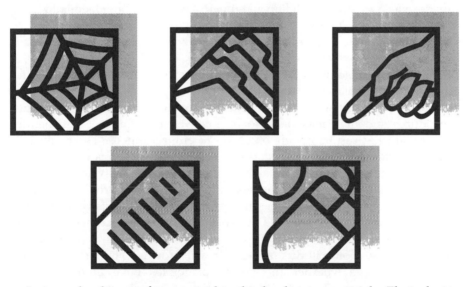

Let us take the set of icons used in this book as an example. Their design was influenced by the need for them to bridge the strong lines of the internal chapter illustration style with the abstract 'scene-setter' chapter heading illustrations. Here, the stronger formal lines in the foreground image are counter-balanced by the offset blurred background. This represents the marrying of the well-delineated figure illustration images and the abstract visual chapter introductions.

As with all icons, the size of the image affects the amount of detail used as well as the concern here with the possible deterioration of detail in the printing process. As depicted, the foreground icon images are recognizable – a pointing finger, a computer mouse, a web, tabbed index cards and a sheet of typed paper. Their labels indicate their meaning in the first case and then once people have assimilated the meaning, the visual image allows faster recognition. This ability for people to short-cut meanings via visuals can be particularly important when used in electronic media because it can help the user to recognize the navigation paths faster and help them understand their location within the application. If the foreground images had been used alone, the visual style would have been simplistic and fragmented in relation to the whole book. The offset background adds a complexity that lifts the icons from being simplistic to better suit the computer-literate specialist audience that forms the readership of this book.

These icons then had to represent more abstract points than the ones described earlier, but they still needed concrete clues within their stylization to help establish their meaning for the reader and to re-establish the meaning every time they are seen. Hopefully, this analysis of the way in which the design of some of the features of an interface assigns meaning will indicate the complexity of maintaining integrity of look, feel and sense in an interface. It is not an easy task, but it does provide the key to good application design. You need to build up an empathy with your audience, and there are several ways to do this. Some of these are outlined below.

Needs analysis was introduced in Chapter 3, *Scoping a project*. Task analysis forms part of needs analysis. This is particularly important if the application is going to form part of the workplace as a job aid, or offer an alternative service to a human one outside normal work hours. Task analysis is the study of how a set of actions are carried out, what processes/ procedures and questions need to be followed to achieve a satisfactory result, and what results match which set of circumstances. The analysis is usually carried out early in the project so that all decisions can be based on the findings. Information analysts will employ the equivalent of a task analysis as they define the structure of the content blocks for a project.

If the type of application does not warrant task analysis then concept testing may help to give a profile of expectations and preferences from the target audience. In concept testing, also called focus groups, people are told what the application will do and what it will provide. Their reactions are monitored to see whether the design principles have predicted their needs/wishes accurately or whether they have common agreement on suggestions that arise during the discussion. Increasingly a form of focus group that operates online and discusses concepts in the equivalent of a chat or discussion group is being used to comment on web pages, for example. This online focus group saves time and money. These groups may be used to tailor the design so that the application matches the user profile better than before. Concept testing used to take place at a stage when there was a very limited prototype or no working prototype of the application. But, because online access is easy, comments can be elicited at any stage of the development. As a result, this version of testing is becoming more acceptable. It is not to be confused with usability testing, which takes place later in the project when a good working model is available. The target group in this case actually uses the application instead of reacting to the ideas that will be embodied in it.

Testing interface design

If there is any way to get the budget to build a prototype application that would include usability testing of the interface, then go for it. Experience can help to predict certain problems with a certain audience but you learn more with every application you work on. There are always a few aspects that do not work out in the way that was planned, but by the time the team has spotted the deficiencies there is often no way back. Usability tests provide a wealth of information, but they are of little use unless they are carried out methodically and professionally. Unless this happens, conflicting results and recommendations will be made.

The theory and practice of usability testing is too great to go into here, but its principles are important, and so some of the insights will be mentioned briefly to encourage you to look into this further.

It is too easy to base interface decisions on your experience rather than on the experience of the target audience. This does not mean that insights gained from experience are not valuable. Nor does it mean that you have to suppress any creative ideas about interface design. It is an evolving area, so there is scope for flexibility and experimentation as long as these are recognized as such, and tried out with the intended audience. It may be that they will experience some difficulties with the interface design. But the important aspect is that you notice where and why there are problems and reach some decisions on (a) how to eradicate them or (b) adding Help to educate the users into using the new aspects successfully.

One of the misconceptions about usability tests is that you need a large number of people to produce valid results. More recent research has shown that up to 80% of the problems were found with between 4 and 5 participants and that 90% were detected with 10 users.

This needs to be put in context, however. It is important that:

- the selection of the participants has been made according to a predetermined profile of user groups;
- the environment for the test has been carefully prepared;
- the participants have been inducted into the test environment and know their rights;
- the tasks to be performed have been created to mirror the aims of the product and the needs of the users;
- the ways of collecting quantitative and qualitative data have been agreed;
- the testing team have been thoroughly prepared and tried out in a pilot test;
- the ways to organize and communicate the data have been agreed.

See Chapter 11, *Testing*, for more information on these and other forms of testing.

☐ The interactive environment

If the purpose of the interface is to make the interaction smooth then this is the criterion that needs to be applied for quality. The users' levels of competence and understanding need to shape the design of the interface. The project manager takes on responsibility for acting on behalf of the users. The biggest problem is deciding what can be assumed as prior understanding of the interactive techniques. This is harder for the general public than for other groups since the application would have to appeal to the naive and experienced user simultaneously.

Any interactive communicator aims to trigger the user's interpretation of the messages embedded in the content. This ability holds the key to good communication with media. But if techniques are used that are alien to the users, they may miss the point completely. If they do not understand the symbolism of the techniques that are used, they will not reap the full benefit from the content. The new forms of interactive structuring employ techniques that take time for users to understand – just as using magnification was outside the comprehension of the tribe in Peru. Understanding, in this sense, is not an innate ability; it has to be acquired. Media techniques are culturally based and depend upon shared experience. The shared experience can be part of a subcultural group or cross-cultural group. Internet users would be a good example of a cross-cultural group that shares common understanding of particular symbolic codes and techniques.

Just as icons are part of the new vocabulary of multimedia, the layering of information associated with Apple Macintosh and Windows has become a common technique. Windowing with option bars and icons has proliferated. The techniques associated with the use of a mouse (point and click) free users from typing in their selections. It becomes easier to organize access to information with small drop-down menus. This approach lends itself to structuring access to a mass of information by splitting it into small pieces. But does your audience have the experience to use this structure efficiently? Will you need to train them in it? Should you stick with established conventions or break them? Should you take some things for granted?

The initial selection screen – the home page for a website and the main menu for an offline application – is very important. They show the scope of the program. They trigger an emotional response as well as a cognitive reaction. They set the expectations and understanding of the user. They give an indication of the scope of the content and the techniques needed to navigate through it. They establish whether there is Help available at all times or whether the user needs to discover aspects about the program. They should set the example of:

1. how users are to select an option – find the links/hot-spots and select, click on an icon which expands into a menu, and so on;
2. how they will know if they have made the selection. For example, the button/hot-spot/picon may change shape, size, colour or stay in a depressed position (simulated by the graphics of course), or you may use a sound to show that something has been successfully selected.

Once users have started to interact with the program you need to establish how they move around in it. Websites are more rigid and share more common features than offline applications in this regard because the browser sets certain parameters that are common. The great majority of users rely on the browser Back button, for example. Despite this, some sites block its use and run the risk of annoying the user. In some instances – such as pages that pass data to a server-side application that then sends a web page in return – using the Back button can stop the site working correctly. In offline applications there are no agreed common navigation conventions. Should the users have an option to select to return to the main selection screen? Should they have a map to show them an overview of where they are? Are they allowed to go up, down, sideways, forwards and backwards, and if so how do they know this? Do they have to complete certain sections before others? How will they know this? This is why offline applications need comprehensive Help sections. The Help is used to train the user in the specific use of that application.

Once certain ways of working have been established, these need to be consistent. The interface and its working needs as much integrity as the other factors we've looked at. If users become confused, lost or irritated by the operational side of the program, their concentration on the content will suffer. They will become demotivated. They will tend to leave the site or

Interface antics.

program before they have found what they wanted or before they've explored all the possibilities.

Designing an interface that helps people to reach all the application information effortlessly is far from easy. It usually provides the longest discussions between the analysts, graphics artists, programmers and producers. The high-level structure will affect how the programmers set up their code. They need to be clear how it is meant to work to ensure that they construct an adequate frame for the application. They will have opinions on what functionality the platform can support, and because they have studied interface design as part of their courses, they often feel that it is their role to design it. The graphics artists feel exactly the same. The interface graphics are one of the prime ways they can exert their creativity and style.

The project manager, working if necessary with other analysts, should have the best understanding of the scope of the content and the client. These have an effect on the interface design. There may be corporate conventions that irk the programmers and graphics artists, but they will have to prevail. There may be special considerations for the intended audience – poor second-language speakers, for example.

Your research on the intended audience and their multimedia literacy level is crucial. It will help to determine the best methods of interaction, their prior experience, whether they will be receptive to innovation, and how many levels of Help they might need.

Sometimes, as with games and activity-based entertainment programs, the consideration is not to make the interaction too easy, as this is not the purpose of the interface. With these the purpose is to excite, surprise, demand attention, and to use fast reactions to interpret a changing environment. These types of application need different considerations for their interface, and many of the guidelines covered in this chapter will not apply.

Online interfaces share more common features than offline. The proliferation of sites a user can access means that there is competition to attract viewers, but at the same time there is recognition that the viewer can move on quickly to a lot of other offerings. Site designs influence each other, so features that work and make sense – such as the control to go back, and a strongly defined selection bar on the screen with a block of text that allows easier scanning of the text than long lines – have become commonplace. If a site is difficult to navigate, you will lose your user to other sites; if the site is easy to navigate but has boring content, you will also lose them. The balance between the user's needs, the content and the style is as true for online as it is for offline.

☐ The use of sound

Sound means any type of audio use. This can include speech, warning bleeps, alarm bells and so on.

When sound became easier to digitize and store on CDs, it became apparent that overuse was unwise. People become irritated by repeated sounds.

Some sounds that are initially attractive or entertaining pall quickly. You need to guard against inappropriate use of sounds at the planning stage, which is difficult, because it is easier to react with your mind than with your ears at this time.

It helps if you take time to look at the use of sound independently of the other factors and see how likely it is for the sounds to be repeated inadvertently. An apposite example might be the use of audio to reinforce clicking on a button by speaking the function of the button. The information is useful at first but annoys users after that. As indicated in Chapter 7 on media selection, you need to consider giving control of volume to the users. This might be by including a control bar linked with the sound (and video) that allows the user to control the volume, pause, repeat, move forwards and backwards, and so on. Control of these could help make the application more versatile for people with hearing difficulties. These users might form a strong subgroup of the audience profile, and if that were the case, their needs would drive the total interface design, not just the use of sound.

☐ The use of colour

Because the use of high-quality colour is easier and more common in applications, and the resolution of screens has increased, some of the initial concerns with the general use of computer screen colour have been tempered. However, the use of background colours, the colour of text against a coloured background, colour linked with layout, and the awareness of colour-blindness in a percentage of the audience still have relevance. The major problems are caused by poor selection of colours in relation to each other, causing difficulties in readability and legibility. A screen is still not as easy to read as print because of screen glare and the nature of electronic text. Because text is prevalent in websites, the lessons learnt in offline production can benefit web designers. Tiled images are often used in the background of web pages without enough thought for legibility, for example.

Graphics artists are important members of the team. They bring their knowledge and skills to bear on the problems of style, design, consistency of visual approach, layout, legibility, and readability. Their training in making the best combinations of colour is invaluable. There can be several uses for colour – attention cue, aesthetic, styling, and branding. As with the use of sound, colour can please initially, then become annoying for users. In online projects, if colour is used badly, then all the factors that applied for offline projects remain true.

One of the problems that still prevail for offline projects is the changes that occur in colours depending on their origins, the platform, the software, and the encoding processes. So even with good planning, colour shifts can occur. Some visitors to the website may have screens with limited colours and they may see something different to the colours intended. It is a good idea for the project manager of offline projects to get the graphics artist to check the effect of the varying processes and to tap into contacts who have used the combinations before to see if there are any adverse but unrecorded reactions. There are the 216 so-called web safe colours that can be used with more reliable consistency. With some applications, colour consistency is vital – medical applications, for example, are notoriously difficult for colour integrity, and can need special processes to ensure accuracy.

Finally, another problem associated with colour remains. There are cross-cultural associations in the use of colour. This is part of the aesthetic appeal of colours, but it may become more important as applications need to reach international audiences. The retail sector has noted the variations in response to combinations of colour. They sometimes adjust the packaging of products for various countries. Some cultures respond better to bright, strong, primary colours, while other cultures prefer pastels. For applications that need to sell, this could be more of a factor than in other types of application. Common examples of Western colour psychology are:

Red = stop, danger, heat, appliance is on, left (port)

Blue = cold, water, sky

Green = go, environmentally friendly, right (starboard)

There is little research in this area at present but it is growing because of the need for internationalization of websites. Companies are faced with the nuances of cross-cultural communication and find that these are not straightforward, have been underestimated and can be costly. (See Chapter 17, *Adapting projects for other languages and cultures,* for more details on these aspects.)

Usability

Many of the main points concerning usability have been indicated already but they have been embedded in the general discussion throughout the previous chapters. Usability concerns all aspects of the design and production and even post-production phases of a project. Ignore it at both your own and the client's peril! It is a concept like 'quality assurance'. It should be part of the responsibilities of everyone involved in the project. It is a major responsibility of the project manager as stated in Chapter 2 because you need to represent the user at all discussions keeping the client and the team focused on achieving results by satisfying the user.

Usability should drive decisions throughout the process of agreeing the overall structure and content, selecting the appropriate media and techniques as well as interface design. By bringing the main concepts together here we hope to reinforce its importance.

So what is 'usability'?

Usability.gov (http://usability.gov) says 'Usability is the measure of the quality of a user's experience when interacting with a product or system – whether a website, a software application, mobile technology, or any user-operated device.'

Computers Solutions Consulting UK approaches it from a slightly different angle and begins to define it in relation to what 'easy to use' means. They find it means the following:

- Effortless – requires little training or mental investment;
- Obvious – the software is clear, instinctual and non-misleading;
- Simple – anyone can use the software;
- Uncomplicated – there are no hidden meanings.

It is clear that if you produce an application that fits these criteria, the users will be able to find what they want or do whatever they need and be satisfied with the time and effort it has taken them. This establishes a good base to work from.

Usability criteria can be applied to the whole application or site and thereafter to each section and screen offered because the user needs to relate to each part for it to be successful. The overriding principles of consistency and integrity of design should hold the experience together.

Often a company imposes its perspective on the application at the beginning of a project. They suggest how to chunk and connect the content according to their professional perspective and this may not be the best way for a non-professional user to relate to it. If the project's target audience is other professionals then their perspective might well match. Jakob Nielsen – a recognized usability guru – investigated a navigation scheme that professionals from the client's company put forward. He compared this with one that was worked out according to how users approached the content. Usability testing showed that 80% used the scheme successfully when it mirrored the user's perspective as opposed to 9% using it successfully when it mirrored the professional perspective. This example is useful to use with clients to show of the dangers of getting the scheme wrong.

It is accepted that users visit and then stay at websites because they find something of interest in the content. If they don't, they leave. The Web itself – or even just one large site – is the equivalent of an enormous bookshop. They have vast amounts of material that the user browses through looking for something relevant for a particular need or something that serendipitously appeals. In offline applications the user has made a choice by buying the application – the equivalent of buying a book from the bookshop.

Gaining the user's attention is the first criterion. In offline applications this might be triggered by the packaging and the content summaries written on the packaging. Or, the user could have been motivated to buy through recommendation, reviews or the influence of advertising. For web pages, the speed of download of the page determines the user's attention above and beyond anything else. If the users are not engaged quickly – by finding relevance in even the fragments of pages that build first as they download – they will move on.

This obviously has many implications for the design of the home page but download times need to be kept to a minimum. You need to catch the eye of the user with headings, text labels or something relevant to what they are looking for so that they begin to relate to the content as the page is forming. Then they will decide if it is worth waiting for or not. Nielsen explains that once you have the users' attention, then they will wait longer as they click through to larger chunks of information and will even be prepared to wait for the download of some video of a topic they know they want to see. This has implications about the best structuring of information on a site – moving from small tasters to larger chunks once the user matches their need to that piece of information.

Sites do have different purposes and so usability guidelines may need to be tailored to suit the need. E-commerce and entertainment or promotional sites are different from informational sites so the following does not automatically apply. Some of the premises are the same but the details may vary. You need to keep an eye on usability guidelines and filter them according to purpose.

It is important to understand and take account of a counterbalance to the measurable aspects of usability otherwise there is a danger of forgetting the emotional reaction that a user can have to the visual, auditory and psychomotor experience of using a website. This is where the concepts of image and branding have their roots and what advertising thrives on. This more subjective approach to design is poorly represented in the usability literature because it is hard to measure. But it should not be ignored either. Curt Cloninger defines this conflict as being between those that see the Web as a fledgling multimedia platform – usually graphic designers he believes – and those that see the Web as data or text driven – the usability experts.

Cloninger is concerned to redress this imbalance and has devised a list of 10 fresh design styles with a hope of developing a more articulate design vocabulary (see www.lab404.com/dan). He places the emphasis on the graphic style and the inspiration that lies behind them. If you are attracted to the multimedia experience of usability, his article referenced later has good references to follow up.

Bob Hughes also places a strong emphasis on creating an 'emotional charge' as the key to success while visualizing a persona representative of the end-user and having an intimate conversation with the interactive medium you are using and the constraints of the situation.

When websites are text dominant, the users employ interpretation techniques appropriate for that medium – skimming, scanning, focusing and extracting meaning from relevant material. The use of other media affects download times of pages that can in turn interfere with the skimming and scanning orientation the users want to perform. Meaningful headings act like summaries for the readers. They indicate the range of material available if they are written effectively. They encourage the users to make decisions on the relevance of the material and whether they will commit time to reading it.

As we have noted, screens are harder to read and people spend less time and effort on web pages than print. This means that you need to make an impact faster. To achieve this:

- organize the content more efficiently
- sequence it appropriately
- use more headings
- use smaller paragraphs
- use shorter sentences
- use lists and tables.

(See the references for sites that offer and maintain usability guidelines.)

If the client is going to provide the material and/or update it, they should be trained in writing for the Web. If you or someone in your team is responsible for producing material, then you need to be aware of the differences and write or edit accordingly. The impact of the information from the site depends on this.

In offline applications the download burden is lifted and all media can be seamlessly integrated and accessed. This opens up the scope for designers but many usability criteria still apply. The main menu needs to indicate the overall structure of the application. The functionality and navigation across the application needs to be consistent. The information should be clearly presented in a layout that is appropriate for readability. Offline applications are still presented on screens and so the limitations of reading still apply.

There are many usability guidelines now available for both on and offline projects and the references will point you to some of the useful ones. It is relatively straightforward to take these on board as a team and you can set the direction as the project manager.

Accessibility

There is growing global recognition that designing applications to allow equal access to the material by people with disabilities is important. In the USA it is a legal requirement and in the UK there are regulations for anyone developing computer-driven systems for government agencies. Companies also have a commitment to provide access to their company computer systems including their intranet for any disabled employees if their work depends on using these systems.

Many equate the idea of disability with physical attributes but the definition can encompass a range of people with special needs. People who have problems with vision, hearing, physical/motor, literacy and learning, and language and communication are included in the extended definition. Some people may need extra input and output devices to help access the material. These are called accessibility aids. Others find difficulty relating to material that uses specific types of media because of visual or auditory problems. The style of the material, the language used and the difficulty level can exclude yet others from abstracting meaning.

All manner of needs can be catered for to a greater or lesser extent. They do not have to involve a great deal of extra work if your company decides what it will address as a matter of minimum policy. Then over and above this, certain projects will need special planning and production to meet statutory requirements. Extra work and care will be necessary too if your client defines particular special needs as a characteristic of their target audience.

It is good to be aware of some examples of accessibility aids that help various disabilities. These tools are being refined and added to constantly so keep up to date with developments by checking out some of the better online information sources from time to time. (See the references for examples of these.)

We'll just mention some examples here to indicate the range of aids available for different purposes. In some cases these may be available free with the computer operating system. Screen enlargers magnify or enlarge parts of the screen so that people with poor vision can read better. Screen reviewers or screen readers translate text on screen to synthesized speech. This helps visually impaired and blind people access the information. If graphics have alternative text labels attached to them the readers will translate these as well. On-screen keyboards provide alternative input to typing on a keyboard via pointing devices or switches. Speech recognition programs allow people to control computers with their voices. There are eye-gaze devices and breath-controlled devices too. People who cannot use standard keyboards may benefit from these.

Apart from generic tools that help in these ways, the design of applications and sites can be made more effective by adopting relatively straightforward techniques. The designers can be reminded about the use of guidelines for colour-blind people and to optimize colours for the visually impaired. Any written material can take account of readability and clarity considerations if the writers are told that these are to be optimized for the client or target audience. The designers and/or programmers will be able to write extras into their code to allows tools for special needs to operate effectively. (Microsoft has a handy tips section for web designers to help with producing accessible sites. See the references.) All these aspects can be implemented as the design emerges. It is far harder to rework and apply these later.

It has become easier to check if your sites conform to the minimum standards to help accessibility because there are several free diagnostic sites. You can run your site through the diagnostics and receive feedback about the relevant items ranked from glaring problems through to minor problems. You can even get permission to display logos showing that your site has passed the test. (See the references for some diagnostic sites.)

The insights into what is considered good design practice across the range of media are important because technology does not stand still. All forms are converging and trying to use as much media functionality as possible. The telcos with their traditional bias in sound have integrated electronic text into their WAP systems and are moving towards integrating video too. Interactive television integrates electronic text data and visual data. (see Book 2 Chapter 1 on Convergence for a more comprehensive understanding of the issues.) The Web is increasing its use of media as the bandwidth allows. For these reasons the principles of design using all forms of media remain important although electronic text has been and continues to be the dominant medium of the moment. The balance will shift and you need to be able to shift with it working from a strong base of understanding about interface design.

THEORY INTO PRACTICE 9

Use the interface assessment form that follows the Summary to assess your next interface after discussions and initial decisions have been made in the team but before the client has been given the decisions. Use your appraisal to go back to the team if necessary for rethinking any issues.

Use it also to appraise any interactive materials you look at to help focus on their true strengths and weaknesses.

■ Summary

- The interface is the infrastructure of the application.

- The use of icons and the method of organization – tree, windows, hypertext – are symbolic, so the users' correct interpretation of their meaning is the key to good design.

- Symbolic structures need special care, explanation and possibly training, when the target audience has little exposure to such concepts.

- Usually, the aim of the interface is to provide smooth, easy access to any part of the program the user wishes, but games, activity entertainment titles or image-aware sites can have different aims.

- The use of sound and colours in the interface also needs attention to ensure best use.

- Usability issues affect all aspects of the design process and are key to a project's success.

- Accessability issues have implications for many projects and may need to be considered across all aspects of the design process.

Tick as appropriate

Application profile   **General interface assessment**

1. User profile   Inappropriate   Appropriate
   a. Naive ☐   Specialist ☐   Mixed range ☐   Match to users   1   2   3   4   5
      General public ☐   Other ☐ ▭
   b. Application use   Match to use   1   2   3   4   5
      National ☐   International ☐

2. Proposed style of use   Disagree   Agree

   Sustained/regular use by people ☐   Functionality matches use   1   2   3   4   5

   Brief/occasional use ☐   Simple functionality matches use   1   2   3   4   5

   Mixed usage ☐   Range of levels match mixed use   1   2   3   4   5

3. Application purpose   Style suits purpose
   To inform ☐   To sell ☐   1   2   3   4   5
   To entertain ☐   For reference ☐
   To train ☐   To educate ☐
   Other ☐ ▭

4. Overall marks for: General impression
                                               Poor   Excellent
   a. Ease of use   1   2   3   4   5   6   7   8   9   10
   b. Design style   1   2   3   4   5   6   7   8   9   10
   c. Consistency of selection methods   1   2   3   4   5   6   7   8   9   10
   d. Consistency of functionality   1   2   3   4   5   6   7   8   9   10
   e. Consistency of visual design   1   2   3   4   5   6   7   8   9   10
   f Clarity of written material   1   2   3   4   5   6   7   8   9   10

5. Overall marks for: Inappropriate   Appropriate
   a. Use of colour in interface   1   2   3   4   5   n/a
   b. Use of graphics in interface   1   2   3   4   5   n/a
   c. Use of sound in interface   1   2   3   4   5   n/a
   d. Use of moving image/animation in interface 1   2   3   4   5   n/a
   e. Emotional reaction engendered   1   2   3   4   5   n/a

6. Accessibility factors employed   Not at all   Well
                                               1   2   3   4   5   n/a

7. Help
   a. Suitability for user profile   1   2   3   4   5   n/a
   b. Amount of detail   1   2   3   4   5   n/a
   c. Tone   1   2   3   4   5   n/a
   d. Effectiveness   1   2   3   4   5   n/a

▉ Recommended reading

Clarke A. (1994). *Human Factors Guidelines for Multimedia*. European Commission RACE ISSUE Project 1065, HUSAT Research Institute, Loughborough Institute of Technology, UK

Del Galdo E. (1990). Internationalisation and translation: Some guidelines for the design of human computer interfaces. In *Advances in Human Factors/Ergonomics 13, Designing User Interfaces for International Use* (Nielson J., ed.), pp. 1–11. Amsterdam: Elsevier

Deregowski J.B. (1980). *Illusions, Patterns and Pictures. A Cross-Cultural Perspective*. London: Academic Press

Dumas J.S. and Redish J.C. (1994). *A Practical Guide to Usability Testing*. Norwood, NJ: Ablex Publishing Corporation

Hughes B. (2000). *Dust or Magic: Secrets of Successful Multimedia Design*. Harlow: Addison-Wesley

Johnson J. (2000). *GUI Bloopers: Don'ts and Do's for Software Developers and Web Designers*, San Francisco: Morgan Kaufmann Publishers

Jonassen D.H., ed. (1982). *The Technology of Text*. Englewood Cliffs, NJ: Educational Technology Publications

Kennedy J.M. (1982). Metaphor in pictures. *Perception*, **11**, 589–605

Maissel J. (1990). *Development of a Methodology for Icon Evaluation*. National Physical Laboratory Report DITC 159/90, Teddington, UK

Marcus A. (1992). *Graphic Design for Electronic Documents and User Interfaces*. New York: ACM Press; Reading MA: Addison-Wesley

Nielsen Jacob (2000) *Designing Web Usability*. Indianapolis: New Riders Publishing

Salomon G. (1979). Media and symbol systems as related to cognition and learning. *Journal of Educational Psychology*, **71**, 131–48

Shneiderman B. (1998). *Designing the User Interface: Strategies for Effective Human–Computer Interaction*, 3rd edn. Reading, MA: Addison-Wesley

Siegal D. (1997). *Creating Killer Web Sites*, 2nd edn. Indianapolis: Hayden Books

UNESCO (1976). *Cross-cultural broadcasting: psychological effects*.

UNESCO Press Reports & Papers on Mass Communication, No. 77.

⬜ References

Institute of Electrical and Electronics Engineers (1990). *IEEE Standard Computer Dictionary: A Compilation of IEEE Standard Computer Glossaries*. New York: IEEE

Corporate Solutions Consulting, *Usability Engineering: Designing for ease of use* UK
http://www.consult-me.co.uk/csc-usability-engineering-page.htm

Accessibility diagnostic sites

Bobby
http://www.cast.org/bobby/

Web Page Accessibility Self Evaluation Test from the Public Service Commission of Canada
http://www.psc-cfp.gc.ca/eepmp-pmpee/access/testver1_e.htm

☐ Websites of interest

Usability

Usability.gov has well-organized material on a complete spectrum of usability issues including checklists
http://usability.gov/index.html

Human Factors International
http://www.humanfactors.com

Weinschenk Consulting
Good quick check lists for Interface Design and Online usability design including e-commerce.
http://www.weinschenk.com/Default.htm

Comprehensive coverage of user-centred web design principles and large set of classified references under Dey Alexander's Web Design Articles section – Empowering Users through User-centred Web Design
http://deyalexander.com (no www)

Usability – the experience perspective

Cloninger C. (2000). *Usability Experts are from Mars, Graphic Designers are from Venus, A List Apart* (e-zine)
http://www.alistapart.com/stories/marsvenus

Accessibility

Microsoft have accessibility tips for web designers and sound all-round information about accessibility issues.
http://www.microsoft.com/enable/dev/web/

General information source
NCAM – The National Centre for Accessible Media
http://main.wgbh.org/wgbh/pages/ncam/

TAP – Technology Access Programme – addresses communication technologies in general rather than just the Web
http://tap.gallaudet.edu/

Betsie stands for BBC Education Text to Speech Internet Enhancer. You can see demonstrations and download the tool to use yourself.
http://www.bbc.co.uk/education/betsie/index.html

Contract issues 2

Project manager's responsibilities

- To understand legal issues that can affect multimedia contracts
- To carry out the company's policy for binding clients and subcontractors to its terms and conditions

9

■ Introduction

In *Contract issues 1* (Chapter 5) we concentrated on establishing ways of working between you and the client. Without these agreements, your work could be affected by hold-ups out of your control, which would impact on your deadlines. We recommended you control these risks by defining the workflow responsibilities between you and the client. Change management principles were also explained, and it was suggested that they were included in the agreement for the way of working.

In this chapter, we shall return to the process of developing more detailed costings that should form part of your background estimates for the final proposal document. After all, you are in business to make a profit, so you have to predict the costs as accurately as possible to stand a chance of coming out on top. Secondly, we shall note the more formal legal details that may need to be addressed.

■ Costing rights and clearances

This is a complex area. The background to the types and the processes involved in rights is covered in Chapter 15, *Rights, copyright and other intellectual property*. If you are not experienced with these, you might benefit from reading that chapter first. Here we're concerned with approximating the numbers involved and their costs, to help stipulate a workable budget. Rights and clearances are a good example of knowledge that applies across many stages of development. The project manager needs the knowledge here to define the budget. Whoever takes on the role of rights clearer needs a good grasp of the varieties, to be able to negotiate the best deal from owners of materials across media during development. The factors that influence clearance costs are similar for most kinds of asset, and you should bear in mind that a clearance for the Web is a clearance for the world.

☐ Still pictures

Any reuse of an existing photograph, picture or slide, or even extracted details from any of these for which neither you nor the client has copyright, will incur costs to clear permission for use. The amount charged varies according to the location of the visual – museum, picture library, for example – who owns it, the purpose for your use, where it will be seen, and how long your programme or site will be in use. This list does not cover all the variables, so you can begin to get a feel for how problematic this is. Unlike Europe, the USA has a tradition of freedom of information that leads to a large number of free sources of assets. NASA is the best-known example. There are also many sources of clip art for which no royalties are payable. It would help if your company found out about free and royalty-free sources, as you never know when they will come in handy.

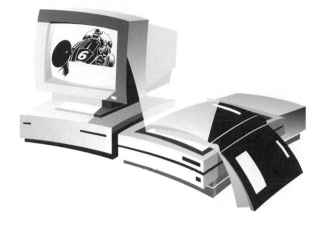

Scanning and rights.

Music

This is the most complex part of rights and clearances. Conditions change depending on the artistes, the length of the music, whether it loops (is played repeatedly), the publisher, and whether it is an original work, library music or a commercial recording. The costs change accordingly.

Voice-overs

These are usually cleared through the voice-over's agent. Rates vary according to the artiste, the length of time spent recording, the type of use, the length of the clearance, and the number of countries the application will be used in.

Video footage

This is rather like stills clearance, and depends on the owner. Costs may depend on the length of the footage, and if the videos come from different sources and have to be edited together you may have to convert them to a common format, which will affect quality and cost. Video footage, if it is being licensed from a television programme, can sometimes contain material with many secondary rights implications including stills, music, artistes and scripts. This can contribute to the clearance costs significantly, and it is vital that a comprehensive scrutiny is made of the rights situation.

Table 9.1 gives a rough indication of some of the variables that can occur, and some examples have been given to demonstrate the variation in costing across the range of media. There isn't a standard rate per photo from museums, for example, so you may be negotiating individual rates from different museums depending on where the originals are kept. Rates vary from

TABLE 9.1 Rights and clearance costing.

Category	Clearance type	Numbers/ length	Market covered	Time cleared	Other factors	Ball-park rate	Total
Stills	Photos from museums	approx. 60	Commercial/ world	3 years		£75–100 B&W £100–150 colour	
Video footage	Library	10 minutes	Commercial/ world	3 years	Technical costs can be high	£250–1000 per minute + nights	
Music	Commissioned Title music	3 musicians 3 minute piece	Commercial/ world	Indefinitely	Buy-out on rights One single payment	£1000 upwards	
	Library (background in 2 sections)	approx. 15 mins	Commercial/ world	3 years	MPCS negotiation	£100 per 30 seconds	
Voice-overs	Professional artistes	2 artistes 1 approx. 35 mins 1 approx. 15 mins	Commercial/ world	3 years	2 payments, one for recording, one for rights	£150 per hour +100% for rights	

country to country. Rates for use on a website may be different from an equivalent offline use.

This list covers 'creative' asset clearances but you might find that fees are due for use of some kinds of computer code – a database for example – particularly with an offline project which is physically sold and distributed. You might find sometimes that the terms under which software can be used change, so just because you have used it before you should not assume that you can use it again in the same way. Of course, sometimes the licence terms for software get easier, but not always.

You should make your client aware of the problems of costing clearances, and stress the estimated cost. You will really only know the true figure once the job is completed; so it may be wise to negotiate an estimate for this part, which you will confirm and renegotiate during the project as you become clearer about the numbers involved. You might negotiate a price for the job excluding clearances, and work on these as a separate costing.

The nature of the task should now be clearer. The complexity should show that a person who will research, negotiate rights, keep accurate records, and keep track of the assets to send back is not performing a trivial task, especially when different types of assets are involved. It may be as well to mention that you are charged penalty payments by some libraries if you do not send the original photo or slide back by a stipulated date. These unknown costs that can occur should be covered by having some of the budget defined for contingency. Also, you should remember that courier companies such as FedEx and DHL may be used to carry the assets, and the cost of shipping is not insignificant. Consider whether your researcher has to travel to look at images.

■ The legal issues

There are a surprising number of multimedia projects that are undertaken on little more than a handshake and often on simple letters of agreement. Also, of course, legal aspects would indicate access to lawyers, preferably specializing in multimedia, and they are expensive professionals. It is true that in most cases, projects progress with some minor hiccups but these are resolved amicably. In cases where things go wrong they can go horribly wrong, and people end up saying 'If only we'd …'. Conversely, if the project is very successful, this can also lead to queries of who can exploit it and how, and who should be getting what from the sales!

The major problem lies in the uncertainty of how to treat multimedia in a legal sense, because it keeps evolving so quickly. In mature delivery media such as broadcasting, music and film the issues of primary rights in materials and the use of the materials for secondary purposes have been sorted out. So, for example, a contract to write and record a talk for BBC Radio might include several clauses explaining in detail what the residual payments are, as percentages of the original fee, for such things as repeats, translations, printing in publications, and sales to foreign broadcasters. See Chapter 15 for more details.

We shall look at several key areas and highlight why some formal agreements might help, but each company has to take responsibility for its own terms and conditions.

☐ Rights and clearances of assets: liabilities

The methods to use when clearing rights are addressed in Chapter 15. Here we shall be concerned with establishing and agreeing which rights and clearances need to be addressed. Your client may give you permission to reproduce, edit and reuse many of the visual assets they have, but they may not own the copyright to be able to give you permission. They may believe they own the images, but ownership of visual images is not straightforward. Visuals prepared for a company brochure may have been given solely for that purpose and no other. So reuse would constitute a breach of conditions from a former contract. Originators of work have particular rights that protect them from other people editing their original work. It is a difficult area, which changes according to country. The client may own copyright for the original purpose of the materials but not have the electronic rights that are required for multimedia.

So it is in your interests to get written agreement, called an indemnity, that the clients own the electronic copyright in all the assets they provide to you, as a safeguard in case of any future dispute over the rights. We note in Chapter 15 that you as developer will not infringe a copyright if you reasonably believe that you have permission to use the asset. But often clients will make seemingly simple requests that can have hidden depths. For example, you might be approached by a company press office to make their press cuttings available to the whole company by putting them on a CD or on their intranet. Unless they have permission to copy the press cuttings they will probably be infringing copyright in the text or any photographs included. This would not be the case if they simply cut them out of the newspapers and circulated a folder with all the cuttings in it. Even if they currently pay a cuttings agency to supply them with cuttings there may be restrictions on what they can do with them.

Other assets you may have to find and clear for the purpose of the project – music, for example. You will be asked for the purpose, audience type, and countries where you want permission to use the application. These are known as the markets and territories you want covered. This is not as simple as it sounds. Many applications begin with one purpose but evolve into others. Material licensed for a CD-ROM in one country may be moved to a website, which is accessible across the whole world. If the rights were originally cleared only nationally, they would have to be renegotiated. An in-house training application may be released on the consumer market after a period of time in the company. The market would have changed, and the necessary rights and clearances may need revision. It is cheaper to negotiate once than have to renegotiate later. For any who still doubt this, consider the possible reclearance costs of the film below.

It has been recognized that reuse of some of the best film footage from television programmes in interactive programs would seem sensible, but many that have proposed this have fallen by the wayside once the cost of re-clearing electronic rights with all those who took part was worked out. As new media use of material becomes more common, the original agreements with both staff and freelancers that govern the use are being updated and clarified.

The duration of rights is also established at the time of negotiation, so you need a good idea of the lifespan of the product to determine how many years to ask for, or you may consider 'buy-outs'. These mean paying a once-only payment by which you get agreement to use the material indefinitely. Exclusivity might also be a consideration, although few rights owners would be willing to give up other use of their asset and, in any case, it would be very expensive. It is safest to assume that any licence of an asset is non-exclusive.

You need a clear directive from the client on their short- and long-term plans for the site or application. You should state what markets and territories you will cover when clearing rights for offline, and how long the clearances will be valid for any project. If you put this in writing and have their agreement to this formally, there can be no confusion as to who should have done what and when, if circumstances change.

If you intend to remake the application or website in another language then you must have obtained clearance for such use. In some cases a rights owner will count a direct translation as part of the original agreement, but in others they will not. It will be easier to cover multiple languages if your agreement provides royalties because an increased number of languages attracts more sales. For a buy-out this argument does not work. A similar situation occurs when an update of the application is required, to change information that has become outdated. The extreme situation in this chain is the derivative, which is another project based on the first.

Other liabilities to note

You will be using other companies' code in the form of libraries, tools and authoring packages under licence to develop your project, as well as producing your own code as and when necessary. You cannot guarantee that bugs from these will not affect the performance of the end-product. This is not as uncommon as it sounds, since multimedia is an experimental environment and code gets used in circumstances that were not originally envisaged, and may therefore fall over. You do not want to be held responsible for problems originating with other people's software, so you should include clauses to cover for this. The same is true of hardware, which can have unforeseen and unstated idiosyncrasies. On a website you may be using CGI programs from other sources including ones in the public domain or open source (which basically means that the code is freely available and can be modified and redistributed freely), and in some cases the licences for these place you under obligations.

Payment structure

You can see that your company will have put in quite a significant investment in terms of time to reach the agreed proposal stage. All this has been unpaid. On a large project, you might be working for a year or more to completion. Even smaller projects can mean considerable outlay of money during the production stages. The company needs to define a payment structure so that payments are staggered according to specific points in the project.

Sign-offs are well defined and represent agreement points, so these might be linked to staged payments. Others follow the computing model and define milestones that represent phases of the project. Payment could be linked to achievement of these. Alternatively, payment stages could be linked to calendar months and achievement of schedule to dates. Yet others ask for a certain amount up front, staged payments through the project, and final payment of the remainder at completion. Whatever option is chosen, some form of phased payment would help your cash flow.

Your client, however, will be interested in containing the costs. This is why they begin by trying to get an estimate from you and then haggle about the fine details of the deliverables to get the best deal for the money.

Effectively, you are signing a fixed-term contract when you agree to the final proposal. It states what you will produce in the time for the money. Your only safeguard in a fixed contract is agreed, comprehensive specifications with as detailed costing as possible done up front; so you have to be confident in your costings.

The alternative to fixed-price contracts, which are notoriously difficult to achieve in any ill-specified projects, is a time and materials contract. This means that you indicate what you expect the cost might be, but that you will keep strict records and bill according to the actual amount it takes. You should be able to see that clearances are so difficult to predict accurately that this approach makes sense. Unfortunately, as time and materials are more open-ended, clients are not receptive to this model although it may be fairer on the developer.

There is another model, which is a shared development where the client clears the rights in the content but the developer undertakes all other work to a budget. This is a likely model where the client is a publisher or asset holder.

☐ Ownership of code and other assets generated

Part of the way developers survive is to build up a stock of code or libraries that help them in the production of other projects. This does not mean that they will produce an application that looks and behaves exactly the same as the original product for which the code was generated. Most often the code is adapted to fit the new requirements but forms some of the building blocks. If your client is not a computer company or a developer they will probably not have any use for the source code that underlies their application. It is best to try to retain copyright in the code but issue a free licence to the client for its use.

The company needs to establish where it stands on this issue so that it will not infringe any rights in reuse of the code later. There is an added problem in that the code used may well be a combination of third-party code as well as its own. This makes it problematic to identify exactly which new code might belong to the client and which you would not have the right to sign away anyway as it belongs to the third party.

Many clients are reasonable once they realize the lack of value to themselves in having the copyright in the code. You might have to agree to provide access to source codes under extreme circumstances, such as your company ceasing to do business.

If clients have been used to commissioning video productions then this will seem a new concept for them. They would never expect a video production facility to retain rights in what they do. It will help if you explain that this is usually the case with software. It is common practice for application software never to be sold but only licensed, with restrictive conditions on usage, copying or decompiling.

☐ Establish your right to demonstrate and promote the product

It is important for winning new business that, as a developer, you are able to demonstrate your capabilities to new clients. Some clients will bind you to confidentiality agreements, and you need to recognize the effect this might have for demonstrating the program after completion. Some clients will not grant permission for competitors to see the product but may be happy for non-competitors to see it. There are several ways to approach this to establish limited demonstrations with the company's permission, but this will be onerous on you.

If the client will be demonstrating some aspects publicly, there should be no reason for their stopping you doing the same. Often confidentiality agreements have a proviso or time limit whereby once the information is in the public domain, then the clause no longer applies. However, it is one more aspect that needs a clear statement, or your company may find that it cannot use the application as part of a repertoire to show at exhibitions or to prospective clients.

Similarly, you should consider what happens if you wish to publicize a project by advertising it or getting editorial coverage in a magazine or on television. Can you show any of it under these conditions?

☐ Moral rights

As developer, your company can ask for a right of paternity to be included in the contract. This will allow your company and its members who worked on the project to have a credit; otherwise, no one is obliged to recognize your involvement once the product is released. See Chapter 15 for more details on moral rights.

☐ Severance

Problems can arise from many quarters that may make it important for your company to extricate itself from any agreement, mainly to protect it from further damage. If your client's company is taken over and you hear that they will be closed down as part of an inevitable downsizing operation, then you may wish to pull out earlier rather than later. Make sure that you still get paid for work done if the project is stopped. Alternatively, if the key person in the client organization leaves and the new person makes it impossible to continue with the project as previously specified, you may wish to terminate the contract.

A severance clause works both ways, so that clients can extricate themselves as well if they have cause.

☐ Force majeure

This refers to the situation where a major unforeseen disaster such as an earthquake or terrorist bomb stops your company fulfilling the contract.

Although unlikely, major catastrophes do happen, and then you want your liability to complete the contract to be contained. This avoids your company being sued for non-completion when it was no fault of your own that you were unable to do so. It costs very little to include in an agreement, but a lot if you don't and you need it.

☐ Which law?

If there is any need for legal action to be taken – over non-payment, for example – then it is to your company's advantage to state which country's law your agreement complies with, and which country's law any proceedings will comply with, since the law on certain points varies around the world. In the USA it varies from state to state. Also, your costs will be easier if the hearings are in your own country. So, again, it is easy to stipulate up front which country's law is to be used, but possibly very costly if you do not.

These are a few of the main considerations, but it is in your interest to establish your terms and conditions and ways of working so that you can capitalize from your time and effort. It should not be the role of the project manager to draft the legal clauses in the agreement, but just to know enough to make sure that the main risks are covered. Each company will have its own way of drafting, issuing and checking agreements: some will do it through the legal section, some with a contracts manager, and some – after guidance from lawyers – will do it on their own behalf.

It is the company's responsibility to have enough support for the project manager to ensure that agreements conform to their requirements.

☐ Freelancer and contractor contracts

When you need to recruit extra people for the team, you also make agreements with them. These will have separate issues that need to be covered, or you may find for example that your graphics artist's company owns the copyright in the visuals that are developed, not your company. Employees are different from contractors as long as it has been established that all work that is created in the course of their work belongs to the company, and this would be stated in their contract of employment. Any of the team, whether in-house or external, has the same moral rights as the company does in relation to the work and the client. So the company may need to establish an overall policy for themselves and employees, depending on how moral rights are treated in their country – if at all. Note that moral rights cannot be signed away to someone else but they can be waived.

The company may be comfortable with employing a contractor who then subcontracts the work, but it may not. Clauses indicating who is responsible for the work and if and how subcontracting can be done are necessary to cover the type and quality of the work. If you have agreed any confidentiality clauses with the client, these usually put the onus on the developer to bind any staff to the agreements, so you might need to be very clear who is working on the project to comply with your confidentiality undertaking.

Again, it should not be the project manager's role to draft the contract agreements, but only to agree the work tasks, the length of the contract, the rate of pay, and possibly payment terms. It is the company's responsibility to provide the standard contract where the project manager completes the relevant parts.

■ Conclusion

The project manager needs to understand the background to many issues about rights, clearances and legal obligations to reach a well-defined contractual agreement with the client. The proposal document becomes part of the agreement, which contains the detailed specification of the work to be done, the time and costs. The more detailed the understanding of what rights and how many will need to be cleared, the better. It can have a big impact on the costs, so it is in the project manager's interest to define this, particularly before work begins. Finally, there are legal issues that are more the responsibility of the company to determine for each project, but knowledge of them is in the project manager's interest to ensure that the project fulfils both the clients' and the company's interests.

THEORY INTO PRACTICE 10

Improve your ability to predict costs on projects.

There are hidden problems that arise with most projects where you need to have allocated a percentage of your budget for contingency purposes. Your company may have a percentage that it recommends that you add on to the cost figure. You need to build up your knowledge about hidden factors to help you predict that your project is likely to run into them. Ask as many colleagues as you can about any overruns on time – remember that time means paying more for your resources and so is an extra cost – and extra hidden costs that they have encountered on projects. Check the percentage of the total budget that these factors cost. Build up a profile of factors related to type of project to define the risk factors and the percentage contingency to cover risks. You may find that some are not risks, but rather costs to tasks that were overlooked. In this case you can detail these into the true costing rather than the contingency.

■ Summary

- Clearances can be complex depending on the nature of the assets and the owners. It will be impossible to cost accurately because there are so many variables. You either need to get the client to agree to an estimated price, which will be firmed as the project proceeds, or work from the top rates that you know to cover yourself.

■ Anything used on a website accessible to the public has to be cleared for the world.

■ There are legal issues that you should understand, although it is the company's responsibility to determine its terms and conditions.

■ Apart from clearing rights in assets you acquire from sources other than the clients, you need to avoid liability if your client gives you assets but does not own the electronic copyright.

■ You need to establish ownership in any new assets created by the project – code, pictures, and so on – and where you stand in development of any derivatives from the project.

■ Other aspects for attention include your right to demonstrate the application, moral rights, severance clauses, force majeure, and which country's law will apply in any proceedings.

■ You are not only involved with contractual agreements with the client. Some of these issues carry over into the contracts needed for subcontractors.

■ Recommended reading

See the reading list for Chapter 15, *Rights, copyright and other intellectual property.*

10

Selecting the team

Project manager's responsibilities

- To match the skills needed to the project requirements
- To check the in-house resource availability – align the requirements
- To determine the roles and responsibilities of the core and extended team
- To interview and select all key team members if necessary
- To establish a list of criteria for each role
- To ensure that the company's policies on contract terms and conditions are carried out
- To ensure that the correct rights and clearances are made
- To provide clear and detailed briefs to those employed

■ Introduction

Although the selection of staff was touched on in Chapter 3, *Scoping a project*, the consideration there was to demonstrate how to assess the cost of the project rather than the skills, but these two happen in unison. The aim of this chapter is to give a more detailed account of the staffing decisions, and to demonstrate the complexity of the process. You need an appreciation of skill sets across several disciplines to be able to match your project needs to personnel requirements, while balancing the cost of the resources against the needs.

■ Identifying the skills needed

The mix of skills needed for any project depends on its content, use of media components, size, platform, and amount of administration. As project manager, it is your responsibility to ensure that resources are available at the right time to keep the project on track. This means that you plan who you need at which points of the project, and then ensure that:

■ these resources are on hand;

■ they are properly inducted into the project;

■ they have been contracted under the right terms and conditions;

- they have the right skills for the job;
- they have the right tools for the job;
- they have a good working environment.

Because of the nature of multimedia, there is often a core team who work together for the majority of the project and then an extended team who are brought in for particular tasks – a video editor or a specialist in CGI programming, for example. The core team may well be full-time staff members from the company, but because the workload fluctuates according to demand, or projects can be long and complicated and therefore lock people into a timeframe, quite often it is necessary to contract-in people to form part of the core team.

According to the company you work for, you may be expected to carry out the interviewing process or there may be a specific personnel role in the company to take care of the search and selection process. In either case it will pay you to define the skills and experience level you need to make sure that you staff the project correctly.

Once you have a feel for the scope of the project and the expectations of the client, you should be in a position to identify the staff needed. Your decisions at this point affect the budget decisions and the costs. You need to assess the position for a core team first by matching the core skills you need with the availability of the nearest match to these in-house.

Once the client has agreed to the proposal, you have to move fast to assemble the team. Situations change quickly. Even though a few of the core team appeared to be available at the time the project was scoped, they might have been placed on another project if the go-ahead for that came first. This can leave you with the difficult task of recruiting very quickly to ensure that the project begins on time. Any delay can be vital to achieving the deadlines, so this is another dangerous time for the project manager – the time between a proposal and confirmation – because some of the circumstances may have changed.

Many companies try to build some flexibility into their organization by having a list of independent contractors that can be brought in for specific projects. A project manager needs to work up a good set of contacts across all the multimedia sectors to help the recruitment process. There are agencies that specialize in multimedia and/or Web design recruitment, and some companies use these to help construct teams. Remember that if you will be using an agency to help, you need to budget for their fees as well as for the staff costs.

Whatever way your company works to solve its staffing needs, someone has to do the interviewing and make the final decision. It is wise to become involved in this process to build up your own skill set. It is not an easy task, and is very time-consuming, but unless it is carried out effectively you could be landed with a poor team for a difficult project.

Your project teams might include the following roles.

Online core team:

- one or more graphics artists/creatives,
- one or more HTML or JavaScript authors (often the graphics artists also do this),
- yourself as a producer/project manager.

Offline core team:

- one or more programmers,
- one or more graphics artists,
- yourself as a producer/project manager.

Extended project team:

- server-side programmers (for online projects)
- video personnel
  - a video director/producer
  - an assistant producer
  - a production assistant
  - a video editor
  - a video journalist
  - a video graphics artist
  - actors/actresses
- sound personnel
  - voice-over artistes
  - sound editor
- general support
  - a personal assistant
  - secretarial support.

Specialist support

- business analysts
- information analysts
- technical analysts
- technical support
- an interface design specialist (GUI or HCI background)
- scriptwriters
- a training analyst
- an instructional designer/interactive designer
- subject matter experts.

On top of this it may be custom and practice in your company that there are one or more managerial people – such as a creative director – who are involved as well.

Because some multimedia specialists have built up experience across a range of skill sets, one person might be able to take on a couple of roles. But when exactly do you need any of these roles, and how do you assess whether you need them? The profile of each skill set and the type of project that warrants their use will be defined to help decision making about resources.

Considerations for interviews: general

It is as well to remember that interviews are a two-way process: you are assessing the candidates, but they are also assessing you and the organization. It is better if a couple of people can attend the interview so that impressions can be consolidated through discussion and comparison. Those interviewing should have:

- established what to say about the company and the project to introduce the candidate to the set of circumstances, the requirements and the set-up;
- established a set list of questions to ask all candidates;
- established the skill criteria needed, and have thought of ways to assess whether the skill set is present at the levels required;
- defined the role needed with the level of responsibility;
- gained an impression of the candidate from pre-reading a CV;
- formulated extra questions specific to the information contained in the CV to ascertain:
  - the accuracy of the information,
  - the reasons for any apparent discrepancies or breaks in employment,
  - the strengths and weaknesses of the candidate;
- put a timescale on the number of minutes to be given to each section of the interview and have appointed a person to be timekeeper;
- allowed a few minutes between candidates to discuss reactions and findings and make notes.

The interviews should start on time, and should progress according to plan. If the plan overruns, any waiting candidates should be kept informed of progress. Some people have the same reaction to interviews as they do to examinations, and it is not an ideal way to form solid impressions. Some larger companies use group interviews for full-time jobs, where the candidates are set tasks to assess their abilities in a range of factors such as leadership, teamwork, and so on.

However, this is not a practice that prevails in multimedia at present. It is a good idea to allow members of the core team to meet candidates for other core team roles because they will need to work together. This can be done after the formal interview while the next candidate is being interviewed. The project manager should then collect any additional comments from the other core team members prior to making decisions.

■ Skill-set profiles: core team

☐ Computer graphics artists

Quite often the HTML/JavaScript authoring for a website is done by the graphics artist or a web author rather than by a programmer, largely because the layout of the page is defined by the HTML. If WYSIWYG tools are used then they may also include basic JavaScript programming for things like rollovers. However for more complicated JavaScript programming, especially if it is important that the pages work on a number of platforms, a specialist JavaScript programmer may be needed. (See Book 2 Chapter 5, *Platform parameters*, for more on this.)

Websites and applications can demand a certain style because of the content, and ideally a graphics artist should be selected to bring the best to the content and to the interactive environment. The development platform and the delivery platform will dictate the level and skill set that are needed for the graphics artist. In the same way, these will affect the skill set needed for the programmer, as we shall see in the next section. The artists will come from either a PC or a Mac background and will have experience in the respective graphics packages and, if appropriate, in web page design.

The artist needs to be both creative and technically minded, since creative ideas in multimedia graphics have to be achieved through technical means. Many adjustments have to be made because the graphics process is not straightforward. Colours can shift quite often as the graphic moves through its various stages to the final image, and for applications where accuracy of colour is needed – selling items that have a range of colour options, for example – this can be a major problem.

The sizing and placement of images cause other problems. Text often becomes corrupted at the last stage. It is difficult for the client to realize how much rework is needed because the graphic may have to be taken back through numerous stages to correct such problems. The technicalities and inconsistencies mean that the graphics artist needs patience and logical, analytical thinking as well as creative flair. Your application may require more of one of these attributes than the others.

The programmer or HTML author and graphics artist have to work closely together. The graphics person constructs the images to a certain stage and then passes them to the programmer or author to integrate them with all the other pieces – sound files, text, position in the program, the means of access to the image, and so on. They work out together exactly how to produce and transfer the images between them. In offline projects particularly, there are often hundreds of images and pieces of images that have to be assembled, so the naming convention for the assets and the version control between them is important.

Online projects make demands on the artists because they have to balance the size and quality of the graphics against the download times. They have to learn tricks of the trade to compress graphics with as little drop in quality as possible but with speed of transfer. Working across browser versions and cross-platform has become a lot more complex over the last couple of years and many companies are limiting their commitment as to how many and which options they will support.

Because people may have worked in various companies with diverse approaches to working, and have different ways of expressing concepts, bringing the core team together can be problematic. Some of the skills overlap, and the graphics artist might have been used to taking the image process further than the programmer expects, or might be used to liaising with clients directly when the project manager wants to avoid this. There may be a strong split between the technical and creative skills. A technical artist may depend on the source images being produced by conventional means and then they scan, adjust, assemble and integrate ready for the programmer. This will always be true for specialist areas such as cartoon images, for example. But if the artist has a strong technical bias, it will affect the resources and costs of the project if you do not recognize that one graphics resource will not suffice. Often this is the case where there is one main artist and input from others as and when needed.

You may find you have to work with an artist who is available in-house but who doesn't have the full skill set you need. The erratic availability of contractors can also mean that you may have to select a person who displays many but not all of the attributes you need. Then you will face decisions of how to build up the balance of skills according to budget.

The project may form part of a set of projects so several artists with a variety of skills might be needed. If there are several people they need to be managed, and a senior graphics artist could be appointed to take on this role, or an art director might be considered.

An art director (or creative director) is usually employed by larger graphics studios as the creative ideas person who is responsible for managing the overall style of projects. You may have a set of projects that need to show continuity of graphic style – a certain look and feel. Also, if you have several computer graphics artists involved in your project, someone needs to coordinate the artistic direction and personalities.

Pre-interview

Although there is usually one main artist for the project, you may need several for different functions during the development, particularly with offline projects. You'll need to define exactly how you intend the project to run with any split of work needed between graphics artists, for example, so that there are no misconceptions about what type of work each artist will be doing. Some tasks are more laborious than creative, and tensions can occur if an artist thinks he or she will be doing creative new work rather than repetitive conversions from source materials. The size of the project will determine whether these tasks are combined for one person to do or whether the tasks are split. Also, one person needs to have responsibility for artistic direction, otherwise clashes in opinions, style and approach will show up in the application.

At interview

The definition of roles is easy to state but difficult to achieve because you will be working blind until the fine detail of the project is teased out: so you can explain to candidates how the graphics appear to split but remind them that the circumstances may change once the project is under way.

It is important to see examples of the candidates' work and understand exactly their role in the production process, whether technical, creative, managerial, or all three. Graphics artists will be happy to discuss their preferences and styles, and might be able to come up with a feel for some treatments for the project once they understand its scope and their expected role. Because interactive graphics production is not straightforward it is a good idea to probe where the candidates have experienced problems and how these were solved. This will give you a feel for the depth of experience and knowledge of the idiosyncrasies of the graphics packages.

You may be working on a project that has a 'house style', and this might mean that the artists will need to adapt their style appropriately. Some find this easier than others, so you should check their disposition for this.

Because the synergy between the programmers or authors and graphics artists is important, it is good to allow them to meet if possible and get their reactions. If the contractors have worked for the company before, it is also wise to gather informal feedback from those that worked with them.

☐ Programmers

This section applies both to programmers as members of the core team for offline production and to their role in the extended team for online production.

The skill set of programmers is wide-ranging. As project manager, your programming resource will be affected by decisions on:

- the development platform;
- the software that will be used for development (authoring, scripting or computer language);
- the delivery platform considerations.

Skill-set profiles: core team

You need to understand what hardware and software you will use in the project to help pinpoint the exact skill set needed in your programmers.

The first major decision may be the development platform that your project will use – Mac or PC, for example. Programmers specialize at this level and then have specialisms within these main groups. There are other development platforms, such as Linux or UNIX, but these are less common apart from server-side development for websites. Often the company will decide which development platform is used. Under the Mac and PC categories there are different sets of authoring tools, although the most common tools are available on several platforms. These packages allow programmers, and non-specialists who have programming aptitude, to develop straightforward applications. You need to have a good understanding of what the tools allow, or take advice from your technical support, to decide whether the tools can fit all the project requirements.

Authoring tools have become much more sophisticated over the past few years, and can cope with far more than they used to, but you need to become informed of their limitations and nuances. Some authoring packages have their own scripting languages. These allow the tailoring of the package to specific needs but add a level of complexity to the skill set needed. Scripting languages bridge the gap between authoring tools and computer languages. The difference in the levels is equivalent to prefabricated house segments (authoring languages), prefabricated building blocks (scripting languages), and constructing your own bricks (computer languages).

A further category of programmer is an analyst or systems analyst. This group have experience in defining the requirements for projects. They are the most likely to convert into project managers since they deal with clients and supervise other programmers to deliver the specification as well as having programming ability themselves. They will have been trained in using structured methods to specify and document computer projects. There are differences in the skill sets required for managing computer projects and multimedia projects, but this group will have a better starting point. The very formal approach to defining requirements by using a functional and technical specification as well as having a user requirements study is seen as over-complex and off-putting for clients in certain business sectors. The principles are sound, but the methods have to be adapted and extended for multimedia.

The application platform does not necessarily dictate the development platform, so a PC application may be authored in a Mac tool set, for example. Sometimes applications need to work across platforms, and this is where wider expertise is needed to ensure that the development takes account of the cross-platform restraints. Of course, developing for the World Wide Web is inherently multi-platform, as different browsers running on a variety of computers should be catered for. You have to be confident that the right decisions have been made about the choice of development hardware and software to fit the delivery platform requirements. If you are non-technical, you need to have complete confidence in the technical support staff and/or programmers who make the decisions on your behalf.

Cross-platform.

If the application cannot be developed in an authoring environment, a programming language will be needed. Although there are exceptions, non-specialists have not got enough experience and training to use computer languages so usually a specialist will be needed. Different languages suit different purposes and accomplish certain tasks better than others. This is why your technical support needs to understand the whole scope of the project to make an informed decision as to what combination of hardware and software will be needed.

Programmers can apply past experience to learn new languages/packages as they work. Some packages share similarities in approach so that the learning curve is relatively fast; others have a totally different approach to their logic, so they take longer to learn if the past experience is not compatible. Quite often the programmers you employ will have to learn as they go along, and you need to be aware of how much extra time you need to build in to allow for their learning. This might sound like poor project management – to employ the wrong skill level – but several circumstances can lead to this. First, you may have to use full-time members of staff with a lower skill level for your project because they are available and therefore it is cheaper for the company to use them than employ contractors. Second, some specialisms within programming are harder to find, and you may not be able to find contractors with the right skills. Third, when skills are scarce they become expensive, so even if you find the right contractors you may not be able to afford them within the budget. In this case you have to gamble on the extra time for someone to gain the knowledge against the speed of experience. This would tend to mean the lower cost for longer or a higher cost for a shorter period of time.

This is a difficult decision, since estimating the time it takes for programming is not an accurate art, particularly in interactive media development.

Considerations for interviews: programmers

Pre-interview

You need to have worked out the skills you want, the skill level you would be willing to accept and 'grow', the length of time necessary to complete the project, and the cost range you could work with within your budget. Ask candidates to bring examples of their work.

At interview

There are good and bad traits within professions that are part of their 'folklore'. Programmers can be creative, versatile, act on initiative, quick thinking, adaptable, precise, accurate, work to timescales, and reliable. However, the profession suffers from labels from the business world that indicate erratic timekeeping (both personal and project specific), poor communication skills, stubbornness, a wish to fulfil themselves rather than the project in hand, and a tendency to be wilful, seeming to live in a world of their own. The problem is that some of the best programmers are not easy to manage.

You have to decide whether solidity or finesse is needed more in the particular project if you end up with a choice of candidates who display different traits, and you need to recognize your own strengths and weaknesses in your management style to assess a fit within your team that you can manage successfully.

If you are technical, you could conduct the interview to assess the technical ability of the candidate. You also need to assess the candidate as a project member. You may well be looking for different attributes than in a full-time employee. Project-specific work can make it easier to manage a more diverse range of people than those you need to work alongside continuously. In a project-specific situation, the expectations are different for all involved.

■ The extended team: skill sets

Video personnel

The use of video in online applications is growing. When a company's image or the information about a key product – a new car, for example – warrants high exposure, or indeed needs to match the exposure level employed in other media, then the pressure mounts to include video despite the restrictions of quality and download times.

At present the shooting of video specifically for online use alone is unusual, and so video production follows offline production paths, and extracts might be used online as well as for other purposes. Another scenario where video plays a part is when a website precipitates alternative media arising from it. So a marketing CD or DVD might well use extracts from the existing website, but because CDs and DVDs set up expectations in the users for audio and video, extras might need to be produced for them. In the case of hybrid Web/CD/DVDs the strengths of each medium are utilized, since the volatile data is kept online for ease of updating while the rest is encapsulated on the disk using an appropriate media mix.

What does this mean in terms of the skill level needed for video online production? It may mean that you need only the expertise to edit and compress extracts of material already produced, to provide online pieces of the best possible quality. Alternatively, you may need to employ a crew to produce major pieces for a hybrid Web/CD/DVD, where stills might be used on the website for continuity of style between the Web and the disk. In between these, for iTV perhaps, you might decide that a video journalist who shoots directly with a digital camera, records commentary and edits items on computer would have all the right skills you need to produce pieces for the particular project. This all-in-one approach is common only for news and some documentaries at the moment but its use may develop in other sectors.

The variety of video that can be appropriate means that you have to recognize and set the quality level of production and the attendant skills needed carefully or your budget can quickly go astray.

If your offline application is going to include video footage, you might need to use a video director/producer, an editor, and perhaps a video graphics artist too. The directors/producers will have contacts and preferences for using certain facility houses, editors and video graphics people, so it may save you some effort if you trust your main video contractor to organize the other video needs. Again, depending on the company bias, you may have access to all the video personnel you need in-house.

The difference between a video director and a producer is not straightforward until you define the roles for a full feature film, where the director has the creative role and the producer is more of an administrator. For shorter pieces of work you need to check what a person will be prepared to do if you interview directors and producers, so that you are aware whether they will collapse the roles together, or whether they expect support themselves. A lot will depend on the amount and type of video footage you require.

As video has become more of a key component in applications, the traditional roles from video production will figure more in multimedia teams. The rise of iTV will play its part in extending the traditional skills too. Production assistants have had a key role in video productions, helping the

Use of video is increasing.

director and producer. The role involves organizing and administration, but can extend to supervising edits, directing part of the shoot, clearing rights, organizing facility houses, and editing scripts. A good production assistant is well organized, used to troubleshooting, well skilled in audio and video production, and has a useful range of contacts.

Personnel with a video background find the seeming disintegration of pieces of a script and the lack of control over the user's sequence of using the material an anathema. Their backgrounds have prepared them for continuity, flow, strong storylines, methods of story development, build-up, characterization and unity of a whole. They lead the viewer through the material. Interactivity destroys this to a certain extent, and it takes time for traditional directors and assistants to come to terms with the changes that are needed in material development. They have a tendency to be critical about the technical quality and the structure of interactive programs that they have seen because they compare them with video programmes. Chapter 16, *Multimedia narrative*, later in the book, looks at the implications of interactivity on the traditional approaches to writing scripts for film and video. It anticipates the skills being needed in iTV.

Although the addition of interactivity and working with programmers is a new area, video personnel are used to dealing with a mix of materials and people. It is possibly a little harder for those coming from a programming background to pick up the creative aspects of audio and video production than it is for video personnel to adjust to interactivity; but it is easier for them to learn the technicalities of audio and video production than it is for video personnel to understand computer graphics and programming technicalities. This might mean that some personnel from a computing or graphics background will claim to have audio and video production skills. You need to decide whether these people have full creative, administrative and technical skills or whether audio and video specialists are needed.

Assistant producers help the producers with the creative direction of the video footage. The producer may delegate some of the responsibility for shots and edits to an assistant but still maintain a strong directional line. This means that some assistants have a wide range of skills and are capable of directing smaller projects. You may decide that an assistant producer could fulfill the role you need, depending on their experience. It would be rare in multimedia to need both producer/director and assistant producer.

Production assistants can be invaluable when a project needs video footage, photos or pictures from picture libraries, clearance of video, sound and graphics rights, or if several strands of the project need to be completed simultaneously because of the timescales. They have an administrative role supporting the director and producer.

The casting and directing of actors and actresses might form part of your overall responsibility. If your footage needs extensive detail such as external locations or studio sets you will need a full production team. This is why and where video footage is expensive and might take up a good portion of your budget. The producer would usually coordinate, recruit and manage the video team, and take care of casting, but you may have to sit in with the client to check that the actors and actresses fulfil their expectations and needs.

So much depends on the scope of the project and the budget that the number of people involved and their roles is difficult to quantify. Multimedia at present tends to expect people to collapse a few roles and responsibilities together because the amount filmed is generally shorter and less complex than for full videos and films.

Sometimes, and this is true for on- and offline projects, you might find yourself in the position of selecting and organizing facilities houses and personnel, such as video editors, to work on pre-shot footage. Your need for a producer or director diminishes in this case, but you still have to clear the rights and re-edit the material to suit the purpose.

Video editors work to directions, so if your application needs existing footage reworked you need to consider whether you can handle the direction or whether you need help. This could depend on your own background and experience and whether the scripts are straightforward. Alternatively, the editor might be prepared to work with the scripts without direction. The range of possibilities within video production and the variety and level of skills within the personnel mean that identification of which personnel are needed and recruitment are much easier with someone who has been part of the industry.

The use of digital video has brought video and computing editing skills closer. Digital footage can be edited on a computer desktop, and even in broadcast production, desktop systems are used for the early offline stage of editing. You might produce your video using broadcast facilities, in which case you will hire these facilities complete with their personnel, and the editing is not really a team-recruitment issue. If you are going to make use of in-house desktop editing for your production then you will need to have a team member who is able to do the work from both a technical and creative point of view. This might be something that a graphic designer can do, especially if the video editing is combined with compositing work, where moving sequences are combined together. Your decision whether to use an edit suite or your own computer could be influenced by cost, personnel abilities, timescale, and the complexity of the editing. However, the creative processes involved with the choice of which edits and video effects will suit the material best are skills that still reside more with video personnel than with computer personnel, although the skill sets are converging.

☐ Sound personnel

The production of audio for a website is basically the same as for an offline application. As with video, some of the production can be done at your desktop.

If you are using audio with graphics and text, you will need to:

- book a studio facility with a sound editor;
- select and book your voice-over artistes;
- select any music needed;
- have all the scripts ready and signed off;
- specify exactly the format in which you will need the material.

You will be asked how long you'll need the studio and editor for, so you have to make sure that you know how much work is involved in the scripts and estimate the amount of time needed to edit the material afterwards. You have to work out the timing sequence of all these aspects so that they come together at the studio. Selecting the voice-over artistes is no trivial task. You'll more than likely have to go through an agency. Your company may hold banks of voice-over tapes from different agencies that you can browse, you may have a voice in mind and need to find out the agent, or you may have specific requirements for voice qualities and need to match them to people. You can phone agencies and put your specifications to them; they will suggest some alternatives, and then send through some demo tapes.

Different prices from different agencies.

The voice-over industry is well structured, and is used to responding quickly to enquiries. The agencies have several questions about use of the voice-over that determine the basic rate for the artiste and any clearance and rights fees. For non-interactive productions the negotiations are straight-forward and clear. They are based on the type of use, type of audience, period of time, and countries for clearance. One of the standard categories that was used – the number of times for broadcast or use – is impossible to predict for interactive media and did cause some headaches for a few years, since the user may or may not access the particular voice-over every time. Because interactive use is now widespread many of the initial difficulties met clearing interactive rights have been addressed and rates are more standardized for a website, kiosk, CD-ROM, DVD or whatever.

It is up to you as the project manager to check that the rates and rights offered match what is needed. Production music recorded specifically for use in film, television and multimedia is available from many sources, and in some cases it is royalty free.

If you are employing production assistants, it is invaluable if they have had prior experience with clearing multimedia rights. As it is an area that is constantly shifting, and the regulators are trying to address the problems, you need to keep up to date with the changes either through them or by yourself.

Voice-over artistes work quickly. They often have sessions before and after yours, so if you have miscalculated the amount of material, or there are too many changes, you will be looking at the hire of all concerned again. The artistes usually charge a minimum of an hour however little they say.

The sound editors will use a variety of techniques to deal with any retakes that are necessary because of mispronunciation, wrong intonation or whatever. The way they choose to operate depends on the sophistication of the equipment they are using. Most studios are digital now rather than tape based and record direct to a computer file. If there are very specific subject terms, it is wise to have a representative from the client at the recording to check the pronunciation.

The artistes should have the script a couple of days before the recording so that they can prepare, although many are excellent sight-readers. The scripts need to have been signed off by the client prior to the recording. During the recording session the editor will mark up the script to show where there were retakes, but you or your delegate should also keep check and decide which out of any that are disputed should be used. The client or their representative might prefer to make these decisions, but they have to be made then and there.

It is important that the editor knows what the tracks will be used for, and the quality level needs to be stated clearly.

Multimedia applications have underestimated the importance of the use of sound, as discussed in Chapter 8. This starts at the script stage, when speech and stills are often put together without the atmospheric use of music and sound effects. However, until the clearance and rights problems are sorted, the expense of quality audio might be too much for many projects, and it is easier to compromise on its quality than on many of the other components.

Audio production is a large administrative, creative and technical part of the project and carries its own risks, which the project manager needs to understand and control. A video producer or experienced assistant producer would have the skills to manage and coordinate the audio production as well as the video if necessary, but they would have to be made aware of the technical specification for the audio so that the next stage – encoding for the website, CD or DVD – can proceed smoothly.

Because the tools have matured quickly, it is becoming easier to encode them. It is so much easier now that graphics artists and programmers can shoot and record pieces of material, then integrate them without the need for all the personnel, studios and facilities houses. If your application needs only this level of quality, there is no reason to go to the expense of full-blown audio and video production. You still need to clear all rights and ensure that there are no accidental infringements such as advertisements on a wall deliberately used as a background in the video, or uncleared use of any music. There are lots of traps to avoid when this in-house approach is taken, and the creative personnel are often not aware of all the administrative angles that need to be covered for legal reasons. If this is the right approach for your project, you have to take full responsibility for ensuring that all the administrative procedures are carried out and recorded correctly.

■ General support

☐ Personal assistant

If the administration in the project is going to be heavy, you may well need a personal assistant instead of or as well as a production assistant. The skills of organizing are parallel, but personal assistants will not get involved with the audio and video production to the same extent. They may book facilities, and arrange and clear rights under your direction if you will be performing these tasks. They should possess secretarial skills so that they can assist in documenting the project and collating scripts as well as contributing to the general communication with the client and team.

If the project is an international one, with all the administrative extras that this entails, a personal assistant may be the answer. If the project involves details of the client's products – a kiosk or a full online retail site, for example – it can be a large task to ensure that the information is accurate and in a form that will facilitate integration.

Clients will be used to changing their details on a daily basis until the products are on sale, and it is difficult to keep track of the current situation on prices, colour descriptions, product dimensions, product specifications, and so on. Unless the application links online to the client database as part of the project specification, you will most likely need to reproduce the details and get sign-off on a version at the time you need to do final integration. You will have to build up the relevant details and keep updating until the last moment.

This is one of those grey tasks that several people might do or share: an instructional or interactive designer might see it as a task to ensure the quality of data and be prepared to take this on; programmers might be persuaded to have this as part of their role, particularly if the technicalities of merging data from the sources can be streamlined; you might see it as part of your liaison and sign-off role; or you may set up a process between companies where your personal assistant will liaise with the appropriate people to maintain the records. A lot will depend on exactly how much data there is, how unstable it is, and how it will be integrated into the application.

The role tends to evolve according to circumstances and the aptitude of the people involved.

☐ Secretarial support

All projects generate a good deal of general administration, and some level of secretarial support is always needed. If you have to type and produce all the documents and letters yourself, make all phone calls to book facility houses, and contact the various contractors, clients and officials, you need to block out at least half of your time for this and have other forms of backup support for the other functions to compensate. Lack of administrative backup is one of the most common causes of problems in multimedia projects, because the amount of time it takes is underestimated and undervalued by managers. This is not a major problem if you do not have to perform several of the core tasks yourself on the project, but if you are expected to do part of the programming, perhaps produce a prototype with an authoring tool, cover all the liaising with the client, and maybe write a script or two while recruiting and managing all the other staff, then the day-to-day administration becomes problematic. This is where the value of being multiskilled can become diminished because it is considered the norm rather than the exception.

If you need to have support, you may be able to identify the busy administrative periods and survive with temporary secretaries. However, inducting people often eats up vital time, and so continuity of personnel across a project needs to be carefully weighed against other factors.

Project managers in other business spheres are not expected to perform any of the core tasks themselves. In many ways, the practical skills are seen as non-management functions and therefore not part of the role. Multimedia roles have not fully settled out yet so the boundaries are not as defined. But the profession is maturing even though it is still going through changes as the technologies change around it. Many more people have not converted through to new media from other areas but began and continue their careers within it.

Specialist support

Business analyst

Increasingly the top management of new media companies are recognizing that it is the initial stages of projects that can be the most problematic. These projects tend to be the larger ones and many are concerned with e-commerce.

Clients have become more informed and more demanding about the results they expect from these new media projects. Sometimes the clients will be fully briefed in their e-business strategy and have very clear business objectives for the project. But you may have difficulty buying in to their perspective because their business is specialized or their way of describing their business processes is peppered with concepts you are unsure of. Some companies have their own cultural stance that is embedded in their vocabulary and takes some time for outsiders to master. You may benefit from having a translator to bridge the gap between their 'business speak' and a new media brief. Having a business analyst who has experience of business practices on the one hand and technology projects on the other might lead to getting a faster working brief than you learning to understand the client's business.

On other occasions the clients' expectations can be unrealistic. They see new media as the answer to all their problems. Sometimes they confuse what new media can achieve on its own and what else might need to change within the company to release its full benefit. If any of these are evident from your first meetings, you may save yourself and your team a lot of time and effort if you offer an e-business analyst or strategist with whom the clients can clarify their ideas. A good business analyst will help the clients produce a clear and realistic brief of what they want and what they say they need in terms of their business. Then you and your team can move forward with far more confidence.

The role of a business analyst or equivalent has become more prevalent as new media has become part and parcel of doing business. The Internet has matured into a key business and public communication channel so that businesses can't ignore it. New media has graduated to being a mainstream necessity. Previously it was marginalized and key business personnel were not often involved. Now new media decisions are part of core business, top management is involved. The decisions warrant attention because the overall performance of the company is linked with them.

There is a skills gap that needs to be recognized here. It is difficult to find business analysts that have a foot in both camps who can bridge the divide to get a clear brief. Clients are wary because some e-businesses have very visibly got things wrong and paid for it by going out of business. Successful e-business models are still eluding definition. E-business strategies are fledgling. This is part of the difficulty for the clients but they must reach their own informed decisions in the risk-filled arena. Your analyst has a difficult role and should not drive the client's business solutions. The analyst should interpret the clients' business solutions into a brief that you can produce with confidence.

Information analyst/architect

An information architect may work side by side with the business analyst and identify the content range and treatment that serves the business strategy. They address the 'who, why, what, how, when and where' high-level decisions about information, its structure and the access within and outside the organization. The key aspect they are concerned with is determining the overall information structure blocks and ensuring that this serves the business in the way that it needs. (See Chapter 6, *Agreeing the content*, for more information about the role of the information analyst/architect and the references at the end for designing information architectures for websites.)

Technical architect

When a project is complex, a good deal of code has to be developed and possibly integrated with other company systems to devise a smooth electronic supply chain. Then a technical architect may be necessary to act as the specialist to coordinate the in-house team and the client's technical resources.

The definition of the exact technical specifications that will be needed is no mean feat under these circumstances. Many e-commerce sites need extended technical considerations so a specialist can be invaluable.

Technical support

The day-to-day running of the technical side of the project can range from straightforward to very complex depending on the mixture of hardware and software that will be used. In some research and international projects your partners might be producing the hardware and software as part of the project, and you may be dependent upon their meeting their deadlines and testing the efficiency of the tools, prior to you using them. Inevitably with new hardware and software the unexpected happens, and it is at this stage that good technical backup is essential.

The company may have a technical director, a production manager, a network manager, a web master and technical assistants, or it may not. It is essential that any work on the project is properly backed up. The administration for the technical side of the project, such as registering software licences, general maintenance, chasing parts and creating backups, can be onerous.

You cannot assume that graphics artists and programmers will perform any administrative aspects unless these responsibilities are defined as part of their role. Depending on where they have worked, this might be considered normal or highly irregular. This is where a good definition of roles, responsibilities and general work practice pays off, because then no one makes any assumption. Very often, it is the assumption that someone else is doing something that suddenly provokes a crisis for the project manager.

The amount of technical support should increase according to the number and type of projects that the company has. If, however, your project warrants extra for the whole period or part of the time, this is yet another resource to nominate and budget for.

An interface design specialist

A GUI (graphical user interface) or HCI (human–computer interaction) specialist might be needed if and when the client demands a strong commitment to image and interface in the design proposal and development. This may arise as a reaction to criticism to an existing website, for example, or as a result of a major competitor adding a radical new look and feel to their website that has been received favourably by the users.

Often general graphics artists or interactive designers fulfil this function as part of their role and responsibilities but if the client wishes you to explain and show how the application will perform in terms of use according to the requirements of the end-users, a specialist will bring the right skill set to the team. The role of interactive designer has some overlap with these specialists but as the names imply, a GUI or HCI specialist brings more precise expertise to the cognitive and perceptive elements of interface design and will employ specialist techniques to test what works and what doesn't, in an effort to refine the interface to the needs of the users.

Scriptwriters

Many scriptwriters could form part of the video personnel team if their experience lies in writing video scripts. If video scriptwriters are employed, they tend to work with the director or producer. But multimedia scripts, as we have seen, can combine any variety of audio, video, interactive instructions, interactive design, and text. You might find one person to write all the scripts for the project, or you might have to employ several for the different parts. Your prime concerns are to:

- maintain quality across the scripts so that every media attribute is used to best effect;
- ensure consistency of style;
- check that there is correct adherence to the overall interactive design;
- keep the scriptwriters on track;
- make sure the scripts keep to the size and specifications worked out for each section;
- determine that each script is technically achievable in the time and budget.

The precise content can take time to determine, and this can sometimes form part of the writer's brief; at other times the subject experts, interactive designers and/or training analysts will work to decide which issues need to be addressed and then work with writers to produce the scripts. The whole area of scriptwriting is one of the least defined in multimedia and therefore one of the hardest tasks to control for the project manager. As each piece of script is addressed, there is a tendency for the writers to want to add and expand the original ideas beyond the scope of the budget or beyond the space allocated for the section, and this needs to be contained. Experience of working with interactive scripts helps writers to understand the new constraints that have to be taken into account, but if they have little experience you need to monitor them closely.

Prior to interview, you need to define a brief to direct the writers. The brief needs to cover the content treatment needed, the scope, style considerations, the audience profile, the company profile, and the timescales. The briefing documents should be written and include as much detail as possible so that there is no misunderstanding later. If there is an overall interactive design, sometimes called the high-level design, the writers should be briefed to explain where and how their piece fits into the overall design. A structure diagram proves invaluable when discussing the project with most of the personnel involved, and always helps scriptwriters. They will have a different approach if they know that they are not responsible for the whole program and will want to ensure that their piece fits the overall specification as well as the individual section brief.

If the writer is meant to take on a fuller role and produce the interactive design as well as the detailed scripts your brief will be different, and you will be checking for a more complex skill set. The type of application will direct the needs for designers and scriptwriters and the precise skills they should have. The script for an advertising agency's website, for example, would need to be very different from a medical education CD.

☐ Training specialist

As already discussed, training has its own approach to defining content and scripts, so if the project is a training application you need to make sure that it conforms to the principles of the discipline. The training specialists you recruit would need to have had experience in training needs analysis if you expect them to define the overall scope of the content. Their role may stop there and the scriptwriters could take over; or, if the training specialists have interactive experience, they may be able to take the project through the next stage of high-level design. They may possibly be capable of writing some or all of the scripts themselves. A lot depends on the application and the experience of the training specialist. So-called 'soft skills' such as assertiveness, leadership and counselling are harder to recruit for than other training areas. You should be looking for a fit, in experience of the content, a match with experience in training analysis for a similar audience, and experience in developing interactive or distance learning materials.

You may find that you need to pair a training specialist with an interactive designer, subject matter experts and scriptwriters at different stages of the content development. If the application is an in-house training program for a large firm, this mix of people would be quite common. If the training specialists were from the client company, and you had to utilize their skills, they might have little or no interactive experience. Then your role would be to recruit enough support staff around them to help achieve the right mix of skills needed for this part of the project.

In developing intranet, Internet and/or hybrid Web/CDs for training, the appreciation of the strengths and weaknesses of the media plus the attributes of the different levels of interactivity that figure in each delivery platform are paramount. The purpose of the training has to be balanced with the way the information is structured. The range and structure of the training information will be affected by considerations such as whether tutor support is built into the package via e-mail, videoconferencing or whatever.

You need to select people for your team who have worked across all forms of training so that they appreciate how to use each element best in the delivery mix. The breadth of skill is difficult to find, and so more than one training specialist might be needed; or a mix of training specialist with instructional designer/interactive designer – as defined below – might provide the solution.

☐ Instructional/interactive designer

One of the key skills you are trying to cover is that of interactive design. Because this is bound up with defining the sections of the content, the interface, and the routing or navigation paths through the material, it spans several of the roles: programming, graphics, scriptwriting, producer, and interactive design. Your programmer or graphics artist may well be experienced in producing the equivalent of a high-level design but not scripts to support it. They may on the other hand not be very experienced or happy in liaising with clients to extract the salient information, and prefer building to a specification that they are given.

An interactive designer takes on some or all of the responsibility of defining content plus specifying the high-level design, and probably can write some or all of the scripts. The fine detail of the interactive design has to be negotiated between all the core team members because they all have relevant input to help shape the decisions. In this way, an interactive designer might sometimes be part of the core team.

If one of your core team, including yourself, cannot fulfil the functions of interactive design, you should consider recruiting an instructional/interactive designer. Other roles will be able to script for text, audio and

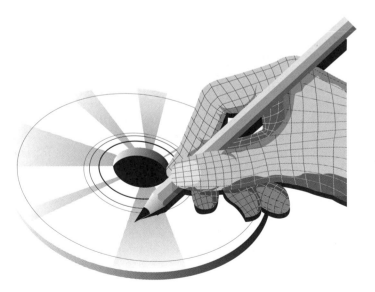

Interactive design.

video, but the 'Help' script for an offline application, which explains how the program works, may also include text, audio and video. This is often forgotten but is vital. It is unlike the other scripts in style and tone. It can be the key to a successful application. As applications are now more complex, the Help script is growing in size and importance. You need to determine whose responsibility it is to take care of this. Online applications can offer direct contact with people for support via the medium, but how this is set up and maintained can be a key decision for the content of the application. Finally, training programs will most likely expect some form of test or exam to check the performance increase in knowledge and skills of the person taking the training. Devising fair and valid questions for a piece of training is not an easy task. Too often this skill set is underestimated and undervalued. The range and type of questions needs to be aligned to the type of content and type of transfer of knowledge and/or skill. The restrictions of online bandwidth affect the ways of testing the transfer of knowledge and skills more than is realized. Because the growth of corporate universities and online training has increased so much, this skill set will gain in importance over the next few years.

Subject matter experts/personalities

Commercial applications tend to use a public figure because the name helps to sell the product. They may be experts in the field or have strong links to the subject. Sometimes, the experts will take an active part in the program by being in the video or doing some of the voice-over. Sometimes they might just endorse the application. On other occasions, they might help to define the content and check the scripts. There can be a pairing between training analysts, subject experts and instructional designers or combinations of these, as and when the project needs it.

It is important that you and your client are confident about the integrity of the content, so it is useful to tap into subject expertise. However, the more people that are involved in vetting scripts, the more problematic it becomes to stabilize them. The subject experts have to be given a clear brief of their roles and responsibilities in the project. If the experts are from the client company, they can influence the project strongly. They can cause havoc if they begin to stray out of their area of expertise into criticizing the interactive structure or the interface, for example.

Their advisory and critical role has to have strong boundaries drawn around it to allow the rest of the 'experts', the core team, to do their job effectively. You need to explain to the client that the experts' advice has to be put into the complete interactive context, and that when this happens some compromises may have to be made. This is more of a problem when the experts suggest complete new areas that need to be incorporated into the application too late for you to reconcile with time and cost.

Subject matter experts and personalities are quite easy to locate and recruit but their guaranteed allocation of time to the project is more of a problem. Your clients will often recommend their preferred experts. It is important that you explain how time-critical their input will be, and get a signed commitment. This applies for all types of project, on- and offline.

THEORY INTO PRACTICE 11

Allocating roles and responsibilities
The checklist at the end of the chapter covers many of the tasks that need to be performed during the interactive media project cycle.

Apply the list to your present or a past project by inserting the team's initials into the relevant boxes to see how the roles and responsibilities pan out. Put 'not applicable (n/a)' where appropriate. Beware any gaps, and ensure they are covered next time.

The listing can be useful during your pre-interview and interview stage. If you are going to use in-house resources, then you can map out their roles and responsibilities, indicate where 'not applicable' applies, and from the gaps that are left get a feel for the personnel you need to recruit and the tasks they will need to perform. You can then make a note of the skills that lie behind the tasks to get a skill profile for the people you need. This checklist would not be comprehensive for international projects where more tasks are used, but it could serve as a starting point for you to adapt if necessary. The checklist can also be found on our website.

■ Summary

- The project manager needs to identify the mix of skills necessary for the project and then assemble an appropriate core and extended team.

- Recruitment is not an easy exercise. It should be handled professionally with good preparation, briefing and role definitions.

- Knowledge of what roles exist and the contribution each can make to the project is important to help in decision making.

- Each role has its own range of skills and considerations. Careful assessment of the skill level needed has to be balanced with the project needs, budget constraints and management style.

- Clear assignment of responsibilities is necessary to ensure that all project tasks are covered. It is a good idea to list all the tasks and assign the person responsible for each as a check that all aspects have been covered.

TABLE 10.1 Project task and skill set checklist.

Client liaison	Initial(s)	Recruitment/selection general	Initial(s)
1. Attend meetings		1. Identify resource needs	
2. Write up meetings		2. Cost resources, align to budget	
3. Be the main telephone/fax/e-mail contact		3. Organize deskspace, equipment, etc	
4. Respond to queries		4. Organize appropriate CVs	
5. Organize sign-offs – proposal, contract, content, scripts, database		5. Select interviewees	
		6. Define roles and responsibilities	
		7. Write job description/criteria	
6. Handle scheduling		8. Define skill mix needed	
7. Monitor budget		9. Interview	
8. Handle disputes		10. Select appointees	
9. Inform on project status		11. Negotiate contracts	
10. Negotiate changes in time and cost		12. Negotiate with agencies	
		13. Induct new recruits to company	
		14. Induct new recruits to project	
Audio production	**Initial(s)**	**Stills/graphics production**	**Initial(s)**
1. Direction/production manager		1. Direction/production manager	
2. Scripts (main and Help)		2. Graphics production	
3. Organize studio facility		3. Picture researcher	
4. Organize recording/edit		4. Rights and clearances	
5. Organize translations		5. Electronic asset management	
6. Direct edit		6. Animation production	
7. Select voice-overs		7. Photgrapher	
8. Select/commission music		8. Lighting	
9. Negotiate rights and clearances		9. 3-D modeller	
10. Liaise with programmers/technical quality assurance, formats		10. Computer graphics	
		11. Scanner/digitizer	
11. Organize M & E tracks		12. Art director	
12. Organize encoding		13. Illustrator/artist	
13. Encode		14. Text/page layout	
14. Monitor and approve costs		15. Typography	

TABLE 10.1 (Cont)

Design and documentation	Initial(s)	Computer and integration	Initial(s)
1. Produce final contract agreement		1. Programmer/software engineer	
2. Carry out specialist analysis if necessary		2. Technical manager	
3. Produce technical specification		3. Network manager/webmaster	
4. Product outline/high-level specification/brief		4. Maintenance	
5. Research and define content blocks		5. Backup/archiving	
6. Research and define detailed content		6. Software librarian	
7. Produce interactive script – interface functions, Help script			
8. Liaise with subject experts			

Video production	Initial(s)
1. Direction/production manager	
2. Identify resources needed	
3. Cost resources, align to budget	
4. Organize recruitment	
5. Select interviewees	
6. Define roles and responsibilities	
7. Interview	
8. Recruit or delegate and recruitment	
9. Recruit: scriptwriters, camera, lights, sound, grips, make-up, continuity, catering, communications, logging, etc.	
10. Negotiate contracts	
11. Negotiate with agents	
12. Organize shoot (locations, props, etc.)	
13. Clear locations, liaise with police	
14. Cast artistes	
15. Organize facility houses/edits	
16. Recruit video graphics: 3-D animator, computer compositor, etc	
17. Direct edits	

TABLE 10.1 (Cont)

18. Edit offline
19. Edit online
20. Approve edits
21. Film/picture research
22. Clearances and rights (footage, pictures, music, voice-overs, etc.)
23. Liaise with programmers/technical quality assurance
24. Monitor and approve costs
25. Organize video encoding
26. Encode video

Database development	Initial(s)

1. Identification of data blocks
2. Link to information architecture
2. Collation of data
3. Verification of data
4. Liaison with clients
5. Integration into project
6. Indexer
7. Help script
8. Spell check and editing

Administration	Initial(s)

1. Typing
2. Filing
3. Answering/making phone calls
4. Collating personnel and project documentation
5. Sending and distributing faxes/ messages
6. Organize meetings, book rooms
7. Organize couriers, cars, post, etc.
8. Photocopying
9. Collect timesheets

■ Recommended reading

Belbin R.M. (1981). *Management Teams: Why They Succeed or Fail*. Oxford: Butterworth-Heinemann

Belbin R.M. (1993). *Team Roles at Work*. Oxford: Butterworth-Heinemann

De Marco T. and Lister T. (1987). *Peopleware: Productive Projects and Teams*. New York: Dorset House Publishing Co.

Honey P. (1988). *Improve Your People Skills*. London: Institute of Personnel Management

Katzenbach J.R. and Smith D.K. (1993). *The Wisdom of Teams: Creating the High-Performance Organization*. Boston, MA: Harvard Business School Press

Phillips N. (1992). *Managing International Teams*. London: Pitman Publishing

Raudsepp E. (1963). *Managing Creative Scientists and Engineers*. New York: Macmillan

Tjosvold D. (1992). *Team Organization: An Enduring Competitive Advantage*. Chichester: Wiley.

Testing

11

Project manager's responsibilities

- To match testing methods to the project
- To devise a testing strategy in conjunction with the team and the client
- To create enough time and budget for the testing to be carried out effectively
- To manage the acceptance testing process in order to get final sign-off for the project

■ Multimedia and testing

There is a good deal of confusion about testing and multimedia. Is testing really necessary? Does it have to be done by people outside the team? Should software testing techniques be applied to multimedia applications? How much does it cost? What's the value? … and this list can continue ad infinitum.

There is also fear of testing, probably linked to the dread of examinations from everyone's school years. It is a subject that is generally avoided in multimedia circles, but hopefully this chapter will show that it is essential to have a testing strategy for each project, and to make clients fully aware of the extent of the testing outlined in the strategy.

The confusion of terminology doesn't help either. Testing and evaluation are the main culprits. They are both to do with making improvements, which is why they are difficult to separate. However, the main difference appears to be that testing implies matching a prescribed set of quantifiable criteria against performance to find errors; evaluation is wider in that it is looking not for specific errors but for improvements to the design during development or when the program is finished. Validation is another term that causes confusion. The problem here is that the interpretation of the term changes depending on the context in which it is used. In evaluation, validation means checking that the methods used are ones that will provide the type of data that is wanted. If one of the needs specified is detailed user reaction to the concepts, it will be invalid to select internal testing alone as a test method, for example.

Testing data categories.

The subject of testing is complicated because there are so many types that can be applied at every stage of a project. Also, the mix of disciplines in multimedia means that different approaches to testing might be employed. Concept testing with focus groups, prototypes, peer review either within the project or with external review of the design documents, usability tests, field trials and acceptance tests are some of the varieties that could be employed.

The type of data collected with any of the processes veers between quantitative and qualitative, objective and subjective, formative and summative. There are arguments for and against all the different methods, and you will have to decide which approach serves the project's requirements, time, cost and quality constraints.

You need to become acquainted with the varieties so that you can devise a testing strategy that will serve your projects. You'll need to understand how to cost the different ways and also consider subcontracting the specialist forms of testing. This whole area can be a specialism in itself. You may have a specialist section in your company devoted to testing so get them to help define the strategy for the project.

As a brief introduction, the varieties mentioned above will be summarized, but it is worth your taking time to explore this area in greater depth with further reading.

☐ Concept testing

This approach comes from marketing. It means trying out the main project ideas on selected groups of people representative of the intended user group. The ideas may be presented in a paper walkthrough or through discussion. This is conducted very early on so it might be prior to any prototype stage of development although with web design it is easier to produce some mock-ups more quickly than with offline applications. The project may not have had complete agreement to proceed, and the findings from the concept groups may influence further agreement. A facilitator opens up discussion around the concepts, perhaps relating them to competitive products. The aim is to check whether the predicted reactions to the new product match the wishes of the users. This is done early in development so that the design can be adjusted in line with the findings, and so that there is more confidence that the intended direction will be successful. Concept testing is synonymous with focus groups. This is a commercial approach to checking out predictions about a product with prospective customers against competing products in the market. Increasingly, focus groups are being used online for websites/pages. The groups can access a special development site and then enter into discussion via a chat facility or forum – also online.

☐ Prototyping

This is derived from software development, and is a mock-up of several of the key features from the program. It is designed to get feedback on the general look and operation of the design as early as possible during development. The practice grew because of the mismatch between the expectations that the clients had from reading the formal specification documents and the reality of the way programs actually worked. This was often explained as the gap between written and visual understanding. The gap caused problems of redesign at a late stage in development, and was costly. Prototypes can also be used with users to gather their reactions to the main operations at a stage where changes in the design can be made efficiently.

With online projects if you set up a password-protected area of a website and put the new design ideas there, then it is easy for any authorized person to have a look and comment, and for you to gather and process the feedback. The ability of a web page to accept updates at any time can be both an advantage and a disadvantage. If you are to have an ongoing responsibility for the site then it is quite reasonable for certain decisions to be taken on the understanding that user feedback may modify them later. But if you are providing the client with something based on a template that they can maintain then this argument no longer applies. It is important to separate the two key elements of a website: the structure and design from the actual content. Some people will find it very easy to imagine a template with changing content but others will not. You could explain it to the client as being like the design of a newspaper or magazine, and so early prototypes of the website may have dummy content in them.

If the website is dynamic, and the web pages are built on demand by a server-side program from a database, for example, then it is likely that this program will be complex enough to need prototyping and testing in the same way as a CD-ROM application. An extra stage here could be offline prototyping followed by online prototyping and even stress testing to see how it performs under heavy use. Of course, a static website can be prototyped offline from a hard disk or CD-ROM, because there is no difference in the way the site performs in running a static site off disk than running it on the server, apart from download times. Adding server-side programming like CGIs to the site changes this because you have to put the site on a server for the CGIs to work, even if you have tested and debugged the CGI program on your computer. This means that a dynamic site may well need its own test server and performance testing before it is released to the client.

☐ Peer review

A faster approach to testing the concepts of design is to get colleagues to bring their experience to bear on them. As indicated, this is important because of the mix of skills needed in the multistrand design. However, this relies on prediction according to factors that have been identified, and prediction is not a science. Experience gives insight but multimedia is relatively young. External peer review can extend the range of experience and insights, particularly if the reviewers are selected for their experience in the respective multimedia application areas. The aim is to refine the design at an early stage to help faster development.

Usability tests

These used to be rigorous tests, usually applied when the project has been integrated and is ready for release. They originated in software development as a method of proving that the program met the needs of the users. In the past the tests were carried out in specially adapted usability laboratories that simulate the places where the users will operate the application. The users might be monitored electronically with cameras, microphones and records of key-presses. They might be observed through two-way mirrors. The very large amount of data collected is analysed to determine where and why the users experienced difficulty so that redesign can take place. Multimedia projects do not usually employ usability tests to the extent of computing application testing, but research projects where data on user reactions is needed, or market-led projects such as applications that are meant to sell products, may have some requirement to apply these rigorous methods for market research.

However, now it is becoming more common to carry out user tests in less formal circumstances with small groups drawn from the target group and try out particular aspects of look and feel and ease of use on prototype sites. This helps companies relate to the market segment and build their knowledge about what works with whom and why. The smaller scale trials with some users are more akin to evaluation and refinement during production than testing but the line drawn between evaluation and testing is often confused, as already indicated.

Heuristic evaluation is also a less formal approach to usability testing that is being used more. This involves a small group of experienced evaluators who use the site individually and comment on its usability. The evaluators confer with one another after they have used the site then report the difficulties they find. The heuristic nature of the evaluation is based on applying general rules that seem to describe common properties of usable interfaces. This is a quick and efficient way of finding the deficiencies of an interface. (See the Nielsen reference at the end of the chapter for more on this form of evaluation.)

Field trials

Here the application is tested *in situ* with the users. They are observed and interviewed. There are a number of different methods of observation and interview that can be employed. The users may also be required to fill in questionnaires. The data is collated and analysed, and the recommendations for redesign are given. Again, this is not as common with multimedia as with software applications, but in some cases, such as accredited multimedia training programs, the accreditation body might need to see that the application conveyed the correct level of information with a certain number of trial users. Some retail applications might also require proof of use in the field.

Less formal and smaller field trials are also being used particularly for web applications for the same reasons as the less formal user tests mentioned above.

☐ Acceptance testing

If there is a clear specification of what is required, then testing can be carried out to prove that the application conforms to the requirements. This relates more to the operation and functional performance of the code, and is derived from software development.

We are going to concentrate on developmental and acceptance testing as they indicate categories of test related to the stage of the project rather than specific methods that will have to be agreed with your clients. Developmental testing means the numerous checks that are carried out during the course of development to ensure that each part of the project meets its specifications. Many software developers have come to use the terms 'alpha test' and 'beta test' in the same sense as developmental and acceptance tests are defined here. These are referred to in the integration chapter (Book 2 Chapter 9), since that is concerned with the influences from software development. This chapter tries to provide an umbrella for all the issues of testing that can be met during projects by amalgamating insights and methods from different disciplines.

■ What is testing?

Testing means examining the project performance according to the specifications that have been agreed. This will include the robustness of the code or compatibility of the website across different browsers, the structure and content of the program or website, the interface, the interactivity, the performance of the program or site under specific conditions, the look and feel and perhaps accessibility issues. It is obvious once stated that unless you have the specifications agreed, you cannot prove that your application passes the final test. You will not be able to draw a line to show that you have completed the contractual agreements. The lack of understanding of what constitutes completion of the application is a risk that you need to control to ensure that final sign-off runs smoothly.

☐ Developmental testing

Another point that is self-evident once stated is that testing the program against specifications is a continuous process during development. Each of the sign-offs that have been suggested is part of the process: the overall

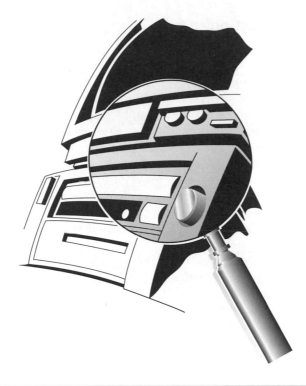

Testing = examining aspects of performance.

structure, text, audio and video scripts, the audio and video edits, the look of the graphics, the look and feel of the navigation. This is not always recognized as being part of the testing process, but it is. A lot of evaluation occurs during project development. Each of the people on the team is concerned to produce a professional product, so they care about their own performance. If it is a good team, they'll monitor each other's performance in a constructive way. But however much they pool their expertise to predict how the users will react and how the code should operate, there will always be weaknesses.

Many of the weaknesses will be spotted and corrected. Some will be noticed and left alone. This might appear to be a strange admission, and you will not find it stated in much of the literature, but it will be true of the majority of projects. Some design errors will be impossible to change because of the repercussions on the whole of the rest of the project. They need to be spotted early in the project to avoid effects on other parts of the application. Sometimes clients insist on certain features that you know will be detrimental in release. (See an example of this in Chapter 14, *Team management principles*, where an executive causes drastic changes to a video sequence.)

☐ Acceptance testing

Sometimes design defects become apparent only in use. One or two factors might show up where what appeared logical from past experience does not apply well in new circumstances. The main problem in trying to get final sign-off is to find what is acceptable for both parties. This can be any point on a scale between 'impossible to use' and 'perfection'. Even the most frequently used and maintained programs, such as word processing software, undergo evolution from the first release to maturity and beyond. Sometimes they are released with a statement as to 'known bugs'. Complex multimedia applications will naturally be able to sustain improvement if there is a proper allocation for an improvement cycle. Now, this is not granting the right for developers to abdicate their responsibility for the quality of the delivered product. It is just trying to establish what is fair and equitable in an unsettled set of circumstances.

The program has to operate without failing. That is the first standard that will not be disputed by both parties. This will drive the acceptance test. But even this becomes problematic. We know of at least three projects where a bug in third-party code in the development software had a severe knock-on effect on the operation of an application. This is actually more likely to occur with offline multimedia because the limited level of code use may not have found all the bugs. This means that the more obscure problems in code occur even when software has been around for some time and appears stable. General use in a new set of circumstances will tease them out. For websites the amount of use is important and difficult to predict. The numbers of users might overload the system, cause the site to slow down or cause some functions to stop working. Load testing and stress-testing of the site may become necessary and in some cases the site will need to be given to a specialized test facility for this. You need to predict and cost the extent of these forms of testing if your client wants them. You may have to convince the client that these are necessary because of the type of site they are building.

HTML is a fairly simple form of code, but different web browsers will interpret the code differently, and it is practically impossible to test web pages on every combination. It is highly unlikely that a bit of poor HTML will crash a machine, but it can make the web page unreadable on one browser but seem fine on another. Unfortunately it is possible for a legal web page to crash a browser. We met a problem whereby a client's website was crashing Netscape online. The problem did not show up when the site was viewed off a disk, and Internet Explorer was unaffected. The problem hit both PCs and Macs. To add to this curious situation the problem appeared after the site had been running happily for several months without change. The bug was finally traced to an innocent-looking background GIF graphic file, and it was replaced.

Perhaps the most common 'bug' on a web page is the broken link. This could be a link to a graphic, and is most likely to happen if the graphic is not in the site being built. It could be an advertisement, for example. Similarly, any links to other sites can change, and although this is a maintenance issue rather than a developmental one, the client needs to be aware that it can happen and it needs policing by someone, or by some program.

With a website, any CGI programs will, again, need testing just as in an offline project. An added problem is that the risk of incorrect input from a user is greater on the Web. The chance of a hacker trying to break your code or get into your site is small, but it exists, and you should make sure that your code traps erroneous inputs coming in through the environment variables that pass parameters to CGI or other server-side programs. You might use JavaScript to validate a form before it is submitted.

You can find tools to check web pages on line: some you download but some you just point at your site and they will report back. At one level there are the validators, of which the grand-daddy is WebLint. A validator will read through a web page and give an output saying where there are errors and most validators can be configured to set the level of rigour required. As well as validators there are sites that will check your web pages to see how efficient they are and offer you suggestions about reducing download times.

What happens when a bug is found in a finished and delivered application? Is it your responsibility? Is it the client's? Is it the original developer's? Here, your own developers fall foul of the problems that others face in trying to reach perfection in software. Remember to include a limited liability clause in your contract to cover this risk. See Chapter 9, *Contract issues 2*.

Defects in the program will range in severity, knock-on effects and frequency. You need to identify the problems, the severity and the effects on the robustness of the program. This will include correcting any data that is wrong, whether it is a typing error, words in the wrong place, text layout and so on, as well as code defects – wrong sequence, failure to operate a navigation path, or corrupted screens, for example. Your aim is to present an application that will work efficiently and perform correctly within a span of correct use. If the specification did not mention it needed to be 'hacker' proof, you do not have a responsibility to test it under the most extreme circumstances. However, users do have a knack of using programs in ways that are not logical. So a span of unexpected use should be tried out as well as expected normal use.

All these points should indicate that acceptance levels should be specified in advance, and that testing has to be systematic and thorough to prove robustness across a span of use.

The test phase is cyclical: developmental refinement occurs to ensure each sign-off stage. The assembly of all the parts according to agreement leads up to integration of the pieces and acceptance testing. This sounds as though there should not be too much to do at the end, if all the pieces have been approved. That is rarely so with multimedia because the integration can have repercussions on previously agreed pieces.

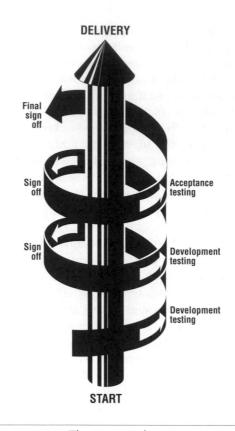

DELIVERY

Final sign off

Sign off

Acceptance testing

Sign off

Development testing

Development testing

START

The test cycle.

For example, the size of text approved in isolation may be illegible because of encoding deterioration, overpowering graphics near it and so on. The colours may shift and in turn affect the legibility of text or clarity of the graphics. A module that worked perfectly on its own may fall over when you try to activate it from a subroutine. The development platform might be different from the delivery platform specification, and someone might have overlooked some of the issues of transfer from one to the other.

A website can be fully tested only when it is up and running on its own server under the anticipated load of accesses. This assumes that you have already tested the interaction between static HTML and dynamic server-side programs, together with such extras as how a submission form might send e-mails. Don't forget that some parts of the picture – the server itself and the mailing program – may not be under your control at all if the site is being hosted by an ISP.

Systematic testing has to be done once all the parts are assembled and integrated. A testing plan should be drawn up to ensure that all paths will be explored and all data checked for accuracy, that all interactivity operates as expected, that the right data appears in the right sequence, and that any records that the user builds up during use are faithful and accurate. Each application will have its own features, so these are examples of the more generic aspects that might need systematic testing.

If an application is complex, and extensive use will be made of it by a range of users, then it becomes more important to use one or more testers from outside the team at acceptance testing. During production, the team will have developed patterns of use for themselves based on their experience of the project. It becomes increasingly difficult for them to predict use from a naive perspective. An external, experienced tester will help to draft a test specification to simulate a variety of experience while checking the accuracy of all the data. It will be necessary to use formal test sheets to keep records of the errors and the sequence of actions that caused them, and to have some code of severity to help decide where correction time will be best deployed. Then, because each error needs to be retested to prove that it has been corrected successfully, the person who corrects it should initial and date the correction and the retest should be initialled and dated. See the sample acceptance test report sheet.

The sheet may seem over-bureaucratic, and it should be adapted or discarded depending on the type of project at the discretion of the project manager and depending on the level of testing required by the client. For more complex projects the sheets can help because there is a tendency for revisions to the code to cause knock-on effects. Retest after retest can take place, gradually whittling away the errors. Because there are retests, it is easy to work on the wrong version, so dating and version numbering become more important. See Book 2 Chapter 9, *Integration*, for a further explanation of version control.

■ What is a testing strategy?

A testing strategy sounds complicated but it isn't. It means stating in writing what measures will be taken to ensure that the final program meets the client's requirements. This will include noting the number and type of sign-off stages, the responsibilities of the team members to meet the technical and functional requirements at each stage, the analysis of the users if applicable, a peer review process if applicable, the building and trialling of a prototype if necessary, and whatever other methods you decide to employ during the development stages.

The developmental testing is part of the testing strategy. You can indicate that prior to and around sign-off points for the project, the team will be testing to ensure that each part of the application meets the specification that has been agreed for sign-off.

If you have agreed to carry out any of the specific tests that occur early in the project, such as focus groups and prototyping, these will form part of the development testing strategy.

TABLE 11.1 Sample acceptance test report sheet.

Project name:	Version number:	Programmer's name
Tester's name:		Date:
Retester's name:		Date:
Machine no./spec.		Platform description

No.	Error description	Priority code	Programmer's comments	Status: Fixed/ Left	Initials	Date	Retest status	Initials	Date

The acceptance test description should be as detailed as you can make it so that it is clear when your team have discharged their responsibilities. If you have had to build a multimedia presentation for an executive, it is straightforward for the individual concerned to try it out and approve it. But if you have a website application with items for sale to the general public, then it can be time-consuming to collect the data to prove its usability prior to release. It is relatively easy to collect the data once the site is live but the feedback will drive adjustments. If you haven't agreed that the adjustments arising from use are post-project and subject to extra costs, you'll find that the client refuses to give final sign-off and effectively gets free updating in the name of the original project.

You may decide that one internal round of testing: record error, resolve error and recheck until satisfied, will be enough. Alternatively you may decide on this and then an external round of testing, perhaps done by nominee(s) from the client company and/or by external testers. Your decision will be based on the complexity of the project, the time and cost of the testing agreed, and the wishes of the client.

Any of the specific tests such as usability and the use of an external tester that occur in the latest stages of the project will form part of the acceptance testing strategy.

A word of warning here about nominees from the client company: often they will ask several others to try the program out and even set up a small sample of use with the target audience. This is acceptable only if that is exactly what you understood was going to happen. If the client expands the testing specification spontaneously then the odds increase against their signing off.

The wider the acceptance testing, the more likely it is that insights about the users will emerge and point towards design rather than code changes. This is normal in emerging fields where user reaction and use are guessed at. This is why small sample user tests are becoming more commonly used as a means of redressing the uncertainty. Unless clients are prepared to pay for these, they need to accept that their application may not be perfect in every detail but that you have faithfully tried to achieve the best given the constraints. Both you and the client will learn from the process, and will be able to assess the user needs better for future applications based on the actual reactions. Until multimedia markets have matured, and sound analysis of user likes and dislikes has been carried out, this will be the situation. It is unfair of the client to expect more, so you need to state and re-state their responsibilities and the risks that they are taking, and spell out the possible consequences.

You can agree that all text will be spelt correctly and that the screen layouts will conform to the agreed specification. You can agree that the program will function as specified, save for code errors in third-party software and hardware. You can agree that the final product will be tested for robustness according to a testing plan that will ensure that all functional paths are tried and that a normal span of use, accounting for some differences in the users, will be tried out. This might specify the automatic web tests that you

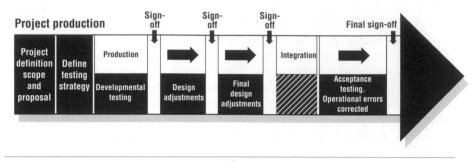

Stages of testing.

will apply and what they cover. All these would constitute an acceptance test strategy that both your team and the client would find acceptable.

So, it is prudent to explain in the strategy plan that the stage for picking up *design* defects is during development, and *operational* errors are the main focus of the acceptance phase of testing. If the client is concerned to refine the design you can offer several alternatives during the development stage, such as a prototype trial, but it must be the client's decision to bear any time and cost implications or sacrifice adjustments to the design. If this is clearly stated and agreed, you will have done your duty both to your client and to the team so that the level of expectations is set. For example, if there was no agreement for a user trial with end-users, and then modifications to the application are made on the results, any request for this would clearly form an extension of the original project in terms of time and cost.

Prediction of use can be based on experience, but actual use will differ. Unless user testing and redesign have been part of the project specification, your part of the contract is to use your knowledge and experience to guess use. The client acts on the users' behalf to vet your specification. If there is no needs analysis as such built into the project plan, the client's responsibility is to act on their users' behalf in good faith, to allow a proper user trial, or to accept tests designed just to test the robustness of the application.

Your testing strategy should be written up as part of your detailed contract documents, and should be alluded to in the scoping document.

Very often the cost of extensive testing and redesign is left out of a multimedia project specification because to do them properly adds so much to the nominal cost of development that a developer fights shy of them. At the very least, the testing time risks being eaten into by overruns. This is more true of offline than of online developments. Multimedia is still a difficult market, so any means of pruning project costs is used to arrive at a proposal cost that will make it competitive. But to ignore this completely by pretending that the development stages of multimedia run smoothly is, in the great majority of cases, unrealistic. The final sign-off will then stand more risk of getting into a never-ending loop.

This can cause dreadful problems for a project manager just at the time that everything seemed to be sewn up. Some projects spin out of control right at the final stage, mainly because of readjustments. The client refuses to sign off until these are completed; the developer is certain the adjustments are extras that should be paid for. Small adjustments can be absorbed, but often there will be one or two seemingly small changes that have large repercussions. It is also likely that your team will be in the process of being disbanded or reallocated onto other projects at this stage, so it becomes far more problematic to implement even small changes.

It is at this point that decisions taken early in the project acquire significance. Did you suggest a structured testing plan as part of the project plan? Did you suggest user trials with prototypes? Did the client reject it? Did they understand the significance of saving money on these items at this time? Did you explain?

If you take the time to plan the testing strategy at the beginning of the project and, if necessary, refine it with your client during development, mindful of time and cost factors, it will pay dividends at final sign-off.

■ Insights into software testing

Acceptance testing in multimedia is the closest to pure software testing because it addresses the code underlying integration. Some of the problems, such as third-party software bugs and corruption of data that was stable, have been mentioned, but some of the insights from pure software testing should be noted.

Testing is a black hole, and the project manager cannot accurately predict how much time and effort it will take to make the program robust. Usually, the deadline for how much time can be devoted to it will be forced on the team by the amount left prior to the release date or handover date to the client. This is why it becomes important to define the priority of defects so that best use can be made of whatever time is left.

There are problems inherent in the nature of changing code, and effectively this is what happens when the programmer addresses the errors found in tests. There is a 20–50% chance of introducing another error. So it is possible for retested code to end up displaying more errors than on first testing. This is not automatically a reflection on the programmer. Testing is like diagnosis; it spots defects that can be symptoms. The programmer may ease the irritation but may not cure the main infection. Other symptoms can then occur that, when studied, show a coding problem that may warrant extensive rework.

Experienced programmers recognize that the more original code is changed, the more likely it is that the integrity of the overall logic will suffer and break down. Another lesson from their experience shows that there are different ways of treating errors. You might be asked if you will take the risk on a 'patch' or 'quick fix', or negotiate an extension from the client, because to address the error in depth might jeopardize the delivery date. You will have to take the decision.

It will help if you recognize that despite the acceptance test being the final test phase for the project, it is the first full test for the integration. So, in effect, the integration stage has a development stage of its own where it needs time to shape up. Depending on the complexity of the application, you should create enough time and space in your project plan for a few test cycles. You might decide to call the first cycle 'integration testing' to allow the recognition that this is the first chance to address the robustness of the integrated code, and then call the retest 'acceptance testing'.

Testing and error correction have traditionally been handed over to more junior programmers. There are dangers in doing this, and you need to make sure that your original programmers are involved to the end of the project. It has been found that other programmers don't have the overview of the project, and therefore address the errors in isolation. They cannot link the symptoms to a main cause as effectively as the original code writers. Fixing errors can therefore take longer for them. Also, there is more likelihood of the introduction of new errors from inconsistencies between the original programmer's code and the new code.

It should be evident that the end of the project is a vulnerable time for the project manager. There are pressures from the team, the client, and the management. These are over and above the pressures from the diminishing time and budget factors.

■ Final sign-off

If the acceptance test is prespecified and understood by all parties, then final sign-off will follow smoothly. It is important to have this agreement in writing just as with other sign-offs. This will act as the end of the responsibilities of you and your team to the client so that final payment can be claimed.

Your specification for the acceptance test can form the basis for the components listed for sign-off but you should add a sentence or two stating that this sign-off concludes the project and that your company has carried out all its obligations according to the agreements.

THEORY INTO PRACTICE 12

Which of the symptoms of a poorly defined testing strategy have you known? Tick all that apply.

1. Clients asking for extras before final sign-off. ☐
2. Clients refusing to sign off the project. ☐
3. Poor version control reintroducing errors that had been corrected. ☐
4. Never-ending testing and error correction cycles. ☐
5. Little testing done because the project ran out of time. ☐
6. No original programmers left to correct errors. ☐

Are you clear now on how to avoid these problems in your next projects?

■ Summary

- Multimedia does not have a strong tradition of testing. Web development is beginning to develop a clearer relationship with the methods of testing from other disciplines.

- There are many forms of testing. Each has its strengths and weaknesses in relation to the needs of an application.

- The project manager has to balance the needs of the application with time and cost factors to devise a testing strategy.

- The client has to agree to the strategy in the full knowledge of what it includes and what it excludes so there are no last-minute recriminations.

- Developmental testing is the combination of sign-offs of the completed parts of the project as well as the natural refinement of the individual assets during the development process.

- Acceptance testing takes place at the final stage of the project to predefined criteria specified in the testing strategy. The integrated code is tested, and the robustness of the project is scrutinized.

- Final sign-off agrees that the team has met its responsibilities and that the application performs as specified.

■ Recommended reading

Brooks F.P. Jr (1995). *The Mythical Man-Month. Essays on Software Engineering*, 2nd edn. Reading, MA: Addison-Wesley

Dumas J.S. and Redish J.C. (1994). *A Practical Guide to Usability Testing*. Norwood, NJ: Ablex Publishing Corporation

Humphrey W.S. (1990). *Managing the Software Process*. Reading, MA: Addison-Wesley

Nguyen H.O. (2000) *Testing Applications on the Web: Test Planning for Internet-Based Systems*, New York: John Wiley & Sons

Patton R. (2001) *Software Testing*. Indianapolis, IN: Sams Publishing

Splaine S. (2001) *The Web Testing Handbook*. Orange Park, FL: Software Quality Engineering

Web Testing Tools and Resources

The WebLint website is at http://www.weblint.org, but the code has not been updated since late 1997. WebLint is a Perl script written by Neil Bowers.

The Software QA and Testing Resource Center website (run by Rick Hower since November 1996) has a range of resources and information on testing. This includes a set of links to testing and validating tools at http://www.softwareqatest.com/qatweb1.html

http://www.netmechanic.com has a range of web-tuning pages including their famous GifBot which will scour your pages and shrink the (data) size of your graphics for you.

One HTML validator can be found on a website run by the Web Design Group at http://www.htmlhelp.com/tools/validator/

Two useful Cascading Style Sheet validators are at http://jigsaw.w3.org/css-validator/ and http://www.htmlhelp.com/tools/csscheck/

HTML and sometimes JavaScript can also be checked in tools like Dreamweaver and GoLive. JavaScript can be debugged in Netscape by typing just the word *javascript* in the input bar at the top of the window. This opens a JavaScript window that gives bug feedback as JavaScript runs in the browser.

12

Archiving

Project manager's responsibilities

- To build into the schedule enough time to archive effectively
- To carry out any company policies for archiving projects
- To rationalize all documentation, assets and budget information

■ Archiving: the rationale

If the project has been a large-scale production then there are lots of ends that need to be tidied up. This can seem like bureaucracy running amok, but once you have been caught out by clients requesting individual graphics from their application for marketing purposes, clients returning after several months to do an update that had never been mentioned, your colleague wanting to see the budget breakdown to help in costing another similar project, another colleague wanting the name of the voice-over artiste and agent, your management dealing with an enquiry from the corporate client company's inspectorate about exactly who had signed off the content in the project a year earlier, an enquiry from the musicians' union about the 15 seconds of a record used, a museum insisting that they are one slide short and claiming four months' penalty fees, and so on, then the value of the time put into archiving in a structured way pays for itself.

Chaotic archiving.

■ What needs to be archived?

Companies may have their own policies for archiving their projects. Many have different systems and locations for storing text, audio tapes, videotapes, code and graphics. There will be different versions of the assets from

Successful archiving.

different stages of the project, and during production you will have held on to them all because quite frequently you revert to parts of an earlier version as the project progresses. Keeping the different versions also allows you to keep a check on how much is changing and whether you could absorb the time and cost or need to renegotiate.

Once the project has received final sign-off, all the assets need to be sorted to ensure cover in all aspects for any further requests. This is an onerous task, which usually falls on the project manager and/or admin assistant as the only ones left working on the project. If no archive check-list is provided by the company it will be in your interest to draft one, because it is easy to forget one or two major items.

You need to make sure that you have scheduled enough time for yourself to archive the project after final sign-off. It will take three to four days of initial administration for a commercial, large-scale project. The amount of text material that will have been generated might fill most of one filing cabinet. You may have electronic folders of text files representing the final web page scripts, drawers full of content documents that helped in constructing the final text scripts, several versions of graphics that led to the final graphics files, a few boxes full of videotapes, copies of the master tapes, voice-over tapes, music tapes, photos, slides, or a stack of CD-ROMs, zip disks or whatever, from testing! You will be pressured to get the graphics and code off the development system to free space for other projects.

So it will help to have a systematic approach to archiving. Now electronic archiving of the texts, including e-mails and formal agreements, budget information, graphics versions and so on, is commonplace. However, there may still be papers and CDs with material from other sources or agencies (museums or music samples) that originated away from you but are part of the production process. You'll need to consider what to do with these and where they are stored.

The company may have defined a set way of capturing the final version of the project – like putting a website copy onto a CD that is then archived with the other pieces of the project or stored separately in a safe for fire protection and security. If there are several places where different parts of the project are archived, it will be wise to have a cross-referencing system of some type.

Archiving of projects is becoming an accepted way of working. (See the references at the end of the chapter to articles on Bulldog's website about companies migrating to complete multimedia archiving systems.) If asset management systems and content management systems are used, they are taking care of some of the archiving aspects of certain types of projects but not others.

As the range and type of projects varies so much, a project manager should know what the company expects archived across all projects and then devise some subsections of extra considerations might apply for other projects.

Formal documents

These will include all contractual documents, such as the final proposal document, any terms and conditions agreed as per the firm's policy, any agreement to ways of working, all sign-off documents for the intermediate stages, and the final sign-off. They should also include all confidentiality agreements from the team members if this was a condition accepted from the client. Copies of all signed contracts drafted for subcontractors or freelancers should be held with the formal documents. All rights agreements for the text, video, audio and graphics assets should be sorted and filed accordingly. You'll need an index of what the files contain for quick access later. Finally, a list showing where assets such as video master tapes, audio tapes, and code backups are being held is necessary for a full formal record to be complete.

Scripts and assets

Text copies of the final scripts for all the components should be held with their electronic files. This will mean sorting out the versions and updating any of the scripts with the inevitable last-second changes that were probably written in on copies. All assets that belonged to the client should be returned. Make a list for the archive files and date it showing exactly what was returned and when.

If you had to use external assets from picture libraries or museums then a similar list should have been compiled for those. Many of them should have been returned and recorded during the course of the project but there are often quite a few of the more important ones left over in case they were needed again. Whoever was managing the rights and clearances for the project should have made good records showing what has been returned and what is outstanding and why.

The company may have a policy to recycle video and audio tapes for other projects, or may choose to archive them as well. The masters may well be held off-site for security purposes so these will need to be clearly marked in an appropriate way for easy identification later if necessary. There may be packaging guidelines for off-site storage that you need to conform to. Wherever audio, video, graphics and code are held, you need to make sure that their location and date of transfer are recorded for the formal set of documents.

Budget information

During the project you will have been monitoring the actual time and cost against the predicted time and cost as stipulated in the final proposal agreement. These are important records, so detailed files are essential. If your finance department has been collating the team's timesheets against tasks or sign-off points, and costing according to the internal and external rates you gave them, then you should already have a file with their information. They should be able to provide you with a detailed copy for the complete project soon after final sign-off. However, for many reasons this rarely seems to happen, so often you have the best understanding of exactly where the project stands in relation to the actual expenditure. Record your understanding.

You need to rationalize the details that you hold with those that the finance section holds. For example, you will have the detailed breakdown of numbers of assets cleared from each source, so it may be easier for you to arrive at a final cost for asset rights' clearances than the accounts section. A lot depends on the accounting system in place and how it records project components. You will then be able to match your figures against the projected figures to get the final picture. You should have been on top of this type of equation all through the project, so that refining the information should be relatively easy.

It is a good idea to write a budget report to put with all this information comparing the predicted and actual spend and the predicted and actual time spent. It will help you for future projects, as well as colleagues and the management, if you indicate the reasons for any overspend in any section or any extra time incurred.

It is easy to forget the causes of problems on a project, but they will help you to become better at predicting time and costs on other projects and to make sharper decisions about risk factors. Some of the factors may point towards organizational issues that should be resolved by management to help all projects to run more smoothly, as well as some showing where you yourself might improve.

The time record systems and therefore staff project spend information are becoming integrated into improvements to standard software packages. Electronic timesheet systems are more common now, and the tasks for each staff member can be pulled into the project plan to update on certain aspects of the project's progress. It is as well to keep track of these developments as there is a point when the saving on admin against the cost of a system will make sense even for a small company.

■ Closing the project

Once all the archiving is in place, all assets have been returned if required, and your work area is probably the tidiest it has been since you started the project, then the project is properly finished. If you don't take the responsibility to do all this at the end, you will find that the project can haunt you as the small requests from all quarters become harder to implement. You will have lost interest in the project, and your own understanding of the files will fade quickly.

Many organizations do not pay enough attention to archiving. You may need to fight to justify the time as legitimate for building into the schedule at the beginning, but it is in your interest. You need to bear in mind that by the end of the project you'll probably hate it, and just want to finish at all costs. It takes mental stamina to persevere with archiving, particularly when your other team members have moved on to more interesting things.

■ Summary

- Spending a few days archiving at the end of a project has good payback even in the short term. Fight for time in the schedule if necessary.
- Archiving is a neglected area. Employ the company's policy if one exists or define and use one yourself.
- A systematic approach to archiving projects will benefit both you and the company.
- File and index all formal documents together.
- Sort out the final versions of all scripts. Return all assets; list and date the returns.
- Trace, list and store all internal assets – video masters, audio tapes, and so on.

■ Gather all relevant budget data together. Write a report on the project management aspects of the project and learn from it for future projects.

■ Recommended websites

http://www.bulldog.ca
  Bulldog addresses digital content management including archiving through its software product. The comprehensive features suit the needs of international media companies but the approach embedded in their system is applicable to smaller companies' projects too. Look at the white papers and a description of their software features.

http://www.rational.com/index.jsp
  Rational has a suite of programs that integrate the project management process and therefore archive many of the pieces of the process across the software team members. Coming from the software development side, it addresses larger e-business solutions.

http://www.macromedia.com/software/sitespring
  Macromedia's Sitespring product offers a set of tools that helps a team leader manage teams and clients. It automatically archives some of the communication and sign-off points, among many other features.

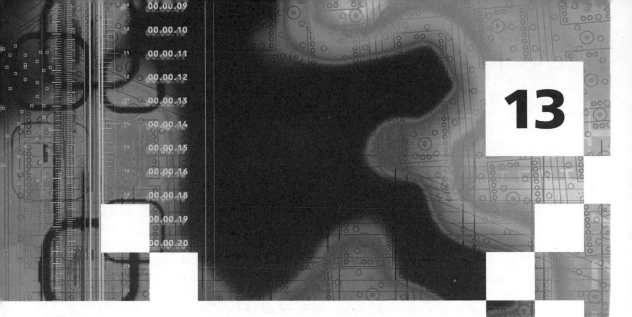

Managing small, quick projects

Project manager's responsibilities

- Not to underestimate the need for using clearly-defined processes
- To recognize that these projects share many of the same stages as larger projects but need to be produced faster
- To realize that processes minimize business risks
- To acknowledge that the time pressure in these projects can drive decisions
- To recognize that small projects can grow into large projects if the clients are satisfied

■ Putting this chapter in context

This chapter stands alone. It is not part of the detailed project management life cycle that has been covered in Chapters 3–12. It has been written to address the needs of multimedia developers who work in circumstances where high-pressured and relatively short turnaround projects predominate. This profile is found more often in smaller companies but is not exclusive to them. These developers want a quick way to relate to project management principles to see if these can be applied to their advantage under their conditions.

With this particular audience in mind, this chapter condenses many of the main principles found in the preceding chapters and streamlines the process to suit the smaller number of people involved in production and the shorter timescale of their multimedia projects. If you, as one of these readers, find you want further explanation, you will be able to go to the more specific chapters in Chapters 3–12, as indicated in the text.

Although designed principally for the readership described above, this chapter can also act as a quick summary of the preceding chapters for the general readership. The main principles are encapsulated into a mini life cycle. There is one important item to note that is new here. This chapter gives more prominence to the business practices underlying the use of project management principles than the main life cycle does because the business risks for small companies are higher. For the general readership then, it will emphasize a different perspective and will be useful for this aspect too.

■ The smaller new media project life cycle

This chapter takes the stance that small projects are still projects and good management is still essential. In many ways, small, quick projects are harder to bring in on time and on budget. They are often performed under stringent time constraints and place the people involved under a good deal of pressure. This chapter looks at the development process taken by a small company when a client approaches them with a project. The approach used here has lessons for other forms of project initiation – the tender process or idea/proposal submission for an in-house project, for example, but this chapter is optimized for the smaller company producing shorter, smaller-scale, client-driven projects.

Some people are critical of the idea of using project management techniques for small projects. They believe that to use them will waste so much time in written work and administration that there will be no time left to get on with production. They think that project management processes are onerous and unnecessary in small projects and are not appropriate. In many ways these perspectives fail to recognize that the principles of project management can be (and often are) applied without the participants being aware of them. If you don't have to generate key documents from scratch for example, but use them as checklists, they can speed up client-facing processes. If there are some 'fill in the gap' templates for key admin processes, this can speed up the process too. More things can be 'carried in your head', passed on verbally to your team or noted down in very few sentences because there are fewer staff involved and easier communication channels between you. Overall, there is less admin and less volume of documentation. But in practice all the tasks need to be done to minimize the risks to your business. Without the key processes in place your business is at risk. We are going to stress the business link to project management more strongly in this chapter than in the general life cycle model because of the increased risks to smaller companies.

In scoping a small new media project you still have the same aim as a larger one – to interpret what your client wants, map this to the capabilities and constraints of a technology system, define what you can produce in a certain timescale for a certain amount of money and work out how you will do it.

It is true that some clients know exactly what they want and articulate their needs clearly. Then your project can begin cleanly and the production process should run smoothly. However, because the range of technology solutions and the variety of functionality available keep mutating, it is no wonder that many clients are unsure of their direction and how the solutions can serve them. They actually want the equivalent of consultancy and advice from you without recognizing this. Because they don't really recognize or rate the advice as consultancy, they expect it to be free. You are prepared to give a certain amount free but the more time and advice you give freely the more money your company is losing.

So what is the difference between small and large projects? Smaller projects usually mean smaller amounts of money will be involved with shorter timescales for development. This will probably mean that your client will not be receptive to having a paid analysis stage to determine precisely what is expected. As explained in Chapter 3, this paid analysis phase is becoming more common across all types of new media project. Experience shows that getting clients to be precise about their needs in terms of what a technology solution can provide is one of the most difficult parts of the project. This leaves you vulnerable. It is difficult to know at the beginning of a project if it will involve a lot or a little effort to define the scope. In the end it comes down to how much you will do to interpret the client's needs for nothing, or whether you indicate clearly the point at which you will begin charging for the time and effort to define what the project really entails. Only then, once you have this understanding, can you say what you will offer to produce for a price. If the client then wants extras or differences over and above your offer, you can re-negotiate the price accordingly.

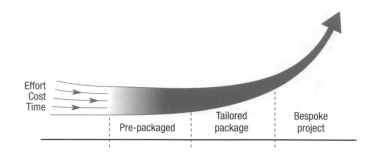

Effort
Cost
Time

Pre-packaged | Tailored package | Bespoke project

The scoping scale for time and effort.

The 'scoping scale' as shown above is a summary of cost versus effort. Companies need to realize that there are different approaches to developing projects and that the approach determines the cost. For the smallest projects it is quicker to offer a predefined package with a price attached and then get the client to refine their ideas against that package deal so that they themselves process and adjust the content to conform to the template. This will be covered in more detail later in this chapter, and involves you in the least effort. In the middle ground in terms of how much effort you put in initially, some interpretation of the clients' needs may be done. You may then map these backwards against a 'packaged' solution that has a predefined cost to help the clients understand what they would get for a particular price and what would be counted as extra. Then you could cost how much effort it would take to add the extras over and above the packaged solution price. This approach then represents a semi-tailored solution. You would use as much of the package templates as you could with extras developed over and above the pre-packaged solution at an agreed cost to suit the particular needs.

For the more complex projects you could start from free interpretation of the clients' needs – perhaps using tools that help determine directions and consensus between groups. There is nothing stopping smaller companies employing similar methods to larger companies if the client will pay for your time and effort – but the freely interpreted, bespoke project is harder to scope. (See Chapter 3, *Scoping a project*, for the alternative methods.) Increasingly more and more pre-packaged deals will be offered to clients who are happy to have a quick and relatively cheap way to ease themselves into a new use of technology. It makes sense for them to minimize their risk by not spending too much. For clear examples of the 'packaged' deal approach see the Demon Internet reference that offers to develop a website, an e-commerce site and a business website cheaply and efficiently.

What is a small project?

This isn't as easy to define as people would think. A lot depends on the type of projects undertaken as a rule by that particular business. For example, a small project for a large company might be a large one for a small company! If we try to define small by monetary value the same applies. For a small company a one-off project of several thousand pounds might be considered a fair-sized project. For a larger company this amount might not be worth their time and effort unless there was the expectation of more and larger work to follow. If we try to define a small project by the numbers of people involved in the development this doesn't follow either. A small team of three specialists might be involved on one project for a long period of time and it could generate a lot of income.

If you can't decide yourself from your own experience what a small project is in your terms, then use the following as a guide.

- A small project might be one that seems small enough to be the equivalent of only a section of your usual kind of project.

- A medium project might be a project of a scale such that you believe you can manage it without any significant change to your usual working methods.

- A large project might be one that needs significantly more resources, or significantly more time than your usual projects. It might even have several components, each of which would make a project by itself.

In this chapter we are going to take the definition of a small project from the perspective of working in a small development company of about seven people. For an online project the discussions will relate to something like the following brief:

Develop a series of web page templates for information on health and diet – in total about 20 screens with four templates that can be edited and amended by the client using a standard WYSIWYG tool.

For an example of an offline project the brief might be equivalent to:

Develop a CD demonstrator to work in a travelling interactive education exhibition on health and diet. It will have three sections with a small interactive quiz and be about 15 minutes contact time in total.

The good news and …

Smaller projects usually involve fewer people especially from the commissioning side of the equation. There may be just one person from the client company to satisfy in terms of what is acceptable. This is a bonus since the difficulty of getting consensus on decisions increases as the number of people involved increases. The reduction in communication between people means saved time and energy, fewer points of confusion, faster agreements on design, faster decisions and fewer people to satisfy. Obviously this streamlines the process on one hand. It's fair to say that often the smaller projects go to smaller development companies and in smaller companies the people tend to be more multiskilled and take on more roles. This also means a faster naturally integrated way of working. On the other hand there is increased responsibility for individuals.

This might mean, for example, that a good graphics artist who has some programming skills might run with a project alone. The design might work well from a visual perspective and the program may operate efficiently but perhaps a more skilled programmer might have made it more effective or added in some useful functionality; or a better needs analyst, business analyst or information analyst might have come up with a more effective structure for the business purposes. Alternatively, a gifted programmer who has worked on a few training projects might run with developing a couple of web-based training modules. He or she might feel capable of deciding on the structure and scripting the content. The training may work without falling over and have structural integrity but the skills of an instructional designer would have improved the users' actual learning from using the module. There are sometimes trade-offs in overall quality with fewer people being used on a project from the developer side. It depends on the type of project, what the client is trying to achieve, and who the target audience is.

Irrespective of the size of the project, you still have to agree what you will produce in what timescale and for what monetary return – this is the same time, cost and quality loop as applied to larger projects.

■ What are the risks?

A generally accepted definition of a 'good project manager' is one who foresees and controls risks. We'll take this as our starting point since for small companies the risks can have more impact than they would in large companies. Therefore the projects actually need better control. We are going to look at the risks in the order of the most serious impact that these can have for a small company. By using this approach the rationale for using the key project management principles becomes clearer but the risk factors cut across the production processes at different points. This explains why the first risk relates to non-payment for the work done. This might occur at the end of a small project that has had a short turnaround time. Non-payment will stop the cash flow and leave a small company very vulnerable. Every small company will recognize that any steps that can be taken to ensure cash flow will be essential. Large companies are not affected so adversely since their cash flow does not become as critical as quickly as a small company unless very large sums are involved. Even though this risk might only surface at the end of a fixed-price project, the way to cover it means taking action at the beginning of your relationship with the client.

☐ Risk 1 – withheld payment

There is a greater danger with small projects that the clients will withhold payment if the agreement is for one fixed-rate payment at the end of the project. They may keep asking for slight refinements knowing that you are likely to comply because the outstanding payment represents a large amount in terms of the time spent. From their perspective they also recognize that they have no opportunity to negotiate once payment is made.

This demonstrates the rationale behind asking for staged payments as opposed to a single payment on delivery. With staged payments the client feels there is always a negotiating stance left to them but the developer receives partial payments to cover work done. Staged payments are harder to justify on smaller projects but cash flow to a small company is crucial. Staged payments mean clear understanding of what the client is paying for and what you are developing so that both are happy. Even on a small project some clear payment points help the process from both sides and even though you may think some verbal agreement was clear at the time, there is always leeway for interpretation unless it is written and agreed.

As you will see from the example below, this written agreement does not have to be onerous and does not constitute a large amount of admin to ensure cash flow. It is only recognized as the natural insurance it is, if and when any problems arise. If it is a natural part of the process, it does not add undue time. If there are standard up-front analysis questionnaires, standard short project milestone payment agreement templates, standard script/storyboard/prototypes, these constitute the middle ground of administration. They will save time once they are in place and allow projects to run more smoothly. However, the time needed to put them in place and refine them is a burden on a small company in the short term. You may begin with the forms given throughout this book and the electronic versions found on the website, but they need adjusting to suit your company's way of working, your client base and the specifics of your type of projects. They offer a starting point.

The amount of administration can be minimized once you have a relationship with a client and both understand each other and the way of working. When there is understanding and trust, the process can be streamlined. You may opt to take the risk and work loosely from the outset to cut corners to win business and this can be fine if your client is fair-minded. But if there are any difficulties once you've established a loose way of working, it is harder to redress the balance because the client has the stronger position. You are, after all, providing services for them. If you state up front the minimum processes you will apply across all projects and explain to the client that there is a minimum amount of documentation you are asked to apply to satisfy company policy from a legal and professional stance, they should understand.

If you accept that you need staged payments, this means you accept the need to provide the client with a written statement of what you are going to produce broken into stages linked to payments. Then you have accepted one of the fundamental principles of project management – a clear definition of what you will do for a certain amount of money. In other words – a defined, written agreement that shows responsibilities on both sides. This is in effect a contract just as your verbal agreements constitute a contract in lieu of written documentation. Your initial specification does not have to be a long legalistic document: it can be several paragraphs covering the following points based on our hypothetical example. (Please note that this is only an example. This book is used throughout the world so you need to comply with your own country's legal requirements and these can vary. Also legalities change from the date of writing and publication so you need to take responsibility to cover the right points for you and your way of working.)

1. A statement of the total payment agreed between the companies and a general description of the end product

General requirements agreement example

Project Name _____

Project purpose/business needs

_____

_____

_____

_____

Target audience:

_____

_____

_____

Outline content and reasons for use:

_____

_____

_____

_____

_____

Company X will pay Company Y _____ amount in _____ stages with an _____ % up-front payment on agreement of this requirement document and the balance as staged payments as set out below:

To produce a CD Master with 4 content sections one of which is an interactive quiz. The total will be approximately 15 minutes of interaction time and contain a range of media including 2–3 short video sequences (Total 4–5 minutes playing time) ready by [completion date].

2. A statement of the next payment stages and a description of the work that will show the stages of the product so that the client will see and agree that the work has been done.

Example description of work representing a partial product.

Demonstration of a prototype where the general look and feel of the main sections and the navigation in and between the sections are agreed. The prototype will use mock content or holding screens and will not represent the final content.

    Milestone 1 Sign-off point and payment point for X amount

    All content sections – text, video scripts and graphics specified and drafted for sign-off but not integrated into the application

    Milestone 2 Sign-off point and payment point for X amount

    Video sequences shot and edited ready for sign-off

    Milestone 3 Sign-off point and payment point for X amount

3. A statement of the final payment and a description of the extra work that will have been done to complete the project

Example description of work representing the move from partial product to completion.

    Integration and delivery of the Master CD where all content has been agreed and works to the look and feel and navigation agreed from the prototype.

    Final Sign-off point and payment point for X amount

    Testing strategy – company standard – no extras requested.

Signed and dated   Developer
Signed and dated   Client

Note: the items in italics will be covered under other risks dealt with later in the chapter.

It would help if you mention to the client in your first meetings how you generally operate and what they can expect. Then when you're ready you can define a few stages of the work linked to milestones and payments and send it through to them to check over. Many companies forget one important item and that is to state at what point you consider a project to start. This is not as straightforward as it might appear. Most companies give a certain amount of free time and hold meetings with the client prior to the actual start of the project. The difficulty here is for both of you to know exactly when the 'meter starts running'. It will help if you agree up front exactly how much of the initial scoping of the project will be done before the time and cost start. This must be true even if you haven't got to the point of signing a formal written agreement. You need to be paid for work done from a certain point if the project falls through before the completed written agreement. Failure to do this traps many a small company. Once you move past some high-level understanding nearer to the detail, you have moved into a cost stage. In the way that the requirements agreement as outlined above is drafted, the start point is clear because once signed, you get an up-front payment to cover the next phase of work and you have both agreed on the work to be done.

Creative companies are particularly vulnerable here because coming up with design ideas and refining them is accepted as part of the initial creative process. But quite quickly the client will be getting free advice and ideas unless the company's policy on where the project is considered to start is stated up front. Creative web design companies are now recognizing that they need to state the start point for charging on interactive projects because it takes more time and effort to agree the components. Also, any rework can take longer than for traditional media. One approach is to define that you have an 'ideas shaping' stage or 'requirements definition' stage that will include mocking up some screens and that this is charged as phase 1 of the project. This is a little different from the approach used as the example in the requirements agreement draft above since it includes some screen samples. This puts more of the emphasis on the visual aspects of the project and is more in keeping with the visually driven approach of some creative companies. Once you define your approach to the processes and your way of attributing costs, this can be stated clearly to your prospective client at the first encounter.

By the time you are able to draft this agreement, you will have spent time discussing the scope with the client. Your ability to write this agreement comes towards the last part of the scoping phase. This may seem a little back to front, but we needed to focus on the highest risk and how to contain it and this agreement establishes the equivalent of your aim for the first phase, your destination point. How you get to this point – the initial stages of scoping, will be covered shortly.

You'll find that something as basic as a completed example requirement agreement form as outlined above will help particularly as one of your client contacts will need to sign it. This helps the client focus clearly on their position and responsibilities. Their company might well come back with some new insights such as having meant five sections plus the interactive quiz and they have two video pieces they want incorporated and so on. Then your new understanding of the scope of the work means that you reassess and renegotiate the fee as a result. Meanwhile you may well decide that because of the timescale you both agree to start the work with the up-front payment while the detail is being worked out.

The risk of withheld payments is more contained using this work process and is covered in more detail in the main body of the book. The principles are the same but the practice varies to suit the occasion.

Risk 2 – changes to the scope of the project

Once you ensure that payment agreement is in place so that cash flow for the company is set up, the next biggest risk for small companies is additions to the scope of the project – known as 'feature creep'. Extras added to a project can move it from being a fair production for the money agreed to being too much work for the money agreed or impossible to achieve in the time.

Changes to the project are in the nature of the business. This needs to be recognized and contingency built in to absorb a reasonable amount of variation. If only a few small changes are made then you will have the contingency leeway to increase the quality of the product near the end by putting time and effort into refining the little things. This can raise the overall quality level by quite a lot. You may decide to have more graphics throughout the text or refine the response times in the navigation, for example. If there have been quite a few alterations that you needed to absorb, you may well not have the time or the leeway in money left to refine the application in this way. Finally, there may have been so many changes that it hardly represents what you started out to produce. You might have worked double or treble the time for the initial amount agreed. This needs to be avoided at all costs and smaller companies have to be aware of how to control changes against time and money because the consequences can mean going out of business.

Changes don't have to be initiated by the client. For example, the tool you thought you could use to produce the application might turn out to be inefficient at a particular routine that is crucial for the functionality. You may have to buy another piece of software and rework or program at a low level to fix the problem. When your best shot from your experience at deciding what can be produced with what effort is wrong, you have to absorb the consequences. Contingency works for both parties involved. You know you will have to meet and accept certain unforeseen circumstances that relate directly to your own working conditions in an unstable environment that are nothing to do with the client.

Although you may already build in a reasonable amount for contingency it only takes one or two medium-to-large knock-on effects from some changes early in the project to absorb it. Then if more changes are asked for what will you do?

This is where the approach that is adopted from project management principles can help. The time, cost, quality triangle helps if you have explained it to the client and they understand how you will apply this through the project – even a short one. You can introduce the concept at the first meeting so that they understand the process. The principles derive from engineering projects but can be adapted for multimedia up to a point. The general use of these principles encourages credibility in a relatively young industry like interactive media. The client may well recognize these principles and accept that they represent a professional approach.

Basically the time, cost and quality principle states that if there is any impact or change to one component, the others will be affected. This means that if the client wants more content and new functionality to go with a new section this adds to the quality of the product and affects the time and cost for development. If the client suddenly decides that because of other things affecting his or her firm they cannot spend as much as they had agreed, then your company getting less money from them will affect what you will produce and the time it will take. Whatever the changes, you need to assess the impact and adjust the costs accordingly.

If you both agree to follow the time, cost, quality project management process there is a mechanism for negotiating any extras produced for time and cost over and above the initial agreement. The client will expect you to assess the impact of any alteration in these three areas and expect extra charges that will be agreed when necessary.

This will make your work process easier. You may not have to use it; but if you haven't prepared your client for it and got them to buy into the process up front, then it leaves you both vulnerable.

The use of the time, cost and quality management principles presupposes that you have both agreed what the project is going to cover in terms of content and functionality, and the timescale for delivery. If you do not have agreement then you can't demonstrate that the client has asked for extras in any of them. So, you can only use the principles once you have reached an agreement. This does not have to be as detailed as you would need in a larger project – as the example has shown – but it should cover enough for you both to recognize when a variation has been asked for.

So how do you get to that agreement stage? Your early discussions should be driven by you using as many means as possible according to your experience to elicit enough information about the project to define the boundaries of a production plan and commit your company to a development time and cost. For the very experienced a project shape emerges within a couple of meetings. They automatically apply the following processes:

- ask analysis questions;
- probe for detail;

- arrange for colleagues to talk some aspects through with the client and report back;
- gauge the psychological needs of the clients;
- attune to the needs of the users;
- assess the politics that might affect decision making and sign-offs;
- process the whole spectrum of insinuations of need until some clear pointers emerge;
- educate the client in company practices.

The experienced take all this on board and more. They filter and define the various communications subconsciously until they arrive at a project shape or structure.

For the less experienced, any aids that can help are welcomed. To keep your questions focused during the initial meetings, a checklist of items can be invaluable. These represent the start points for discussion and the clients' answers may need further probing for clarification. You may want to add in extra sections once you find a special need, for example. The checklist cannot be the solution, only an aid. It can just be used as a prepared tabular form in which you handwrite a few sentences on the major pieces of the project. Then you can photocopy and give it to the client to establish if you are both clear on where the discussion has led.

Some people feel that this makes the process too formal and can indicate that they do not trust the client. This needs to be assessed for each situation but unfortunately once the timescales are short, the decisions are made faster and the people involved are rushed. The details are forgotten quickly because of the pressures on both parties and each side remembers some aspects but forgets or embellishes others. This happens and is not a conscious attempt by the client to ask for something different; they may genuinely believe that they had conveyed something different to you on certain aspects. Vice versa, it is easy for you to interpret something that was said in one way when they meant it to be interpreted another. Clarity is important even if it is just getting to a first-level agreement.

The essential aspects to cover are:

1. The timescale
2. The agreed cost
3. The size, general functionality or interactivity needed and the range of media that will be used.

In a quick project you need to get to the level of detail where you can point out when any extra or variation tips the balance from the project being achievable for the time and money to not being possible in the time and for the money. If you have a sheet to fill in as you talk to the client in the first meeting or two, this will help focus you both and move you towards the agreement document. This type of aid relates to an approach that falls in the middle of the scoping scale for time and effort (Figure 13.1). It focuses you both on high-level understanding rather than detail and allows for some open discussion and interpretation.

☐ Sample quick scoping checklist 1

Client name

Client address

Client contact numbers/e-mail

Project name

Date

Purpose of project

Target audience

User reaction
General emotional reaction you want from your users to the interactive experience?

What will they want from your site?

Project type

Web pages

CD

CD with web links

Presentation/speaker support

Kiosk

WAP

Project description

Comments/ rough cost estimate

Timescale

Size

Content

No of web pages/screens

(a range between x and x)

No of sections

Names of sections

Reasons for content choice

Interactivity type

Main screen options (No)

Search facility (Type – keyword/free text)

Database (estimated range/number of items)

Static screens/pages with links/buttons

Animation/movie with links

User profiling

Quiz/scoring

Help

Media

Text (approx no of screens)

Graphics (approx no)

Animations (approx no)

Audio clips/commentaries
(No of minutes, stock or originate)

Music clips
(No of minutes, library or original)

Video clips
(No of minutes, stock or originate)

Extras to check
Site or application examples the client likes or dislikes

Translations are not needed
Who to maintain
Present set-up. Contact:

Company practices explained
Requirements agreement document

Standard testing strategy
(agreed people to comment, etc.)

Admin procedures followed
(turnaround, sign-offs, 30 days 'bug fix' term post-completion etc.)

Payment structure

Budget range available
Up to

Date
Developer signature

Date
Client signature

The sample sheet gives some pointers but it still needs to be tailored for each project. Items that don't apply can be crossed out while others can be added in. It is only going to be an estimated guess so it is useful to put a range on everything. If the client knows that you're expecting to produce between 12–15 web pages in total and you put a range on the estimated price, you'll have established the marker to use later in the agreement document. In the end if they agree they want 25–30 you can both understand that it has gone past the estimate range and you need to establish a new cost as a result.

This form of exercise establishes the understanding of a certain amount of work costing one price and by implication more work costing more. It can be bounced back and forth during early meetings helping to firm up the process as you both define more detail of the project. (See Chapter 3, *Scoping a project*, for an expansion of these principles.)

Small companies do not want to get dragged down by admin procedures and that is justifiable but only up to the point that the lack of procedures doesn't jeopardize the company. It does take a bit of time to adjust some template forms like the one above to suit your clients, your projects and your company, but then they can save time and help identify gaps in both your own and the clients' understanding of the scope of the project.

☐ Risk 3 – visual mismatch

This means the client asks for changes because of a mismatch between what they had in mind and what they see before them.

This difficulty is not the same as the client asking for extra features as described in Risk 2. This relates far more to the problem of discussing a visual product in non-visual terms as both you and the client try to describe what the one wants and the other will produce. This is more of a problem in offline projects than online because web pages are usually much easier to change than an integrated application on a CD-ROM would be. It is common with online projects to ask the client for examples of other websites they like or dislike in order to help this process. However, smaller, quicker projects need to get sample screens and layouts in front of the client as soon as possible to move towards agreed layouts and colours.

It is a good idea to draft a flowchart or a site map as early as you can in the scoping phase to help the client understand how the pieces will inter-relate. This can be refined in parallel with the requirements as a visual record and it is certainly a good idea to include one with the requirement agreement document to offer an alternative visual representation of the 'bones' of the project. (See Chapter 3, *Scoping a project*, for more on the visual techniques that can be employed and the pros and cons of them.)

Smaller projects can mean that some screens are drafted earlier than they might be in larger projects and on less understanding of the detail. But some of the major look and feel criteria can be established and refined as the detail firms up. You might present a few mock-up designs that have some placeholder graphics, false titles indicating where selection lists might be, a logo in a couple of positions for comment, some different colour combinations to prompt reaction and so on. Asking up front about the general emotional response that they expect from their typical user can help focus the direction for the creative style and it helps keep the client thinking about other people's responses rather than their own. The mock-ups may have to take into account that a couple of extra content sections might emerge in the detail and need to be represented and linked to from the front page. So these mock-ups will already be designed from the idea of some flexibility and scalability because there would still be unknowns in the content.

In effect, in smaller projects the stages of production are collapsed even more than in larger projects. This working environment brings its own special constraints but as long as you design to accommodate some variations, the shape of the look, feel and navigation can be tweaked into the final result. The important thing to recognize here is that the clients will be working under the same focused time constraints as you. They should appreciate that everything has been done in the time that can be done because they have been pushed to keep up with the processes. Then if a few things emerge in the detail that usually would necessitate rework of the main components, such as perhaps re-jigging the front screen and navigation, they will compromise more than in larger projects because there is no time left. This is only true on small, quick projects.

If time is not the driving force, the client will not compromise and will expect the rework needed to accommodate the knock-on effects of the late but important content details. In this case, collapsing the production stages when not driven by time constraints can lead to late rework. As explained in Chapter 11, *Testing*, it is common for stable code to develop problems because of rework on other parts of the program even given the advances of object-oriented coding. So minimizing conditions that lead to rework is a sound policy.

There is another consideration about a small project versus time constraints. Even if the client has not imposed a strict time limit because of their company deadline, your company has to define a strict time limit or you'll spend too long on the project for the money you will get for it. This is the hardest set of circumstances because the client will expect the rework and revisions and you will have an alternative but very necessary internal time limit.

In this case, you need to have stated how much time your company would be able to put in for the money and include a defined revision cycle for the project. During the project you will have needed to control the sign-off points by agreeing a turnaround time and the number of named people that you would accept comments from for adjustments to the look and feel, navigation and any code errors. This is the equivalent of defining your test strategy for the project as described in Chapter 11.

You need to have explained that once the final version is handed to them they have a defined period to find any 'technical' bugs and that you would fix these within the original cost agreement. However, because the look and feel and navigation paths had been agreed along the way with the specific people the client had suggested, any extra work apart from code deficiencies would be subject to extra costs.

This gives you some control over rework being asked for because of subjective responses to the look and feel and explains where the paid work finishes.

☐ Risk 4 – 'passing the buck'!

The clients say the program is not what they wanted or does not perform in the way that they expected. This can be linked to refusal to pay the last payment and even demands to pay back other instalments. Beware company politics!

There is no guarantee that a small project means it is an easier project to scope. Often it is harder than many people realize to refine content into small, neat chunks or for a program to be contained in a simple structure. If you have to make decisions about the structure blocks before you can properly analyse the whole, there may well be gaps. This is a big dilemma for small projects because the time for analysis is pared to a minimum. The clients tend not to be receptive to paying for an analysis stage as they will have a tight budget for the project. To them, of course, it may not be considered a small project. Without strong, clear direction from the client on the content, the size and the number of the main pieces needed in the program, you will not know what you are getting into.

Also, without some checks on what the company is trying to achieve and what they are expecting as a reaction to the program from the users, you will be left vulnerable if the clients turn round at the end and say it isn't what they want. Even if you have just one or two statements of what the client wants to achieve as the main focus of the program, if you can produce these and demonstrate what you did from your experience to try to achieve them, you will be seen to have fulfilled the brief.

However, the main problem might be that your client had not really defined the reasons for the program in line with the company's direction or agenda. Once other managers in the company see the program, they might well react negatively and your contact will need you, the developer, as the scapegoat. Or once the program is in use the client may find that the users are not reacting as the company wants. This is when those statements of purpose (or business objectives) and reasons for content selection (that are in italics in the agreement document) become so important and any indications in the scoping checklist as outlined below that lead to that section being completed also gain importance. It is true that sometimes you will advise on content areas because the client asks. You can offer your opinion based on experience and the understanding you have of their objectives. You cannot be held responsible for their lack of definition of the purpose of the application nor for the way it is used if they have agreed to your definition in the agreement based on your prior discussions.

Because these areas are the *raison d'être* for the project, they are important but they are the most difficult to define in a short time. (See Chapter 3, *Scoping a project*, for a clearer understanding of how to elicit better definitions.) Some quick e-mails to the client after initial discussions and after mulling over your ideas on these issues are a good idea. They help you both to confirm early in the project the direction you are taking as a result of the 'objectives' of the program in relation to what the user will be able to do with it. How you intend lining these up should be the cornerstone of the project – as long as the client can furnish you with the right information to do this.

So this brings us back to how to get a good but quick up-front analysis. If it is not appropriate to use the more thorough processes of getting consensus of direction and need from your clients as described in Chapter 3, *Scoping a project*, and if the clients do not come back to you with a list of their objectives and expectations as suggested in the Scoping Questionnaire in Chapter 3, the fastest way to drive direction is to have a checklist of what you are prepared to provide for this particular type of small project. You may classify these lists as business-to-business, business-to-consumer or consumer-to-consumer for example. Then you and your client tick the list for the ones that they agree with and add any extras they may want but not necessarily have in the time. This will set the direction if nothing else has. This means that you have to draft a set of small checklists for the different types of project you do. Many items may be the same but the target audience, the market sector or the premise of the project might need emphasizing by some additions.

Sample scoping checklist 2 for small projects

Small business-to-business website

A typical user will want to access:

(a) basic information about the company

(b) information about services offered

(c) a client list and reference quotes

(d) 2 client case studies

(e) contact information

(f) request/download company brochure (only offered as PDF file)

   Possible extra:

(g) awareness raising factsheet/quiz to identify need for service

The developer undertakes to provide:

Home page that   1. Clearly identifies the company

                       2. Contains the company's logo if applicable

                       3. Identifies the main content blocks of the website

                       4. Establishes the look of the rest of the site

Select one of the adjectives that best describes the emotional reaction you want to get from your user to the look

(a) follow existing branding look

(b) moody

(c) neutral, transparent but clearly presented

(d) jazzy

(e) cool

(f) traditional business

(g) modern, contemporary business

(h) homely, cosy

(i) mystical

(j) intriguing

(k) techie

(l) outrageous

(m)high-tech

(n) high-tech design

(o) humorous

(p) developer to decide from experience

(q)

5. Establishes the feel of the rest of the site through

(a) Conventional lists/topic choices

(b) Choices need to be discovered

(c) Choices non-conventional

(d) Lists/topic revelation to be set by developer in accordance with look set
    from above

(e)

Rest of site	
	(a) Looks and feels consistent with home page
	(b) Carries through colours
	(c) Colours vary per section
	(d) Maximum of 4 pages of information on any section
	(e) Maximum 2 graphics per page

Technical attributes	
	Graphics to be optimized for speed of download
	Home page to download within X seconds
	Site to work with version X Explorer only on PCs
	Basic content description and keywords meta tags
	No animations (no use of flash)
	No video
	No audio
	No database development
	No translations/foreign versions
	No maintenance agreement
	No search engine registration
	No hosting of the site

Test strategy (standard)
(a) Iterative internal peer review (design) at all stages
(b) Iterative code testing (at all stages)
(c) Client to test and report at sign-off stages with ▢ named company
    people only
(d) Integration and web testing pre final delivery
(e) No user trials
(f) No field trials
(g) No focus groups
(h) Code error correction post final delivery within 1 month

Admin attributes
(a) Turnaround time for clients to return/report or provide assets ▢ days
(b) Named sign-off
    Delegate sign-off with full authority
    (in case of sickness, etc.)

Payment structure
Company standard (Up-front payment followed by staged payment linked
to milestones to be set out in the agreement document.)

Signed and dated – developer
Signed and dated – client

The emphasis is clearly on the users and what the company will want them to have access to. You also try to elicit bare information about the type of emotional response the client wants to get from a general user to aid the graphic look and feel. This should help streamline the visual direction. Then you drive the requirements by stating how much you will offer under the umbrella look and feel, what you do not offer, the work process you will employ including the sign-off procedure, the payment structure and the testing strategy your company will apply as standard. If the client wants any differences or extras, they will need to define precisely what they want in reaction to your strong guidelines. This directive approach lies closer to offering a predefined package on the scale shown in Figure 13.1. However as soon as the client adds to or responds against any of the points thereby indicating a definite need, the project will move on the scale towards being a more expensive bespoke project.

So you can move from a loose approach even with a small project if you are confident in analysis, interpreting needs and handling clients. You can have a half-way approach where the discussions firm up through an outline scoping checklist that you tweak as your discussions and understanding of the project firm up. Or, you can become more directive with the scoping checklist example 2 as above. The different approaches allow the relationship with your clients to influence you but contain the business risks you operate under for your company. They clearly show your responsibilities for the scoping phase of the project. The success of the project and the success of your company depends on this.

THEORY INTO PRACTICE 13

Company business risk appraisal
Using the four categories of risk emphasized in the chapter apply them to your present company practices with your colleagues.

Where are you most at risk?

What can you do to minimize the risk?

Can you define any extra risks in your company based on your experience?

What can you do to minimize these?

	Risk Factor				
	Low				High
	1	2	3	4	5
Risk 1 Withheld payment	☐	☐	☐	☐	☐
Risk 2 Changes to the scope of the project	☐	☐	☐	☐	☐
Risk 3 Visual mismatch	☐	☐	☐	☐	☐
Risk 4 Passing the buck	☐	☐	☐	☐	☐
Risk 5	☐	☐	☐	☐	☐
Risk 6	☐	☐	☐	☐	☐
Risk 7	☐	☐	☐	☐	☐

Strategies to minimize risks:

■ Summary

- Smaller companies are more vulnerable to impact from project risks than larger companies.
- A good project manager minimizes risks.
- To maintain cash flow, use a requirements agreement to define the project development linked to staged payments.
- To control changes, apply the time, cost, quality principles starting from an agreed project development plan.
- To align visual understanding, use application maps/flowcharts for a visual overview of the project, use fast sample screens to establish look and feel.
- Agree in writing, the business premises underlying the project. Show how you relate to these in the treatment to insure against any business/political shift in the client's company during development.
- Establish your company practices about sign-off, turnaround, testing, etc. as well as payment.

■ Recommended reading

As this chapter was based on experience, there is no reading material recommended.

References and websites

Example of restricting your clients' choices to aid a clear brief:

Demon Internet ISP offers a template set of options for people to set up a website. The look and feel is set, colour chosen, options (extra charges attached). Clear, clean, basic but unambiguous.
http://www.demon.net/products/netlaunch/index.shtml

Similar offer to set up an e-commerce site. More choice but still clear and straightforward.
http://www.demon.net/products/demonpowertrader/index.shtml

Set up shop offer for small businesses – similar to above.
http://www.demon.net/products/demoncommerce/

Flowcharting and idea mapping tools

Ryerson's school of Radio and TV ongoing research into charting multimedia, see Resources – Flowcharting
http://www.rcc.ryerson.ca/rta/flowchart/index.html

Axon Idea processor also possibly for eliciting concept maps with new clients. A visualization tool for thinkers it says!
http://web.singnet.com.sg/~axon2000/

Pre-packaged online work flow aids

http://www.macromedia.com/software/sitespring

Self Development

■ Introduction

In this edition we have enlarged the self-development concepts to form their own section and kept the life-cycle project management processes together in the first section. The work context in any management role now expects people to take the initiative in their own development. So it is with this in mind that we have built up the related concepts that can influence your role without necessarily being embedded in the life cycle.

You'll find that Part II covers some generic concepts and some specialist concepts for project managers. *Team management, Rights, copyright and other intellectual property* and *Marketing and marketing research* have a wider application than the specialist project manager knowledge related to *Multimedia narrative* and *Adapting projects for other languages and cultures*.

Interactive media professionals do not have a defined career path. It is difficult to find training specifically for them because the roles fluctuate and the volatile technology keeps forcing more and more diversity into the roles. Many of the new media companies have not invested in training or if they have offered it, they offered general management training or IT related management training.

Part II builds a portfolio of middle management knowledge and skills that have direct relevance for new media professionals.

Team management principles

Project manager's responsibilities

- To negotiate with higher management on behalf of the team
- To motivate the team and set the direction for them
- To create good communication between the team members
- To employ a variety of management styles appropriate for the occasion
- To take account of lessons learnt about successful management of multidisciplined teams
- To identify and remedy any deficiencies in the team in functional, decision-making and interpersonal skills
- To resolve problems occurring in the teams
- To recognize and address environmental factors affecting the team

■ The project manager and team culture

Most multimedia projects take place in a team culture. A good team culture can be defined as having the following characteristics:

- everyone pulling together to achieve well-defined tasks
- respect for each other's skills
- a sharing of success and failures
- mutual support when needed.

The team will be affected by outside conditions such as recognition within the organization, being valued, being treated fairly, receiving support, and receiving adequate resources. A team culture will often take its lead from the organization culture but it can develop its own. So the manager has a dual role: to try to provide the conditions that will help to motivate the team to work well together, and to create an open, constructive working atmosphere to allow the individuals to achieve their best in a way that also serves the project best.

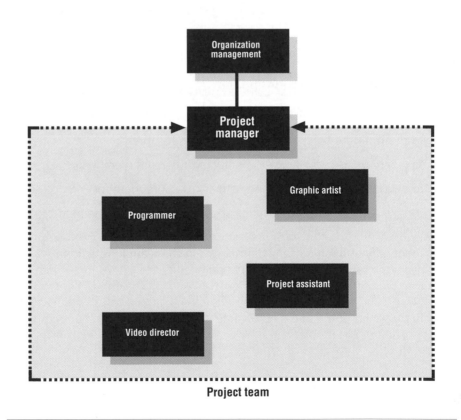

Project manager's position.

To provide good conditions, the manager has to negotiate with higher management for the necessary resources. You may need to justify how they will improve the success criteria of the project. As the team's representative to higher management, the manager takes the lead on their behalf. For many, this representation role appears a contradiction of the idea of leadership. Leadership seems to imply being in front of others, being ahead of them, making the decisions for them, but this is true only in some cases. Team leadership is also about being the representative of the team's needs, views and skills.

It is not easy to create an open, constructive working atmosphere. Individuals have their own aspirations, their own personality traits, their own strengths and weaknesses, their own defence mechanisms, and their own ways of interacting with other people. It might seem impossible to unify a disparate group who come from different disciplines, with different skills and different ways of describing multimedia. However, the team will respond to the tone and form of interaction you set. You can be the catalyst by being open and informative, supportive and straight-talking.

Team leadership is also about giving direction, but this should not be confused with being directive. Setting the direction in a multimedia project means performing all the background tasks that have been described in the preceding chapters and helping to define exactly what each member needs to achieve and how each task relates to the whole project. The administrative tasks, such as defining everyone's role and responsibilities, in themselves set a working direction, and this in turn gives unity of purpose. Maintaining the overall vision of the application also helps to set a direction. Individuals can become too involved with their own particular pieces to maintain the overview. Constant focusing on the needs of the user also sets a unifying direction for all concerned.

As discussed in Chapter 2, project management principles were generally derived from engineering projects. The background to the general management concepts of 'a manager' or a 'a leader' has been based on historical models with some insights coming from military models, and others from hierarchical business models. Just as the engineering derivatives for project management needed adjusting for multimedia project management, so the traditional principles underlying concepts of managers and leaders cannot be transferred directly to multimedia management. The difference that has been identified is one of managing creative teams. The research concerning successful multimedia managers has not been applied directly to multimedia teams, but roles such as theatre director, conductor of orchestras, and TV programme production have now been studied, and provide a contrast with other management models.

The main differences between traditional managers and managers of creative teams seem to relate to the dynamics of interaction with team members. For successful creative team managers, the old authoritarian role of manager appears to change to more of a collaborative role. The manager also retains more of a 'hands-on' approach to the task in hand, whereas previous models have stressed leaving one's specialism behind, trading it for new management and administrative functions. They are also more part of the team than removed from it, spotting role gaps and filling them. It is a more fluid role in concept than previously.

More of these emerging principles will be covered later in the chapter. The key point being made here is that we cannot blindly apply previous concepts about team management to teams working in emerging media sectors. The introduction to management styles that follows is presented in this spirit. It appears that the successful creative team manager shifts styles and this is reflected in the scenarios covered below.

■ Management styles

Setting a direction for the team means encouraging them to share the vision of the end-product. Being directive, on the other hand, is linked to management style. There are many ways of defining management styles but we'll concentrate on directive, consultative, collaborative, and delegation. Good managers employ a mixture of styles appropriate for the occasion and circumstances. The hard part is recognizing which to use, and when.

The *directive* style is appropriate when you have the knowledge and experience to make the necessary decision, you have to accept the responsibility for your decision, and the decision is needed quickly. Under these circumstances, you make the decision and then direct the team members to carry it out. If you communicate this to the team in an open manner, you can be directive without making them feel manipulated. They may challenge the decision from their perspective and experience. You should see this as a chance to broaden them by giving an explanation, rather than as a challenge to your authority – as long as you are confident that you are right.

If, for example, your client phones you to request an immediate demo of work in progress because a new divisional manager has been appointed who

Management style: directive.

is re-prioritizing the workload and the whole project might be in jeopardy, you would be justified in directing the team to stop work and pull a demo together. This may well affect their schedule and cause rework later. However, faced with the alternatives of no project or some downtime, you have no choice. The important thing for the team to recognize is that your use of authority is not arbitrary.

Management style: consultative.

You can employ a *consultative* style when you need to make a decision and you are fairly confident about it but you have some time to check the views of team members. They may influence you or they may not. You have the time to think things through and take all aspects into consideration before reaching a decision.

Collaborative decisions occur when you recognize that you do not have the right knowledge, skill and experience to come to a conclusion yourself, so you seek the team's views to pool experience and take a decision based on the majority view.

Collaborative decisions may not involve the whole team. You may seek the views of some of the team who have the relevant skills, and take the decision based on their expertise.

In multimedia management, where there are so many strands of expertise, often you do not have the same level of knowledge and experience in specific areas as members of the team, so you will need to collaborate with them often.

However, sometimes you will be forced into making decisions in time-critical circumstances where you cannot contact the right team members. Both sides need to recognize the constraints and accept that some decisions may not always be the best. They can be the best for the time and the circumstances, which may be your only consolation. You will maintain an open and honest atmosphere by admitting that the decision was forced and that you were aware of the risks but that you were left with no choice.

Management style: collaborative.

This can happen, for example, at a meeting with the client very late into the project, where they suddenly include an important visitor from their head office who states an opinion contrary to the one your client has stated in a video presentation in the project. You can see that they are as surprised as you, but they agree with the visitor wholeheartedly. You are placed in a very unfortunate position. You cannot embarrass your main client in front of their visitor by explaining that they have already stated their original position on camera and signed off the video, which has been encoded and integrated into the relevant section.

But once the visitor departs you have to address the situation. You recognize that there is no way that you can now keep that opinion in the section but also you cannot rework it in the time and money even if the client agrees. There is little else to do but suggest that you'll look at the section and try to edit the offending part, or cut it out. The client insists that the new position has to be included. You know that a new video clip is impossible, and that the client will not move from their demand. The stakes are too high for them. You appreciate their circumstances. At the same time, you realize that your knowledge of the specific content is not accurate. The scriptwriters would be the ones to comment on the impact, and usually you'd have telephoned them. But as their work was finished a few weeks earlier, their contracts have ended and they are no longer around. With a public launch in a few days, you decide to go for the lowest common denominator – to cut out the old message and then insert the new one with text and graphics, knowing that this is against the design continuity of the application but is achievable.

When you and the team fully analyse the situation back at work, the new slant actually has much more of an impact than imagined because several of the associated ideas are affected as well. The whole section needs rework rather than one contained piece. So much is affected that it becomes better to scrap the video and reform the section into text, some saved audio, and new graphics. Your team are furious with you, and your client is furious – more with themselves and their top management for not communicating changes in policy faster to them – but they take it out on you. However, a decision had to be taken and the consequences accepted as part of your responsibility.

With hindsight, there might have been alternatives if you could have thought things through and talked things through. But with other pressing points on the meeting agenda, you needed many decisions and agreements, not just to firefight with that one. Your only consolation might be that other project managers would understand, and if you'd warned the client not to include time-sensitive information in a video, they had ignored the advice!

Management style: delegation.

Delegation means that you transfer the powers of decision making on some matters to members of the team. But you must meet certain conditions to be seen to delegate otherwise this can be abdication not delegation. If you delegate, you need to make clear:

■ how far the delegation is allowed;
■ that you delegate with complete authority within the limits set;
■ that you will support all decisions made on your behalf.

If you fail any of these criteria, you have not delegated effectively. There is nothing worse than a manager who confuses delegation with abdication.

This can lead to unclear ideas of how far, when, and to what level the other people can make decisions. With no clear boundaries and with a confusing brief, it is easy to make mistakes. If your own manager has abdicated not delegated, you'll quickly find that there will only be support as long as you are right!

For example, you may decide to delegate the video production to a video director who would take care of the casting, the shoot and the edits, and hand you a master tape. You could allocate a budget from your budget for the completed tape and then monitor the spend. You might prefer to take over at the encoding stage so that the key points for you to monitor would be the quality of the content, the technical quality, and the compatibility of the tape source. This would then be delegation. The video director would know the precise tasks, the authority limits of the budget, where you would want sign-off, where you would take over, and the criteria for acceptance of the tape.

This has been a quick overview of some of the styles that have been identified. It is impossible to cover this area in greater depth here but it is important to introduce it as a topic because your performance as a project manager can be affected by your management style. Many multimedia project managers do not recognize the extent to which good people management contributes to successful projects.

It would be a good idea to include some more reading on management styles in your own development plan for the next year to get a better appreciation of the insights that can help with managing people.

■ Teams: lessons learnt so far

From Chapter 10, *Selecting the team*, we understand how to identify the technical or specialist skills needed for a particular project and recruit accordingly to make sure all the tasks are covered. But this is not the complete recipe for success. A project needs enough people in the team with a capacity to bond the individual pieces together. This means that they are willing to attend to detail and compromise their individual professional drive for the sake of the total project performance. The project manager needs to take the lead in this. A good team needs the complete set of technical or functional expertise, problem-solving and decision-making skills, creative skills, and interpersonal skills.

The problems of managing talented specialists have been recognized in investigations into teamwork. As indicated earlier in the chapter, research is beginning to recognize that traditional models of manager, leader – or whatever title is applied to the project manager of teams where creativity is necessary – need modifying.

We'll look at two approaches here. The first looks at managers of creative teams. The second is based on insights from managing IT teams. Interactive media development has elements of both, and so both are seen to have relevant contributions to make.

Effective team leaders and successful teams: is there a formula?

■ Successful managers of creative teams

John Whatmore (1997) has studied creative teams and has found the following elements of successful leaders:

- Strong experienced leadership. This was equated with experience in the design domain, with strength of personality and a democratic style.
- Leaders as part of the team. They used an empathetic approach to motivate the team. They immersed themselves in problems and helped the team to cooperate towards mutual goals.
- Care in selecting the team. The manager takes responsibility for selecting the team and defines their role in achieving the project goals.
- Provision of freedom and trust. Effective managers set realistic parameters while giving freedom of expression and trust to the individuals to 'produce the goods'.
- Encouragement of collective working. The work process is transcultural and transdisciplinary, and the project manager needs to be right on top of the progress to understand whether to swing the balance at a particular point or task, and if so, when.
- Support and protection for the team. Because the creative members of the team have skills that are hard to define and defend, the project manager creates a shield from outside influences to allow the creativity to flourish. They champion the team's beliefs outside the group.

■ Being there and being sensitive. Effective leaders of creative teams exert influence more by what they do than by what they say. They are there when needed for support of any kind. They relate sensitively to the individual as well as to team needs.

These key points represent a shift from how traditional management effectiveness has been perceived, and pave the way for new models to emerge. Over the last few years more has been done to try and understand the successful creative team because cross-functional and cross-disciplined teams have become increasingly necessary.

Barlow (2000) points out that with technology changing so fast, the traditional management role disappears even in the IT arena. Whereas previously the manager decided on the tasks, apportioned the work and judged its effectiveness, this does not happen as much now because it is more than likely the younger programmers know more than their bosses about the newer computer languages.

Furthermore even though they at least share a common perspective because of their discipline root and may relate to complex concepts within their discipline at a high level, once they are part of a team of mixed disciplines – as in web development – they meet a new kind of complexity where different perspectives conflict with each other. As well as the knowledge sets being different, there are differences in cognitive style, cultural background, personality and values, making collaboration even more difficult. In turn this makes it harder for the team to trust one another.

The next consideration is the complexity of the problems being solved. At a macro level these can be divided into structured and ill-structured problems. Problems where a structure can be perceived are of their nature easier to solve. The ill-structured problems display incongruities that make them difficult to solve. In multimedia development an example of this might be when stakeholders have values and goals that conflict about what they want in a website. Also, the team might have values and goals that conflict about the solution of how the site is to be structured, what it is to contain and what it is to look like. It is understandable given these examples that conversion to one set of goals and values is improbable but the process of attempting to solve the common problem can have spin-offs because people can adjust or shift their perspectives as a result of being involved.

A jointly understood compromise may help move people towards a solution and this might be achieved by using a process where the diversity of expectations of the people involved is made explicit. Then there can be an agreed move towards commonality or a compromise. Another tack might be an agreement to differ strongly on some aspects to highlight areas where there is more common ground between the participants.

Kaufmann (1980) investigated whether the approach to problem-solving made any difference. He found that easy problems presented in words were solved quickly. Medium-complex problems were solved better when represented in pictures. Complex problems were solved best by people getting physically involved with the actual problem and manoeuvring pieces of it until it was solved. This may have implications for the way the web team communicate their ideas to one another in the initial stages of design but the use of visuals to indicate structure and content of a website also has implications for clients and/or users. The rationale of using some visual methods – flowchart, idea maps, or site maps – is explained in Chapters 3, 4 and 6.

Barlow stipulates that one of the criteria for successful creative teams is that once they have decided on a course of action, disagreements about the goals, facts and criteria remain. He defines the knack of such a team working together in relative disagreement after seeking any clarification and simplifications that are possible but recognizing that consensus is impossible. Interestingly, Barlow came to the conclusion that one of the most effective techniques for guiding a team lay in focusing them on the benefits and effects desired by the customers. This supports the project management premises already put forward in the rest of the book but now are cited within the team perspective. He found that an even more effective technique for successful teams lay with defining the relative incremental cost of each benefit for the customer and balancing that against what the customer was willing to pay. This has obvious parallels with the project management techniques of establishing time, cost and quality already covered in scoping a project and in dealing with changes in a project. Lastly, he found that getting the team to position alternatives they had against criteria of the clients – a decision criteria matrix – was indicative of success. This technique was discussed in Chapters 3 and 4 and is extended under project management principles to include criteria derived from the users as well. All these techniques, Barlow found, stimulated more complex understanding of problems within a team that in turn released more creativity from the team about moves to a solution.

■ Characteristics of successful teams

Another approach to defining the characteristics of successful teams has been taken by Meredith Belbin (1981, 1993), who offers detailed insight into personality mixes, teamwork, success and failure. Personality attributes and behaviour characteristics can account for the success or failure of projects. Interaction skills within the project team can make or break it. Although Belbin's experiments were conducted with management teams selected on the basis of extensive psychometric testing, the personality attributes could be applied to any set of individuals who need to work in a team setting.

The use of psychometric testing as part of multimedia recruitment would not fit into the way the industry works at present. It is difficult enough to find the right technical and creative skill mix. But the project manager can benefit from understanding group dynamics, and may use the knowledge wisely to help in difficult situations.

Belbin's findings that appear to have relevance for multimedia will be summarized in the following paragraphs.

The premise that very high levels of mental ability in all team members make the best combination proved disappointing. It appeared that critical debate was a characteristic of these teams, and that there were difficulties in their reaching coherent decisions. They were difficult to manage. The emphasis within teams of high mental ability was analysis not synthesis, and in teamwork the analysis needs to be synthesized to move the ideas to tangible development. The teams performed best if there were one or two people of high mental ability and worst if there were none. The profile for teams from high-technology areas was one of high mental ability, and so there could be correlations between multimedia teams and these findings.

There is little that the project manager can do, as many of the necessary skills for a multimedia team warrant high mental ability. Critical debate is necessary in a creative, high-tech field, and specialists thrive on it. It forms part of their drive and motivation, both of which you need in the project. But if you recognize that the avenues explored lack cohesion, and no one else in the team provides a unifying stance, it becomes your responsibility. There will be a balance between allowing constructive debate and letting it run away with itself.

High-tech teams also portrayed the inability to have a rounded approach to viewing problems. This is a weakness associated with teams that have a concentration of specialists. Specialists were often found to have anxious-introverted personalities, and this was also noted as a cultural prevalence in high-tech companies. If the specialists had risen to management levels, they continued to display specialist tendencies. This also showed in the types of project that they selected. The projects tended to aim high within the specialisms rather than consolidating and refining known techniques.

There is a dilemma here because the literature has also shown that every project needs to be personally challenging for the team to give their best, otherwise they become bored or indifferent. The specialists may only be employing these principles, but because they are specialists they aim higher than others would. Again, you have to find the balance between personal challenge and achieving the project within time and budget. The business principles will help give the rounded perspective needed, or you might opt to invite a business specialist into some of the initial meetings to add balance.

The other option might be to share the criticisms of high-tech teams with your team as part of the critical debate. People can learn. They can begin to recognize when the team displays these tendencies and can move towards accepting the need to balance them. They may come up with some surprising strategies to compensate for them.

This would seem to leave multimedia project managers themselves in a vulnerable position. As indicated in earlier chapters, they often still carry a split role within the project, acting as specialist in one area and general project manager in the others. It is important that your own specialist views, as well as those of the other specialists, are considered within the business context of the application so that the criticism of narrowness in the team vision is avoided.

There are some points in favour of the project manager being a specialist where other specialists are present in the team. They are difficult to manage but they are more predisposed to respect people who are achievers within a related specialism. It will not make the role easier necessarily, but it will be easier to voice your opinion with confidence.

Belbin noted that if teams were composed around those who showed creative criteria, there appeared to be weakness of follow-through. There was an abundance of ideas but they were not utilized effectively. A team needed a creative source, but also needed the backup of people who would create the opportunity for the ideas to move into action. There are by definition many creative people as part of the multimedia team, and so this might present possible difficulties.

From Belbin's research, the team leaders who were most effective with computer application development teams were selected not for their experience and seniority in the field but for 'chairmanship' qualities. These were defined as the ability to recognize the strengths of the others in the team, to explore options that were raised, to back the right person at the right time, and to obtain good results. This does not, and could not, define how the leaders knew who to back or when and therefore influence the final decision. The data seems to support the thesis that the leader should not be the cleverest person in the team but should appreciate the strength in others, help them communicate in ways appropriate for the whole group to understand, and keep them focused on the objectives. However, the tasks that the team need to perform can also define the type of leader that is needed. If the team has been in a rut, someone who is extrovert can galvanize it into action and drive it forward, and therefore might be more appropriate than the 'chairman' character.

Eight role types were defined as necessary for potential management team excellence:

- a solid organizer;
- a catalyst who would draw the best from other members;
- someone with drive and a readiness to challenge;
- a creative, imaginative person;
- someone with the capacity to shape the ideas into action by using contacts and resources outside the team;
- a hard-headed judgemental figure;
- a person who responded well to people and situations and who would engender team spirit;
- someone with the capacity to follow through.

These roles represent the concept of an 'ideal' team mix where there is balance for the variety of management tasks that could arise. Often, each team member may have to fill a few roles as and when they arise. The dynamic nature of teamwork means that the needs shift, and therefore team members adjust their roles to cover the needs.

It was very difficult to find the last type of team member – the one who would finish the task and follow through on the detail. Many managers admitted that they lost enthusiasm for the tasks once the exciting and challenging first phase of definition had passed. This dwindling of interest is unfortunately characteristic of multimedia projects and project managers. The production phase is often beset with adjustment after adjustment for a variety of reasons, and this is wearing for the team.

THEORY INTO PRACTICE 14

If you are working in a team at present, put the initials of the team members most likely to fulfil the role types into Table 14.1. The names are shorthand for the roles described above, so refer to that paragraph for confirmation of the role types. They are not the original names used by Belbin, and have been adapted to suit a multimedia audience, but the role types conform to the original research.

Remember, one person can switch between several roles over the course of a project if necessary, although one role tends to dominate. It there are any gaps left, what are you going to suggest to try to achieve a balance for the team?

TABLE 14.1 Team role profile

Role type	Team member's initials
Solid organizer	
Catalyst	
Driver	
Creative	
Explorer	
Judge	
Carer	
Completer	

The end of the project spins out. Everyone wants to reach the final sign-off but it is the hardest to get. There is also a problem of reallocation of energy and resources from the team onto new projects, as these are phased in while the old ones are phased out. The team members are invigorated with the new, exciting challenges. The old project's appeal becomes stale.

This, one of the hardest phases for project managers, is made worse if the lack of finishing power is part of their own weakness. If the team members lack the will to complete tasks, and this is more characteristic of creative and analytical personalities, there is a problem in keeping the team on track to the end. It becomes the project manager's responsibility to get the project finished. The management of the company needs to recognize these problems, which are inherent in this type of teamwork, and back the project manager in the allocation of enough time and resources, as well as giving encouragement to the team to finish.

The other role that is a problem to fill in a team is the one of handling conflict or difficult situations. There is a tendency for the team members to opt out of this and leave it up to you even if the cause is related to a particular team member. The move between a hierarchical system where the team leader is accepted as the one who is directive, and the open team structure where whoever has the best fit of skills for the task takes the lead, is a strange feature of team interaction. There will be situations during the course of the project that need strong, hard decisions.

Take for example a graphics artist who likes working at night and so ends up arriving for work late in the afternoon. This becomes the norm. It is true that in multimedia there is tolerance for erratic hours, because the team will work hard and long to reach a milestone. But if the work habit of one member means that the rest of the team find it very difficult to communicate the necessary tasks, then some action has to be taken. The behaviour increases the time taken to complete a phase, and the error rate for the work is likely to increase because of the miscommunication. You will have to decide the course of action. If, after explaining the reason for the request, the team member fails to rectify the situation, what are your options?

You will need the backing of the rest of the team to take further action or you risk alienating them, but if they agree with the problems it is causing, and that the member's actions are detrimental to the project, you have the backing to become more formal with the treatment, which could lead to a change of staff for the sake of the project. The main problem lies in getting a replacement up to speed versus the disruption caused by the present situation, but the longer the situation remains unresolved, the more unsettling will be the effect on the team. You will need to take the lead in these situations because you have the nominal authority and the links to higher management. The main problem is the switch between the open, less formal management style that you need to adopt to allow the ideas to flow within the team and the traditional role of a strong director.

The only other way that these tough team problems are resolved is by getting the core team to commit themselves to mutual accountability for the project. If your company employs performance monitoring, there could be scope for doing this so that team objectives are set rather than individual ones. This might exert more influence over the team needing to work together and accept mutual responsibility for achieving the total project rather than expecting to fulfil the specialist role only.

If the team is performance driven and the tasks have been determined and agreed between all, then this should help keep the group working towards common goals and feeling mutually responsible for achieving them. Then the team itself should help to coerce errant members, because everyone's work is interdependent.

Belbin's work has moved on now to encompass the ideas of balance between a team role, a work role and a professional role and how these differ for an individual within an organization. He has devised a colour-coded approach to help managers and jobholders define tasks and responsibilities in a way that allows flexibility and individual as well as joint responsibility. This is aimed at making the appraisal process better for both manager and jobholder.

There is now a quick online team role analysis offered by Belbin with accompanying reports (see the references for details) but remember that the role names were adapted here for the work set. It is easy to transpose the principles to the labels used as the standard by Belbin if you want to try this out with your team.

There has been some criticism of Belbin's approach to defining teams based mostly on questioning the validity of the self-perception of a team member. Critics feel that self-perception does not give a balanced understanding of a person's role and should be counterbalanced by opinions of other members of the team. Also, his research approach has received some criticism since the teams he based his findings on were ad hoc teams put together in a training setting rather than real teams operating in their own environment. These criticisms are offered as a balance and you need to read the original works to decide how you might apply the principles to best effect.

■ How the organization can affect team management

Because it is hard enough to recruit the functional skills for the core team, balancing the interpersonal skills so that there is a blend that will cover the eight role types may be like looking for needles in a haystack. The mental ability, creativity, and personality factors needed for multimedia development almost seem to work against teamwork and project management.

But an understanding of the blend that can provide a good team mix is a tool in itself that should help you to analyse some of the problems you'll experience better than before. It may provide some answers to the need for key extra resources that might have to be brought in at various stages as cement, for example.

In Chapter 2, specific examples were given to show how the structure of the organization you work for can affect your role as project manager. It can influence your team management if the in-house team members report to a functional boss as well as to yourself. The team members can have split loyalties, which may affect their work on the project. They may be pulled to work in different directions by both of you and find it difficult to reconcile their duties to the project and to the company at large. The company management needs to recognize this potential conflict and define the respective roles for the functional manager and the project manager so that the team is clear how they should relate to both.

The team will need frequent meetings to communicate how individual parts of the project are progressing and for you to pass on detailed information of the client's latest reactions. The organization can facilitate these meetings by having meeting rooms that are accessible and well laid out. People can take communication seriously or not, but the environment can help to provide the right stimulus for good communication. There is nothing as frustrating as holding a team meeting in the corridor or in part of an open-plan space with the constant noise of telephones ringing, copying machines, and interruptions from other people. Clear communication in a pleasant room takes a shorter time and causes less disruption of not only your own team's work but also that of other people, than the disorganized, patchy communication that takes place in crowded environments.

The layout of a meeting room can influence contributions from the team, so you need to recognize this and organize the room accordingly. A round table or a circle of chairs gives the best non-hierarchical feel to a meeting and encourages everyone to contribute. If you are trying to engender an open, constructive team culture, the circle will help. An oblong table encourages a hierarchical feel, particularly if you sit at the head of it in the traditional leader position. If you have no choice in this, at least sit on one side instead of at the top of the table.

Pointing out environmental factors is not popular with companies, although they are one of the few factors they can control or influence. Take the previous example of the graphics artist who had antisocial hours, which made it difficult for the rest of the team. The artist may well have said that the reason for the hours was that he or she was more productive when it was quiet in the office than when it was hectic. In this case, how would you deal with the situation?

Open-plan offices are common in multimedia companies, and the variety of tasks and people needed creates a busy, communication-rich environment. This in turn creates noise. The type of task that people have to complete affects the level of concentration. Multimedia is characterized by specialists' constructing pieces of the project. Concentration is needed here. There is also a good deal of demonstration and discussion to refine the parts as they are integrated, as well as general meetings to communicate both inside the team and to a larger group of company management and clients. It seems self-evident that the environment needs to support contemplative work and communication.

If environmental problems are genuinely affecting the performance of your team, the least you can do is voice your concerns to company management with any suggestions that could help in the short term. Perhaps working from home for a number of days with definite meetings in the office on regular occasions might suit some parts of the project. Perhaps reallocation of members of the team within the building or rooms could help. Perhaps the team themselves could come up with some suggestions.

De Marco and Lister (1987) correlated environmental factors with best programming performance in their surveys of programming projects. If the space was quiet, private, large and protected from interruptions, performance was on average 2.6 times better. Of course, this was part of a larger context of research, and the ability of the programmers was also taken into account. De Marco and Lister's description of how interruptions affect concentration flow is interesting. It takes about 15 minutes for someone to focus at the right level of concentration for intellectual work to flow. If they are interrupted it takes another 15 minutes to settle back into the same level. This means that phones ringing, colleagues interacting, and enquiries can be extremely disruptive for productivity. This can certainly affect your project. If there are any strategies that you can use to influence environmental factors, use them.

There are laws governing the ergonomic layout for workstations, the amount of space, lighting conditions, and the amount of use of screens. These vary from country to country. There are concerns over issues of eye strain, repetitive strain injury, and the effect of emissions on skin diseases and on pregnant women. As project manager it is in your interest to keep abreast of the regulations to ensure conformity. The health and safety aspects of the environment are the employer's responsibilities, but the welfare of your team is yours for the duration of the project.

THEORY INTO PRACTICE 15

Think of the project manager or manager you have admired most to use as your role model.

Using John Whatmore's elements of the successful creative team leader as a checklist, how does your manager line up? Do the criteria work for your role model? Are there any noticeable omissions? Would you add any extra criteria? How would you measure up if your team was asked to do this exercise?

List the functional/technical, decision-making/problem-solving and interpersonal skills for your role model. List any weaknesses. Then list your skills in these areas together with your weaknesses.

Finally, draft the same list again but write it from the perspectives of your team members or colleagues, or, even better, ask them to fill the list in for you. What would they consider your strengths and weaknesses in a management role?

Compare the lists and decide on your own development needs from them.

■ Summary

- ■ The aim is to create a good team culture of cooperation and effectiveness.
- ■ Team leadership means representing the team to management as well as setting the direction for the project.
- ■ As project manager you'll need to employ a variety of management styles to suit different circumstances.
- ■ The use of project management principles has been equated with success within creative teams.
- ■ Effective managers of creative teams exhibit behaviour that is different from traditionally accepted models of management.
- ■ Personality traits of multimedia teams can cause problems for performance management.
- ■ The environment can affect the team's performance.

■ Recommended reading and references

Belbin R.M. (1981). *Management Teams: Why They Succeed or Fail*. Oxford: Butterworth-Heinemann

Belbin R.M. (1993). *Team Roles at Work*. Oxford: Butterworth-Heinemann

De Marco T. and Lister T. (1987). *Peopleware: Productive Projects and Teams*. New York: Dorset House Publishing Co.

Honey P. (1988). *Improve Your People Skills*. London: Institute of Personnel Management

Katzenbach J.R. and Smith D.K. (1993). *The Wisdom of Teams: Creating the High-Performance Organization*. Boston, MA: Harvard Business School Press

Kaufmann G. (1980) *Imagery, Language and Cognition*. New York: Columbia University Press

Phillips N. (1992). *Managing International Teams*. London: Pitman Publishing

Speake T. and Powell J. (1997). *Skills for the Missing Industry: An Exploratory Study*. Sheffield: DFEE

Tjosvold D. (1991). *Team Organization: An Enduring Competitive Advantage*. Chichester: Wiley

Whatmore J. (1997). *Managing Creative Groups: What Makes People Good At It*. Horsham, West Sussex: Roffey Park Management Institute report.

☐ Websites/articles/resources

Christopher M. Barlow (2000) *Creativity and Complexity in Cross Functional Teams*. Stuart Graduate School of Business, Chicago
http://www.stuart.iit.edu/ipro/papers/html/barlow.htm

Meredith Belbin's official website – there are lots of unofficial ones!
http://www.belbin.com/home.html

Articles critical of Belbin

Self-Perception is no Basis on Which to Build a Team
Barbara Senior, Nene College

Management Team Composition: A Spurious Balance?
Dr Chris Dawson, Ms Pat Lord and Mr Gary Pheiffer, all at Thames Valley School
of Management
http://www.solent.ac.uk/sbs/iconoclastic/list.html

Team resources – general

Center for the Study of Work Teams (University of North Texas)
http://www.workteams.unt.edu/index.htm

Rights, copyright and other intellectual property

Project manager's responsibilities

- To ensure that all assets used in the application are cleared for the correct use

- To avoid the rights status of the whole application being compromised by uncoordinated rights issues

- To consult expert opinion if there are any doubts

■ Rights and wrongs

Suppose I came round to your house for dinner one evening, and you showed me a beautiful model boat you had made. It had taken you several weeks to build it, and you had lovingly fashioned every plank on the deck and every line in the rigging yourself. It was well made and I liked it. To quote the Bible, I coveted it. So on the way out of your house I hid the boat under my coat and walked away with it. Is that theft?

Once I had reached my house I took your boat and put it into a machine that made copies of it: each copy indistinguishable from the original. I took those copies down to the market the next day and sold dozens of them and paid you nothing. Have I done anything illegal or immoral?

Suppose I came round to your house for dinner one evening, and you played me a beautiful song you had written. It had taken you several weeks to compose it, and you had lovingly fashioned every nuance in the melody and every line in the lyrics yourself. It was well written and I liked it. To quote the Bible, I coveted it. So on the way out of your house I remembered your song. Is that theft?

Once I had reached my house I took your song and sang it into a machine that recorded it and then made copies of it. I took those copies down to the market the next day and sold dozens of them and paid you nothing. Have I done anything illegal or immoral?

In law a copyright is as much an object as something you can touch. It can be traded and it can be passed on to your heirs. Unfortunately it is also intangible. You cannot actually touch it, and so it does not match our usual understanding of a property.

Copyright is one important aspect of what are called intellectual property rights (IPR). This chapter has two aims. First, it will provide some background to copyright itself, and why it is important, and second it will outline some of the rights models used in the media to see whether they can be applied in a particular multimedia application for the licensing of IPR and assets. There is a caveat. Intellectual property is a complex area of the law, and expert advice should always be sought if there is any doubt. It also differs from country to country, and even the basic philosophy behind rights differs between countries. The growth of the Internet has complicated the issues even more. This chapter is intended only as an introduction and not as a user guide.

■ In the beginning

Copyright as a concept in English law has its roots in new technology. In the second half of the fifteenth century the invention of printing made it possible for books to be mass-produced, and as a result unauthorized copying of literature was a possibility. The book printers – the stationers – formed themselves into a guild, and were granted a royal charter in 1556. Under this charter lawfully printed books were registered with the guild, and the guild had powers to act against unauthorized copies.

The first copyright act in the UK dates from 1709, and gave the 'sole right and liberty' of printing books to authors and whoever they assigned rights to. Protection was for a period of 14 years from publication but could only really be enforced if, as before, the book was registered with the Stationers' Company.

Later revisions of the law widened the net to include other creative works such as engravings and music. Eventually the emphasis on copying had to be extended to embrace rights of usage for performances of music and drama, and eventually sound recordings, cinematograph films and broadcasting joined the fray, the concept of what is still called **copyright** extending to embrace new means of distributing intellectual property.

From this beginning has come international agreement on the protection of intellectual property. This covers inventions, copyrights and, to a lesser degree, designs and a recent addition, moral rights. To a great extent the introduction of moral rights into English law reduces some of the differences from, say, French law. The English approach has been that protection of copyright is protection of the material benefit of exploiting that right. This is why English law protected the rights of printers. The French and Belgian perspective is that copyright is in some way a recognition of the artistic achievement of the author. In fact in French law it is not copyright that is protected, but *droit d'auteur* – the right of the author.

☐ Getting a copyright

In US, UK and European law a copyright is created at the same time as the copyright work. The situation used to be different in the USA, where you had to publish using a particular notice of copyright, or in some cases register a copyright for it to be in existence, but this situation was anomalous and recently changed (although, before an infringement suit may be filed in court in the USA, a work of US origin has to be registered and there are other advantages relating to damages among other things). Registration fixes a date on your work. An alternative way of doing this would be to send yourself a copy by registered mail, which fixes a date to the copy in the envelope as long as it remains unopened. However, it is possible for two people simultaneously and independently to produce the same thing, so this method isn't infallible.

You can have copyright in a work of art (painting, drawing, sculpture, and so on), literature (prose or poetry – even the source code of a computer program), music (more on this later), and in a photograph, movie, or television programme. There has to have been some effort exercised to create a copyright, so that by photocopying a drawing you do not create a new copyright – you only risk infringing the original one. US law requires that creative effort took place before a copyright is created. The condition, in English law, is sometimes called sweat of the brow, and is less demanding.

The advent of electronic reproduction and wide area public networking through the Internet has confused the copyright situation, and the law keeps changing to cope with it. Until the twentieth century there was no need to recognize that there could be copyright in a photograph or sound recording, and as time has gone on whole new issues have been added to intellectual property, such as 'look and feel': can you protect the way your user interface works? – Apple and Microsoft have been battling over this issue for many years. Recently an important US court held the menu commands of a leading spreadsheet program to be uncopyrightable.

International agreement on copyright has been based on a series of conventions that are ratified by governments. Since the distribution of intellectual property is an international business it is only equitable that a country should expect the same kind of protection for its citizens' work in a foreign country as it gives to its citizens itself – or indeed gives to citizens of foreign countries. Needless to say, some countries have taken a more lax view of this kind of protection than others have, as any visitor to certain parts of the Far East may have found.

Although copyright protection is automatic in the USA and UK, it is considered good practice to assert the copyright by printing a notice such as © 2001 Elaine England and Andy Finney. Other phrases such as 'all rights reserved' and 'if you copy this we will send the boys round and sort you out' or the prominent FBI shield that you see on American videos are arguably a bit over the top. The reason for them is to remove any possibility that a defendant in court could claim he or she didn't know the material was copyright. This is of course no defence to a primary infringement, but it could be considered to be mitigation since ignorance of copyright is widespread. Primary infringement is the initial production of an infringing copy. In cases of secondary infringement, ignorance can be a defence in the UK. This would happen if, for example, you imported an infringing work or licensed the work and it was reasonable for you to believe that the person who provided the material owned or had cleared the rights. Even if an infringer acknowledges that 'copyright infringement is theft', as they say, there is also an attitude that copyright owners are rich and would not miss a few bucks. But we all have the potential to be copyright owners, and deserve not to be ripped off.

When you produce a copyright work as part of your employment, the copyright usually rests with your employer. However, when you commission a freelancer to produce it for you, the ownership of the copyright will usually rest in the first instance with the freelancer. For this reason, a commissioning company will often take copyright in a commissioned work under the terms of the contract, and this is probably the best way to avoid confusion. This situation is complex, especially when contributors are contracted via an agency, and a detailed discussion of this problem is beyond the scope of this chapter.

If you have to decide about copyright ownership you should think of it in terms of future use. If you as creator will have no further use for the work then you lose nothing by assigning copyright or granting an exclusive licence. Assigning your rights means that they are no longer yours: you have sold them, and an assignment is always exclusive.

As commissioner you have to be able to use the work for its intended purpose, which may or may not require you to own the copyright. (Computer program code is a special case, which is discussed later in this chapter.) Beyond these issues, the copyright in something is as much a part of the deal as the money paid, and can be negotiated, since the copyright has a value in itself that is distinct from ownership or use of the work. It is also unrelated to the time it took to create the work, since a Picasso sketch remains a Picasso sketch whether it took him ten days or ten seconds to draw it. To be safe, all copyright assignments and licences should be in writing. In fact, under US and English law, an assignment of copyright can only be made in writing.

Moral rights

Moral rights are a relatively new addition to intellectual property in English law. This provides a method in law for you to be credited for your work (called paternity or attribution) and for your work to be used only in ways of which you approve and without unauthorized changes (integrity). Given the interactive nature of multimedia, moral rights are quite significant, especially integrity. It is worth noting that you can do anything with a work if the author consents. In the USA, moral rights are narrow and usually apply only to visual arts.

The composer of a piece of music has a moral right for the music not to be edited. You should not cut out the verses to leave just the chorus or change the order of the verses. If you design an interactive application that allows the user to do things like this then you risk a claim for conspiring or inducing infringement of the moral rights of the composer. For this reason most music publishers will not allow you to include a song in your multimedia application under circumstances where the user can change the music because they do not have the permission of the composer to do so. Music will be discussed in more detail later.

When a graphics artist builds a montage of images from many sources there is a risk of infringing moral rights. A particular photographer might take exception to having something extracted from the image or to having the image cropped. Juxtaposition of one image with another might be problematic for reasons other than copyright because it is possible to libel someone by publishing an unwisely montaged or positioned picture, so great care should be taken with this. Is it real or is it PhotoShop? An extreme example would be to build a photograph of a notable teetotal politician drinking a glass of water into a montage so that he appears to be drinking in a vodka distillery. Because computer technology is now quite able to produce images of non-existent objects, such as the scenes of ancient Rome in the movie *Gladiators*, in a way that is very difficult to distinguish from reality, this problem is only going to get more difficult.

Because moral rights are new to English law there is less guidance on what can and cannot be done than there is with more established areas of copyright. One possibly contentious area arises because the author or authors of a computer program have no rights of paternity or integrity. This is because computer programs are often written by large teams. But does this also apply to multimedia? As a creative person your future depends on people recognizing your past work, and it is important that credit is given where it is due. There will be instances where, as a multimedia developer, your client will attempt to deny you a credit. Your only straightforward way of achieving your just credit is to insist on it in your contract with the client, rather than by relying on the law. Conversely, many commissioning contracts will include a clause waiving moral rights.

Exceptions

One problem with copyright, if taken to extremes, is that while the owners have their rights, the rest of us should also have some leeway to enable life to go on; and the concepts known as fair use (fair dealing in the UK) and insubstantial portions come into play. In law, and in the right circumstances, these are two important exceptions to infringement. A critic reviewing a book has the right to quote from it without asking permission. A student studying the works of an artist has the right to photocopy illustrations to include them in a research paper as long as you give sufficient acknowledgement to the author and the work itself. You can quote a small (insubstantial) extract from a literary work, again with an acknowledgement. Reporting of current events and news gives a lot of leeway: but note that this exemption does not extend to reproduction of photographs.

In the USA there are also exceptions for parody and even some commercial use may be fair if it does not injure the copyright owner.

Unfortunately we cannot always benefit from these exceptions in websites and multimedia productions. Recently, in English law, it has been ruled that some of the exceptions to infringement do not apply if you are making a commercial product, and a multimedia title for sale would be commercial. The term 'insubstantial portion' does not necessarily mean that anything short is OK, and two obvious exceptions to this are the denouement of a mystery novel and a line of poetry. The test is always one of degree, and there are no hard-and-fast rules about what constitutes an insubstantial portion. Importantly, this kind of exception applies only to literature, not a film or a piece of music for example, so you cannot argue that a four-second sample from a hit record is fair game because it is an insubstantial portion.

Alongside the exceptions included in copyright legislation there has to be an element of common sense. It is very difficult to judge whether a photograph will work in a montage or on a web page without trying it out. Here, technology is actually making things more difficult for us. In the old days, to make a mock-up of a page of a magazine, you might cut out copies of photographs from the colour supplements and paste them onto a piece of paper. That does not infringe copyright in the photographs. Doing the same thing on a computer involves scanning the photographs, and so you infringe the copyright unless you already have permission to scan the image into the computer. In this case the intention is the same, but changing the means by which you carry out your intention has led to a possible infringement.

One very constructive idea to get over the mock-up infringement problem has been implemented by some stock photo libraries, who give you a blanket permission to reproduce their images for mock-ups and many even supply low resolution images for this very purpose.

Music

One area of copyright that causes confusion is music, and it is worth going into this rights situation in some detail. The confusion arises because there are several different rights in music, which have grown up in custom and practice over the years.

Once you write a tune it is copyrighted, and you have the exclusive right to exploit that tune, which you might do yourself, or by licensing the rights to a publisher, who then 'works' the tune on your behalf for a fee. (You can license the rights for either the full duration of copyright or for a limited time.) Once upon a time music was 'plugged' by a song 'plugger' going to the

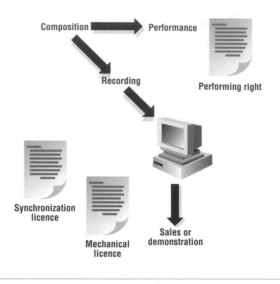

Music rights.

office of a band leader and playing the tune on a piano in the hope of the band's performing it. Today a 'plugger' is more likely to be taking a disc jockey out to lunch.

If you grant permission for someone to perform your tune in public, that is (logically enough) called the performing right. In the UK, performing rights in music are administered by a body called the Performing Right Society (PRS), and they collect money from radio stations, concert venues and the like. In the USA the equivalents of PRS are ASCAP, BMI and SESAC. In offline multimedia you are unlikely to have to deal with the performing right although, because of the similarity of wide area network distribution (for which read Internet) to cable, you may find that a performance licence is needed for something on a website. (Note that the Digital Performance Right Act and the Digital Millennium Copyright Act in the USA specify a number of ways in which sound recordings are handled in the digital world – of which more later.) If one of your multimedia productions is played at an exhibition, and it contains music, then permission is needed, otherwise the performing right is infringed. In the UK it is usually the responsibility of the venue to cover any fees due for public performance of music, and they probably have a blanket licence for this purpose, as do many bars and shops.

If your tune is recorded, another permission is required covering what is called the mechanical right. This right, administered in the UK by the Mechanical Copyright Protection Society (MCPS) and by the Harry Fox Agency in the USA, is quite distinct from the copyright in the recording. If you include a record or CD in your multimedia application you will need permission and a licence covering the music, which will come from a music publisher, and a separate licence for the use of the recording, which will come from a record company. This need for a dual licence has led to some publishers setting up special libraries for use in film and television – and now multimedia – where all the rights are controlled by the publisher, so they become a one-stop shop for music. Using these recordings is always cheaper, so library (sometime called production) music should be your first choice for music in multimedia.

With library music the licence is usually called a synchronization licence because the music is mostly used synchronized to images in films and television, and this generally does not attract a royalty payment, just a fee based on duration used. You and the library publisher can also negotiate for reductions, royalties or whatever you jointly agree.

Another significant benefit of library music is that it is provided specifically for you to tailor to your needs. The publisher will expect you to edit it to fit your requirements. This will not be the case with a commercial gramophone record where you would normally have to explain in some detail just what you want to do with the recording before permission is considered. The British Musicians Union also considers that interactive multimedia (and presumably use of a website) is a different usage compared with sale of a record or CD, and might require that you pay another session fee; this fee would be in addition to a licence from the record company and the publisher. The session fee is the fee paid to the musicians for playing the music at the recording unless they were members of a regular group, in which case they would probably receive royalties from sales.

When you license a music recording from a record company, the company may have to pay royalties to the principal performers from your usage, depending on the contract between the record company and the artistes. In many cases, use in multimedia, whether online or offline, would not be covered by their contract, and the record company would have to negotiate for the right with the artiste before being able to license it to you. This may be impractical, and so the record company would have to refuse you a licence.

Alternatively you could get the music specially composed and recorded, and a surprising number of multimedia projects do this. This ignores what a good library publisher can offer, but it does ensure that you have original music, which might be very important to your application. If you do commission music, you should make sure you take further exploitation rights. This would enable you to use the music in a sequel, or to release a record if (say) your games theme was a hit.

The World Wide Web

In general, countries want to make the effect of new technology on copyright fit into the existing legal framework. At its root a website should be viewed legally as any other publication. It has more similarity with a magazine or even a television programme than with a CD-ROM because it is (or should be) a living updated thing. Legally, websites can be considered to be cable programmes, and this is the basis on which music is currently licensed for them in the UK. This definition excludes videoconferencing, Internet telephony or chatrooms because these are two-way interactive things, but this is exceptional.

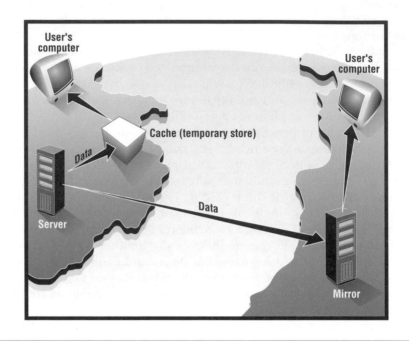

Caches, mirrors, and Web linking.

The technical way in which a website makes its way from the original server to the viewer's screen means that copies of the site can exist in caches and sometimes on mirror sites. All web browsers use local caches to stop re-downloading of data that has already been downloaded, and some Internet service providers have caches to reduce long-distance download times for pages frequently viewed by their customers. In an extreme case the original site, the cache or mirror and the viewer can be in three different legal jurisdictions.

Whereas a cache is a necessary and automatic part of the functioning of the Web, a mirror is not. (A mirror is a copy of a site on another machine, usually in another part of the world, to expedite access from a distance.) This means that it could be argued that anyone publishing material on the Web knows that transient copies will be stored in caches and so implicitly authorizes them. This is not so with mirrors, and explicit permission must be sought to mirror a site. An alternative point of view is that a cache is a necessary backup of software (the HTML being computer code) and so is legitimate, but since your browser will work if you turn off the cache this argument might not be so solid.

There are some programs that download a site quickly to allow you to read it offline at your leisure (you can do this with Internet Explorer for example), and the otherwise transient caches of Netscape Navigator and Internet Explorer can themselves be accessed offline either using programs such as Netscape History or by the simple expedient of configuring the browser to work offline.

Caches and mirrors may also disrupt the usual logging of accesses of the site's pages, and if this is a crucial part of an agreement for advertising then we have a problem. In some cases a cache will check to see whether a page has been updated, and this shows on the site log in a distinctive way.

Linking from one page to another is a key part of the Web, and it is assumed that anyone can link to anyone else freely. When I find someone has linked to my pages I am delighted. However, not everyone would be so happy under all circumstances. A link can be seen as an endorsement or possibly as a claim of authorship. Under some circumstances it can be defamatory or encourage copyright infringement. Also, consider the use of frames to show another website as if it were part of yours or using the image source HTML link to bring someone else's image into your page (known as inlining). In neither case is there any copying done since the final page is assembled only in the viewer's browser window but both of these instances go beyond simple display of a web page and so may well go against any implied licence.

The much-publicised case between two newspapers in Shetland seemed to revolve around whether just linking to another page could infringe copyright. In fact the result does not appear to have related to this issue but rather around copying of headlines on the Web pages themselves. The Web community could breathe again.

Parts of the 1998 Digital Millennium Copyright Act (DCMA) in the USA served to clarify some things about rights on the Internet, sometimes picking up from the implied licence. For example, ISPs were not to be liable for transitory files working their way through an ISP's system on their way from sender to recipient. Another section regularizes caching, but emphasizes that the caching must not interfere with mechanisms for counting hits.

In 1995 Congress created a Digital Performance Right in sound recordings and the DCMA added webcasting to the kinds of performance covered. In this case, webcasting was to be administered by a statutory licence, and also the production of ephemeral recordings in the process of preparing such webcasts (for example, by compiling recordings together into a sequence) would not infringe.

Domain names are a complex area in their own right. Although domain name registrars operate a 'first come first served' system for granting use of names this has to be seen in the light of other legislation. In registering a domain name you may be at risk of infringing a trade or service mark. You might think that companies who have such rights to names have registered the relevant names but this is not necessarily so. Where the domain name includes the trade mark, or is deemed to be close enough to it to cause confusion, then registration and/or use of the domain is likely to attract a lawyer's letter at the very least. You need to be careful to avoid this, possibly by searching the relevant trade mark registry. But marks can be used and recognized without being registered. You should be especially careful if your client insists that you register a particular domain name and should make it clear that you cannot take responsibility for any issues arising from this.

There is an interesting reverse use of trade marks in respect of domain names. The dilemma is that when new top level domains (TLD) are announced, they are often not available for registration for some time. But a company with trade names to protect will reasonably want to have the relevant domains in, for example .shop or .info. In this case, one way to 'reserve' the domain name is to register the whole domain name, including the TLD part, as the trade mark.

There are so many interesting points arising from the way the World Wide Web works (in the meaning of 'interesting' used in the famous Chinese curse 'May you live in interesting times') that it may be that the only solution is to widen the scope of fair use and fair dealing to take account of it. This is a point made in Graham Smith's book *Internet Law and Regulation*, which is in any case a good place to start if you want to explore this field further.

Databases

A database consists of a collection of items that are stored in such a way that they can be found in a systematic way. If the database consists, for example, of photographs or articles from a newspaper then these, individually, are copyright. If there is creativity (or even just skill) applied in the selection or arrangement of the contents then the database is in itself copyright. Even if the contents are not copyright then a new European right called *sui generis* is applied, which protects the database for 15 years from publication. In the case of a living updated database this could continue forever.

The *sui generis* protection of a database is a European concept and not an American one. The European protection is given only to 'owners' who are Europeans (as in the European Union), and this protection is not currently extended outside Europe unless similar protection is given to European databases in the other country. This means that an American database does not have this protection in Europe because the USA does not have the required legal concept. There have been moves to provide protection for databases in the USA but, at the time of writing, they were still being discussed in Congress.

The public domain and clip media

Copyright does not last forever. As the concept of copyright in law developed, so the time for which a work was copyright grew. At the beginning of the twentieth century copyright in the UK lasted only for the greater of 42 years from the date of publication or seven years after the death of the author. In the following 100 years the period has grown to allow the heirs of the author more time to benefit from the work, until the period in Europe reached 70 years after the year of death. This was 50 years in the UK until copyright was harmonized within the European Union.

In the USA the duration is much more complex than in Europe. Pre-1979 works are protected for an initial period of 28 years, renewable for a further 47 years. A work that first expired after 1963 was automatically renewed, but complex rules govern who actually receives the renewal rights. The duration of most copyrights in America is now the same as in Europe: life plus 70 years.

Any assumption that a work is out of copyright is fraught with danger, and you should seek professional advice, but in general a literary or artistic work is in copyright in Europe until 70 years after the end of the year in which the author died. This becomes more complicated for a translated work, where the translator has rights too, and similarly for illustrators and engravers.

In Europe, a sound recording expires 50 years after publication. So if you have an original 78-rpm gramophone record from before the late 1940s in your possession – an old Caruso recording, for example – then the recording is no longer in copyright. The tune, however, could well be in copyright since its copyright lasts for 70 years after the death of the composer. Similar arrangements apply to photographs, but for movies – known as cinematograph films – the situation is complicated since performance in public was not seen to be a publication. So some movies have surprisingly long copyright lives. The situation is not simple, and undoubtedly you can imagine the complexity of rights in a production containing multiple media forms, each of which has different copyright terms and needs world rights.

Incidentally, you should assume that a transcription onto CD of an old recording is copyright, especially if the sound was cleaned up in the process. It is possible to fingerprint digital files to identify the source, so if you wish to use an old record, you should clean it up yourself.

So now we come to the Mona Lisa. Since Leonardo da Vinci died over 70 years ago, the picture is out of copyright. It is so old that copyright did not even exist at the time. Therefore you might assume that you can include an image of the Mona Lisa in your application without permission. Unfortunately this is not the case, and the reason will become clear if you consider how you would acquire an image of the painting; stealing it from the Louvre is not an option.

If you owned the Mona Lisa you would have the right to control access to it and, as a result, to control reproductions. This is true of any collection of out-of-copyright works, usually in the hands of museums or art galleries. They will grant permission for reproduction, for a fee, as if the work was in copyright and they owned the copyright. The agreement you sign with the gallery allows you to use the image for a specific purpose. If you use it for another purpose you are not in breach of copyright but you are in breach of the contractual agreement. There will be a copyright in the photograph you receive from the library as well.

Going to the gallery or museum and photographing the picture yourself would not infringe copyright, but the museum would presumably allow you entry only on condition that you did not take photographs, or that if you were to do so, they would not be for publication. This is a contractual obligation on you, but it could be invalid if it was not brought to your attention before you bought your entry ticket. The Van Gogh museum in Amsterdam has a more straightforward approach. They do not allow anyone to take a camera inside. Incidentally, if you were able to take a photograph through an open window, you would not have infringed copyright or any contract. Whether the resulting image would be good enough to publish is another issue altogether.

In general the terms out of copyright and in the public domain are used to mean the same thing, but they are not exactly so. Copyrights expire after a time, but the owner has the right to give them away before this time if he, she or it (because an organization can own copyrights) so desires. The owner can also allow people to exploit the work without payment, with or without conditions attached. This is known as placing it in the public domain. However, just because an author places something, such as a piece of software, in the public domain does not mean that it is out of copyright. Often conditions are attached; so read the small print or the 'read me' file. The copyright on something placed in the public domain in this way will expire at the usual time.

NASA, like other US government agencies, places its material in the public domain. This means that you can use images from the space probes free of charge (apart from paying to get the picture itself). However, NASA does state that you cannot use the images in such a way as to suggest that NASA endorses your product. So there is a condition, albeit a relatively small one, attached. Since 1978 works of the US Government have not had copyright protection at all (Section 105 of the US Copyright Act), but this was not intended to extend outside the USA, which raises the question of European use and even of export outside the USA of finished works incorporating such material.

Some companies produce libraries of assets that are supplied royalty free for you to use on paper or in multimedia applications and Web pages. This is clip art, or clip media. This material is often still in copyright, and it is not really in the public domain either because you may have paid for a book or CD-ROM that contains it, and your use of the material is restricted. There is probably a restriction to make sure that you do not produce more clip media disks from their clip media disks, and you might be restricted to a certain number of images in a single production. But you do not have to pay anything else to use the material in as many productions as you like.

CD-ROMs of clip media range in price from tens to hundreds of pounds/dollars. You can even buy clip art in books, and the Dover Books series of clip art and design are a notable example of this. They often reproduce illustrations from Victorian books and magazines because they are, in themselves, out of copyright. If you own or have unrestricted access to hundred-year-old copies of the *Illustrated London News* or *Strand Magazine* (with its original Sherlock Holmes stories and illustrations) then you could exploit their contents because you have the actual out-of-copyright originals, assuming that the author and illustrator died long enough ago.

It is possible to obtain free material such as clip media by downloading it over the Internet. You should assume that something you can download is available for you to use only if you are explicitly told that this is the case. Usually there will be a page of contractual terms and conditions that you agree to by clicking on the link to start the download. Because Web pages can so easily be taken apart it is sensible to include a copyright notice on any image on a page as well as on the page itself, but bear in mind that the attitude to copyright on the Internet is loose, to say the least, and you should assume that someone somewhere will copy. On the Internet, infringement is considered to be the sincerest form of flattery.

As a multimedia developer you must think not only of the rights you take in assets you license but also of the rights you can take in any work you commission. You could be commissioning artwork from a graphic designer, photographs, music, or scripts. There is even the software written by your programmers.

As a rule of thumb you should explicitly acquire rights in any work done for you by your staff or freelancers. This would be included in the contract for the work but, for you to be sure, it has to be a contract with the person doing the work, not an agency or subcontracting company. If you are acquiring rights from a freelancer or subcontractor then he or she must be able to pass on those rights, and should indemnify you against any claims should that turn out not to be the case. You can acquire rights in future work if it is appropriate, and in Europe it is important to obtain all appropriate waivers of moral rights as well.

■ Some rights models

In order to make use of someone else's intellectual property in a project you have to get permission, and this will result in the granting of a licence for the use of the copyright material. It can be difficult to describe the rights involved, so one approach is simply to describe what the project is, how it will be used, and who will buy it. In some forms of media a number of specific rights have grown up that define the uses you can make of the material you have licensed. For illustration, here are a few examples:

■ **All rights**. As the name suggests, this type of agreement gives the developer all the rights for exploitation of the material. In practice this might be the kind of right taken in a small interview or script rather than a substantial contribution to an application. In the case of small contributions this kind of agreement might attract only a small fee, or maybe no fee at all. However, since an all-rights contract with no residuals (residuals being payments for further use of the material beyond the original purpose) is biased in favour of the producer or publisher rather than the contributor, it should be used with care. You should be careful when licensing material that was originally covered by all-rights agreements. With older material it is also possible that an all-rights agreement might not include new media, on the basis that such things as websites were not known when the author signed the agreement. Similarly, a broadcaster's all-rights agreement might cover only broadcasting, and so on.

■ **Non-theatric**.   In audiovisual publications, a non-theatric right is one that excludes broadcast, home video and theatric rights. This sounds a little back to front, but basically broadcasting is usage for radio or television transmission (and possibly cable), theatric is performance where the public pay to see the material (as in a cinema), and home video is performance where the public pay for the material. Non-theatric covers use in training, business, education, conferences and exhibitions. This is the case even if the public pay admission, because they are not paying specifically to see the material.

■ **Home video**.   This right, applied to videos, allows you to sell or rent the material to the general public. The equivalent for audio is the gramophone right, whereby record companies pay musicians to include their contributions on records.

■ **Internet** or **interactive right**.   This is a term that has recently been applied to a permission to use material on a website or on a CD-ROM. By definition, such a right is for the world.

■ **Flash fees**.   Still images, when used on television, are sometimes paid for on the basis of the time they are on screen. The common, but essentially impossible, question from picture libraries for multimedia is 'How long is it on screen?' Music will usually have a rate dependent on duration, but you do not 'still frame' a piece of audio. However, you could repeat a loop of music under a menu, for example. In this case you should negotiate a special rate for the use.

The terms used above are some that you might come across, and they are not platform specific. There seem to be two schools of thought regarding the licensing of assets for multimedia. The first says that the licence should relate to the market for the product. Terms such as non-theatric apply to that method of licensing. The second school of thought says that the method of delivering the material is more important than the market, and will want to license differently for analogue and digital, for interactive and linear, and for on- or offline.

Split market.

Similarly you have to consider whether a foreign language translation of a website or an application that otherwise remains the same should require renegotiation of the licence for pictures or music. With a website it may be the head URL that distinguishes one site from another as far as licences are concerned.

One model, adopted by at least one major multimedia developer, is to acquire rights for all versions on all platforms for the life of the product. The 'life of the product' is a vague term, which has as yet remained untested; it probably allows revisions but does not allow the material to be used in a project on another subject.

In the offline world, licences are also granted for territories. These may be language specific (such the amusingly named GAS – Germany Austria Switzerland), or regional (North America or EU), or historic (British Commonwealth). World rights used to be considered to be all-encompassing, but the advent of satellites has led to a solar system or universe territory. Remember that anything you put on a web page can be seen anywhere in the world, whether you intend it to or not, so a licence for the Internet is, by definition, a worldwide licence.

One usage issue that is exercising some multimedia developers is the question of contribution: 'Just what is the contribution of this asset to my project?' This is obviously a question that you should be asking when you assess a fee, but it can also become a negotiating point. Does an image that is seen only if the viewer navigates his or her way down through five levels to a particular screen of explanatory detail carry as much weight as an image in the main menu or home page?

The risk of following this path of argument is that, rather than lowering the fee for the less-seen image, it raises the fee for the one in the main menu. The question has to be judged on the basis of what is actually being bought. In practice it is the right of reproduction of the copyright image, related to the intended use, that is being bought. Trying to quantify how likely it is that a viewer will see the image is akin to differentiating between different pages in a book. (But book licences do distinguish between the 'ordinary' pages and the cover or frontispiece.)

Because of possible ambiguity and misunderstanding, it is dangerous to rely on terms such as 'non-theatric' or 'interactive' instead of a clear specification in a licence of exactly what media, platform and so on is actually meant. A licence should also say who owns the rights not expressly granted in the licence.

The already confusing rights situation in multimedia is compounded by different asset owners applying different models. Picture and music libraries work differently, and two picture sources may operate in different ways as well. Since there should be a known status of rights for the whole multimedia application, it is important not to risk one asset's compromising the others in terms of such things as the duration of a licence, or territories in which the application can be sold. Failure to pay attention to this can result in the rights in the whole product being affected by the lowest common denominator of rights in its individual assets.

This is perhaps less crucial for an online project such as a website than it is for a CD-ROM, simply because a website can be changed at any time very easily whereas a CD-ROM would, in extreme circumstances, have to be withdrawn from distribution and destroyed.

Royalties versus buy-outs

Should you pay royalties or pay a one-off fee for use of material? And if you buy out rights, what multiple of the standard fee should be used?

Obviously, if the multimedia project is never sold then royalties based on sales are impossible. A web page is never sold since it is usually freely viewable by anyone who accesses the URL. However, a web page can attract income through advertising or other means, so it is possible for there to be an income stream without actual sales.

Although a creator has every right to share in the profits from his or her work there are compelling reasons why a buy-out can be a fair offer. In a small market it might be a very long time before a royalty stream amounts to much. A buy-out on the basis of an estimated number of sales may lessen the opportunity for making more money in the long term but it does give the asset owner 'money now', which may be much better than 'maybe more money much later'. Look upon it as repositioning the risk, and consider the interest earned by investing the extra money instead of waiting for a royalty trickle.

From a practical point of view it can be difficult for multimedia developers to administer royalties if they are small companies. Often the applications are made for clients who pay the developer a fixed fee for the development, and the developer may not get any royalties, which does not provide a basis for any downstream royalty payments to asset owners. Clients may not be willing to undertake to pay royalties because they had no control over the negotiations.

In more mature media, such as books, television and records, companies have whole departments that handle royalty tracking and payments, and in time multimedia publishing will probably follow this model.

☐ Rights in code

The situation for rights in computer code is a little different from that for rights in assets because of the way code is written. It is often built up of fragments, libraries and routines that were written for other projects to carry out certain tasks such as drawing a picture to the screen or synchronizing sound and pictures.

It is custom and practice for software not to be sold but to be licensed. If you produce a multimedia application for a client you should not assign the copyright in the code to the client because that will make it difficult for you to reuse that work. Clients ought to accept this, but it does mean that you need to state it explicitly in the agreement with your client. You will, of course, have to grant a free licence to use the code, otherwise they cannot make use of what they have paid for, but they will not own it.

As a developer contracting software from a programmer you will have the opposite point of view, and will probably want to make continuing use of any code written for you. This means that you will have to explicitly take the rights you need from the programmer. If you have contracted a company rather than a person you need to be sure that they can assign you these rights because they have taken them. Should you ever want to license rights in code to your client then you have to have the rights yourself first. It's a basic rule – you cannot license rights you do not have.

A further point is that computer programs are specifically excluded from moral rights in Europe, although it is not clear how this exclusion would apply to multimedia applications given that they also contain literary, artistic, musical and other kinds of work. You might want to include a clause in any contract you make with your client to ensure that you get due credit for your work.

■ How to negotiate

There are no hard-and-fast rules, but a few guidelines will be helpful.

- Be fair and honest. Few rights holders are going to cheat you; they are just after an honest income. Similarly, you have a right to pay a fair price.
- Set yourself a target price, based on experience, but don't be unreasonable or inflexible. The more you do this, the more you will have a feel for costs.

- Accept that some rates are just not negotiable, because the owner does not want to negotiate.

- Be prepared to say 'Sorry, I cannot afford your rates' – but make sure you have time to change your plans for the project.

- Remember that the asset owner who has only one asset to sell may want more money than a library.

- If you run into trouble with an asset after an offline application is 'finished', never admit that to the asset owner. Balance the cost against the cost of changing the application (plus a new asset) rather than your original target price, since paying an extra 100 for the picture will cost you less than paying 200 to go back and change the application. In general, because of the way websites are built, this is less of a problem on the Internet.

- Be consistent in your description of the usage to be agreed. This is much more important than worrying about one picture costing too much, since one asset that cannot be used in Japan means your whole application cannot be used in Japan.

- If the man with the big cigar says that the voice-over fee is $20,000, accept that he is really trying to say 'Go away!'.

- Build up working relationships with asset owners, partly because it will make the negotiations more convivial, but also because buying in bulk can be cheaper.

- Don't confuse the technical cost (such as dubbing the film or photographing the picture) with the licence fee, and make sure you know which you are paying and when.

- If your source is not already digitized, you can offer to return a picture to a photo library quickly. They might lower their fee as a result. For a bulk deal you could even scan the images on their premises with your equipment. Don't forget to ask for permission to digitize images as part of the process of deciding what to use.

☐ The rights checklist

- Can we administer and pay royalties?
- What is our target fee for any particular kind of asset?
- What delivery platforms are we licensing for?
- Are we offline or online or both?
- Is the fee tied to page impressions on the website?
- Is excerpting for promotional editorial or advertising of the application included?
- What is the duration of the licence?
- What territories are covered?
- Are foreign language versions covered?
- How do the agreements relate to my expected pattern of sales in these territories and languages?
- Are further editions of the work covered?
- Are bug-fixes covered or would they be considered new editions?
- Are derivative versions covered?
- Have the asset providers indemnified us against claims for infringement should they not have true title?

■ ... and finally, jurisdiction, distance selling, patents and data protection

One of the more significant things that the Internet has done to communication is to internationalize it. Anything you put on your website can be seen by people in most of the countries in the world. Before the Internet, worldwide publishing involved making licensing or distribution deals with different people in different countries, and arranging for shipping of items of software between continents. Now all that it takes is to tell someone that your URL exists and say 'Please come and look'. Unfortunately this raises the issue of legal jurisdiction. Jurisdiction is basically the law you come under.

This could be important in multimedia publishing on the Internet, partly because everything you publish that way is available internationally. Just because your website is situated in Denver, Colorado doesn't mean that you

have to clear rights only for the USA. People in the UK or Egypt or Russia or New Zealand can see what you have published. But rights are not the only issue. A libel committed on the Internet, such as in a Usenet newsgroup, could be read anywhere, so a legal action could in theory be taken anywhere. The state of Minnesota declared that its consumer protection legislation was applicable to any online purchases – even if the purchase did not involve a buyer, seller or recipient in that state. Basically the internationalization caused by the Internet lays any Web publisher or supplier – including you with your home web page – open to action anywhere in the world. So be careful.

The territorial restrictions placed on DVD (in its movie form) by the film companies are a similar issue to that of jurisdiction. Here, DVD disks have a territory flag in the data that says which part of the world the disk is licensed for. A disk licensed for the USA will not, for example, play in a European or Japanese machine. It is likely that any equipment or technique that might be employed to circumvent such a restriction would be, in itself, illegal ('protection against circumvention of technological measures used by copyright owners to protect their works' is specifically mentioned in the Digital Millennium Copyright Act and similarly in European legislation). This might become a multimedia issue if you were to produce a movie-playing application that played a DVD movie disc on a computer but ignored the territory flag. In any case, since DVD movies are encrypted you will have to have a license to decrypt and display the movie and this licence will itself place restrictions on what you are allowed to do. (Notwithstanding the open publication of decryption codes on a number of websites!)

While it is beyond the scope of this chapter to go into detail about law covering selling on the Internet it is worth mentioning two points. First, sales taxes and the way they are charged have usually worked on the basis that if a buyer and seller are in different countries then no sales tax is due: in the USA this has applied to buyers and sellers in different states. In Europe this is changing. Value Added Tax, the equivalent of sales tax in Europe, has complex rules applying to sales between countries in the European Union, and in principle, sales of goods or services to someone not registered for VAT (usually a home consumer rather than a business) are counted as if the buyer and seller were in the same country. In this case tax is applied in the seller's country. The rules if the buyer is VAT-registered are less straightforward and are known as the rules of 'place of supply': if you are VAT-registered then you have to know about these before you issue an invoice. The complication comes when you are supplying what are called 'electronically delivered services' and this includes sales of anything which is downloaded across the Internet. In this case the 'place of supply' is the country in which the buyer is, not the seller because the rule says this is 'where the service is enjoyed'. As a result, if you are in the EU and you make enough supplies of this kind to customers in other EU countries, you may have to register for VAT in your customers' countries as well as your own. This rule does not apply to physical goods bought over the Internet which are then shipped to the buyer conventionally. If in doubt, check with UK Customs and Excise or your equivalent VAT authority.

The reach of VAT may even cross the Atlantic since, at the time of writing, it is being suggested that American companies (and others outside the EU) who provide 'electronically delivered services' to non-business customers in Europe, such as downloads of software bought over the Internet, should collect VAT just like they would collect sales tax from someone in the same US state. The reasoning behind this is that, as downloaded software cannot be checked and taxed at the border like a physical package, then the government is losing out on some tax money.

Finally on the sales front, recent harmonization of legislation called the 'Distance Selling Directive' is being introduced across Europe to provide consumer protection for any remote selling, including by telephone and the Internet. It will place obligations on the seller, many of which are common sense but also many of which are new.

And so to patents.

You cannot copyright an idea, only the form in which the idea is expressed. The idea that a television transmitter and receiver could be put in an orbit so high above the earth that it appeared to be stationary, and could then be used to relay television signals, cannot be copyrighted. It could be patented – or could have been in 1944, when Arthur C. Clarke wrote his famous *Wireless World* article on the subject. The article itself, being the expression of the idea in literary form, was copyright, and indeed will be for at least the next 70 years since, at the time of writing, Mr Clarke is still very much alive.

A patent is a document given to you by the government granting you the exclusive right to exploit and control exploitation of a process for doing something. You have to be able to describe the process in such a way that any reasonably capable person could carry out the work from your description; so you cannot be vague and, say, patent time travel without describing how to do it. The process must not be obvious (patently obvious?) since there has to have been an inventive step in the process that you have seen but others have missed. Finally you have to have done it first. If you were beaten to the idea by someone who can prove it then your patent will not be granted, or could be declared invalid, even if you genuinely knew nothing about the other idea. This is called prior art.

Prior art can come from the craziest places. One, possibly apocryphal, instance tells of a patent examiner who was trawling through literature to see if a particular new idea had been described before. He finally found a reference, but it was not in a scientific journal or a PhD thesis: it was in a comic book.

In most countries you have to keep quiet about your invention, since disclosure can invalidate the patent as well. So do not be tempted to give a learned paper on the subject too soon. Timing is critical, and swear everyone you discuss it with to secrecy – that is, non-disclosure.

If you have been granted a patent, you have the right to control use of your idea for (in most countries) up to 20 years from the date of filing. A patent does not actually have to be taken out by the inventor. Often employers will take out patents based on work done by their employees. The employee will be the inventor but the employing company will have the patent rights if the work is done during the course of the inventor's employment.

The process of getting a patent is both time-consuming and costly. It is important that a patent is carefully worded so that it can stand up to scrutiny for inventiveness. A particular kind of lawyer called a patent agent should be involved in this process. Currently there is no such thing as an international patent. The patent will have to be applied for in every country for which protection is required. This should be the countries in which your product would be used or manufactured. You have the right to stop both sales and manufacture of an infringing item – or to negotiate a royalty payment.

In Europe a computer program cannot, as such, be patented. However, a technical process can still be patented even if a program is key to how it is done. It is the technical process that is patented, not the software behind it. But this distinction is more easily seen in an industrial context than in the kind of work done in multimedia. The UK Government Intellectual Property website explains that a program to improve translation between two languages would not be patentable because translation was not a technical process. A program to improve image manipulation would, however, be patentable.

However, since software patents are granted in the USA that would not be granted in Europe, it is important that possible patent infringement is considered when learning from other people's techniques on the Internet. The risk is probably slight, especially given how much code is freely available under such things as the GNU Copyleft [sic], but should not be ignored. Fortunately, the possibility of multimedia per se being covered by a patent seems to have gone away, although the patent in question was still under discussion by the US Patent Office and its owners at the end of 2000.

A final point is that in the process of granting you the 'letters patent' the government will also publish your invention. This will happen even if you decide not to pursue the patent.

As the inventor you have the choice of patenting your invention. If you decide not to patent it you should consider finding a way of establishing your prior art by publicizing your idea. If you do this, someone else trying to patent the same process later on will not be able to gain a patent and so stop you making use of your 'own' invention. Altruistically, publishing your idea allows other people to make use of it. It is the equivalent of shareware.

Although you cannot copyright an idea, and many ideas cannot be patented or would not be because of the cost and time involved, you can protect your idea by contract. If you need to discuss your idea with anyone you should get them to sign a non-disclosure agreement (NDA) in which they agree not to disclose your idea. That will afford you a measure of protection, and, along with terms and conditions of trade, every company should have a stock NDA.

Data protection is a broadly European concept in law, and it is a particularly important issue for websites which have customer relations management (CRM). Basically, under English law, anybody who controls data relating to living people may have to be registered under the Data Protection legislation. The definitions of a data controller and a data subject, and the eight Data Protection Principles, are carefully set out in the UK Act and in the guidelines for registration.

The eight principles can be summarized as follows – the data must be:

- fairly and lawfully processed;
- processed for limited purposes;
- adequate, relevant and not excessive;
- accurate;
- not kept longer than necessary;
- processed in accordance with the data subjects' rights;
- secure;
- not transferred to countries outside the European Economic Area without adequate protection.

If you produce a database that contains personal information about living people you are a data controller and must be registered. There are exceptions for data used for business marketing and personnel purposes, and for 'household' information such as Christmas card lists. The 1998 UK Act changed some of the ways that the data protection legislation worked.

Data protection is not dealt with in the same way by every country. There is no such thing in the USA at a national level but it is clear that not having an arrangement for transferring data between Europe and the USA would be a serious problem as you will see from the final principle listed above. To resolve this, the EU and US administrations came up with the 'Safe Harbour' principle whereby individual companies would agree to comply with the principles of data protection. In this way the safety of the data is guaranteed by the American company rather than by the law.

THEORY INTO PRACTICE 16

Study some licence agreements and other contracts to help you understand how agreements are drawn up.

Some of the references below, Henry, for example, contain sample contracts you can look at.

Perhaps your company has agreements from previous projects you can look at as well.

■ Summary

- Copyright is a property like any other and, as such, should be respected. A copyright is automatically granted when certain kinds of work are produced, including artistic and literary ones. In some countries, besides the copyright by which the owner controls reproduction, there are moral rights that protect integrity and paternity.

- Any asset you wish to use in multimedia is going to have copyright implications but music is perhaps the most complex of these with composer, publisher and sometimes recording company having a stake in the exploitation.

- There are exceptions which allow some limited use of copyright material without the need for clearance, but usually free use is possible only when the work is out of copyright.

- Selling something on the Internet can have legal implications beyond the sale itself.

- Ideas cannot be copyrighted, only the expression of them. If you have an idea for a process for doing something then a patent may be the appropriate course of action.

■ Recommended reading

You should always take careful legal advice on rights issues, but it is useful to have some basic background. Most of these books are based on English law. When reading books on copyright, make sure that they are up to date.

Dworkin G., Taylor R.D. (1989). *Blackstone's Guide to the Copyright Designs and Patents Act 1988*. London: Blackstone Press
This book is a straightforward introduction with useful reference tables and a copy of the Act itself.

Henry M. (1994). *Publishing and Multimedia Law*. London: Butterworths.
This book covers more law than IP. It is fairly expensive but includes 52 sample contractual documents on paper and PC disk.

Holyoak J. and Torremans P. (1998). *Intellectual Property Law*. 2nd edn. London: Butterworths
This book is aimed at students, and gives substantial background on all aspects of intellectual property including patents and copyright. Some international issues are covered as well.

Smith G.J.H. (ed.) (2001). *Internet Law and Regulation*, 3rd edn. London: Sweet & Maxwell

Stim, R (1999) *How to License and Clear Copyrighted Materials Online and Off*. Berkeley, CA: Nolo Press

Strong W.A. (1999). *The Copyright Book: A Practical Guide*, 5th edn. Cambridge, MA: MIT Press
This is a guide to US law for non-specialists.

Whale R.F., Philips J.J. (1993). *Whale on Copyright*, 5th edn. London: Sweet & Maxwell

☐ Recommended websites

Nolo's website at http://www.nolo.com is an all-round resource for US law.

The US Copyright office has various documents on its website including one on basics of US copyright law and a summary of the DCMA. Their site is at http://www.loc.gov/copyright/

Many aspects of UK Intellectual Property law are outlined on http://www.intellectual-property.gov.uk/

The Chartered Institute of Patent Agents (Staple Inn Buildings, High Holborn, London WC1V 7PZ) publishes information leaflets that explain the functions of a UK patent agent.

The UK Data Protection Commissioner is now the Information Commissioner, which might change the web URL. But for the time being it is at http://www.dataprotection.gov.uk/.

Multimedia narrative

Project manager's responsibilities

- To keep up to date with influences on multimedia design and practice
- To be able to understand concerns of members of the team about narrative structures
- To be able to evaluate applications in terms of narrative structures if necessary
- To be able to discuss narrative implications with clients in an informed manner
- To be able to anticipate the complexity of the production process regarding the type of multimedia narrative production

■ Rationale

Why have we decided to include a chapter on multimedia narrative in this edition? Although researchers have been looking into the concepts of interactive narrative and interactivity for over ten years, it has not had a noticeable impact on mainstream production of applications in the way that software concepts such as human–computer interaction, navigation, usability and interface design have. This is not meant to demean the research efforts; we just feel that now the timing is right for the work to be recognized and built upon.

This is due mainly to the growing importance of interactive TV (iTV). Because entertainment has been such a large part of the televisual experience, interactive entertainment will become the focus of more activity. As a result, scriptwriters who convert to interactive scriptwriters will want to find groundwork to help them face the new challenges. The concepts of 'narrative' and storylines have more affinity with scriptwriting and storyboards than with other forms of writing for media. As a result, the principles of interactive narratives may well find a better reception with this influx of interactive writers from a new background.

The dominance of web-based applications is another aspect that could have contributed to the lack of interest in interactive narratives. This is because the move from developing offline applications to online ones caused a dip in the use of media. This was a result of the broadband issues. (See Chapters 7 and 8 and Book 2 Chapter 3 for more on this.) The restrictions kept people focused on the use of interactive text and still images rather than on the use of all media together. This meant that content developers did not have to consider how to integrate several forms of media interactively nor take account of the impact this can have on the way the user relates to the information provided. Now this is changing. The use of websites as adjuncts to TV programmes is becoming the norm. This blend of media is a stepping stone for users to move towards using full interactive TV. Added to this, the increase in broadband on the Internet will allow designers to increase their use of media. They also will face new challenges to integrate all the media in an interactively coherent and meaningful way for the user.

The background research into multimedia narrative provides insights to help all those involved in structuring content for an interactive context. It provokes thought around communication issues in ways that other research does not. It raises questions that need to be answered in order for the design of interactive applications to progress.

■ What is multimedia narrative?

To answer this we need to understand what narrative is – and this isn't straightforward. There are different perspectives since there are many

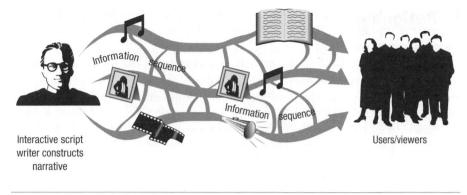

Multimedia narrative construction.

forms of narrative. There are the oral, storytelling traditions of narrative. Oral narrative varies in itself depending on the form of communication. This may be face-to-face or distance communication. It also changes according to the medium used for communication – the radio or telephone, for example. Then there are the written story conventions of narrative from classic literary novels to science fiction. We have even developed filmic traditions of narrative.

These all relate to a person or author constructing a sequence of information that they then convey to the listener or reader using audio, text, stills or moving images. But the communication process is not complete unless the person receiving the information interprets the sequence to extract the sense from it. Some narrative research addresses the one half of the communication process and others concentrate on the other. We will cover the basics of both perspectives.

We have explained a little about the 'grammar' of films where collapsed time, cutting shots and flashbacks are conventions of narrative that have emerged through use in films and TV (see Chapter 7). This also happens in the storytelling in a novel, where the overt chapter-based structure allows plenty of scope for parallel stories which can be resolved at the end of the book. All the other kinds of narrative have their own forms of 'grammar' that build up expectations in the person receiving the information.

Researchers of media have defined the elements or building blocks of convention that people attune to over time and then use to decode the stream of information that they meet. For example, fables have a moral outcome to them and people predict that there will be a resolution of good and evil in the story. To bring this more up to date, the highly successful Mills and Boon romantic novelettes are written to a tightly defined structure. Although there are many authors and many stories, the story lines, the characters and their behaviour are written to a code. The main structure revolves around a couple who fall in love but there is an obstacle for them to overcome before they can be united happily. This is formulaic writing with the guidelines even specifying how far into the story the first kiss between the heroine and the hero needs to happen. Whether you like it or not, narratives can be, and are, written to formulae and they can be commercially successful.

The simplest definition of narrative is a storyline that has a beginning, a middle and an end (and, to save you asking, they occur in that order). There is a linear unfolding of events. But narrative does not only apply to stories. Once you take the perspective that narrative is about the structure underpinning forms of communication, it can be applied to all information that is passed between people. In live communication, some context needs to be established to start the communication, an exchange of information takes place and the communication is concluded. In communication through media, the author still has to establish a context that the intended recipient will recognize, provide structured information exchange using conventions established for the medium in use, and conclude the communication in an appropriate manner

Multimedia narrative has the added characteristic of interactivity – of choices for the receiver of the communication. Previously the author of the communication has forged a pre-planned structure through the storylines or communication and this has left the receiver in an interpretative, overtly passive role. Once choices can be made through interactivity, the passive role becomes active. One of the interesting spin-offs in this discussion of 'grammars' is the difficulty of labelling the receiver of the interactive information. The word 'reader' for text communication is considered a passive label. A television 'viewer' is also a passive label. People who use computers for whatever communication purpose are called 'users' – an active label. What label then will be applied to people using iTV? The term passive here is used in the physical sense since the listeners and viewers are active mentally; interpreting and predicting events, relating them back to previous occurrences and so on.

The change in role for the recipient of the information in an interactive context is just part of a subtle but significant switch that causes a reaction rather like ripples from a stone thrown into a pond. Once the recipients of information can decide a pathway through the choices made available to them, their role shifts. They begin to forge their own structure within a structure. By constructing the story threads or linking threads between information, they take on the partial role of creator or author. A professional interactive author, on the other hand, does not just construct one pathway through a narrative but needs to construct several so that the users can create a pathway that suits their interest. This isn't as easy as it might appear. It is true that there are often several strands to a storyline in conventional media so this doesn't represent a change. But there has always been a single resolution to the strands where they come together through carefully crafted jigsaw pieces of storyline falling into place. There has always normally been one end.

As soon as the user has a choice at critical points in the narrative, the author needs to cover all the alternatives and craft the strands into a larger but still coherent whole structure. However, the more choices there are, the harder it becomes to contain the overarching structure. There are some tricks of the trade emerging. For example, the author can ask closed questions instead of open ones, restricting the number of possibilities for the user. Consider the difference between 'Would you like a drink?' and 'Would you like tea or coffee?' The closed question controls the expectations of the user and contains the interactive path structure.

If we take the example of two people meeting and exchanging a conversation for a couple of minutes, the context and meaning that is shared between them is crafted between them. A meeting of two different people would produce another unique exchange. Even if the two sets of people were asked to discuss the same topic, their actual conversations would vary. Conversation is the closest model for interactive communication that I can think of and ought to give an indication of the possibilities when there are choices available on both sides. Returning to our previous examples of recognizable narrative structures – how would you write interactive fables and romantic novelettes?

It is difficult to keep the threads of interactive storytelling weaving into a coherent path. So to help interactive writers, software tools are being developed. These can prompt the author to recognize 'loose' story threads that need to be bound back into the main story structure, for example. Attempts have also been made for computers to generate complete stories as well. (See the references for more information to follow up on a couple of these tools if you are interested.)

The tools have had limited success so far but Bob Hughes acknowledges that the quest has produced some interesting results and the spin-offs may well prove invaluable tools in their own right. I see this quest as the equivalent of speech recognition tools. It'll take some time, but it'll get there and be worth it.

However, we need to query whether clutching on to previous narrative tenets is actually just clutching at straws. Should stories have a neat ending? Is getting lost in hyperspace through over-clicking on links always a bad thing? Are there positive aspects to these seemingly unruly interactive narrative experiences that can be worked to advantage? Janet Murray believes that just as film grammar conventions took time to emerge and relied on creative people who could forge the medium, the tools and the imagination together to produce a visual vocabulary, the new challenges of digital design will need their own creative gurus. She takes a positive view towards the differences that digital design allows and in her courses has helped designers towards crafting interactive content by analysing the general tools of their digital trade. These include database design, simulation techniques, mapping information in spatial terms and so on. These lend themselves more to structuring content in a digital environment rather than trying to pull conventions straight through from text conventions. For those who want more than an introduction to the basics of digital narrative her book, *Hamlet on the Holodeck*, is essential.

■ Broadening the definition of 'narrative'

The previous definition in this chapter took the stance of an author constructing a story. The very word 'narrative' places the emphasis on the creation of the story or the teller of the story. We have understood that the continuity of the story line and its resolution are important factors.

If we change the emphasis to the person receiving and decoding the information or narrative, the cognitive attributes that allow the person to make sense of the created structure become part and parcel of the communication process. In other words, if the messages are not received or if the narrative is not understood then they cannot fulfil their purpose.

It is a chicken and egg situation. The receiver needs to have enough recognition of the context and form of the implied narrative structures to be able to extract the meaning that leads to understanding. The meaning unlocks the purpose of the narrative communication whether that purpose was enjoyment or fuller understanding of a topic, or information to help decision making, or whatever.

The multimedia narrative communication process.

This approach to narrative, where cognition plays a part, widens the emphasis from the creator of narrative to the creator of clear communication. Clear communication concerns more than those deemed authors. Those involved with designing interactive instruction or those involved in designing interactive business communication need to know which mechanisms of interactivity will work unconditionally with their users and which might need guidance or tuition to release the meaning. There's a need to understand more about the cognitive processes that people utilize when they are interacting with multimedia applications. Lydia Plowman gives a clear description of the mental processes related to reading text as a pointer to the complexity of decoding multimedia narratives.

Reading is not a straightforward linear movement, a merely cumulative affair; our initial speculations generate a frame of reference within which to interpret what comes next, but what comes next may retrospectively transform our original understanding. As we read on we shed assumptions, revise beliefs, make more complex inferences and anticipations; each sentence opens up a horizon which is confirmed,

challenged or undermined by the next. We read backwards and
forwards simultaneously, predicting and recollecting, perhaps aware of
other possible realisations of the text which our reading has negated.

(PLOWMAN 1996)

These mental actions can be applied to the way a person relates to other media as well but they do not give the complete picture because multimedia demands more from the participant. This is the gap in our understanding. We need to understand more about the internal cognitive reactions of the users to interactive applications.

Lydia defines why multimedia is different and the reasons that researching the cognitive processes it can generate are so complex. These include:

- media formats switching frequently between video, text, animation, graphics, sound and silence;
- the combinations of different media on the screen at the same time;
- the users' possible control over pace, sequence, choice of activity and input;
- the possibility of group usage and the communication between the people about the decisions to use with the application.

All the combinations of these elements and the purpose of the communication embodied in the interactive application can cause differences in the way an application is structured and interpreted. This then is the true scope of the interactive writer's task.

The focus on cognitive processes is where the overlap with HCI (human–computer interaction) research, information design and interactive instructional design occurs. However, the forms of interactivity that serve entertainment purposes have tended to be excluded from these areas of research but are not excluded from multimedia narrative research. Interactive entertainment has had its own healthy market through games and now that there are more possibilities opening up for interactive entertainment via the TV and mobile communications, a winning formula – the equivalent to interactive soaps – could open up new markets. The stakes are high.

You may wonder where computer games fit into this. Is there not a narrative element to Lara Croft swinging through the jungle and exploring pyramids; and is there not even a narrative form to 'shoot-em-up' games of the Doom and Quake variety?

The answer is that games run the whole gamut from simple dice-throw decisions to complex rule-based narratives. When is a narrative not a simulation and when is a simulation not a game? It is difficult to make a clear-cut distinction when even a flight simulator can include the story of flying from New York to Los Angeles.

It is also worth considering the role of text-only games in the development of non-linear and interactive narrative. Games like the 'Hitch-Hiker's Guide to the Galaxy' date from the early days of PCs and some were even written for mini-computers and mainframes. They allowed the user to decide on paths and strategies. A significant difference is that a true interactive narrative has no 'right' path, unlike most games. This compounds the difficulties of writing the options in the story because you can no longer use the short-cut of only having a single path that actually goes anywhere. The stage is set and there is a need to understand the complexity of media, the physical and mental interaction around all the forms and the implications for those constructing the applications and those using the applications whatever type of communication or narrative is being used.

■ Managing the development of narratives

The principles that have been covered so far have identified some of the variables within multimedia narrative. But there is also a tension between the creative use of narratives and the pragmatic use of narrative structures that can affect the management of a multimedia project.

Claus Rosenstand places the concepts of narrative in a business context and identifies the impact for a project manager. This is closer to the perspective we adopt in this book because of the link with the business model and role of the project leader. It begins to explain some of the tensions that project managers come across during the project in terms of conflict of narrative perspectives.

He identifies a tension that can develop when there is a mismatch between the business quality needed for a project and the narrative quality needed for the content. He sees the client determining the business quality while the user is more concerned with narrative quality of the application. The quality levels may not coincide because the project is put under time and cost parameters that determine the quality level that can be achieved for the client – the business quality. However, if the user were to be placed first and the quality of their experience was paramount (narrative quality and the quality of the user experience become synonymous here), then the time and cost to develop the most beneficial product might well be very different. So the project manager can be squeezed between trying to suit the client while also trying to serve the user.

He also discusses the potential conflict between the software production process and the content production process. These two can also interfere with one another. The software process may want to develop a refined and well integrated structure but the content narratives may encourage non-linearity, and flexibility.

The factor of the amount of control that the user has over the application becomes important in a project because, Rosenstand concludes, the complexity of managing the development of multimedia products increases when more narrative control is given to the user. Our guess is that once this increases, the complexity of the software functionality increases too.

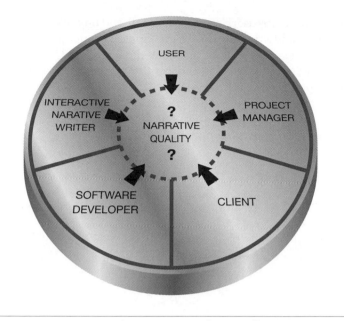

Perspectives on narrative quality.

This brings us closer to being able to rationalize some of the apparent contradictions that are met during the production process. The client, the project manager, the software developer, the content author and the end-user all have different views on the best narrative quality for a project. This helps us extend our understanding of the overall quality of a project and further research may lead to practical ways to reconcile the different perspectives so that the production process is made easier.

■ In the meantime

The World Wide Web is gradually establishing some forms of commonality that users can recognize. For those that have seen it developing over a period of years, there are expectations of a 'back' button, of denoting active links by underlining or colour, of the layout of a news site, of functionality expected according to a site's purpose and so on. There have been fads and fashions that have gradually firmed up as the users' reactions have been noted in terms of returns to the site, bookmarking a favourite site, length and breadth of use among others. Elaborate first-page site maps died as the result of users discounting the sites because they wouldn't wait for the graphics to load up, for example. This is the definition of web grammar and narratives in action. In the end, as with all the other media, it will be what works for the audience that will emerge as the key to success. Some of these elements will be constants and others will delight because of their creative innovation and deviation. They in turn will get integrated into the main-stream and be replaced with other innovations.

THEORY INTO PRACTICE 17

Sensitize yourself to narrative structures by monitoring your own reactions to them. Choose a communication medium – a TV programme, advert, book, conversation, e-mail, theatre or whatever. Concentrate on your reactions to the medium and note them down.

- What cognitive reactions are being triggered in you?
- What is triggering them specifically?
- What narrative techniques has the initiator of the communication used to provoke/evoke a response in you?

■ Summary

- The increased opportunities for design in broadband and the rise of iTV give multimedia narrative research more currency now.
- Narrative structures have varied across media but all have evolved recognizable conventions.
- Interactive narratives allow the user choices and this opens up the boundaries. There are currently no conventions.
- Just as with previous narrative forms, interactive authors rely on the user to interpret and assign meaning to the narrative structure.
- More research is needed to understand the cognitive processes employed in understanding interactive narrative forms.
- Multimedia narrative forms can be creative or pragmatic and this may cause tension between different people involved in development.
- The amount of control the user is given over the narrative process has an impact on the development process.

■ Recommended Reading

Hughes B. (1999) *Dust or Magic: Secrets of Successful Multimedia Design*. Harlow: Addison-Wesley

Murray J. (1997) *Hamlet on the Holodeck: The Future of Narrative in Cyberspace*. Cambridge, MA: MIT

Plowman L. (1996). Narrative, Interactivity and the Secret World of Multimedia, *The English & Media Magazine*, **35**, Autumn, pp. 44–8

Rosenstand C.A.F. (2001) *Managing Narrative Multimedia Production in Virtual Interaction: interaction in Virtual Inhabited 3D Worlds* (ed. Lars Ovortrup). Springer: London.

☐ Websites of interest

General information about narratives

http://hotwired.lycos.com/synapse/braintennis/97/31/index0a.html
> A chance to interact with a novel interactive webtext interview structure with opposing narrative experts – Janet Murray and Sven Birkerts

http://ic.www.media.mit.edu/
> Research papers and more on narrative structures from the Interactive Cinema group.

http://jupiter.ucsd.edu/~manovich/home.html
> Lev Manovitch – artist and new media writer, describes his book *The Language of New Media*, to be published by MIT, articles and research on narrative.

☐ Narrative tools

See the following websites for details

http://www.mercurycenter.com/svtech/news/special/storytelling/story.htm
> Digital Storytelling resource that leads to tools and more sites of interest.

http://216.25.53.29/trans-tex/index.html
> This has Applescript, Eliza and Azile. The first allows you to create shortcuts in editing content/text. The others are classic question generators that try to simulate natural conversation in the style of a psychiatrist.

http://www.robotwisdom.com/ai/crawford.html
> This explains and gives background information on Frasmatron – a story generation engine by Chris Crawford

http://www.erasmatazz.com/index.html
> This is Chris Crawford's website where you can access the story engine

☐ Acknowledgements

Bob Hughes, author of *Dust or Magic*, and Claus Rosenstand of InterAct for their helpful comments and references

Adapting projects for other languages and cultures

Project manager's responsibilities

- To recognize that these projects can have special needs and require specialist skills

- To recognize that these projects can range in complexity from dedicating a couple of members of your team to requiring a specialist company (or subcontractor)

- To recognize that these projects can have an impact on all aspects of design from layout to servers used

- To separately specify the needs for this type of project

- To educate your own company in the potential complexity of localization and internationalization projects

■ Background

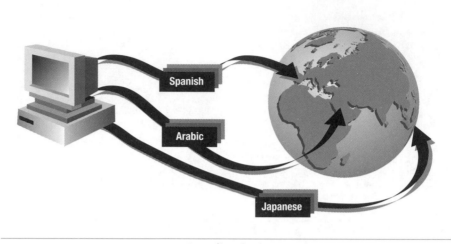

Localization.

The adapting of applications for other languages and cultures gives rise to two extra types of projects called localization and internationalization. During this chapter we will cover the difference between these types. We will address localization first where a project manager is concerned with altering a website or offline application to suit markets other than the one for which (probably in which) the original product was developed. This at the very least means translations are necessary but until a person becomes involved in a complex localization project and mixes with specialists from the field, it is difficult to appreciate how involved and specialized the process can be. As indicated in the specification questionnaires in Chapter 3, localization projects warrant a separate questionnaire in order to cover the span of issues that it may contain.

We will touch on many of the aspects that you need to take on board but we will not follow through with a localization project management life-cycle example as this would need a separate book. These projects can be highly specialized and cover elements of project management that are not generic. It will quickly become apparent that if a company wanders into a localization project unprepared, it will underestimate all the factors of time, cost and quality that need to be addressed in order to keep the project on track.

Localization in multimedia means adapting online and offline applications for local markets so that the product can be distributed globally. As the impact of the Web becomes more universal and the users of the Internet shift away from specialists to the general public, the use of local languages becomes increasingly important. This increases as e-commerce spreads since more commodities are sold if the goods and services are offered in the appropriate language. Carter Doughtery (2000) cites a US company as reporting that people are three times more likely to buy products if they are promoted in their own language. This explains the rise in the need for localization skills and its emergence as a growing market sector for developers. More multinational companies are seeing it as a necessary part of their business strategy so that their products and services are introduced simultaneously in many countries.

Apart from the promise of increased sales of commodities if people can relate to the products in their native language, adapting existing titles or sites is cheaper than producing them from scratch. Peter Looms (1996) identifies that an adapted title costs between 10–50% of the original development.

■ Assessing the scope of a localization project

The specialist knowledge required for this area comes from being able to identify the level and the implications of localization processes. These can range from translating some of the voice-overs of an offline application into another language, to multiple language translations of the whole software application from the code, button and label names, the text content, the visual content, the audio content and the knock-on effects these can have on layout and associated materials like manuals or printed matter accompanying an application.

There is another approach to localization projects where your own company might identify a foreign product that would suit your country's market. In this case, you might need to negotiate the licensing and royalties deal with the owner of the product, localize it and market it into your country through an advertising campaign. These extra stages would need to be factored into the project cost. However, although this approach was possible with several of the larger companies some years ago, many have now developed their own localization programmes. They recognize that the return on the investment of localizing for markets of other languages has grown in line with the established base of hardware.

Until you unpack the implications, you will not be in a position to realize the possible extent of localization projects.

▢ Specialist factors affecting localization projects

Localization projects are sometimes referred to as internationalization projects. The difference lies in the emphasis that the project takes. The more the emphasis lies with the software engineering or the code of the application, the more it veers towards internationalization.

Lionbridge defines the difference as:

■ Localization refers to the process of preparing a software application and the supporting documentation and packaging for specific target languages and cultures through translation and cultural adaptation.

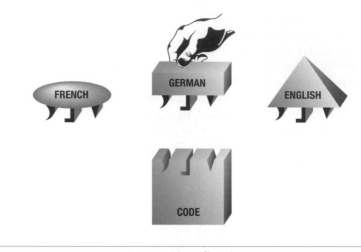

Internationalization.

- Internationalization is the process of designing and developing, or re-engineering an application, so that it can be adapted to various locales without software engineering changes.

The company goes on to make the case for employing internationalization before localization of the product because it can eliminate the need for re-engineering a product for each localized version. This can reduce the costs of localisation later by 40–60%. This needs to be put in context however. Multimedia tools are easier to internationalize than some multimedia applications. Take for example a history product. Different countries have different perspectives on historical events. (The Swiss edition of the *Chronicle of the 20th Century*, for example, has very little mention of the Second World War since Switzerland was neutral.) The product would not sell as well if the cultural perspective were not taken into account as well as the change in language and the content edited accordingly. Software tools have little or no content so the impact of localizing them can be more straightforward.

Bearing this in mind, in the rest of the chapter, we will be referring to localization with the understanding that internationalization can be part and parcel of the total package needed.

The processes and tools used within the localization project life cycle can differ from those used in other projects and this is not usually appreciated. It depends on the scope of the localization. There are separate localization project management tools, separate translation software aids and programming packages that allow underlying code to be translated across several languages. In the end, it will depend on the project needs, how much or how little you will need to do to accommodate the requirements.

The processes involved are intertwined with the business drivers just as with general multimedia project development. Because the needs are precise, the solutions need to be tailored as well. You have to consider what the client – or you – wants to achieve with the translations and this determines the precise amount of fine-tuning required for the translations.

Each language encompasses a range of styles that are used appropriately for a particular situation. There are levels of formality, politeness and specialist vocabulary. Just because a person speaks a language does not automatically mean that he or she can successfully translate any and every word in that language. The translator has to be proficient in the specialism that is being translated.

Take for example a medical application aimed at medical professionals. Would every English-speaking person understand enough to be able to transcribe the content in their own words to show they had understood what they had read and record this accurately enough for others to understand? Would they be able to pronounce the specialist words correctly?

Similarly, what about producing an application for teenagers? What nuances of language appeal to that age group in the native language? Once you recognize that there are many aspects of your own native language that lie outside your own expertise then the difficulties of translating through to another language come into perspective. How could the nuances of 'teen speak' from the one language be translated effectively into another language?

When Dorling Kindersley produced interactive CDs, they integrated the localization process into a prototype stage related to product development. The prototype and dummy packaging were sent for appraisal to their international partners. The culturally dependent problems were identified and dealt with at this stage. The company had their own proprietary tools that were used to assemble the separate language components once their international partners had developed them. Each international partner worked with a dedicated DK localization team since the details down to conventions for naming files were part of the process and needed to conform. DK have stopped producing interactive CDs but are involved with international online projects where this expertise will be valuable.

As this example demonstrates, the business sector that will use the programs will affect the level and preciseness of the translation of the content that is needed. The expected use of the information also has an impact on the process. There is a certain level of translation that is needed for people to gain the gist of what is meant. But another level of translation is needed if they have to act on the information and carry out tasks related to understanding it. This can happen when they may need to operate machinery or make choices to invest money as a result, for example. Then very clear, unambiguous translation is needed.

The difference between these types of needs is defined in the specialism of localization as 'in-bound' and 'out-bound' communication. So an automatic text translation package might be applied when fast but less accurate information transfer is acceptable in a written form; however, specialist highly accurate translations can be needed when the information will be used to influence others or help in decision making or carrying out processes.

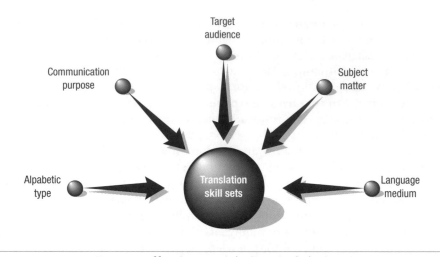

Factors affecting translation and design.

A translator might use an automatic translation package to begin the translation process (in-bound) and then refine the sense according to the particular needs of the user (out-bound). Some translations software packages refine through use and 'learn' to give better renditions for a particular specialism. In this case the translators' job gets a little easier because of the package as they add specialist terms and nuances into the package. This increasingly saves time and effort.

By now you should be getting an impression that who will use the translation, how they will use it and what they will do with the information, are all contributing to the scope of this type of project.

The type of language used – written, audio or visual can also demand different skills and affect the people involved in the translation process. Translating for the written word involves certain language skills whereas translating for another to speak in the language is rather different. The sentence structures change, the vocabulary changes, the sense becomes coloured by the particular tone and style of the piece. This happens even when you move from written to spoken word within a formal set of circumstances. For example, a written statement about the side-effects of a new drug for a medical audience would sound out of place if the written words were just read out loud. If a doctor was interviewed about the side-effects of the drug, the same information might be covered but in a very different way.

It should now be apparent that the subject matter and the medium of communication will affect the localization project as well. Let's extend the previous medical example. Consider localizing a complete online and offline printed version of a database of drugs and their side-effects. If this were to be used as a resource for a worldwide medical audience, the volume of the material across the range of media – online and offline text – becomes an extra factor to be taken into account.

There are even further considerations once we get to this point where rather than developing a website and then considering what extra effort is needed to move it through to different languages, it is better to know from the outset if the whole needs to be developed for multilanguage purposes. Peter Looms identifies two strategic approaches to this – 'global culture' and 'multicultural'. With the first – global culture – the developer contains the design to suit the same target group in different cultures. An example of this sort of global group might be IT professionals across countries. They share the same professional backgrounds in different countries and share concepts and technical terms. With the 'multicultural' approach the content and presentation needs to be tailored to the users in each market. The purpose may help determine the approach since passing on professional information might be treated as a 'global' approach but trying to sell anything would point to a 'multicultural' approach.

If the 'multicultural' approach is taken, there are considerations of browsers and their role in multiple-language use, the internationalization of HTML and other web mark-up languages and if servers are multiple-language proficient.

An operating system destined for world use might be considered devoid of 'content' in the form accepted for applications produced for general users, but even this, for example, includes manuals, and multimedia Help functionality, among other content aspects. It is specialist subject matter. Translating this into other languages means preparing the software to be independent of language, designing an international-aware user interface and software architectural issues.

With more e-commerce happening via online sites, the cross-cultural legal differences cannot be forgotten in localization or liability may result. The tax on goods sold varies between countries and needs to be taken into account. Different countries have different legal requirements so that products sold in one country may not be legal in another, or sale and return clauses may vary across countries. The freedom of speech of the USA does not sit absolutely with the English law of defamation, for example, and affects certain content publication on websites. Whose responsibility is it to monitor the content and under what legal system? So, the localization team may well need their work checked by a legal representative. Market considerations become more critical as competitors strive to reach sectors before their rivals. In this case, if the application has been developed along internationalization premises, the time-to-market is decreased for the localized versions and upgrades are faster, easier, and more cost-effective.

Cultural differences will operate at different levels according to the application and will necessitate a thorough appraisal to make sure all practical and aesthetic differences are accommodated. Take for example the translation of a website into Arabic or Japanese. The first is an example of a bi-directional language: the second is double-byte.

In a bi-directional language (where script and numbers are written starting from different directions) the computer will have to be able to display writing that runs from right to left, rather than the Roman convention of left to right. This is further complicated in some cases, such as Arabic, where the shape of a character changes depending on where it is in a word. (This can happen in Roman script where sophisticated typesetting will allow ligatures – characters that join together – but this is not a necessary aspect of the writing and is often ignored.)

A double-byte character set is one where the 256 possibilities in an 8-bit byte are not enough. Basic ASCII actually uses only 7 bits and so runs from zero (or 'null') to 127 which is usually 'delete'. This gives enough scope for English letters and numbers plus some control codes such as line feed, carriage return and tab. Adding another bit allows more characters with accents (like acute and umlaut) but even this is not enough for even the relatively limited set of characters used in Europe. Ironically, if it wasn't for mathematics and engineering, the Greek alphabet might not have made it into the 8-bit set.

The solution for the rest of the world is to use 16 bits (2 bytes) that allows thousands of characters to be represented, including the original 8-bit sets. With this, languages such as Hindi, Thai, Inuit, Chinese and Japanese can take their rightful place in the information society.

These examples show some of the practical differences that multilingual translations can create. It is now well known that the space needed for different languages varies and can have a major impact on the application's interface and layout. If button names become appreciably longer or take two words instead of one in translation, the screen layout can be compromised. If we imagine the impact on the complete use of text within the application, then the effort to translate can quickly mean redesign as well.

Sometimes the changes in technology happen so quickly that there are no words in the other language to represent the new concepts. This can mean that the translators have to make up new words from prefixes, stems and suffixes of other words in the language. Sometimes, when the language doesn't work through words but through concepts like Chinese and Japanese, this can mean completely new words or use of what is, for them, a foreign word. Then the users have to be trained in the new meaning through glossaries and use in context.

☐ ... and yet more

Localization can affect the whole set of processes described during the life cycle of project management. The quality assurance cycle is greatly increased because each of the languages needs to be checked against a set of criteria agreed for the project. The colour and graphics may need to be changed to suit the culture as well as the language itself. The testing procedures increase as well. There are software tools designed to help these processes and these are being refined quickly because this sector of business is growing rapidly. Even if your company has not been involved with localization before, it may well be in the future.

A 1999 study by a New York research firm, Allied Business Intelligence, estimated that localization comprised 32% of the $11 billion world market for translation and it was growing.

Some companies only learn the true worth of having good localization techniques applied when sales of their products are affected through underestimating of the importance of translation. The 'Nova' car translates into 'Doesn't go' in Spanish, for example and failed badly after being launched in Mexico. Rolls-Royce had a near miss when they almost named a car 'Silver Mist' which, in German and politely put, translates into Silver Manure!

■ ... and does it matter?

The shift that online commerce brings to a company that moves it from being a local to a global business gradually underpins its whole approach and processes. Whether you like it or not any website can be seen internationally. You will pick up visitors from within your own language group and probably even visitors who do not speak your language very well. They are unlikely to know the limitations of their knowledge of your language. It may not be appropriate for a very small operation to produce several versions aimed at different cultural and linguistic groups but at the very least you should consider any negative impact your site might have in a culture different to your own.

Localization and internationalization are part of the globalization business switch. They can be applied to front-end and back-end processes. A change in one affects the other and it may well be that if you don't take this into account sooner rather than later, your business may be wrong-footed and new rivals can move in.

James Murdoch (2000) set this scene in relation to broadcasters and their attempt to rationalize the digital onslaught from various quarters in the TV industry including the impact of the Internet. He redefines the approach that TV companies should take regarding production and distribution of materials. He demonstrates that the concept of English dominating the global digital audience for any form of communication is flawed. In fact, Mandarin, English, Spanish and Hindi are the four languages with the most speakers and irrespective of where the speaker is located, their preference is communication in their own language. He believes that production centres cannot survive as monoliths broadcasting worldwide. '... each must be a series of local businesses, each carefully focused on the key language groups and local cultures that make up their respective audiences'.

It has taken these traditional forms of communication quite some time to recognize what global business means and how it affects core processes. Companies going online should perhaps keep an eye on the shifts that will drive localization and internationalization projects.

THEORY INTO PRACTICE 18

Check out the automatic translation packages available freely with some search engines. (AltaVista and Google offer slightly different types.)

Search for a term used across the world in all languages. You could try an international brand name, for example. When the result summaries come back, check for any in other languages. Select the translation option. Try a few languages as the translations are better in some than others.

Evaluate the service through the result. Does the translation:

(a) Make perfect sense

(b) Make enough sense for you to understand the gist

(c) Make very little sense despite using words in the translation language you have chosen

(d) Make no sense

Consider if the translations offer you enough for 'in-bound' communication as described above. Check on how the tools are progressing by re-doing this exercise in a few months to see if they are being improved.

Although the automatic translation tools should demonstrate the need for professional translators, remember that these are free and generic rather than specialist. It is remarkable that they manage what they do, given the complexity of languages, and they are improving all the time.

■ Summary

- The need to develop local language sites increases as more people from more countries go online.

- Products sell better if people can read about them in their native language.

- Localization projects range from small cosmetic changes to complete rewrites from the code up.

- The scale and type of work affects the tools and processes used.

- The subject matter and the purpose of communication can affect the level of specialist translation needed.

- Extra factors may need to be taken into account such as legal issues, special needs of some languages, materials associates with the application, quality assurance across cultures.

- Shifting market sectors and native language access to information may have far-reaching consequences and need monitoring.

■ Recommended reading and references

Doughtery C. (2000). Globalization translates into Localization, *Washington Times*, 24 April

Looms P. (1996). Localising multimedia CD-ROM titles – a strategy for survival. *Interactive Multimedia International*, June, **10** (6), 6–7. (Interactive Media Publications Ltd London UK)

Lionbridge is a US-based, dedicated localization company http://www.lionbridge.com

Murdoch J. (2000). *You Say Tomato: Language and Growth in the World's Major Media Markets*. Speech at The Edinburgh Television Festival 27 August 2000.

Nielsen J. (1996). *International User Interfaces*, New York: John Wiley & Sons

☐ Useful websites

Rubric has a website that provides a range of information on localization but more from the software than cultural point of view. It lists books of cross-cultural communication and localization as well as offering its own handbooks on localization processes. http://www.rubric.co.uk

Global Reach keep an estimate of the numbers of users per language on the Internet at: http://www.glreach.com/globstats/index.php3

Web Word article has a comprehensive list of links and relevant resources:
Rhodes J. (2000) *Usability Around the Globe: Resources*, on Web Word 2 Jan 2000 http://webword.com/moving/global.html

ACM SIGCHI Intercultural Issues – collections of links to relevant references and resources http://www.acm.org/sigchi/intercultural/

Lerner M. (1999) *Building worldwide Web sites. Make sales (or just friends) with a Web site that speaks the visitor's language*, Author and President of Learn the Net.com September 1999

Find at IBM Developer Works Library:
http://www–106.ibm.com/developerworks/library/web-localization.html

☐ Acknowledgements

Peter Looms of Danmarks Radio/Television/Online for his help and comments on this chapter.

Marketing implications for interactive systems

Project manager's responsibilities

- To understand online marketing concepts
- To recognize the implications for interactive website design, particularly e-commerce sites
- To focus the project team on marketing issues when appropriate
- To influence the company's use of marketing principles in its own site
- To liaise with marketing staff, if part of the company

■ What is marketing?

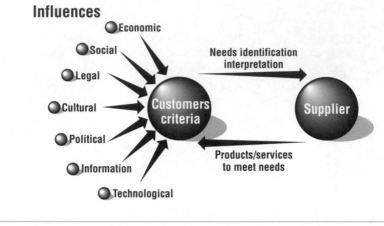

Influences
- Economic
- Social
- Legal
- Cultural
- Political
- Information
- Technological

Customers criteria

Needs identification interpretation

Supplier

Products/services to meet needs

The marketing perspective.

For many, the concept of marketing is linked only with advertising and selling. However, it concerns a wider two-way process of exchange in which the supplier identifies, anticipates and satisfies customers' wants, and the customers choose to buy because the goods or services meet their criteria. This is a continuous process since the customer's criteria change according to many influences – economic, cultural, legal, technological, social, informational, and political. The supplier needs to recognize any shifts in requirements and even anticipate these to satisfy the customer before the competition does, or risk losing business.

☐ What is online marketing?

The same principles apply for online marketing as stipulated in the general definition above. Your clients supply goods and services to customers online and want to know their needs better to anticipate and provide better services and goods. Since the previous edition, the understanding of the potential of online marketing has moved through some embryonic stages and is beginning to mature. Now your clients want to utilize the interactive technology links with their customers and potential customers to help the marketing cycle. Web developers are actively involved in the process because the technology tools they use, the approach to design and even the definition of relevant website content can be affected by a marketing perspective.

The path that links products with their target market is referred to as the marketing or distribution channel. The Internet has become a distribution channel. It is an excellent example of a technological influence that has changed and continues to change the behaviour of the customer. The web community has developed its own cultural, social, and informational require-ments. It has driven new legal, political and economic imperatives. (See figure.) Because this new culture and its requirements are contained in a technological framework, web developers and marketers have to work together more. They depend on integrated processes to distribute goods and services, and process consumer information.

Even though the Web has enormous potential as a distribution channel because of the numbers of people using it, understanding what people want or will tolerate from the interactive channel, what they will give in terms of information about themselves, how they will relate to the channel in terms of advertising, what they will wish from direct e-mail marketing and so on, is problematic. Early on the potential was exaggerated and uninformed. Then the lack of performance by some dot.com companies has unsettled investors and e-clients. Over-emphasis on the use of media-rich technology for technology's sake instead of working from a clear understanding of the customer has been identified as a strong contributor to even a large com-pany's downfall. Spam clogs the Web up and sullies the potential customer's attitude towards personalized targeted mail. Banner ads are often ignored. As more is known about the attitudes and behaviour of particular online customer groups, the informed marketing cycle will evolve to suit it.

Why are these concepts important?

If your company is producing e-commerce sites these concepts are useful to understand your clients' drive to know their customer base. On the other hand, your clients may expect you to immerse yourself in their business to fully understand their strategy and to tailor their website accordingly. They'll appreciate you being knowledgeable about their market sector and you may well need to get up to speed quickly. You may find that many of your clients already have understanding of marketing issues but want advice from you about the latest online trends for their sector to decide if they should utilize extra techniques in their site. So there may be many reasons why taking a marketing approach to a project will be needed. It would be foolhardy not to take the basic concepts on board to apply to your own company and website. After all, you have competitors and you need your clients. You're part of a market sector too.

Marketing principles and new media

The concept of marketing has gradually been recognized as a determining factor that can affect the philosophy of companies. If all sections of your client's company coordinate their efforts towards putting the customer first, this is a sign a company is applying the marketing concept. There is also an emphasis on profitability rather on the volume of sales, on relationship and loyalty rather than anonymity and quick sale.

The key principles of marketing and distribution have been difficult to apply to online media until recently. These principles are: know your customers, know your competition, know your strengths, know your market, know how to reach your customers with information and products and know how to keep your customers.

Even when these principles are applied in a mature market, marketing is not an exact science and many predictions are wrong. But all decisions have to be made on available data, so market and competitor intelligence and the interpretation of this information are important aids to targeting the market or a particular part of it. This is why traditionally the larger corporations invested in technology trials and used their marketing departments to process the data. Even a little information on an emerging market might allow the development of a strong product line or service ahead of the competition and establish the company's credibility with their customer base.

Now technology tools allow the equivalent of trials to a targeted section of people online, automatic processing of the data and reporting to the clients. They can then use the intelligence to refine their product or service and release it to a wider audience. Alternatively, the client may offer the product or service to a narrower, more specific but more responsive set of customers as a result of the intelligence. This form of survey and trial becomes more accessible to more companies as a result of the tools and the customer's access to technology.

■ Know your customers

From a marketing perspective it is essential to know who your customers are and what they want so that you can meet their needs and increase response to you ahead of the competition. It may seem an easy question but it isn't as straightforward as it seems. Are your customers those who commission the project from you or are they the end-users who use the deliverables you produce? We've argued in previous chapters that the end-user's needs should take priority and you should be their champion when allowed. But quite often the people holding the purse strings will interpret the business needs without taking the user or customer into account. However, if the clients are market driven, they are likely to have an interest in the users and their profiles already. They will be informed about them. They will be interested in getting feedback from them in as many ways as possible. They will be able to direct you knowledgeably. If your clients do not show this awareness you may be able to influence them with your market knowledge and advice, get them to pay for an appraisal of their online market sector to help drive their decisions, or encourage them to gather the information themselves as part of their decision-making process.

Dislikes

Lifestyle

Preferences

Predisposition

Tolerance

Likes

Know your customers.

In marketing terms, knowledge about the users is needed so that certain customer traits can be identified. Then the market can be divided into certain types of customer behaviour and wants. This leads to products and services being developed specifically for particular segments that are identified. But the 'free' culture of exchange of information and goods that underpinned the Internet has meant that traditional ways of identifying trends are confused. Marketing companies have been trying to establish new business models for the new ways of doing business. But they need access to the same sort of information to base their decisions on as they did in non-interactive media – their customers' wants, needs, likes, dislikes, aspirations, beliefs, attitudes, lifestyles, and sense of humour. Then they can design websites that provide experiences to suit the trends. Equally, the online tools and techniques allow more personalization and this is emerging as a new model.

Whereas traditional marketing was only interested in trends that showed large and lucrative segments, now it is far easier to tailor offerings for a smaller but still lucrative segment. In the end, if you satisfy a single customer who you then retain and who comes back for more later, this customer is more valuable than the unknown casual shopper. The increasing sophistication of the technology used in call centres is being refined to serve an individual as well as possible – to tailor the service to suit that specific need at that moment to encourage loyalty. The same trend is happening on the Web because the technology is capable of it if the customer is ready to accept it.

Knowing your customer base and understanding it is still the most important driving principle from a marketing point of view, even in inter-active media. If you have this information from your client then you can tailor the website accordingly to reach the right people with the right mes-sages. Just because it is easier to retain large amounts of data on customers via interactive channels, this does not exempt companies from local and international legal requirements concerning data protection and privacy rights. It is important to have proper legal advice when devising your online marketing strategy. (See Chapter 15, *Rights, copyright and other intellectual property*, for more on this.)

■ Know the competition

Know your competition.

The companies that are successful in terms of repeat custom and sales are offering goods and services that meet the needs of their particular market. By studying what is on offer and comparing it with what others offer, you'll begin to understand the concept of competitive edge.

If you try defining competition in terms of your own company, you will find that it is even more difficult than knowing your customer. Your competition can originate from several sources – direct, close, similar products, substitute products and indirect competition.

We'll talk through an example of defining competition from an interactive point of view here but you may well need to apply these principles on behalf of your client or ask your client to give you this information as part of your analysis.

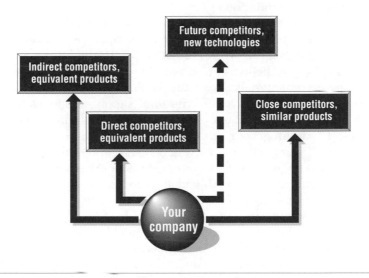

Identify your competitors.

Your direct competitors are usually the easiest to identify. In interactive media terms they will be other companies who compete for the same group of clients/customers and offer the same type of applications. Let's say that your company specializes in developing online history resources based around the standard curriculum for junior schools. Your direct competitors would be similar firms with a similar orientation.

Close competition offers products that have similar benefits for similar customers. If you specialize in schools, and another firm is producing historical edutainment titles that can be suitable for schools and home use, they would be close competitors.

If we continue the education scenario, a museum might have a special historical exhibition developed around resources they have. They might produce an associated CD for sale in their shop or a resource pack plus online resources for teachers as either a follow-up or substitute if the teachers and classes can't visit the actual exhibition. Would you have considered the museum a competitor?

Substitute products are ones that might be bought instead of your online offering. In the case of this museum exhibition, the museum shop may be selling general books and videos on historical aspects as well as their own based on the exhibition. The substitute products – the books and videos – might prove more popular than others in the shop sales. Looking at this in a wider context, educational video titles and of course, books, offer information in ways and at prices that could influence buyers away from other resources. Perhaps the museum featured here should have considered producing their own video and book as 'substitutes' for the CD. Then more of the sales would be of their own titles, and so make a return on the investment in the original exhibition.

It is wrong to become complacent about the competition, because the worst threat might come from an indirect competitor. Broadcasters, for example, are experimenting with interactive TV. In the future, TV or cable companies might offer schools an interactive package. The schools would receive many more materials across the whole curriculum for a year's subscription than they might get from the total supply of educational online packages from several suppliers. Both you, as a multimedia educational company, and your direct competitors might suffer in this case. Your indirect competitor, the TV or cable company, may offer a different form of product, which can appeal to and win away your customers. Alternatively, you might have watched and planned for this change in the market and have built bridges with the emerging competitors. Then, instead of selling to the schools yourself, you might be looking to produce for the TV or cable company instead. The Internet's success came quickly and was a surprise to many businesses. It was an indirect competitor to software developers but suddenly, because of its popularity and the computer literacy of its users, it offered a realistic market platform and possible distribution channel for interactive products.

Returning to knowing the competition for your clients, it is often valuable to get your clients' reaction to some of their competitors' websites. With your wider understanding of competitors including immediate, close and distant you may widen the sites that you look at together to get a rounded view. Your client's perception of their competition can affect your design of their site.

Alternatively, some marketing companies are offering the same market analysis of online competitors as they offered for offline. This can include their use of online advertising, its impact, customer reaction to the competitor website and so on. They use online tools to conduct surveys and the data is immediately processed into competitor reports. Your client may hand you reports like these to take into account as part of their brief to you. Unless you know the principles, you will not necessarily appreciate their significance. Your clients on the other hand may not be aware that such services exist for online market intelligence. You might recommend they use them to get a better idea of what they want as part of the analysis stage prior to production. You might contract in that service on their behalf since online market survey companies often design websites too and you wouldn't want to lose your client to them.

■ **Know your strengths**

Know your strengths.

It is probably easier to get your clients to define their strengths in relation to those of their competitors and close competitors. They ought to know where their competitors are succeeding better than they are in a particular market segment and why they are better. Their website may need to capitalize on their strengths and help to redress the balance. However, their online customers' profiles may be so different from their offline ones that the site might need to have a different emphasis while retaining enough of the recognized brand image. A well-known method to help focus the client with this type of analysis is known as SWOT. This asks a company to consider its strengths, weaknesses, opportunities and threats. Your clients may already have a SWOT analysis and this can help you make decisions about content and look and feel.

Your clients' strengths are their competitive edge and you need to consider whether you are representing their entire online potential in relation to the online market opportunities. You can also consider whether the strengths can be enhanced or focused because of online opportunities to give better results. At the same time, once your client recognizes their weaknesses and can explain them to you, you are in a position to use the site to start counteracting them. The same is true of any threats the client identifies.

If you are in a position of matching the analysis of the clients' strengths to the profile of their online market, you should be able to assess which areas of their online business can serve the market best. However, the state of the market will be important here. In an emerging market like online, companies take business from wherever it is offered rather than target specific areas, because opportunities are diverse and uncharted. As a market matures and segments, then companies that have gathered intelligence within the market begin to specialize and line up with particular needs.

Again, it is important that you recognize that these principles can and should be applied to your own company and your own site. Often, your clients will use your site and those of your previous clients to get an impression of your approach and you need to be as aware of your own strengths and weakness and begin to address these to keep up with your own competitors.

■ Know the market

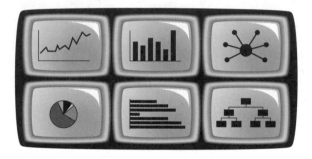

Know your market.

Larger companies pay for market research and use the information for competitive advantage. They have been the only ones who have the capability to do such large-scale research in new and emerging markets until now. However, analysis tools for online surveys and web traffic analysis tools can now provide any company with its own research relatively cheaply. You need to realize though, that formulating questionnaires to give clear and relevant information needs specialist skills. Also, web analysis tools process the data in different ways. So you'll need to understand which ones are better for particular purposes or market sectors.

Once a new market becomes big enough, marketing research companies start to do their own research because they know there will be enough people interested in buying the reports based on their data. Gradually, as market segments mature, the research companies follow the trends and write more targeted reports to sell. These can be a useful source of information about your client's market sector, so even if they have not tapped into them, you may find the information invaluable. It is important to have current information and to ensure that it is reputable if your client is to take notice. (See the references for some general marketing research companies that cover online and technology sectors.)

Increasingly because the tools are integrated into the systems and sites of the companies conducting the business, marketing data is being collated directly rather than through an intermediary. Clients can have far more intelligence and more quickly about online consumers than they have ever had before. What data is collected and how it is presented and interpreted is vital since it drives business decisions. There can be too much data and it can be misinterpreted with disastrous consequences. Interpretation of data is also an area where expertise is still needed.

Research companies will employ their own research techniques, and some of these will be addressed later in this section, but less formal sources can also be invaluable. Articles in e-zines or the trade press can indicate where a client's competitors are putting effort into a new initiative. Attending exhibitions and monitoring competitor trends/products/pricing is also fruitful. Online forums and discussion groups can indicate attitudes and opinions. These form part of a micro picture about a market that you tap into if necessary to help understand your client's business. More rigorous and formal methods need to be applied to gain a macro picture of what is happening and where key players are heading so if your client has bought or subscribed to market research about their sector, this can help you form decisions.

If your client has a marketing section but they are not directly concerned with the commission, you may consider interviewing them to get salient information about the market issues as they understand them to help you formulate decisions about the content, functionality and look and feel for the site.

Your clients themselves may gather information continuously about total sales in relation to products and geographic variance, for example. This will allow them to see whether their general marketing strategies are working, and to help identify trends. This type of data is called continuous marketing research. Research companies also employ this method of continuous research to build up macro marketing trends. They may decide to gather data on an emerging market every year, for example. They will cover the same ground to monitor shifts and so identify emerging trends, scale of operation, increased investment and so on. With established market segments, they may produce more regular reports – monthly breakdown of interactive sales by sector and country, for example. The opposite of continuous research is ad hoc research that is carried out for a specific reason. This might be to help a company make a particular decision – to find out why a popular series has dropped sales, or why hits on a highly popular website have declined and are therefore putting the advertising revenue it gets at risk, for example. The feedback can help the company decide what to do about the problem.

If you are revamping a client's website, it is important to understand their dissatisfaction with the old site and what they want to achieve with the new one. Often, there are marketing issues driving the revamp that need to be elicited so that you can take the best direction.

Returning to the gathering of data, there are two major categories – quantitative and qualitative. Most marketing research data is quantitative. This means that the information can be conveyed in a numerical way. The number and total of sales are obvious examples but percentage sales to age groups and success rates on repeat sales are also quantitative. Many questionnaires are devised to be analysed numerically. The continuous research reports will have processed the data collected from their questionnaires into graphs, charts, percentages and so on to help people compare one set of figures against previous results. In the early phase of gathering market data online, people were preoccupied with click-throughs (the number of times people clicked on an advert or link to get to the site). This has become more sophisticated with leads generated and sales or conversions made as a result of click-through that can then be linked back to the cost per lead of the initial ad placement or the sales return on the initiative or promotion made. Other measurables include 'stickiness' or increased time spent on a site as a result of a make-over perhaps, or a re-editing job on the clarity of the information. You can measure loyalty increases by people who bookmark the site, join the opt-in mail/personalization scheme, want a free newsletter, or return for more sales, among others.

Qualitative data is reflected in descriptions and unstructured reactions. This type of research is used to predict customer behaviour/attitudes and so tailor a new product to suit as yet unrecognized needs. Inductive methods such as asking the interviewee to project into a situation and comment freely on their reactions are used. To keep costs low, qualitative research is frequently conducted using focus group discussions. The qualitative research methods are found most helpful in establishing the categories of market segment. The concept of lifestyle – leisure activities, interests, social habits and so on – for example, has largely replaced that of social class as being a key determinant of customer behaviour. This type of data research has become more prominent for the web community because it has been recognized albeit slowly, that consumer behaviour online cannot be predicted by data that was gathered about previous offline behaviour.

The sources of marketing information are either primary or secondary. Primary data is that collected by direct involvement in such methods as observation, surveys, interviews, inductive techniques, and experimentation. Secondary sources are those where the data has already been analysed and collated in some way. This can come from internal company records such as sales records, loyalty card information and/or return business – if these are appropriate for the products or services in question, for example. Alternatively, the data might be compiled from records of use of a website. The external sources of data will come from market research reports, trade reports and so on.

It is important to check the reliability and accuracy of the information. Reliable information means that the same results can be repeated or reproduced. The information also needs to be valid. This often depends on the size of the sample used to collect the data and whether the sample was representative. You need to consider: if the information were extended, would it be true of the market as a whole? Relevance is another principle to apply. If product groups are lumped together and you need information on a specific type of product, can you use the information? Finally, you need enough data to make the decisions you want, and another reminder that the information must be current. Markets can shift quickly offline but online can shift even faster.

■ Know how to reach your customers with information and products

Know how to reach your customers.

It seems common sense that if you are in business to produce products and services, your customers will buy more of these if they are easily available, the price is right, and they compare favourably with competing products and services. The key has been distribution or access to the goods and services. With the World Wide Web it might appear that these issues are solved at a stroke but they are not proving as simple as that.

If we take offline interactive media goods such as CDs as a historical example we can draw parallels. One of the first attempts at establishing a distribution channel for CDs was to sell the applications side by side with the hardware in major media hardware chains. This included audiovisual and computer chains. In the next phase, the applications were more readily available in the larger shops of the stationers' chains. These shops were the type that sold audio CDs, videos, and limited computer accessories. Finally, dedicated software stores for a range of computer-related software and multimedia applications were established in the major high streets. Distributors have emerged and have refined into ones for particular sectors – games and education for example. (If you need to find a distributor, you'll find them listed in the multimedia directories – see the references.)

When it comes to the Internet, many falsely believe that the distribution problems are over because all potential customers need do is search for the sites and the browsers are there to help them. However, how and why sites are accessed, either directly or via searches, is not straightforward. Just as with CDs initially, people don't know where and how to find the goods they want. The search engines work on key terms so if the customer's search terms do not match the key terms by which the page is indexed then there is a mismatch: no hit. Even with advanced searches the potential customer can have a bewildering choice with many still not fulfilling the need exactly. The search engines also offer predefined categories to help target the search better. Sometimes this can help but at other times you can go round in circles. Often it depends on the type and purpose for the information you need so that general health topics might be under the health subsection on the search engine's front page but if you chose this because you wanted to find statistics on arthritis for a country, it wouldn't help you.

This is similar to the query about CD location initially – should they be in audiovisual or entertainment shops? Is the information you need from a website under business, leisure, cultural and so on. Classification of information is a major problem and getting bigger. Companies and organizations with large amounts of material have already had to face these problems when they digitized and classified their material for internal digital access even prior to distributing it online. Picture libraries, general libraries, and publishers are examples of such organizations that have faced these problems.

As a web developer, you need to understand the customer search and the search engine matching process that is done through the use of meta tags for content and keywords in the headers of your web pages. These are hidden but used to classify the information. (See Book 2 Chapter 2, *The Internet*, for more on this aspect.) Search engine optimization techniques can help your prospective clients get better access to your site. It is straightforward to apply and makes sense. There are a range of strategies: from selecting an easily remembered domain name – preferably the same or based on the company's name unless it has already been taken – embedding the best keywords in the meta tags to match words customers might search on, paying a premium to be processed by the search engines faster than normal to get into the system, and even paying to ensure that your company comes on the first page of search results for a given keyword. Apparently most people appear not to spend much time cycling through tens or hundres of results that may be found as a result of a search. (See the reference to Search Engine Watch for more about these 'paid placement' and 'paid inclusion' practices.)

Standards are emerging about how information should be 'tagged' or identified so that groupings of similar material can be made more efficient. The IEEE is active in developing standards of classification across several sectors. For example, they are defining meta tags for learning technology so that similar types of content can be identified and classified together. (See the references for their website.) MPEG-7, a strand of the Motion Picture Expert Group, is developing an ISO standard for metadata describing audio-visual material to assist with indexing for libraries and media archives – a Multimedia Content Description Interface. These initiatives and similar may well help in the long term.

Finally CDs got their own stores on the high street, if you remember the example. What would this mean as an equivalent on the Internet? This is proving important because parallels are emerging. The recognition that online community groups are self-selecting, have common interests and share similar needs for certain information, goods and services has emerged as an equivalent of a megastore of attraction. The news and information relevant to the common interest forms the community and attracts the people back to the same place regularly. They build up trust in the community and it acts as an umbrella for the spin-off goods and services that are promoted through directories, adverts, news items, etc. all with instant links through to their websites. The community itself becomes the brand and instils loyalty through the information passed freely between the participants. Specialized services can then be offered at a premium both for members of the community and for the sellers of goods and services.

The concept of brand in the traditional sense remains important in attracting customers to a site so if your client has a strong well-recognized brand, their website should be integrated into their complete marketing strategy across all the communication channels. A strong brand means that people will know what to expect and have trust in the company. However, the site should still offer some extras for the customers that suit the functionality of the Web over and above their usual relationship with their retailer or service provider.

But what if the client doesn't have a strong branding? How will you attract customers to their site? Affiliates may be an idea worth considering. This is a group of sites that can serve the same customer base but have complementary products and services. They all link to and promote each other's sites so that awareness and traffic increase for all. Affiliates agree percentage payments for sales that occur as a result of click-throughs from the others or similar type of deals. Strong brands also use the affiliate strategy because of increased sales and spin-offs. Alternatively a prominent brand may host the equivalent of a shopping mall where websites compete with any others in the mall including competitors. The rationale is that they will get more traffic than if their site were alone.

Adverts can also play their part in leading people to a site. It is important that a website presence is integrated with a company's whole strategy because if people become interested in the company through offline adverts it is easier for them to check up on offers via a website than by phone. Site names can be easier to remember. Phones are only manned at certain times whereas websites are accessible 24 hours. It is still surprising that companies often forget to put their web address on all communications that are linked to the company such as press releases, company brochures, compliment slips, headed notepaper and so on. People appear to be more attracted to a site through offline means than by web-based advertising. Banner adverts have to be placed carefully and timed carefully if they are to have impact because many users ignore them when they are focused on attaining specific information from the web page. Reading habits change on the Web because of the environment and so things that have worked offline are not guaranteed to work in the same way. It is this refining of marketing strategies to suit the new context and user behaviour that is desirable and will ultimately produce results.

All this is part of knowing how to reach your clients' customers with information and products but again it has relevance for your own company within its own sector and for your present and future clients.

■ Know how to keep your customers

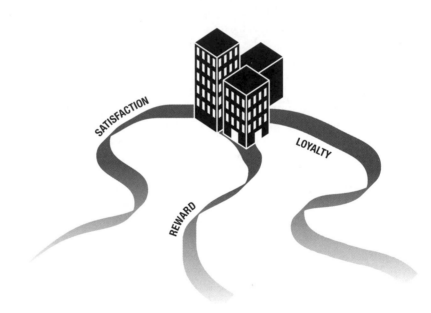

Know how to keep your customers.

Traditional marketing has recognized the true value of retaining customers and the sense in developing loyalty and trust. A satisfied customer will spread the good news and will be as beneficial in attracting new clients/customers as other marketing techniques. We have seen the rise of loyalty programmes with loyalty cards and reward schemes. Companies have recognized that profiling the information on buying habits helps them respond to market forces faster and helps them plan new goods and services.

Now there is increasing emphasis on customer relationship management (CRM) particularly from the service sector. The idea of a relationship means being in tune with a customer's attitude, lifestyle and aspirations. To achieve this the company needs precise information on a customer to tailor information and products to them. The information may come from any communication source – phone, fax, e-mail, website interaction, and conventional mail. It is integrated into a customer profile. This amount of information will only be given freely if and when the customer trusts the company across all its aspects from the quality of its service, how it deals with people, the quality of its products and the security of its transactions. Companies are increasingly asking the person's permission to send specific information to them so that they do not injure the relationship with unsolicited mail. As indicated before, this raises aspects of data protection that need to be adhered to and these are covered in Chapter 15, *Rights, copyright and other intellectual property*.

Building a relationship implies time, effort and interaction. Online technology provides more and cheaper interaction opportunities with a client. So utilizing the interaction points is important for building the relationship. These happen within a context that is equally important. Companies that buy into this marketing perspective want their websites to reflect their integrated strategy. They will look for a strategic process implicit in aspects of a website that will satisfy new and old customers – a process that will lead new customers through stages to loyalty and old customers to continue to be satisfied and rewarded for their custom.

Multimedia companies that work with marketing clients may well need to talk in terms of strategic customer phases being covered such as – awareness, attraction, interaction, community and loyalty, for example. These phases can be linked to specific techniques that will be part of a Web presence such as online advertising, affiliate programs, targeted e-mail or permission-based mail, newsletters, online competitions and reward programmes.

◼ An introduction to market analysis

Although we touched on broad methods such as quantitative and qualitative research in the section above, it will be useful to explore some techniques further.

A marketing research company will gather different types of data according to the needs defined in the brief. The information will be processed and presented in a variety of ways. One of the common techniques used is a perceptual map or matrix as demonstrated below.

If you had commissioned a market research company to evaluate the perception of a client's website (Number 1) against competitors in the market segment, they might collate the results in this way. This would demonstrate

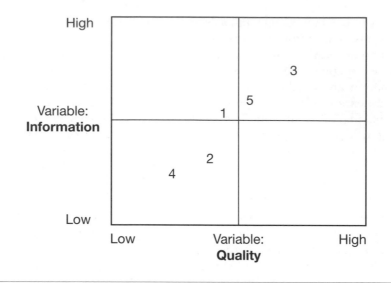

Perceptual map of multimedia competitors.

the position in relation to coverage of information and perception of the quality of the information provided. You would be able to discuss strategies for changing the perception of the company for the better while trying to increase the quality of information in line with what the respondents said they valued. Other variables can be used for the axes, but the variables should be ones determined by the client as important to them during the research.

Another form of analysis that is used in marketing research is the Pareto method. This is valuable in defining which segment of the business is making the best contribution and what customer group might be the most valuable to target. If we apply this to an e-commerce website, the contribution analysis of customer accounts to sales might be applied. The analysis helps to decide which type of product group offers the best return and where the effort for winning a particular type of business might make a big difference. It can also point out products that have not made an impact for the online business and might need rethinking for this customer group or even be discontinued. The example chart opposite demonstrates this in a figurative way. Each dot represents a type of product that a hypothetical client company produces and shows the value on the return for the company. Each dot might represent a product type.

These few examples provide a basis for understanding where and how marketing analysis can begin to serve a company. Although marketing is a relatively new discipline it has made a significant contribution to business studies, and is refining its techniques to help business decision making all the time. It needs professionals well versed and trained in its discipline

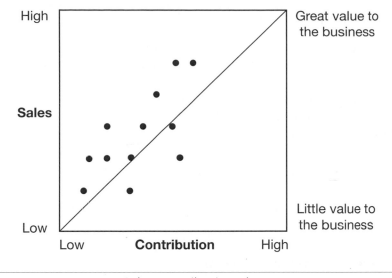

Sales contribution chart.

to perform the collection, analysis and interpretation of data. The intelligence that they can give a company needs to be considered carefully but cannot be ignored. We hope that this short introduction will encourage professionals to be receptive to marketing information and better informed as to the value of the decisions taken in relation to the business objectives.

What of the smaller companies that cannot afford to have marketing personnel or to commission research? These need to rely on surveys and reports produced for the industry. A listing of relevant companies and the types of report they offer is given at the end of the chapter.

THEORY INTO PRACTICE 19

Choose three of your close competitors and check out their websites.

Make a note of the information they give, the way it is classified, the description of the services/products that they offer.

How would you describe your experience of using the sites? What are their strengths and weaknesses?

Look at your own site and perform the same analysis as objectively as you can. What are your strengths and weaknesses in relation to those of the three competitors? What would you suggest from a marketing perspective as a make-over for your own site?

■ Summary

- ■ This chapter defines the principles behind online marketing and explains the relevance of them for a multimedia project manager.
- ■ The possible implications for web development are covered. The marketing perspective can affect all stages of development from analysis, content definition, look and feel, functionality, tools used, information gathered and processed.
- ■ The key concepts of know your customer, know your competition, know your strengths, know your market, know how to reach your market and how to keep your customer are covered.
- ■ Some insights into marketing analysis practices are outlined.

■ Recommended reading

Adcock D. Bradfield R., Halborg A. and Ross C. (1995). *Marketing Principles and Practice*, 2nd edn. London: Pitman

Forrest E. (2000). *Internet Marketing Research: Resources and Techniques*. Sydney, New South Wales: Mcgraw-Hill Australia

Hagel J. and Armstrong A.G. (1997). *Net Gain: Expanding Markets Through Virtual Communities*. Cambridge, MA: Harvard Business School Press

Hanson W.A. (2000). *Principles of Internet Marketing*. Cincinnati, OH: Thomson Learning

Henning K. (1998). *The Digital Enterprise: How Digitisation Is Redefining Business*. London: Random House

Judson B. (1996). *Netmarketing*. New York: Wolff New Media

Kim A.J. (2000). *Community Building on the Web: Secret Strategies for Successful Online Communities*. Berkeley, CA: Peachpit Press

Newell F. (2000). *Loyalty.com*. New York: McGraw-Hill

Tapscott D., Ticoll D. and Lowy A. (2000). *Digital Capital Harnessing the power of Business Webs*. Boston, MA: Harvard Business School Press

The IEEE standards groups work across sectors to establish international working practices
http://grouper.ieee.org/groups/index.html

MPEG-7 The Motion Picture Expert Group are developing the Multimedia Content Description Interface
http://www.mpeg-7.com/

Search Engine Watch is a useful site for webmasters to understand the extra services that various search engines offer, including 'paid inclusion'.
http://searchenginewatch.com/webmasters/paid/html

▢ Technology/media market research

Directories

The Multimedia and CD-ROM Directory (2001). London: Macmillan Reference

Agencies

Pull together various reports from sectors
Global Information Inc
http://www.gii.o.jp/english/plms.htm

Companies

These produce reports on various aspects of the markets. Some reports are continuously updated and revised; some are specially commissioned as trends appear.

OVUM Ltd.
http://www.ovum.com
INTECO
http://www.inteco.com
CIT Publications
http://www.telecoms-data.com
SIMBA
http:// www.simbanet.com
TFPL Multimedia
http://www.tfpl.com/TFPLhome.htm
FT Media
http://www.ftmedia.com
Cyberatlas
http://www.cyberatlas.com

Companies specializing in Internet research

Zona Research
http://wwwzonaresearch.com
NOP Research Group
http://www.nopres.co.uk
A.C.Neilsen
http://www.acnielsen.com/ and
http://www.eratings.com/

☐ General recommended reading for developers

Burdman J. (1999). *Collaborative Web Development: Strategies and Best Practices for Web Teams*. Reading, MA: Addison-Wesley

Friedlein A. (2001). *Web Site Project Management*. San Fransisco: Morgan Kaufmann

Vaughan T. (1998). *Multimedia: Making It Work*, 4th edn. Berkeley, CA: Osborne McGraw-Hill

The Multimedia and CD-ROM Directory (1998). Vol. 1 Marketplace. Vol. 2 Titles. London: Macmillan Reference

Glossary

2.5G Intermediate stage between current mobile telephones and **3G**. See **HSCSD**, **GPRS**, **EDGE**

3-D Three-dimensional, appearing to have depth.

3-DO Obsolete consumer multimedia player.

3G Third generation mobile telephone systems, another name for **UMTS – Universal Mobile Telecommunications Services**.

8-, 16-, 24- or 48-bit image The more bits a colour image has, the more colours can be shown in it. An 8-bit image can have 256 colours because 8 bits can be used for numbers from zero (00000000 in binary arithmetic) to 255 (11111111 in binary arithmetic). However, these colours can usually be chosen from a larger palette of perhaps millions of colours. If the 256 colours are all shades of grey then a photographic-quality monochrome image can be reproduced. A 16-bit image will have thousands of colours, and can look photographic in many circumstances. For a truly photographic colour image the millions of colours available in 24 bits is necessary (or even more). Note that on the Apple Macintosh an 8-bit matte or alpha channel can be added to the 24 bits, and the image can be referred to as being 32-bit. Also the PNG graphics format can handle 48-bit colour images with an alpha channel.

- 1 bit gives you two colours (usually black and white).
- 2 bits give you 4 colours.
- 4 bits give you 16 colours.
- 8 bits give you 256 colours
- 16 bits give you 65,536 colours.

- 24 bits give you 16,777,216 colours.
- 48 bits give you 281,474,976,710,656 colours.

16 by 9 Aspect ratio (width to height) of widescreen television (conventional TV has an aspect ratio of 4 by 3).

above-the-line cost A cost that you would not be paying as part of the overhead of running the company. Your in-house resources and/or staff are a below-the-line cost whereas a freelancer hired for a particular job is an above-the-line cost. These two kinds of cost are both real, since somebody has to pay them, but your attitude to them is likely to be different.

acceptance testing This is testing that is applied according to pre-determined parameters agreed with the client at the end of the project to show the project conforms to the standard expected and warrants payment.

accessibility Designing websites and other programs to give equal access to them by people with disabilities. In the case of web design it includes designing the page or a version of the page that makes sense when read by a speaking web browser (screen reader).

adaptive palette A relatively limited palette of colours that is calculated so as to best reproduce a full colour image. Often 256 colours but sometimes less.

ADPCM Adaptive delta (or difference) pulse code modulation. Delta PCM is a sound-encoding method that reduces the data rate by storing only changes in the size of samples rather than the absolute value of the sample. The adaptive part is where the encoding of the difference values adapts so as to more accurately follow large changes between samples.

ADSL Asymmetric subscriber line (or loop) which is a means of carrying very high speed data down a conventional copper telephone cable over distances of a few kilometres.

agent A piece of software that is empowered to act on the user's behalf, to carry out tasks like network maintenance or to book a holiday. A mobile agent is an agent which is able to move around a network from computer to computer in order to do its job.

aliasing Occurs when the way something is recorded produces errors that look or sound as if they should be parts of the real thing. The wheels of racing covered wagons in a Western movie, which often seem to be going backwards, do so because of aliasing. In this case the 24 frames per second of the film is not fast enough to accurately record the motion of the wheel. In digital audio it is possible to produce false sounds if the rate at which the sound is sampled is not fast enough to accurately represent the waveform. See **anti-aliasing**.

alpha channel Besides the red, green and blue channels of an image that determine the colour of each pixel, there can be another channel that sets how transparent the pixel is. This is known as the alpha channel. The effect is similar to a matte except that a matte is usually only 1 bit deep so that the transparency is either full (so the background shows through) or opaque. In television this is known as *keying*.

alpha disk The disk on which an alpha version of an offline application is distributed.

alpha test The first test of a complete or near-complete application, usually by internal users. The term originates from computing, and is not always used by web agencies and multimedia companies originating from other disciplines.

always-on A mobile phone system where data connections are charged by data transferred rather than by duration of connection. Also used to describe an Internet connection using, for example, ADSL where users do not have to dial in to connect.

ambient noise or **ambience** Extraneous sounds intruding on a sound recording due to such things as traffic, distant voices, bird song and the like, possibly including the **echo** and/or **reverberation** of the room.

analogue Strictly speaking an analogue is any kind of representation or similarity. However, analogue is used in multimedia (and in audio and video and electronics in general) to differentiate from digital. In digital, a signal is turned into a series of numbers, and the numbers are stored or transmitted. In analogue the signal itself is either stored or transmitted directly as a waveform, or is converted into another medium that can follow its variations and itself be stored or transmitted. Whereas analogue systems are prone to distortion and noise, digital systems are much less susceptible.

animatic An application that demonstrates and prototypes the final application.

animation Simulated movement of objects using computer or video effects. A simulation of a building rising from its outline foundations to completion is an example of an animation.

anti-aliasing In graphics it is possible for edges of objects to look jagged because the resolution screen display is unable to accurately represent the object itself. To alleviate this problem the colours of the pixels around the edge of the object are mixed gradually between the object and its background. In this way the colour resolution compensates for the lack of spatial resolution that causes the jagged edges. By definition, this technique cannot be used where only pure black-and-white pixels are available. Some computer displays will now automatically anti-alias text to make it look cleaner on the screen.

applet A very small computer application (usually in the Java language) downloaded from a website to run on the user's computer as part of a web page.

application A general term for a multimedia (or any kind of software) title or project.

application-based program A program that is either self-contained or which runs entirely within one environment, such as an authoring package.

artefacts Disturbances and defects to an image or sound that are not supposed to be there, but which are the results of errors in digitization or display.

ASCII American Standard Code for Information Interchange – the main standard for representing letters and numbers in computing.

assets The media components of an application or web page – audio, video, graphics, animations, text – that combine to form the content.

authoring tool A computer program designed to be simple to use when building an application. Supposedly no programming knowledge is needed, but usually common sense and an understanding of basic logic are necessary.

B2B Business to business: trading between two businesses carried out electronically. See **B2C** and **C2C**.

B2C Business to consumer: trading between a business and consumers carried out electronically. See **B2B** and **C2C**.

back-end A computer program whose operation is not apparent to the user, such as a supporting program on the server which provides information that the web server can send to the user over the Internet.

bandwidth The amount of data passed along a cable or communications channel of any kind. Sometimes the data channel, or pipe, is described as *fat* if it has a high bandwidth and can carry a lot of data quickly, or *thin* if it cannot. Bandwidth is usually expressed in bits per second or bytes per second. Because of this confusion you should be clear whether bandwidth is being expressed in bits or bytes to understand how fast the data can be transmitted.

banner advertisment An elongated narrow advertisement placed on a web page. There is a 'standard' size for banners of 468 by 60 pixels. Usually, clicking on a banner takes the user to the advertiser's website.

BCPL A computer language, one of the ancestors of C and C++.

bearer A protocol that transparently carries another protocol.

beta If your application or website has 'gone beta' then it should be finished but needs testing. This testing may be carried out by people outside the production team and even outside the production company.

bi-directional language Enabling a computer to cope with a language that reads and writes from right to left – like Arabic or Hebrew – as well as left to right as in English. The individual languages would of course be uni-directional. This goes hand-in-hand with being able to handle many more characters than the standard European-centred ASCII text. See also **double byte.**

bit The smallest unit in binary numbers. A bit can have a value of either 0 or 1. The number of bits used to represent a binary number limit the maximum value it can have. For example a 4-bit number can have values from 0000 to 1111 (0 to 15 in decimal).

bit depth In graphics, the more bits a colour image has, the more colours can be used in it. An 8-bit image can have 256 colours, but you can usually choose those colours from a larger palette of perhaps millions of colours. If your 256 colours are all shades of grey then a photographic-quality monochrome image can be reproduced. A 16-bit image will have thousands of colours, and can look photographic in many circumstances. However, for a truly photographic colour image, the millions of colours available in 24 bits is necessary (or even more). Note that on the Apple Macintosh an 8-bit matte or alpha channel can be associated with the 24 bits, making 32 bits. See also **8-, 16-, 24- or 48-bit image**.

bit rate reduction Audio and video engineers often use this term to mean compression of data, as the term 'compression' has another meaning, especially in audio. See **compression**.

bitmap A graphic image that represents the image by a matrix of pixels, usually going from top to bottom, left to right. Bitmap images usually have a resolution in pixels per inch and a size in pixels.

blanking In analogue television, the time between the end of one TV line and the start of the next (horizontal blanking) or the end of one field and the start of the next (vertical blanking or vertical interval).

Bluetooth A short-range high-speed wireless data standard especially promoted for consumer and mobile telephony use. Named after a Scandinavian king. See also **Wi-Fi.**

boiler plate A standard form of contract that is then modified or qualified to make up the contract for a particular agreement.

Bookmark A function of an application whereby users can store their place so that they can quickly go back there later, even saving the Bookmark for retrieval many days later. The electronic equivalent of a piece of paper between pages of a book.

browser A piece of software that allows the user to look through a number of resources, usually held in a variety of formats. A web browser is designed for viewing World Wide Web pages on the Internet. Netscape Navigator, Internet Explorer and Opera are examples of web browsers.

buffer A place for temporary storage of data, often to smooth out differences in speed between a data input and output.

build The process of taking all the component parts of a multimedia application (or indeed any piece of software) and making the finished version.

bump mapping In computer graphics, a technique for giving a surface texture to objects by slightly distorting the shape.

buy-out Paying for all the necessary rights in one go rather than paying royalties.

byte In binary arithmetic, and hence in computing, a byte is an 8-bit number and can have a value between 0 and 255.

C, C++ Powerful computer languages, often used to write sophisticated code to carry out specialized or difficult tasks in multimedia applications. C++ is more recent and is designed for object-oriented programming. Java is based on C.

C2C Consumer to consumer: trading carried out between consumers, like auctions or jumble/yard sales, carried out electronically. Also see **B2B** and **B2C**.

cache Computer memory or disk space used for temporary storage of data in order to speed up a task. A web browser has a cache on disk to hold recently downloaded pages and graphics so that if a page is revisited and has not changed the information can be quickly loaded from the local disk rather than downloaded again over the network.

call centre A centralized enquiry centre that people phone for information relating to a business, its services and/or products.

carousel A model for interactive television where a sequence of information is transmitted repeatedly.

cartogram A style of illustration in which a map shows statistical information in a diagrammatic way.

CD burner A machine that can write compact disks, including CD-ROMs. The disks were originally called WORMs (write once read many) and so sometimes the machines are called WORM burners. The term CD-R is more common now, and there is a re-recordable version called CD-RW, which has limited compatibility with standard CD-ROM drives.

CD-i Compact Disk-Interactive is an obsolete interactive multimedia platform that uses a television monitor with a CD-i player as the delivery system. Primarily developed by Philips for the consumer market, it allows use of all media on the system. It has its own set of authoring tools, and conforms to the Green Book technical specification standards. With the decline of consumer CD-

ROM, CD-i remained in a niche market for training and other professional applications primarily because of its inexpensive player cost and use of a television set rather than a computer monitor.

CD-ROM Compact disk read-only memory has progressed from allowing only text and data onto the disk to now include audio, graphics, animations and video. It conforms to the Yellow Book and ISO 9660 technical specifications. CD-ROM drives vary in the speed for transferring data but for multimedia delivery you need to allow for potential users having drives that are not the fastest available.

CD-TV A short-lived obsolete consumer multimedia system based on the Commodore Amiga.

cellular radio A system for radio communication that uses a large number of low-powered transmitters, each operating in a small area called a cell. Mobile telephones use this system and as the telephones move their connections move from one cell to another.

certificate An electronic document that authoritatively identifies a web server so that secure (HTTPS) transactions can take place. Without a valid certificate a web browser will not set up a secure link.

CGI Common gateway interface: Internet standards for the passing of information between applications such as web browsers and pages and the server. Programs that make use of this, called CGI programs, allow sophisticated generation of web pages based on dynamic data, and mean that such things as forms and databases can be used on the Web.

change management A system set up by developers to monitor and control the number and type of changes made during development, whether the changes originate in-house or from the client. Also known as *change control*.

change request form The document used to request a modification to an already agreed specification. Used in **change management**.

channel See **distribution channel**.

character generator A piece of software or hardware designed to make captions for video and superimpose them on the picture.

chat and chuck Name given to very cheap and disposable mobile telephones.

chrominance The colour part of a colour television signal, as distinct from the brightness part, which is luminance. Often abbreviated to chroma.

circuit switched data In mobile telephony, a dial-up call where users have continuous use of the circuit and pay by duration of call. See also **always-on**.

clearances The overall term for copyright and similar permissions.

client side A process, such as display of a web page, which happens on the user's local computer rather than on the server.

clip art/media Illustrations, photographs or any other media items available, usually inexpensively or even free, for use in productions with no further payment. See **royalty-free.**

codec A piece of software that compresses and/or decompresses audio or video. Stands for coder-decoder.

coincident needles A stereo meter for showing volume of sound where the two needles of the meter, representing left and right signals, revolve around the same point.

coloured In audio, the detrimental change in a sound due to the influence of the physical environment (such as the room) or distortions in the recording system.

competences The definition of skills evident from practices carried out in the workplace. This term has become prominent in training circles through the link to NVQs (National Vocational Qualifications). These are new-style qualifications that are concerned with accrediting people for the skills they employ naturally as they carry out their work.

compile To take the source code of a computer program and turn it into machine code using a compiler. The source code is written by the programmer. Extra code from programming libraries is incorporated at this time. The opposite is **interpreted**.

component A video image in which the colour information is kept separate from the luminance or brightness information. Usually two signals are used to represent the colour information. This is similar to RGB, and the RGB signals can be extracted from the three components. The components are also specified to take into account the eye's response to different colours.

composite A video signal in which colour and brightness are encoded together in the same signal. PAL and NTSC are composite television systems.

composite image In video, an image in which colour and brightness are encoded together in the same signal; in graphics, an image made up of several other images, blended together.

compressed but lossless A compressed signal from which the original signal can be retrieved without any changes or errors.

compressed with loss A compressed signal from which it is impossible to retrieve the original signal, in which a version of the original is retrieved that is satisfactory for its intended purpose. Also known as **lossy**.

compression In computing, reducing the amount of data needed to carry something; also known as **bit rate reduction**. When the term 'video compression' is used it will almost certainly have this meaning, and will refer to such systems as MPEG and Sorensen. In audio, reducing the dynamic range (range of loudness) of a sound recording.

computer-based training Often referred to as CBT, computer-based training is a method in which some or all of the training content of a course is turned into an interactive computer program.

concept map A visual representation to help show relationships between different items.

concept testing Testing of ideas on an audience chosen from a sample market. The

aim is to check the feasibility of the ideas for the market before incurring expense implementing them. The method for implementation can but may not involve interactive methods. Concept testing originated with marketing, and may be called *focus groups*.

conforming In video editing, taking the edits noted from an offline edit session and using them to edit the real high quality recording for final distribution. If done automatically based on the list of edits it is known as auto-conforming.

contention ratio In an ADSL connection, a measure of the number of other users sharing your connection to the Internet. This will be a small number, typically less than 100, and it assumes that few users will be demanding bandwidth at any moment. Not all ADSL systems make the users share the connection.

contingency In project management, predicting the need and reserving funds, time and/or resources to cope with unforeseen circumstances that affect the project schedule. Multimedia project management needs more contingency than many other forms of project because it is a volatile environment.

contouring An artefact in graphics reproduction whereby smooth changes of brightness or colour become changed so that discrete steps are seen. Sometimes also called **posterization** (especially when used for artistic effect) or **quantization**.

convergence The gradual merging of computing, broadcast media and telecommunications technologies.

cookie A small amount of data stored by a browser on behalf of a web server to help track a visit to a website.

copyright The right of a creator of a work of art, literature, music, and so on to have control over the reproduction and exploitation of the work.

credit The linking of people to the tasks they performed. This is normally done by listing the name and function performed, as in credits at the end of a television programme. The crediting of personnel in media is very important and is often governed by agreements between production companies and unions.

critical path The identification of the optimum sequence to carry out tasks to achieve a project on time and within budget. See also **task analysis** and **network analysis**.

CRM Customer Relationship Management. A system based on collecting information on each customer from many sources within an organization into a central electronic file and using this to tailor information on goods and services to their needs.

cross-platform Describes the development of applications that will run on more than one delivery platform.

CUI Concept User Interface. These are tools that help a group of people debate, define and rank their most common important concepts. These tools can be helpful in the analysis of requirements for a project.

custom palette A palette of colours chosen specifically to represent an image.

DAT Digital audio tape, a format using 4 mm tape in cassettes originally designed for digital audio (48 kHz sampling 16-bit) but also used to store data when it operates as a streamer tape format.

data protection The concept in European law whereby personal information is protected and the organizations who use this data and the use they can make of the data are registered and regulated. See **safe harbour.**

debug To study an application with the intention of removing any errors found.

deck The equivalent of a website in **WAP**. The analogy is a deck of cards.

decompile To take the machine code version of a program and change it back into something a human can understand.

decryption To remove the encryption from something so that the original is produced.

delivery medium The system used to distribute an application. The World Wide Web can be considered to be a delivery medium.

delivery platform The multimedia system or systems that people will use to interact with the application. The total specification of the platform is important so that the application is developed within the capabilities. A web browser can be considered to be a delivery platform.

development platform The multimedia system that is used to develop the application. This may not be the same as the delivery platform. It is important that the final application is tested on the delivery system to check that it will perform on the specified platform.

development testing This is iterative testing applied naturally during the development of a project to ensure that all the pieces work.

diaphragm In a microphone, the membrane that is vibrated by sound and so causes the production of an electrical signal that represents the sound.

digital In a digital system, the signal (including such things as sounds and pictures) is turned into a series of numbers, and it is these numbers that are stored or transmitted. In an **analogue** system the signal itself is either stored or transmitted directly, or is converted into another medium that can follow its variations and itself be stored or transmitted. Whereas analogue systems are prone to distortion and noise, digital systems are much less susceptible.

direct competitors Companies that are in the same line of business, competing for sales from the same people.

discovery learning A learning situation that is structured to allow the learner to explore and find answers rather than be told the information.

discrete cosine transform or **DCT** A mathematical technique for transforming a bitmap of an image, which contains individual dots of the image from left-to-right and top-to-bottom. The DCT analyses the image block by block to find the large areas of colour and the fine detail in them. The resulting file can then be analysed to determine what can be removed without seriously affecting the look of the image. This is the basis of **JPEG** and the first stage of **MPEG** compression.

distance learning A learning situation in which the student studies a course away from the institution using any medium that is provided. This may include interactive programs. See also **open learning centres**.

distribution channel A well-defined and sustained system for moving goods from production out to the people who will buy the products.

dither Small, seemingly random perturbations to a signal or image designed to fool the eye or ear into thinking that it has greater quality than it really does. In graphics a dither is a seemingly random pattern of dots of a limited range of colours that, when viewed from a distance, appear to have a greater range of colours. When digitizing a signal, a dither is used to reduce the effect of digitizing errors because our eyes and ears are less distressed by noise (which dither looks like) than by the sharp changes in a signal that the dither disguises.

DLT A streaming tape format used for data backup and also used to send DVD masters to replication facilities. Has replaced **Exabyte** for these purposes where large quantities of data are involved.

document-based programming Programming in which the format of the document is standardized and one or more applications can be used in concert to read or display it. The World Wide Web is an example of this.

Dolby The company (and inventor) famous for a system for reducing noise in an audio recording and for systems providing multichannel (surround) sound in cinemas and the home. The name is often used ambiguously for either. Dolby is a trade mark.

domain name The Internet equivalent of a street address, showing the route to a particular computer. The name will end with the top level domain name (**TLD**), which designates a user sector, primarily in the USA, such as .com for commercial, .gov for government or .edu for education. There are also internationally agreed country names used as TLDs such as .us, .uk, .fr and .dk, and a machine will usually be situated in that country. New TLDs are occasionally added. The US sector top level domains are often used by organizations wishing to show an international presence even if they are based outside the USA. In an e-mail address the domain name appears after the @ symbol. An individual computer can have a fully qualified domain name (FQDN), which uniquely identifies it. Every FQDN must have a corresponding **IP address** but the reverse is not true.

Domain Name Registrar A company authorized to sell domain names and arrange for them to be made available on the Internet.

Domain name system Usually just called DNS, this is a distributed database on the Internet that maps domain names to IP addresses and vice versa.

dot com company Usually used to refer to a company that exists and trades solely in cyberspace. The name comes from the top level domain where many businesses have their domain names.

dot pitch The distance between dots of phosphor on a colour television or monitor tube. Figures of 0.23 to 0.28 millimetres are common and a smaller dot pitch means a higher resolution is possible.

double byte The use of 16 bits (two bytes) that allows all the characters needed for all world languages to be represented in software. This includes Hindi, Thai, Chinese and Japanese, for example and the standard for this is called Unicode. Most Western European languages can be represented in 8 bits using the **ASCII** standard. Also see **bi-directional**.

dpi The density of dots in an image or on a computer screen. Most computer screen displays are 72 or 96 dpi (dots per inch).

draw object In graphics, an image that is defined in terms of simple graphics 'primitives' such as lines, arcs and fills.

drop frame In NTSC television time code. A time code format which adjusts to compensate for NTSC not having a whole number of frames per second by dropping some time code numbers to keep in step.

dub To copy something, usually an audio or videotape recording. A dub is the copy itself. In digital terminology a direct digital copy is often called a *clone* since it will be indistinguishable from the original.

dumb terminal A computer terminal with a keyboard and screen that does nothing other than show a display generated at a distant computer and send back your typed input.

DVB Digital video broadcasting system used in most of the world apart from the USA. Also a mark used on European digital televisions to show that they will receive digital TV programmes.

DVD Digital versatile disk. Originally called digital video disk, this is the successor to CD-ROM and has many incarnations. The capacity of a DVD disk is much greater than that of a CD-ROM because the system packs the information more tightly on the disk, has the possibility of two information layers per side, and can have information on both sides of the disk. As with CD, recordable, re-writeable, audio and ROM versions are possible. DVD Audio is one of two new formats designed to supersede compact disc audio, the other is **SACD**.

DVD-ROM Use of DVD to hold a large amount of data (up to almost 18 gigabytes), which can then be accessed by a computer. Basically the equivalent of a big CD-ROM.

dynamic range In audio, the range of loudness or volume of a sound.

dynamic web page A web page that is composed by a program running on the web server computer based on factors such as the kind of request from the browser and what information is currently available. To the browser it looks exactly like a static page.

e-business or e-commerce Business involving goods and services carried out electronically, usually via the World Wide Web.

echo In audio, delayed and distinct individual repeats of the original sound, either due to sound bouncing off the walls of the room or deliberately added electronically. Famously used on the vocal of Elvis Presley's 'Heartbreak Hotel'. See also **reverberation**.

EDGE Enhanced Data Rate for GSM Evolution, a 2.5G mobile technology.

educational technology The study of the ways in which the use of media and structured approaches to organizing material can aid teaching and learning.

edutainment A term derived from the words *education* and *entertainment* coined to describe a category of interactive titles. These are designed to be used in the home to inform and motivate through the use of media.

electronic programme guide A guide to what is available on the channels of a digital television system, shown on the system itself and enabling viewers to actually call up programmes. More usually called EPG. In a multi-channel world, if a channel is not listed in the EPG it is virtually invisible to viewers.

electrostatic Describes a system for microphones, and less commonly, loudspeakers and headphones, whereby electrostatic charge is used to detect or cause the movement of the diaphragm.

emulator A system that pretends to be something it is not, such as a software system that pretends to be a piece of hardware or a software system that pretends to be another software system.

encryption Changing a data file so that it is unrecognizable but can be turned back into its original form on receipt, if the receiver has the key to decode it.

environment map In computer graphics, a method of reproducing reflections on the surface of an object by determining an image of what the object 'sees' from its position and wrapping the object in this image.

environment variable Information passed to a web server when a distant browser requests a 'page'. It includes information on the computer making the request and what web page included the link being followed (if any).

EPG See **electronic programme guide**.

evaluation Often confused with the term 'testing' and used interchangeably, but when used in a strict technical sense, there are differences. Evaluation of an application is the broad appraisal of any factors that influence the development, delivery and reaction to it. See also **testing**.

Exabyte A type of computer streamer tape using 8 mm cassette tape in the same format as Video-8 but now largely replaced for professional applications by a format called **DLT**.

exclusively assigned rights Copyright passed on to someone else so that the original copyright owner no longer has rights in the material.

external clients People who are not part of your organization who commission you to do a piece of work. They define the brief and specifications. Budgets are agreed and negotiated between you.

Extranet A private network whereby the main company allows some other companies to share some or all data on their **intranet** with strict controls on access.

e-zine An electronic equivalent of a magazine.

fair dealing or **fair use** In copyright law, an exception to infringement under certain limited circumstances because your usage of the material is very slight and/or under circumstances where free usage is seen as reasonable. Examples of this include use of extracts from books in a review and limited use in education. What constitutes fair use differs from country to country and is often misunderstood.

feature creep A gradual and insidious increase in the capability of a piece of software as it is developed, usually without any overall plan of implementation.

field trials The use of the product *in situ* with the intended users prior to release to identify problems for correction.

file path The combination of disk or volume name, directory names and filename that uniquely identifies a file on a computer.

firewall In networks, a computer which monitors traffic flowing between the Internet and an internal network so as to prevent unwanted connections such as hacking.

fixed-term contract A contract that cannot be extended beyond its original duration without positive action being taken by both parties. To extend the term either a new contract would be written or a new clause added to the original contract.

flowchart A diagram that shows step-by-step progression through the content blocks of the proposed website or program.

focus groups See **concept testing**.

force majeure A condition in a contract where neither party has control over the circumstances. This might include war, loss of electrical power and acts of God.

formative A term used to describe evaluation processes carried out during the development cycle. These are contrasted with summative evaluation processes, which occur at the end of development. In this context, team review meetings that occur during the project could be called a formative evaluation process. See **summative**.

frame-grabbing Synonymous with digitization of video but dating back to the days when computers had to digitize frames individually.

frames In video a complete single image, which forms part of a moving sequence of images. On the Web, a technique that allows several distinct parts of a web page to be defined, and which can be defined separately by the author. Often used to allow an index to be shown alongside the different things referred to in the index.

front-end A computer program that provides interface and setup procedures for a less user-friendly but probably more powerful back-end program. On a web server this might be the programme that formats web pages having drawn information from a back-end database.

FTP File Transfer Protocol. Protocol for transferring files between computers over the Internet.

fully qualified domain name (FQDN) see **domain name**.

functional specification A document that says how an application works. The application will be written by referring to this if part of company policy.

gallows arm A kind of microphone stand with a vertical part to which is connected a horizontal extension. This is like the arm of a gallows, and it is used to extend across a table (for example). The mic is fixed to the end of the arm.

gamma The relationship between the brightness of an original (such as a digital image) and the way that signal is displayed by a monitor or on a printed page.

Gantt chart This is a chart that shows progress in relation to a timescale, often used in planning and tracking a project. It was named after Henry Lawrence Gantt, an American engineer.

gateway A computer which connects one system to another, for example a local network to the Internet. In **WAP** a gateway translates and mediates between web pages using **HTML** and WAP phones which use **WML**.

GIF Graphics Interchange Format: a standard for 8-bit graphics, widely used on the Web.

One version of the standard allows part of the image to be defined as transparent.

gigabyte 1024 megabytes.

global culture An international group of people who share similar needs for communication based on profession, business sector, hobby, interests, or whatever.

golden master The final version of an application; the one that will be distributed.

GPRS General Packet Radio Service, a 2.5G mobile technology.

GPS Global Positioning System, a satellite-based system provided by the US Government (mainly military) which allows a GPS receiver to pinpoint its location and altitude on Earth. Precision of the system was initially limited to protect military interests but this has been improved. It is also possible to use a local fixed beacon to augment the satellites and give very high accuracy. May eventually be incorporated into mobile telephones and motor vehicles.

grabber board A piece of hardware that takes in an analogue signal, usually audio or video (where it is a frame grabber), and digitizes it for storage in the computer. Incorporation of audio-visual ports in computers and the advent of DV (digital video camcorder format) make this kind of card obsolescent.

graduated mask In graphics, a mask that determines how much of a second image shows through the first. It is graduated because it has values such that a mix of the two images is seen.

graphical structure editor In programming, a programming environment whereby the author can lay out the relationship between sections of the application in a graphical way, like a flowchart.

GUI Graphical User Interface.

hacker A person who uses considerable computing skill in deviant ways, including introducing computer viruses into a computing community. The term is also used less often, and informally, to denote a skilled computer programmer with no malicious intent. Similarly *hacking*.

half-toning In graphics, a method for reproducing shades of grey by using black dots of varying sizes. See **dither.**

hardware A piece of equipment; as distinct from software.

HCI Human Computer Interaction.

header The invisible part of a web page in which formatting information for the page and meta tags are placed. See also **meta tag**.

high-level design A first attempt to define the interactive structure and content of a program. The term comes from software engineering. See also **outline design**.

hits, hit rate Either the number of individual requests for data that a web page receives or the number of different visitors who have called that page up. This latter is now more usually called **page impressions**.

host machine The computer on which a program runs.

hot-spot A section of an image on the screen that instigates an action when the pointer enters or clicks in it.

HSCSD High Speed Circuit Switched Data, a higher speed version of GSM and a **2.5G** mobile technology.

HTML Hypertext mark-up language: the system used in web pages to describe a web page and its contents. Eventually a combination of XML and Cascading Style Sheets (CSS) will together describe the contents and define how they should be displayed.

HTTP Hypertext transfer protocol: the Internet communications protocol used in the World Wide Web. Basically, a browser calls up a web page by sending an HTTP request to the server. HTTPS is the encrypted and secure version of HTTP.

hybrid Web/CD A multimedia application that needs both a web connection and a CD to function fully. This could be a CD-ROM that updates itself from a website or a website that uses a CD-ROM to hold large multimedia assets such as movies.

hypertext Non-linear text that is read by following jumps and links in the text itself.

icon A pictorial symbol or representation used on the screen to denote an active area. It will allow access to further data or trigger an interactive reaction of some type. It has become common for a text explanation to appear when the user positions the cursor over the icon to help the user understand its significance. See also **picon** and **micon**.

ICT Information and Communication Technologies. Term used as shorthand in describing aspects of convergent technologies.

image map A graphical menu of a website usually put on the front page. This has fallen out of favour as it often took so long to download.

IMAP Internet Message Access Protocol. A recent alternative to **POP** for e-mail.

i-mode Web service provided by NTT DoCoMo in Japan for mobile telephones.

implied licence In the context of a website it is usually assumed that the web pages are published so that they can be viewed across the Internet. Any other use of the pages, such as extracting images from them or displaying them out of context, would breach this implied licence to view. Many websites now have an explicit set of terms and conditions under which the site is viewed.

in-bound communication Communication that only needs to be understood enough by the person receiving it to fulfil a specific need. The need can be linked to various levels of understanding – gist, relevance, decision, action, etc. Here the context is understanding a level of another language enough to understand the message without actually seeing a correct translation.

indemnity A guarantee that if any cost is incurred as a result of your action, you will cover it.

indirect competitors Companies that are in related lines of business to you who may win sales from your potential customers with their products.

information architect Helps users find and manage information successfully by designing organizational and navigational systems (also called *information analyst* or *information strategist*).

inlining Linking to someone else's image so that it appears to be part of your web page even though it does not reside on your server. Potentially a breach of copyright because of a breach of the **implied licence** under which web pages are published on the Internet.

instructional design The study of methods of teaching and learning with particular reference to the selection and use of media to aid instruction. The term is widely used in the USA. Europe tends to use the term **educational technology**.

instructional designer A person who applies the principles of instructional design to convey information using a variety of media and methods.

insubstantial portion In copyright, a small proportion of a literary work that can be reproduced without infringing copyright.

integrity (of moral rights) The author's right for the work not to be changed.

intellectual property A general term for rights such as those protected by copyright and patents.

interactive design The definition of how to structure the content and interactive paths through the material for an interactive application.

interactive television Interactivity applied to broadcast television. As yet this is ill defined, but certainly includes multimedia electronic programme guides, information systems, and adjuncts to the transmitted programmes allowing viewers more involvement.

interactive video An interactive system that uses an interactive videodisk to deliver sound and pictures and combines them with text, sound and graphics from a computer source. More a system of the 1980s, used by large corporations for training, its use has declined. Also denoted by IV.

interface The way an application is designed for people to use. This includes the screen designs, the use of icons or menus, the way interactivity is set up, and the overall structure of the application.

interlaced Describes a television picture that is made of two halves, which interlace with each other like the teeth of a comb and the spaces between.

internal clients People – part of your own organization – who define a piece of work for you to do. Budgeting for the work might be affected by company practices.

Internationalization producing software in a way that facilitates adaptation to suit other languages and cultures without the need for re-programming.

Internet A worldwide interconnection of computer networks, originally set up between the American military, its suppliers and research base to make a network that, by virtue of its multiple interconnections, would be safe from destruction. Up to the 1990s the Internet was largely the preserve of the academic and research communities, but the invention of HTTP, HTML and the World Wide Web has made the Internet the latest mass communications medium.

interpreted In computing, a computer program where each individual command is translated into machine code instructions for the computer before moving on to the next one. The opposite is **compiled**.

intranet A local area network, such as in a company, which operates using Internet protocols and systems. This will now usually include a local implementation of the World Wide Web with web pages read by browsers. Intranets have changed the way most large companies communicate with their staff.

ionizing The process of electrically charging something by removing or adding electrons.

IP address A number, in the form 123.123.123.123, which uniquely identifies a computer on the Internet. See **domain name**.

IRC Internet Relay Chat, a protocol for typing messages between computers in real time.

IrDA Infrared communications standard used in mobile telephones, **PDAs** and lap-top computers for interconnections and connection to fixed devices such as printers.

ISDN A digital phone line which provides a link of either 64 kilobits per second (European standard) or 56 (US standard) per channel with a minimum of two channels. ISDN stands for Integrated Services Digital Network.

ISP Internet service provider: the organization that connects you to the Internet, usually by means of a dial-up telephone connection with a modem. Some ISPs operate nationally and internationally (such as AOL, MSN and Demon), while others operate locally.

iTV See **interactive television**.

jaggies See **staircasing**.

Java A computer language based on C and devised by engineers at Sun originally for use in cable television set-top boxes. It allows efficient sending of small applications (applets) across the Internet, which are then executed on the user's computer.

JavaScript A scripting language that runs in recent browsers and allows more sophisticated control of pages and interaction than HTML. No relation to Java.

JPEG A standardized method for compressing still photographic images with high rates of compression. Almost always **lossy**. The acronym JPEG stands for Joint Photographic Experts Group.

kilobyte 1024 bytes of data (not 1000).

layer (of graphics) Several layers of images can be combined together in graphics to make a new single image. The relationship between the layers is controlled by their alpha channels.

leadership The employment of appropriate management styles to ensure and maintain progress of a team towards common goals.

lean back Like watching television, at a distance, as distinct from **lean forward** and sometimes known as couch potato.

lean forward Like using a computer, close to the screen, as distinct from **lean back**.

learning styles Part of the theory of learning, which indicates that people develop preferred ways of learning. This has implications for designing learning materials so that people can process the information in ways appropriate for their preferred style.

letters patent Formal term for the document that defines a patent.

library music Recorded music produced especially for use in film television and other audiovisual productions. Usually available for licence based on a standard rate card. Also known as **production music**.

limiter In audio, an electronic circuit that automatically controls volume to stop short peaks of volume exceeding a certain amount.

link On the Web a word, phrase or graphic on a web page that, when clicked by the user, sends an HTTP request to the server, usually calling up another web page. Sometimes referred to as a *hot link*.

load balancing Sharing the traffic on a website between a number of server computers in order to handle very high numbers of hits. See **scalability.**

localization Using translation and cultural adaptation to produce software and support materials ready for use in particular languages and cultures.

location-aware or **location-based services** Services provided to a mobile telephone which take account of where the phone is located, to offer lists of nearby restaurants for example.

log Record kept by a web server of every HTTP request it receives, with details including the time and date, who asked for the page, and how much data was transferred.

look and feel Common name for the interface of an application. See **interface**.

lossy In compression this means that the original data cannot exactly be retrieved from the compressed version. This does not necessarily mean that the effects of the compression are visible or audible.

luminance The black-and-white or monochrome part of a colour television signal or picture.

machine code Zeros and ones in a program that a computer can execute directly.

magneto-optical disk A type of disk used for data storage for which both a laser and a magnetic field are required to write data.

mainframe A very large computer – in capability if not in size. Probably run by a dedicated team of people and able to handle many tasks simultaneously.

market research Information about the changing behaviour of people and their habits, gathered by a variety of methods and organized into statistical or analytical representations.

mark-up language A system of marking text so that it can be understood or displayed correctly using a computer. **HTML** is hypertext mark-up language.

master tape The definitive and original recording of something.

mechanical right The right to record a piece of music.

megabyte 1,048,576 bytes of data – 1024 kilobytes.

memory leak A bug in a computer program which causes it to gradually fill up its available memory and finally crash.

menu A set of options listed or otherwise available on screen for the user to select. A main decision point in an application might be called a *menu screen* even if it does not contain a conventional menu list.

merchant services Service to facilitate trading, primarily used to mean accepting payment using credit cards. The merchant service is usually provided by a bank and ultimately has to link to a bank. May include online validation of the credit card transaction so that the merchant (i.e the online shop) can safely dispatch the goods.

meta tag A tag which is placed in the header of a web page to pass control or similar information to the web browser or indexing program that reads the page.

MHEG ISO standard for the definition of multimedia and hypermedia objects.

micon An icon that has moving images. Few make the distinction between icon and micon and generally icon is used to cover all selection images. See also **icon** and **picon**.

middleware Software that manages interaction between different programs, especially in a network. It might link a web server and a database.

MIDI Musical Instrument Digital Interface. A standardized way of describing music and how it is played so that a MIDI-compatible instrument can then provide the sound.

milestone Defined key points of the project's development. Milestones are often linked to the end of a phase of development, and can be linked to phased payment stages of the project as well.

MIME Multipurpose Internet Mail Extension. A standard way of identifying what a file is so that it is handled correctly by web servers and other computers.

mirror site A website that contains the same content as another website. This is usually done so that access speeds can be optimized depending on where in the world the user is. Mirroring a website requires permission, otherwise it is infringement of copyright.

mobile agent See **agent**.

modelling In 3-D graphics, building a scene by defining objects in the scene and arranging them and their environment.

modem Stands for modulate-demodulate and usually refers to a device that takes digital data and converts it into an analogue audio signal so it can pass through the telephone system. The signal is converted back using another modem at the other end. The term is also used for any similar translation and so an ADSL system would include ADSL modems (see **ADSL**).

montage A single graphic made from several sources.

moral rights Rights, related to copyright, which protect a work from unauthorized changes or misattribution without the author's permission. This is currently mainly a European concept but is applied to works of art in US law.

morph To change one shape into another in a smooth transitional movement.

MoSCoW This is an example of one approach to eliciting client needs in a project where you define the items the client *Must have, Should have, Could have* and *Would like to have*. This approach derives from Rapid Application Development programming techniques.

MP3 MPEG Audio Layer 3. One of the ways of compressing audio in the MPEG family of standards, widely used on the Internet.

MPEG Motion Picture Experts Group; a group of ISO standards for compression of video and definitions of multimedia objects.

MPEG audio The MPEG standard includes three levels of audio. Level 1 is used for DCC (digital compact cassette), Level 2 is usd in DVD and digital broadcasting and level 3 (better known as **MP3**) gives the best compression and is widely used to compress audio on the Internet.

MPEG-1 The version of MPEG that compresses video to a data rate of around one megabit per second. The quality is similar to that of S-VHS.

MPEG-2 The version of MPEG for broadcast quality video at bit rates of the order of 5 megabits per second. Digital television, digital versatile disks (DVD) and Sony's Betacam-SX use MPEG-2. (MPEG-3 was to have dealt with high definition but it was eventually included in MPEG-2.)

MPEG-4 An extension to MPEG introducing object-oriented structures to audio and video and compression for low bit rates.

MPEG-7 An extension to MPEG to provide a standard framework for indexing audio-visual material. (There is no MPEG-5 or 6

and the number 7 is the sum of 1, 2 and 4. The next MPEG is MPEG-21 which is a multimedia framework allowing an overview of all aspects of content delivery covered by the other MPEGs.)

multicultural Communication that needs to be produced specifically for different languages and cultures.

multimedia narrative The structure underpinning forms of interactive communication. Interactive narrative allows the user to take control of the sequencing of information and this is what differentiates multimedia narrative from more traditional forms of narrative.

multiscan Referring to a computer monitor that can work with a range of displays.

multi-session disk A CD-ROM that can be/is written to more than once with each new set of data being added onto the end of the rest until the disk is full.

multitasking Able to do more than one task at once.

needs analysis The primary stage of a training project where the definition of the criteria for success takes place. The competence level of the target audience and the gap between this and the proficiency needed is analysed.

Network Address Translation (NAT) A way of 'hiding' the IP addresses of the computers on a network from the Internet at large. This might be done for security or to avoid unnecessarily using up Internet IP addresses.

network analysis Also referred to as *critical path analysis*; this is the definition of the core tasks and the dependent tasks needed to complete the project. These are mapped out in a network diagram to show their relationship to each other. See **critical path**.

newsgroups See **UseNet groups**.

non-disclosure agreement A contract, usually brief, whereby one party agrees not to disclose information given to it by the other party. Usually known as an NDA.

non-exclusive rights A licensing of rights that still allows licensing to other people.

non-linear In audio-visual production, the use of a computer to edit digitized sound and/or vision. Synonymous with *random-access*.

normalizing In audio, adjusting the volume of a digital audio file so that the loudest parts have a predetermined value, often 100%.

NTSC The analogue colour television system used in North America and Japan, with 525 lines in a frame and approximately 30 frames per second. See also **PAL/SECAM**.

objective A precise definition of a result that is wanted, in terms that will allow the result to be measured. Objectives are used particularly in education and training applications where the results of learning need to be stated, and ultimately measured, to demonstrate the effectiveness of the materials. Objectives are often confused with aims. Aims are more general statements of direction rather than measurable statements.

objective evaluation Evaluation carried out with preset criteria that give a measurable indication of the results. See **subjective evaluation**, **qualitative evaluation** and **quantitative evaluation**.

object-oriented programming Programming as interaction between self-contained mini-programs or objects.

offline A multimedia application that works in isolation on a computer and does not need a network connection. A CD-ROM application is an example of offline.

offline editing Video editing with working copies of the 'real' videotapes and low-quality equipment in order to prepare for **online editing**.

on-demand services A method of providing entertainment and other audiovisual material to consumers (and others) whereby they can demand a particular item, such as a film, and it will be sent to them immediately down a communications link. Some early video-on-demand systems even sent MPEG-1 video to consumers down their telephone lines.

online Applications that operate over a network, particularly the World Wide Web.

online editing Video editing with the 'real' videotapes on high-quality equipment or using a computerized system but with high quality digitized audio and video.

open learning centres Centres usually set up in the workplace where a variety of learning and training materials are gathered for people to use. They can have access to the materials as and when they want. Many use interactive materials as well as videos and books. This approach to learning reflects the need for quick access to training in organizations that are changing faster than ever before.

open plan An office arrangement that assigns space according to changing need. There are no or few permanent partitions between desks, so that the space can be reorganized efficiently when needed. An extension of this principle allocates desks and even computers to workers as they are needed, and is known as *hot desking*.

operating system The lowest level of computer software in a computer. It manages the operation of the hardware and provides the programmer with ways of controlling the machine. Often the term *operating system* is taken to include the graphical user interface as well.

option bars Part of a graphic on the screen that provides hot-spots, buttons or icons grouped together for the user to make a choice.

OS Operating system.

out-bound communication Information that is distributed to numerous people who are likely to have specific uses for the communication. Therefore the accuracy of the information is important and in this context the accuracy of any translation from another language to retain its integrity becomes important.

outline design The first attempt to define the interactive structure and content of a program. The term comes from interactive training design. The later stage from this discipline is called the *detailed design*. See also **high-level design**.

palette The colours available for use in a graphic.

PAL/SECAM The analogue colour television systems used in Europe and most of the world outside North America and Japan, with 625 lines in a frame and 25 frames per second. See also **NTSC**. SECAM encodes the colour information differently to PAL and is used mostly in France, the Middle East and Eastern Europe.

pan Moving the viewpoint of a camera from side to side by swivelling it and not actually changing the location of the camera.

Pareto method An analytical representation of data in graphical form; used to help identify the products that can make the best contribution to the company.

patent The right to exclusive implementation of a process as defined in the patent document.

patent agent A lawyer who drafts letters patent.

paternity The moral right whereby you have a right to be identified as author: also known as *attribution*.

PDA Personal Digital Assistant. Very small hand-held computer also known as a palm top.

peer review Appraisal by colleagues or people performing similar jobs, where the sharing of experience and insights is used to adjust, in this case, the design and functionality of the application.

perceptual map Analytical representation of the results of a survey; used to understand the relative positions of two variables plotted in a matrix.

perceptual matrix See **perceptual map**.

performance monitoring A management process in which people agree criteria of acceptable achievements for a period and review performance according to the criteria at the end of the time. The performance agreement might be linked to bonus payments. Any shortfall of performance accredited to lack of skill might prompt training initiatives.

performing right The right to perform a piece of music to an audience.

Perl A computer language widely used on web servers to produce dynamic web pages based on data received from users. It has powerful string manipulation capabilities, which make it well suited to generating HTML on the fly.

personal construct Term originating with George Kelly, a psychologist from the 1950s who devised techniques for people to define and prioritize concepts that were important to them. A personal construct is the construction and interpretation of meaning by an individual.

personal video recorder (PVR) A set-top box television receiver which also contains hard disk storage and can record programmes for time shifting just as a VCR does. But a PVR can do more than this; the two main features being the ability to pause live programming and for the box to learn your viewing habits and record programmes speculatively to offer you later.

picon An icon that shows a realistic image or picture rather than a representation or symbolic image. Few make the distinction between picon and icon, and generally icon is used to denote all selection images. See also **icon** and **micon**.

pilot projects Experimental projects designed as a run-up to a full-blown development.

pixels Picture elements, the basic building blocks of a picture: sometimes used to be called *pels*.

placeholders A temporary use of images, audio and/or text that are representational of the navigational feel of the final version but not part of the real content.

plug-ins Small extensions to the functionality of a piece of software such as a web browser. The use of the term *plug-in* refers to the ease with which they can be added, usually involving simply copying the plug-in into a particular computer directory.

PNG Portable Network Graphics. A graphics standard devised to replace GIF but giving much higher quality and more versatility. PNG can be used as an archive format.

POP Post Office Protocol, one system used to handle mail boxes for e-mail users. An alternative is **IMAP**.

port (number) A software identifier saying how a computer should treat an Internet request. Web pages are usually requested from port 80.

port (to and a) Move a computer program from one machine/platform to another.

portable document format A standard for encoding documents in a file so that the look of the document, including its fonts and graphics, is retained no matter which computer it is shown on. Devised by Adobe.

posterization Reduction of the smooth variation in colours in an image to a series of discrete steps. Also known as **quantization** and **contouring.** Although this effect is usually seen as an error, posterization is sometimes used for artistic effect.

POTS and PANS Light-hearted terms used to describe changes in telecommunications. POTS are Plain Old Telephone System and PANS are Positively Amazing New Stuff (or similar).

pre-alpha A very incomplete version of an offline program.

pricing policy The decisions made on the price of goods based on the understanding of the market, competitors' prices and what people are prepared to pay.

primary colours The smallest set of colours which can be combined to produce virtually all other colours. For light these are red, green and blue and when combined produce white. For pigments they are red, yellow and blue and when combined these colours produce black.

primitives Basic building blocks of a computer system.

prior art In patents, a patent can be invalidated or refused if the idea has been publicized before or already existed (uses 'art' in the same way as the term state-of-the-art).

production music Recorded music produced especially for use in film television and other audio-visual productions. Usually available for licence, based on a standard rate card. Also known as **library music.**

programming language Since computers can work only with zeros and ones it is rather difficult for mere mortals to program them. To alleviate this problem, programming languages have been developed that understand almost real English.

progressive scan A television picture that scans each line in order as distinct from **interlaced.**

project management The specification, planning and control of time, cost, quality and resource issues to complete a project on time and within budget.

project manager A person who carries out project management. Used here to describe the leader of a multimedia team.

proposal The document in which the developers outline the application content, development schedule and cost for the commissioners of a project.

prototype A limited working version of the application; used early in the project to get reaction to the general design and interface so that adjustments can be made.

proxy server A computer that sits between a computer and the Internet and helping to handle transactions such as web page accesses. A proxy is commonly used to locally store distant web pages that are frequently called up so as to speed up the apparent web access and reduce network traffic.

psycho-acoustics The science of hearing, taking into account the psychological aspects of the way the brain interprets sounds as well as the pure acoustics and physics.

psychometric tests Psychological tests that use measurable factors to attribute a score for the person being tested. The tests are used in recruitment and career management decisions, particularly in large organizations.

public domain Used to mean out of copyright and so freely available for use. This is not strictly true since copyright material can be placed in the public domain by the owner with the intention of it being freely available but while still retaining the copyright.

pushing the envelope Trying something new, usually without sufficient experience and with an element of risk.

qualitative data Information collected by less structured means than quantitative data, e.g. free response questions, and relating more to impressions and feelings.

qualitative evaluation Evaluation that takes into account a wide variety of factors that might influence the results being analysed. The attitudes of the users, the culture of the institution or country and the general environment would be examples of qualitative factors. See also **quantitative evaluation**.

quantitative data Information collected by methods that can then be processed and represented numerically or statistically.

quantitative evaluation Evaluation that is concerned with measuring the results against predetermined criteria to assess whether they have been achieved. The number of times that Help is used might be used as an indicator of how effective the interface of an application is, and the percentage of correct responses after obtaining Help might be used to indicate the effectiveness of the Help messages. These would be examples of quantitative measures of evaluation for multimedia packages. See also **qualitative evaluation**.

quantization An artefact in graphics reproduction whereby smooth changes of brightness or colour become changed so that discrete steps are seen. Sometimes also called **posterization** (especially when used for artistic effect) or **contouring.**

quantizing Inaccuracies in the digitizing of a signal caused by the integer distance between levels of sampling.

RAM Random Access Memory; basically the memory in a computer.

ray tracing A technique used in computer graphics to produce realistic images by following the path of light as it travels from the light source, via the objects in the scene, to the observer.

refractive index The amount by which light changes velocity when it passes between media, usually between air and glass or water. The refractive index is different at different frequencies and therefore colours; hence a prism is able to break white light into its constituent colours.

relational database A database with a complex structure allowing the data items to relate to each other in many ways. If the relationship is simple the database is often called a *flat-file* since its structure resembles that of a card index.

render In computer graphics, to build an image.

requirements agreement A document explaining what the client wants from the program that indicates the range and scope of the work you will produce according to the time and cost you define.

residuals Extra rights in a licence that are not involved in the primary use but which may be applied later. Also called *secondary rights*.

return on investment (ROI) A measure of the effectiveness of capital invested in a project, calculated by expressing average profits from the project as a percentage of average capital invested in it.

return path In an interactive system, the way a user can send data back to the interactive system in order to control it.

reverberation In audio, delayed repeats of the original sound, either due to sound bouncing off the walls of the room or deliberately added electronically, which are so close together as to be indistinguishable. See also **echo**.

RGB Red, green, blue: the three primary colours of light from which virtually all colours can be built. Also refers to an image that stores the three primary colour components separately.

rights Permission to reproduce and/or sell something.

RISC Reduced instruction set computer: a microprocessor with relatively few built-in operations but which can execute what it has extremely quickly.

ROI See **return on investment**.

role-play A technique used in teaching and psychology, in which a person acts out a situation, perhaps from different perspectives, to get insight into decision making and reactions.

royalties Payments based on the number of copies sold or distributed.

royalty-free A copyright licence which allows the licensee to use the material without any further payment. A similar term is **buy-out**. See **clip art/media** and **royalties**.

run-length encoding A form of compression that stores the colour of a pixel followed by how many subsequent pixels are of the same colour. This works best with images made up of large areas of flat colour, such as a cartoon.

run-time The execution, or running, of a program.

SACD Super Audio CD. One of two new super-quality digital audio formats designed to supersede compact disk audio (the other is **DVD** Audio).

safe harbour A principle whereby individual American companies agree to comply with the principles of European data protection so that they can be legitimate recipients of data. See **data protection**.

sample rate The frequency with which an analogue signal is sampled on digitization. For accurate representation the sample rate must be at least twice the highest frequency in the signal.

scalability The ability of a website (or any other system) to function under very high load.

scan To convert a flat image such as a photographic print into a digital form by measuring the relevant parameters of sections of the image in an ordered fashion, usually left to right, top to bottom.

scanner A device that converts a flat image such as a photographic print into a digital form by scanning across it.

screen reader An accessibility tool that translates computer screen text into speech for visually impaired people.

screen resolution The number of pixels on a screen. The most common in multimedia is 800 by 600 pixels.

scripting languages Computer languages that are designed to be used without detailed knowledge of programming. They are specialized to particular tasks.

scriptwriter A person who writes TV, radio or film scripts for entertainment or documentary programmes.

seamless branching in DVD, a technique to allow users to choose different paths through moving video without there being any discontinuity.

segment An identifiable part of a market that has enough common needs to influence products being designed for it.

server In a local area network, a server is effectively the hard disk that is not on your own computer but elsewhere. You can use it to store your files or you can look to it to supply material available to the whole network. In a wide area network or video-on-demand system the server is the centralized repository for data. On the Web, a server is the distant computer that holds the web pages and responds to your requests for them.

server side A program or programs running on the server to dynamically produce, find and/or format information to be sent to the browser.

session fee A payment for performing in a music recording as a session musician or recording a voice-over. A principal performer would probably take royalties on sales, not a session fee.

set-top box A computer-based system that is designed to be like a piece of home entertainment hardware (for example, a VCR or CD player), and may actually sit on top of the television set. Satellite receivers and decoders for video on demand and digital TV are usually referred to in this way.

severance In employment, the terms under which the employment is ended.

sibilance Exaggeration of 's' sounds in a voice, sometimes natural but sometimes caused by poor acoustics or microphone placing.

sign-off The signature of a person given the authority to agree that a phase of work has been completed satisfactorily. Sign-offs are often linked to milestones in the project, which can coincide with staged payments.

simulation A technique used to reproduce a situation as realistically as possible to allow people to develop the skills needed to handle the situation. This is often used in management training. The easiest computer-based example to quote is that of a flight simulator used to train pilots, and in many ways this kind of simulation is better known as **virtual reality**.

site map Graphical or topographical representation of the structure of a website (see also **image map**).

slippage The amount of time that has been lost according to the agreed schedule and the present project position.

SMS Small Message System, a method for sending short text messages between mobile telephones.

software A computer program or computer programs in general. Usually used to differentiate from the equipment or hardware.

source code The human-readable version of a computer program before it is compiled into machine or object code.

spam Unwanted and unsolicited e-mails: junk mail. Named after a song in a Monty Python sketch.

speech recognition The identification of spoken words by a software tool. The words are digitized and matched against coded dictionaries to identify the words.

spider The agent of a web search engine that automatically surfs the Web, following links and indexing pages.

staircasing Appearance of lines on a screen that are almost, but not quite horizontal, and under some circumstances will appear jaggy. Also referred to as **jaggies**.

standards conversion In television, conversion of a video signal between the PAL and NTSC standards or vice versa. Changing from PAL to/from SECAM and between high and standard definition is usually referred to as *transcoding*.

standing waves In sound, self-reinforcement of a sound wave when it is reflected back on itself by a wall or the end of a tube. Between two walls this will reinforce certain frequencies and so colour the sound.

Star A configuration of a cable television network where there is a distinct path from the cable centre to an individual subscriber.

static web page A web page that is fixed and stored on the server as a simple text file.

storyboards A scripting convention that includes mock-up visuals; used in video production originally, and now sometimes used in multimedia projects.

streamer tape Magnetic tape, usually in cartridges or cassettes, onto which computer data is recorded or streamed for archiving and backup purposes. The most common formats are DAT; Exabyte and DLT.

streaming On the Web, playing of an audio or video file over the network so that it is heard or seen instantly as it arrives. The audio or video file does not usually remain on the user's computer, and it is possible to stream a live event, rather like a radio or TV broadcast.

style sheet A document that defines how the parts of a web page are to be displayed based on markup tags in the text. These could be a simple redefinition of the standard HTML tags or they could be completely unique to the page, possibly working in conjunction with **XML**.

stylus In computer graphics, a special pen without ink that is moved across a special tablet in order to draw a line or shape on the computer screen. In audio, the tip, usually diamond, on a gramophone pick-up that actually makes contact with the disk groove.

subcarrier A secondary frequency added to a signal in order to carry extra information, such as colour in a TV signal.

subjective evaluation Evaluation that is based on observation and analysis of non-quantifiable factors, and is affected by the experience and bias of the evaluator. See also **objective evaluation**.

summative Term used to describe evaluation processes used at the end of development. This can include testing but could also include such practices as the end of project review, or debriefing procedures. See also **formative** and **evaluation**.

SWOT A method of analysing a company's position against competitors by defining its *Strengths*, *Weaknesses*, *Opportunities* and *Threats*.

synchronization licence A licence to take music and synchronize it with pictures in a film or video.

synchronization pulse Part of a video or digital signal that identifies a position in the signal, such as where a frame of video starts.

take In a take, or a recording: an attempt to record something. If you have to try again, then you do another take.

talking head In film or video, a sequence which only shows a single person speaking, possibly direct at the camera.

task analysis Identification of all the processes and subprocesses needed to complete a project.

TCP/IP Transmission Control Protocol/Internet Protocol is the protocol used to pass messages around the Internet and in many ways defines the Internet.

technical specification Document describing a task to be undertaken in terms of the equipment and techniques required.

telco Shorthand term used generally for a telecommunications company.

telecine In television and DVD production, the machine that scans the film and produces a television signal from it. Now often working digitally and in high definition.

telemedicine Remote access to medical facilities using audio and, especially, video connections. The implementations can range from diagnosis assistance to remote participation in surgical procedures.

telephony Ordinary telephone traffic, in which people talk to each other.

teletype A teleprinter or telex machine, used to communicate with computers before monitors, or VDUs, were available.

TelNet System for remotely controlling a computer as if you were sitting at its own keyboard.

testing The use of methods and procedures to check the performance of an application according to predefined criteria. Testing is often confused with evaluation. It can form part of evaluation, which has a wider remit. See also **evaluation**.

texture mapping In computer graphics, adding a texture to the 'surface' of an object drawn in 3-D.

time and materials contract A contract for work in which the cost is directly related to the time spent and the materials used. It is the opposite of a fixed-price contract where the fee for the job can only be changed by renegotiation.

time code Information added to video and to audio for video, to uniquely identify the individual frames. This is a great help when editing. Time code can be displayed or even recorded on top of the picture in which case it is referred to as *time code in vision* or *burned-in time code*.

time-based media Media that change over time, such as audio and video.

time-lapse photography Photographic technique in which a camera remains fixed in position and records events in detail by taking pictures at intervals over a period of time. The film is then speeded up when shown, to allow people to see the changes take place in seconds rather than days. An example would be the change of a flower from bud to bloom to death.

TLD Top Level Domain. See **domain name.**

transcribe To make a written copy of a document or communication.

tree and branch A configuration for cable TV networks where there is no individual path between the cable centre (head end) and a subscriber.

trimedia Media production where content is produced for radio, television and the Internet simultaneously.

uncompressed Describes the original form of an image, sound or other data.

Uniform Resource Locator (URL) The full string that both defines the path to a remote service on the Internet and also says which kind of transaction is requested. The most common is to start the URL with http:// which means that the user wants a web page, but there are alternatives. A URL is a special case of the more general Uniform Resource Identifier (URI).

Universal Disk Format (UDF) A standard for computer storage directory structure (etc.) defining the dataspace on a DVD disk but which can also be used with other media. Optimized for large files.

Universal Mobile Telecommunications Services (UMTS) A plan for mobile telephony that includes high data rates and the use of multimedia. Better known as **3G** (3rd Generation)

Unix A computer operating system used extensively in tertiary education, industry and for Web servers. Linux is a version of Unix.

usability laboratories Specially constructed rooms where people are observed using applications and their actions are recorded on video, through the computer and on paper by the observers. The information is analysed to indicate the effectiveness of the program and to make recommendations for improvements.

usability testing The recording and subsequent interpretation of people's usage of a computer-based system through a combination of methods that can include observation, electronic records, and video taping. See **usability laboratories.**

UseNet groups A long-established system of bulletin boards distributed around the Internet. Sometimes called **newsgroups.**

user profile Information about the way a typical user would interact with the program.

user requirements The needs of the users; studied to determine how the application should be structured and how it should operate. Similarly *user specification.*

validation An appraisal of the methods that have been used to check that they are consistent with the results. It is sometimes used with the sense of evaluation but strictly it is part of an evaluation process. Also sometimes used with the meaning of field trial as validation exercise. See also **field trials.**

version control or **tracking** In software development, keeping track of changes to the software so that development is cordinated. This is especially important where more than one person is writing code.

vertical blanking interval (VBI) The part of a television signal between the bottom of one picture and the top of the next. Used for teletext, closed captioning, time code and test signals. In computing the VBI is useful because it provides time to change a displayed image.

video CD A compact disk, actually a Mode 2 CD-ROM, which contains MPEG-l video and audio, and can be played on a television or PC screen like a videocassette. Although this early digital videodisk has not been widely accepted by consumers in the West, it is very popular in the Far East.

video compression Reduction of the amount of data needed to carry something; also known as **bit rate reduction** to avoid confusion with dynamic range reduction in audio which is also known as compression.

video conferencing Basically the combination of a telephone conference call and television or a video telephone. Recent video-conferencing systems operate using personal computers, allowing both ends of the conference to work together on documents that each can see.

video on demand A system whereby a home subscriber can access television material stored remotely on a server. Some systems use high-bandwidth cable and others use ordinary telephone wires for the link between the server and the consumer's television. See also **set-top box**.

videodisk See **interactive video**.

virtual machine A layer of software between a computer program and the computer such that the interface between the program and this software is standard no matter what actual machine is used. The new software exists in different versions for different machines.

virtual reality A 3-D visual environment which reacts to a user's presence and input so as to give the impression of actually being there. Non-immersive VR uses a screen whereas immersive VR is shown using goggles to give a pseudo-realistic stereoscopic view.

voice-over An audio commentary that accompanies video or graphics. Hence *voice-over artiste*, a person who reads the commentary.

walled garden A self-contained mini version of the Internet which a service provider

produces in order to provide a 'safe' web experience to its customers. This might be to avoid certain kinds of content (a school might do this to limit pupils' web access) or to make sure available material is in the right format for cable TV or **WAP**.

WAP Wireless Application Protocol – web-like system for use on mobile phones. Uses a mark-up language called **WML** which is based on **XML**.

waveform A visual representation of a signal, usually electronic in nature, that changes over time, such as recorded sound.

Web browser A piece of software that takes as its input a web page – with all its text, images, links and even sounds and moving images – and formats and displays it on the user's computer.

Web editor Either a person who is responsible for the content of a web page or a piece of software used to lay out web pages.

Web pages The individual documents, based around HTML, that make up a website. Analogous to the pages of a magazine.

Web Safe palette A set of 216 colours which will always reproduce correctly in a web page. It is not 256 colours because some places in the computer's palette are reserved for the windowing environment.

web surfer Person who accesses the World Wide Web and looks at websites.

website A group of web pages and possibly other networked resources that are designed to be viewed as a distinct entity in the same way a magazine is made up of pages and separate articles.

web-television Display of web pages on a television set rather than a computer screen.

white balance A setting of a camera to make sure that what is white in a scene is recorded as white by adjusting the relative proportions of the primary colours and so compensating for the inherent colour of the light source. Also known as colour balancing if carried out after recording.

WHOIS A part of the DNS which allows you to look up who owns a particular domain name. See **domain name system**.

wide area network Computer network that extends beyond the home or office building or complex. Often consisting of linked local area networks, as in the Internet.

wide latitude Of film, able to record a wide range of brightness levels in a scene, or cope with under- and/or over-exposure.

Wi-Fi Trade-mark name used to denote IEEE 802.11 standard wireless network as used by companies including Apple and Lucent. Has 11 megabits speed over a medium range sufficient for use in buildings or a close neighbourhood.

WML Wireless Mark-up Language. Based on **XML** and similar to **HTML**. Used to mark up web pages for **WAP**.

WMLScript Extension scripting language for **WML**. See **JavaScript**.

World Wide Web (WWW) The multiplicity of HTML documents on websites spread around the Internet. On a technical level the Web uses Hypertext Transfer Protocol (**HTTP**) for communication between web browsers and web servers, although other Internet protocols such as **FTP** (File Transfer Protocol) are also used in tandem.

WORM In data storage, Write Once Read Many, a type of computer disk that can be written to but not changed. Often used to denote a CD-ROM that has been written rather than pressed or replicated. The process is known as burning a WORM or burning a CD.

WYSIWYG Describes an application that shows you the end result of your work exactly as it will be seen by the end-users: What You See Is What You Get.

XML eXtensible Mark-up Language. A very versatile mechanism for defining ways of marking up documents which can be used for web pages and many other media.

zoom To increase the focal length of a lens in video or photography. It magnifies the scene and looks similar to, but not exactly the same as, moving closer to the subject.

Index

Note: When page numbers are highlighted in **bold**, the reference appears in the Glossary.

3-D animations 167, **392**

acceptance test report sheet 255, 256
acceptance testing 247, 250, 252–5, 255–6, 260, **392**
accessibility aids 195–6, **392**
accreditation 71
accredited multimedia training programs 249
action replays 159
ActiveX 58
activity-based entertainment programs 190
actors 228
actresses 228
administration 35, 277
Adobe Acrobat 171
advertisers 160
advertising 24, 49, 184, 193, 194, 210, 385–6
  banner 373, 386
agreements
  confidentiality 210, 211–12
  contractual 8, 117
  international 321, 322
  non-disclosure 343, **407**
  requirements 11, 278–81, **411**
  verbal 127, 277
  written 277
Allied Business Intelligence 367
alpha test 250
Amazon 72
analogical graphics 169
analyst 223
animation 6, 70, 135, 167–8, 169–70, **393**
animators 35
Apple Macintosh 188, 322
application architecture 88
application map 47, 88

archiving 12, 173
  budget information 267–8
  chaotic 264
  closing the project 268
  final proposal document 266
  formal documents 266
  needs 264–6
  script and assets 266–7
  successful 265
art director (creative director) 221
artistes 231
ASCAP 326
assessments 144
assets 65, 206–8, 209, 266–7
  production 12
assistant producers 228, 231
attribution 323
audience, intended 190
audio 165–7
author 135
authoring 34
  languages 223
  tools 223, **394**

back-end (server) development 47, 48
back tracking facility 173, 189
background noise 167
ball-park costs 120
bandwidth 54, 157, **394**
  restrictions 239
banner
  advertisements 373, 386, **394**
  graphic 152, 184
Barlow 308, 309
BBC Radio 205
Belbin, Meredith 309–10, 311, 314
beta 97, **394**
beta testing 74, 250

bi-directional language 365, **394**
blind people 196
BMI 326
boiler plate 119
Bookmarking 173, 355, **395**
branding 64, 135, 185, 194, 385
breach of conditions 206
breath-controlled devices 196
broadband 348
broken link 252
browser 47, 48, **395**
budget 7, 153–5
  for CD-ROM 36
  media components 154
  offline projects 153–5
  online projects 153
  resources 155
  vs time information 32
  see also costs
burden of proof for transfer of information 144
business analyst 135, 233–4
business strategist 45
buy-outs 207, **395**
  rights and 336–7

cache 328–9, **395**
carousel 6, **395**
cartograms 182, **395**
cartoonists 35
cartoons 167
CD, presentation 70
CD-ROM 49, **396**
  budget for 36
  copyright 332, 336
  final sign-off 127
  licensing 206
CGIs 208, 248, 253, **396**
change management 120–3, **396**
change request form 121–2, **396**
chat group 186
chatrooms 328

cinematograph films, copyright
331
clearances *see* rights and
clearances
client(s)
dissatisfaction 289–91
knowledge 374–6
reaching 383–6
responsibilities 118, 125
retaining 386–7
varieties of 8–9
client-side development 47, 48,
396
clip art/media 202, 330–3, **396**
copyright 332–3
Cloninger, Curt 194
cocktail party effect 171
cognition 38
colour 220, 254
shifts 191
use in retail sector 192
colour blindness 172, 196
communication of change 121
competences 143, 144
competition 376–8
competitive edge 376
component integrity 141, **397**
computer graphics artists 220–2
computer languages 223
computer program
patenting 342
rights 337
Computers Solutions Consulting
UK 193
computing consultants 35
concentration flow 316
Concept System 46
concept testing 186, 247, **397**
concept user interface tool (CUI)
46, **398**
confidentiality agreements 210,
211–12
consistency 185
constraints 155
online or offline platform 152–3
content
agreeing 146–8
definition 132
general principles for
establishing 148–9
importance of 132–4
influences on
business and retail 142–3
limitations 144–5
training applications 143–4

quality 134
whose role to define 134–6
content and media definition 92
content blocks 135
content clusters 46
content integrity 145
content management system 59
content structure maps 146
contingency 281, **397**
contingency costs 96
continuous market research 381
contracts
agreeing how to work together
117–19
background 112–13
change management 120–3
contractor 211–12
definition 112
education and 125–7
fixed-term 209
freelancer 211–12
refining the proposal into
113–17
responsibilities 124–5
stages of a project 123–4
time and materials 209, **414**
contractual agreements 8, 117
control of time 29–30
convergence 197, **397**
copyright 12, **397**
clip media 330–3
computer program code 323
databases 330
definition 320
exceptions 324–5
expiry 332
infringement 323, 331–2
international agreement 321,
322
jurisdiction, distance selling,
patents and data
protection 339–44
models 333–8
all rights 333–4
flash fees 334
home video 334
Internet or interactive 334,
336
non-theatric 334, 336
rights in code 337–8
royalties versus buy-outs
336–7
moral rights 323–4
music 324, 325–7, 331
negotiating 337–8

obtaining 322–33
origins 320–1
ownership 323
photograph 331
phrases 322–3
public domain 330–3
still images 334
world 335
World Wide Web 327–30
core team 217
corporate image 70
costs
ball-park 20
contingency 96
resource 115–16
rights and clearances 202–5
shipping 205
couriers 96
creative brainstorming 37
creative websites 9–10
critical path analysis 19, 21, **398**
cross-component integrity 141
cross-platform 224, **398**
cultural differences 188
in colour 192
see also language
customer relationship
management (CRM) 343,
387

data fields, definition 134
data protection 339–44, **398**
Data Protection Principles (UK)
343
database engine 133
database functionality, definition
134
dating 255
deadlines 37
decision criteria matrix 309
decoding techniques 160
delivery platform 7, **398**
Demon Internet 274
demonstration programs 166
derivative 208
design defects 258
development team 34–5
development time 122
DHL 205
diagnostics 196
diagrams 182
digital audio file 165
Digital Millennium Copyright Act
(DCMA) (1998) (USA) 326,
329, 340

Digital Performance Right Act (1995) (USA) 326, 329
directive management approach 36
disabilities, users with 195
discipline 38
discovery learning 164
discussion group 186
dissatisfaction, client 289–91
distance education/learning 144, **399**
distance selling 339–44
Distance Selling Directive 341
distribution channel 372–3, **399**
distributors 383
documentation 121
domain names 329–30, **399**
Dorling Kindersley 363
dot.com companies 373, **399**
dotted line responsibility 30
double-byte characters 365–6, **399**
download
    speed 193–4
    times 167
drama 158
droit d'auteur 321
duration of rights 207
DVD 157, 161, **400**
    marketing 226
    territorial restrictions 340
    videos 73
DVD-ROM 73, **400**
dynamic web pages 48, **400**

e-commerce 1, 47, 133, 194, 233, 234, 235, **400**
    native language and 360–1
editing 155
editor 135
education 117, 164
    contract and 125–7
    distance 144, **399**
    graphics and 168–70
    offline 72
    scoping and 72
    video for 163–5
    see also training
educational technology 144, **400**
edutainment 72, **400**
e-learning 1
electronic timesheet systems 268
electronically delivered services 341
e-mail project diary 22

emotional charge 194
English language 147
engravers, rights 331
entertainment 73, 133, 194
    activity-based programs 190
environmental factors 315–16
e-publishing 133
ergonomics 316
evaluation, definition 246, **401**
executive summary 86
Exit 183
external charge-out rates 114
external clients 8, **401**
external tester 257
eye-gaze devices 196

fade-out 166
fade-up 166
fair use 324, **401**
Favourites 173
feature creep 281, **401**
FedEx 205
films 159
    grammar of 159, 349, 351
    library 95
finish date 98
flash fees 334
flashbacks 159
flowcharts 46, 47, 136, 169, 288, **401**
focus groups 186, 247, **401**
focusing 194
force majeure 210–11
foreign broadcasters, sales to 206
formats 141
framing 162
freedom of information 202
front-end (client-side) development 47, 48, **402**
front page 137, 138
full screen 157
functional managers 31
functional websites 9–10,11

games programs 133, 190
    text-only 353–4
Gantt chart 18, 22, **402**
global culture strategy 365
grammar of film making 159, 349, 351
graphic roles 34
graphical user interface (GUI) 235

graphics 135, 167–70
    in education and training applications 168–70
graphics artists 135–6, 191

hacking 253, **402**
hardware amortization 95
Harry Fox Agency 326
headings, meaningful 194
Help screens 6, 92, 188, 189, 190, 239
heuristic evaluation 249
high-level design 236, **403**
Hitchcock, Alfred 162
home page 88, 168, 188
hot-spots 137, **403**
house style 222
HTML 90, 122, 220, 252, 254, 328, 329, 365, **403**
Hughes, Bob 194
human-computer interaction (HCI) 182, 235, 348, 353, **403**
hybrid 70
    CD-ROM 53
    projects 6
    Web/CD/DVDs 226, **403**
hyperdocuments 173
hyperlinking 171
hypertext 172, **403**

iconograms 182
icons 181, 182, 185, **403**
ICT (Information and Communication Technologies) company 45, **403**
illustrators, rights 331
image 64, 185, 194
    maps 137, 184, **403**
    size 185
immersive virtual reality 159
in-bound communication 363, 364, **403**
indemnity 206, **403**
information
    layering of 188
    structure 88
information analyst/architect 45, 63, 135, 234, **403**
innovation, managing 29
instructional design 144, **404**
instructional designers 135, 232, 238–9, **404**
integrity 323, **404**

intellectual property rights (IPR) 320, **404**
interactive design 236, **404**
interactive designers 135, 232, 238–9
interactive development companies 9
interactive drama scripting 141
interactive entertainment 348, 353
interactive television 2, 49, 161, 197, 226, 348, **404**
interactive training and education 24
interactivity 227–8
interface **404**
    accessibility 195–7
    definition 180–1
    design 181–97, 348
    interactive environment 188–90
    target audience 185–7
    testing 187–8
    use of colour 191–2
    use of sound 190–1
    usability 192–5
interface design specialist 235–6
internal charge-out rates 114
international projects 73–4
Internationalization 69, 360, 361–2, **404**
Internet Explorer 252, 329
Internet service provider (ISP) 53, 329, **405**
Internet telephony 328
Internet/CD hybrid 53
interviewing 217
intranet 1, 46, **404**
IT sector 2

Java 58, 122, **405**
JavaScript 58, 220, 253, **405**
jurisdiction 339–44

Kaufmann, G. 308
Kelly, George 46
key deliverables 97
key development stages 96
kiosks 158, 160, 166, 167, 183
knowledge 143

language(s) 1–2
    authoring 223
    English 147
    multiple 208
    native 360–1
    remaking in another 207–8
    scripting 223
    of teenagers 363
learning styles 163
learning theory 169
legal differences, cross-cultural 365
legibility 191
library (production) music 327
licensing 209
lifestyle, concept of 382
line length 172
linking, web 328–9
Linux 223
literacy, multimedia 190
live maps 137
localization 67, 69, 361, **405**
    extent 367
    importance 367
    scope 361–7
    specialist factors 361–6
log analysis 59
logical graphics 169
logos 196
look and feel user interface 132, 322, **405**
Looms, Peter 365
loyalty 382, 386

Mac tools 223
main menu 188
market analysis 387–9
marketing
    CD 226
    channel 372
    competition, knowledge of 376–8
    customer knowledge 374–6
    definition 372
    market knowledge 380–3
    online 372–3
    principles and new media 373–4
    reaching customers 383–6
    retaining customers 386–7
    strengths, knowledge of 379–80
marketing analyst 45
markets and territories 206
meaningful headings 194
Mechanical Copyright Protection Society (MCPS) 326
mechanical right 326, **406**

media
    and message 155–7
    scripting 139
medical applications 363, 364
meeting location 315, 316
meeting room layout 315
meetings, initial 42
MEPG–7 385
meta tags 88, 384, **406**
micons 182, 184
Microsoft 173, 196
    on copyright 322
Microsoft Project 19
MIDI 165
milestones 96, 97, 208, **406**
mirror 328–9, **406**
moral rights 210
morphing 155
MoSCow 57, **407**
MPEG 157, **407**
MPEG–2 157, **407**
multicultural facets 67, **407**
multicultural strategy 365
multilingual facets 67
Multimedia Content Description Interface 385
multimedia, definition 5
multimedia narrative 348, **407**
    definition 348–51, 352–4
    filmic tradition 349
    managing development of 354–5
    oral narrative 349
    quality 354–5
    recipient of information 350
    written narrative 349
multimedia projects
    client-centred multimedia project cycle 11–14
    emerging models of development 9–11
    resource costs 115–16
    varieties of client 8–9
    varieties of project 7–8
Murdoch, James 367
Murray, Janet 351
music copyright 324, 325–7, 331
    costing 203
Musicians Union 327

NASA 202, 332
navigation 193, 348
needs analysis 186, 258, **407**
Netscape History 329
Netscape Navigator 329

Netscape online 252
network analysis 19, 20, 21, 22, 28, **407**
network manager 235
Nielsen, Jakob 193, 194
non-disclosure agreement (NDA) 343, **407**

object-oriented programming 29, **408**
office automation 173
offline client-centred project scoping questionnaire 105–9
offline project 5, 6
online client-centred project scoping questionnaire 76–82, 99–104
online communication 64
online interactive media scoping questionnaire 49–68
  client's previous multimedia experience 49–50
  statement of what client wants 51–2
  type of project 52–4
    access and use 62–3
    benefits/achievements wanted 60–1
    browser/platform expectations 58–9
    budget 67–8
    content (existing assets) 65
    emotional reaction considerations 63–4
    hybrid Web/CD 53–4
    importance ranking 56–7
    internet/intranet/extranet 52–3
    market sector of the client 54–5
    media mix 64
    mobile 54
    project bias 55–6, 67
    site maintenance 59–60
    size of section 57–8
    special considerations 66–7
    time for development 65–6
online project 5, 6
online training 145, 164
on-screen keyboards 196
operational errors 258
organizational structure 30–4
origins, multimedia 16

out-bound communication 363, 364, **408**
ownership of content 72

panning 162, 163
paper-chase reaction 147, 148
parallel action 159
Pareto analysis 388, **409**
partnerships 34
  with consultancies 135
patent agent 342
patents 339–44, **409**
paternity, right of 210, 323, **409**
PC tools 223
PDAs 54, **409**
peer review 247, **409**
perceptual map/matrix 387–8, **409**
performing right 326, **409**
Performing Right Society (PRS) 326
personal assistants 35, 232
personal construct theories 46, **409**
photo libraries 325
photograph, copyright 331
picons 182, **409**
pictograms 182
picture libraries 95, 228, 384
picture researchers 35
pilot projects 153, **409**
place of supply 341
placement of images 220
Plowman, Lydia 352
plug-ins 167, **409**
point of information 70, 71
portable document format (PDF) 171, **410**
post-meeting responsibilities 74–5
Power Mapper 137
preference selection 92
presentation 70
primary data 382
printing in publications 206
prior art 342, **410**
producer 228
production assistants 228, 230
production manager 235
production music 327, **410**
profit margins 96
programmers 224
  interviewing 225
  skills 222–5
project assistants 35
project cycle diagram 12

project management **410**
  limitations 19–22
  cf. multimedia project management 17–30
  effect of multimedia on 28–30
  quality in interactive media 22–5
project manager 31, **410**
  ending project 312–13
  management styles 302–6
    collaborative 303, 304
    consultative style 303
    delegation 305–6
    directive 302–3
  position 300
  responsibilities 124–5
  role 39–40
  role types 311–12
  successful managers of creative teams 307–9
  successful teams 309–14
  team culture and 300–2
  team management 314–16
promotional sites 194
proposal 11, **410**
  aim of 84–5
  balance 93
  content 85–6
    executive summary 86
    general introduction 86
    general treatment 87
    offline projects 91–5
    online projects 88–91
    reasons for choice 87
    statement of client's wants 86–7
    statement of user needs 87
  content and media definition 92
  cost/payment 94, 97
  description of the human resources 96
  limitations of the proposal 97–8
  on- and offline projects: common ground 95
  outline diagram of proposed structure 96
  time for testing 97
  variations on the treatment 95–6
  work breakdown and schedule 96
prototypes 247, **410**

prototyping 127, 248
psychometric testing 309
public domain 330–3, **411**
publishing 24, 71–2

qualifications 143–4
qualitative data 382, **411**
quality
    definition of 25
    of content selection 143
    level of, in program 143
    link with time and cost 25–8
quality assurance 192
quality assurance cycle 366
quantitative data 382, **411**
questionnaires 48
    offline client-centred project
        scoping 105–9
    online client-centred project
        scoping 76–82, 99–104
    online interactive media
        scoping 49–68

rapid application development
    (RAD) 29
readability 191
RealAudio 165
RealVideo 152
re-clearing of electronic rights,
    costs 206–7
recycling 267
reference 73
reliability of information 382–3
repeats 205
representational graphics 168–9
requirements agreement 11, **411**
responsibilities
    client's 118, 125
    dotted-line 30
    post-meeting 74–5
    project manager 124–5
retailing 33–4, 192
reviews 193
rights and clearances 90, 94,
    267
    choice of law 211
    costing 202–5
    force majeure 210–11
    legal issues 205–12
    liabilities 206–8
    moral rights 210
    ownership of code and other
        assets generated 209
    payment structure 208–9

right to demonstrate and
    promote the product 210
    severance 210, **413**
rights clearer 35
role conflict 30
role-plays 163, **412**
rollovers 184, 220
Rosenstand, Claus 354
royalties 336–7, **412**
rule of thirds 162

Safe Harbour principle 344, **412**
salaries 95
sales contribution chart 389
Save 184
scanning 194
scoping 7, 11
    analytic techniques 45–9
    benefits 275–6
    client's brief 42
    definition 274–5
    offline 68–74
    risks 276–93
        changes to the scope of the
            project 281–4
        client dissatisfaction
            289–91
        general requirements
            agreement example 278–81
        visual mismatch 288–9
        withheld payment 276–8
    sample quick scoping
        checklists 284–7, 299–3
    of small new media project
        273, 291–3
scoping questionnaire 48
scoping scale 274
screen enlargers 196
screen glare 191
screen readers 196, **412**
screen reviewers 196
scripting 147
    for linear media 139
    for multimedia 140–2
scripting languages 223, **412**
scriptwriter 135, 236–7, **412**
search engines 384
secondary data 382
secretarial support 35, 232–3
section audit table 89
security of online transactions
    56
semiotics 182
sequences 164
sequencing 155

server-side development 48, **412**
SESAC 326
session fee 327, **413**
set-top box 6, **413**
severance 210, **413**
shared development 209
shipping costs 205
signature tune 166
sign-off 114, 119, 208, **413**
    archiving documents 266
    authority 148
    dates 123
    final 127
simulations 163, **413**
site maps 88, 137, 288, **413**
size of image 185, 220
skills 143
skimming 194
Small and Medium Enterprises
    136
small project
    rejection by clients 289–91
    new media project life cycle
        272–94
soft skills 237
software **413**
    development phases 43–4
    sector 2
    see also computer languages
Sony 173
sound effects 166
sound personnel 229–31
space, ease of reading and 172
spam 373, **413**
special needs, users with 195
specialist programmers 35
specification phase for software
    development 43
speech recognition programs 196,
    413
staff
    extended project team 218
    general support 232–3
    interviews 219–20, 225
    offline core team 218
    online core team 218
    selection 216
    skills
        core team 220–5
        extended team 225–31
        identifying 216–17
    specialist support 218–19,
        233–40
staged payments 208, 277
start dates 98

static web pages 48
stationery 96
still images 162
   copyright 334
   costing 202
storyboard approach 147, **413**
streaming 160, **413**
stress testing 248
structure diagram 236–7
structure maps 137
structured learning 164
style police 69
subcontracting 211, 333
subject matter experts (SMEs)
   136, 239–40
sui generis 330
superimposition, picture 168
sweat of the brow 322
SWOT analysis 379, **414**
synchronization licence 327, **414**
systems analyst 223

task analysis 186, **414**
taxes 340–1
team culture 300–2
team leader, project manager as
   34–9
technical analyst 135
technical architect 234–5
technical assistants 235
technical consultants 35
technical director 235
technical support 35, 235
technical writers 136
teenagers, language of 363
television 159
tendering 8, 43–4
terms and conditions 117
testing 12, 67, 144, **414**
   acceptance 247, 250, 252–5,
     255–6, 260, **392**
   alpha 250
   beta 74, 250
   concept 186, 247, **397**
   definition 246, 250
   developmental 250–1
   field trials 249–50
   interface 187–8
   integration 260
   peer review 248–9
   prototyping 247–8, **410**

psychometric 309
   sign-off 260
   software 259–60
   stages 258
   strategy 255–9
   stress 248
   test cycle 253–4
   timing 97
   and trials 90
   usability 186, 187, 249, 257,
     415
text 170–4
   bubbles 184
   size 254
tiled images 191
time constraints 57, 96, 289
time control 29–30
time, cost, quality principle 25–8,
   282
time-keeping 313
time-lapse photography 155,
   415
time record systems 268
timescale of project 38
timesheets 31–2
trade mark 329–30
training 164
   accredited programs 249
   content and 143–4
   graphs and 168–70
   interactive 24
   offline 70–1
   online 145, 164
   video for 163–5
training analyst 45, 135, 237–8
translation 206, 363–4
translators 35
   rights 331
trash can icon 183
treatment, definition 132
tree structure 181, 182
Truffaut, François 126
trust 120
typography 171

Undo 184
UNIX 223, **415**
usability 173, 348
   guidelines 194, 195
   testing 186, 187, 249, 257,
     415

UseNet newsgroup 340, **415**
user interface 38

validation 246, **415**
validators 253
Value Added Tax 341
VCRs 161
verbal agreement 277
   in short project 127
version control 121, **415**
version numbering 255
video 159–65
   background factors 157–9
   for education and training
     163–5
   costing of footage 203–5
   visual grammar 161–3
video conferencing 7, **416**
video editors 228–9
video encoding 171
video footage 70
video graphics 70
video graphics artists 35
video personnel 225–9
video producer 231
videoconferencing 328
visual impairment 196
visual mismatch 288–9
voice-over artiste 21, 94, 229–30,
   416
voice-overs, costing 203

WAP systems 54, 197, **416**
web agencies 1
web editor 136, 140, **416**
web master 235
web safe colours 192, **416**
Web search engine 88
Web/CD hybrid 53
WebLint 253
website **416**
   detail 137–40
   structure 136–7
Windows 172, 188
withheld payment 276–8
workstations 316
written agreement 277
WYSIWYG 220, 275, **417**

zooming 162, 163, **417**